Encountering Religion

An Introduction to the Religions of the World

Edited by

Ian S. Markham and Tinu Ruparell

BLACKWELL
Publishers

Copyright © Blackwell Publishers Ltd 2001
Editorial matter and arrangement copyright © Ian S. Markham and Tinu Ruparell 2001

First published 2001

2 4 6 8 10 9 7 5 3 1

Blackwell Publishers Ltd
108 Cowley Road
Oxford OX4 1JF
UK

Blackwell Publishers Inc.
350 Main Street
Malden, Massachusetts 02148
USA

British Library Cataloguing in Publication Data

A CIP catalogue record for this book is available from the British Library.

Library of Congress Cataloging-in-Publication Data

Encountering religion : an introduction to the religions of the world / edited by Ian S.
Markham and Tinu Ruparell.
        p.   cm.
    Includes bibliographical references and index.
    ISBN 0–631–20673–6 (alk. paper) — ISBN 0–631–20674–4 (pbk. : alk. paper)
        1. Religions.   I. Markham, Ian S.   II. Ruparell, Tinu.

    BL80.2.E493   2000
    291—dc21

                                                                        99–085999

Typeset in Bembo on 10.5/12.5pt
by Graphicraft Limited, Hong Kong
Printed in Great Britain by TJ International, Padstow, Cornwall

This book is printed on acid-free paper.

Contents

List of Contributors — ix
Preface — xi
Acknowledgments — xiii

1 Studying Religion: Issues in Definition and Method — 1
Elizabeth Ramsey and Shannon Ledbetter

Defining Religions — 1
The Study of Religion — 6
Approaches to the Study of Religion — 10
Academic Disciplines and the Study of Religions — 14

2 Religion and Sociology — 21
Julie F. Scott and Irene Hall

The Sociological Perspective — 21
The Development of the Sociology of Religion — 23
Researching Religion — 28
The Main Interests of the Sociology of Religion — 32
The Sociology of Religion Today — 40

3 Religion and Psychology — 44
Carl Williams

A Psychological Approach to Religion — 44
The Beginnings of a Psychology of Religion — 46
Psychoanalytic Approaches to the Psychology of Religion — 48
The Objectivist Approach to the Psychology of Religion — 52
Transpersonal Approaches to the Psychology of Religion — 58
Conclusions — 64

4 Religion and Scripture: The Function of the Special Books of Religion — 68
Alex Smith

Key Questions Regarding Scripture's Characterization — 69
Judaism — 70
Christianity — 74
Islam — 78

Hinduism 82
Buddhism 85
Sikhism 87

5 Religion, Ritual, and Culture 96
Seán McLoughlin

From Beliefs to Practices 96
Some General Approaches to Ritual 98
Durkheim and the Function of Ritual 100
Rites of Passage 101
Secular Rituals? 103
Culture 106
Religion and Culture 109
Ritual, Symbols, and Power 112
Conclusion 114

6 Religion and the Arts 117
Shannon Ledbetter

Platonic Opposition to Art 120
Medieval Use of Art as a Route to the Spiritual 122
Islamic Integration of the Rational with Art 123
Victorian Culture 124
Theological Perspectives on Art 127
The Modern Confusion 128
Case Studies 133

7 Secular Humanism 139
J'annine Jobling

Historical Survey 141
The Enlightenment 142
Worldviews 149
Case Study: Religion as Oppressive 152
Ethics 155
Modern Expressions 157
Conclusions 160

8 Hinduism 163
Tinu Ruparell

The "Hindu Mind" 163
Worldviews 168
Institutions and Rituals 173
Modern Expressions 182
Women in Hinduism 184

9   Buddhism   190
David Torevell

   Historical Survey   191
   Worldviews   194
   Institutions and Rituals   200
   Ethical Expression   204
   Role of Women   206
   Modern Expression   209

10   Sikhism   215
John Parry

   Historical Survey   216
   The Sikh Belief System   221
   The Human Condition   224
   Rituals and Institutions   227
   Ethics   232
   Engagement with the Modern World   236

11   Chinese Religion   240
Jack Leung

   Mythological Rulers   244
   Historical Survey   244
   Worldviews   250
   Ethical Expression   255
   Role of Women   259
   Rituals and Institutions   261
   Calendar   264
   Engagement with Modernity   265

12   Judaism   272
Elizabeth Ramsey

   Historical Survey   274
   Worldviews   278
   God   280
   Election   281
   Torah   282
   The Land   283
   Institutions and Rituals   284
   The Main Festivals   285
   Ethical Expression   288
   Modern Outlook   290

Secularism 292
The Holocaust 293
Israel 294
Jewish Humor and Story 295

13 Shintoism 297
Ian Markham

Shintoism in the Past 298
Shintoism Today 304

14 Christianity 309
Alex Smith

Historical Survey 311
Second and Third Centuries 313
Third and Fourth Centuries 314
The Middle Ages 316
The Reformation and Counter-Reformation 319
The Modern Period 321
Worldviews 322
Institutions and Rituals 326
Ethical Expressions 329
Modern and Future Expression 332

15 Islam 337
Victoria La'Porte

The Life of the Prophet Muhammad 339
The Sunni\Shia Split 341
Sufism 344
Worldviews 344
The Philosophical Tradition 346
The Prophets and the Message of Jesus 348
The Significance of the Prophet Muhammad 350
Life after Death 351
Institutions and Rituals 355
The Role of Women 356
Modern Expressions 365

Bibliography 372
Index 375

Contributors

Prof. Ian S. Markham is Liverpool Professor of Theology and Public Life, and Foundation Dean at Liverpool Hope University College. His research interests include ethics, philosophy of religion, and pluralism.

Dr. Tinu Ruparell is Lecturer and Research Fellow in Religious Studies at Liverpool Hope University College. His work centers on comparative philosophy of religion, Hinduism, continental philosophy, and science and religion.

Irene Hall lectures in Sociology at Liverpool Hope. Her research interests are in community and research methods.

Dr. J'annine Jobling is a lecturer in the Department of Theology and Religious Studies, Liverpool Hope University College. She researches primarily in the field of twentieth-century theology, especially with relation to feminism, postmodernism and hermeneutics.

Dr. Victoria La'Porte lectured at Brunel University between 1996 and 1999. She currently lectures at Liverpool Hope University College. Her areas of research are in Christian Theology and the relationship between Islam and the West.

Shannon Ledbetter is currently the Developments Officer in the Department of Theology and Religious Studies at Liverpool Hope University College and lectures in Christian Spirituality and Pastoral Theology. Her research interests are in Social Theology, Religion and the Arts, and the Theology of Work.

Jack Leung taught Buddhism at Liverpool Hope. His research interests focus on classical Chinese thought, the history of western interpretation(s) of Chinese religious traditions, and orientalism in comparative theology.

Dr. Seán McLoughlin lectures in Theology and Religious Studies at Liverpool Hope University College. He researches in the area of Muslims in Britain.

The Rev'd Dr. John Parry is a minister of the United Reformed Church who teaches World Faiths and Missiology at Northern College, Manchester. He previously had regular contact with Sikhs in both India and the UK.

Elizabeth Ramsey is Senior Lecturer in Theology and Religious Studies at Liverpool Hope University College. Her research interests include Jews, Judaism, and the impact of the Holocaust.

Dr. Julie Scott is currently a lecturer in the sociology of religion at Liverpool Hope University College. Her research interests include the embodiment of belief among Protestant fundamentalists; religious meaning systems; contemporary western religiosity and secularization.

The Rev. Alex Smith is assistant priest at Christchurch Priory, Dorset. He was for many years senior lecturer in Theology and Religious Studies in Liverpool Hope University College. His research interests include church history, liturgics and the nature of scripture.

Dr. David Torevell taught Christian Theology, Buddhism, and Religion and Film at Liverpool Hope University College. His interests lie in the above-mentioned subjects as well as Religious Education.

Carl Williams is a lecturer in the Psychology Department at Liverpool Hope University College. His research and teaching interests include: transpersonal psychology, parapsychology and the psychology of exceptional human experiences.

Preface

No education is complete unless it has included study of the world religions and the phenomena of religion. The contributors and editors of this textbook stand in the firm belief that, as we begin a new millennium, the truth of this statement holds even more sway; and it is to the fuller understanding of all that falls under the purview of "religion" that the present text aims. *Encountering Religion*, and its associated text *A World Religions Reader*, together form what we believe to be an excellent tool for teaching and learning in the area of religious studies.

The challenge of creating a new textbook in religious studies is both daunting and extremely rewarding. We set ourselves the task of providing, within two companion volumes, most if not all of what a teacher and student of religion requires for a fuller understanding of this immensely complicated field of study. Thus *Encountering Religion* covers the "major" world religious traditions, including their histories, main beliefs and practices, ethics, views of women and contemporary expressions. This is cross-referenced to a new edition of *A World Religions Reader*, which provides primary source texts for these traditions. As secular humanism is now arguably the predominant conversation partner for religion, particularly in the West but gaining ground elsewhere, we begin with a discussion of this tradition – setting a context of sorts for each religion which follows. In addition to this, and filling a lacuna in many existing introductory textbooks, *Encountering Religion* presents discussions of methodological and other aspects of the study of religion, such as its definition and modes of study, the psychology and sociology of religion, the role and nature of scripture, religion and the fine arts, and the relationship of religion to culture. We have, therefore, attempted to bring together in these two books, elements satisfying the main teaching needs: methodology, content, skills, and primary readings. The resulting volumes should form, therefore, comprehensive, user-friendly textbooks for any student working in English in the field of religious studies. They will be appropriate for courses in comparative religions or the study of religion at universities, colleges, polytechnics, and institutes of further education worldwide, as well as excellent introduction and reference books for the interested reader.

Dedicated specialists have written each of the chapters, and thus each contribution is somewhat different in style or flavor. However, unlike such edited volumes, we have worked together both on our own chapters and each other's and have tried, where possible, to tie the chapters together harmoniously. The heart of this operation was the Department of Theology and Religious Studies at Liverpool Hope University College, and the book is a truly collaborative project. To ensure coherence, each chapter was read and discussed within the department. Monthly seminars ensured that material was worked and reworked in the light of the other chapters. The result, we trust, is a volume that shares the same expectations of our anticipated readers: it is accessible, clear, and accurate.

As a teaching tool, *Encountering Religion* includes at the end of each chapter a full glossary as well as bibliographical material. However, sensitive to the debates surrounding pedagogy, we want the book to impart both information and skills, believing firmly that these two elements cannot be separated as they have been in the past. To this end, along with the substantial content and information in the book, we ensured that every chapter includes classroom exercises that will help develop certain skills (from teamwork to evaluation, analysis, and critical reflection). We want to make sure that this is a volume that can be actually used in the classroom.

As we have already noted, this book is intended to be used with *A World Religions Reader*. While it is, of course, possible to use each text alone, teachers who choose to use both in concert will find that the two volumes work very well together. So, for example, to facilitate cross-religious comparisons, each chapter in the two texts is structured in the same way: the introductory material revealing a sense of the "spirit" or "mind" of a tradition, Worldviews, Institutions and Rituals, Ethical Expressions, and Modern Expressions. However, we have not been held captive to this structure and, where in certain traditions it has been found less appropriate, other structures have been used. Contributors responsible for the chapters have used the structure flexibly and the editors have endeavored to allow each chapter its own distinctive feel while maintaining an overall coherence to the whole.

No textbook on religion can hope to be complete. There are numerous elements of each tradition we have had to neglect, many historical expressions left out, and much discussion concerning the method and theory of religious studies omitted. Also, for various technical and methodological reasons, certain chapters had to be very limited in their scope. While we regret these deficiencies, we found they could not be avoided in a project such as this. While referring the reader to the bibliographies, in defence we submit that to include all of the missing parts would have resulted in a work much larger, substantially more expensive and hence of limited use in the classroom. Thus the sometimes dense chapters which follow have made conciseness a virtue, avoiding overly abstruse discussions, and communicating what we consider most important in an empathetic way.

We shall not belabor this preface further, allowing rather what follows to speak for itself. However, we would like to affirm the view that the study of religion leaves no one unaffected. It is impossible to grapple with the metaphysical themes in this book without having one's own metaphysics challenged. This is the joy and reward of religious studies: one is embarking on a journey that will thrill, inspire, sometimes annoy, and most certainly challenge. We trust that this volume will do just that.

TR, IM

Acknowledgments

This is a team effort. The vast majority of contributors work at Liverpool Hope University College. Dr. John Parry (Sikhism) and Dr. Victoria La'Porte (Islam) became honorary members of the College for the purpose of this volume. Each chapter was discussed in a Hope seminar, and we are grateful to all the participants at those seminars: the book is all the better for those constructive discussions about the issues. Particular thanks are due to Catherine Moorhead who helped us organize the final manuscript, and to the staff at Blackwell Publishers, particularly Joanna Pyke, Clare Woodford, Alex Wright and their scrupulous copy-editors, for their patience and support of this project. Thanks are due also to our University administration, especially Professor Simon Lee and Canon Dr. John Elford.

The team would like to dedicate the book to the memory of Elizabeth Scantlebury (1953–96). She was a much loved teacher of Islam and a popular member of the Department of Theology and Religious Studies at Hope. She would have loved this project: we are sure that she would have been pleased with the result.

Finally, the Editors would like to thank their wives – Donna and Lesley – and children – Kiran, Sacha, and Luke – for their love and support, and for tolerating our absence as we completed the task of editing.

Ian Markham   Tinu Ruparell
Liverpool Hope University College

The authors and publishers gratefully acknowledge the following for permission to reproduce copyright material:

S. Thobani, Indian Woman, Bulletin of Concerned Asian Scholars in Kim Knott "20/20 Visions" published by SPCK in 1992. Reprinted by permission of SPCK;

Extract from "Petals, poems and a sense of shrine" by Paul Valley, taken from *The Independent*. Reprinted by permission of *The Independent*;

Extract from "The Great Learning and the Mean in Action" by E. R. Hughes, published by J. M. Dent. Reprinted by permission of David Higham Associates Limited;

Extract from "Mencius" translated by D. C. Lau (Penguin Classics 1970) Copyright © D. C. Lau 1970. Reprinted by permission of Penguin Books Limited;

Extract from "I Ching" Classic of Changes by Cary F. Baynes, published by Princeton University Press, USA. Reprinted by permission of the publisher.

The publishers apologize for any errors or omissions in the above list and would be grateful to be notified of any corrections that should be incorporated in the next edition or reprint of this book.

Chapter 1

....

Studying Religion: Issues in Definition and Method

Elizabeth Ramsey and Shannon Ledbetter

Defining Religions

The Study of Religion

Approaches to the Study of Religion

Academic Disciplines and the Study of Religions

Encountering Religion is a textbook about religion. While this might sound straight-forward, right at the outset we confront our first difficulty. What exactly do we mean by religion? If the word religion is going to be used at all, there is obviously a need for a working understanding of what the word religion means, in order for any useful communication to be possible. However, as we shall discover, it seems that any single attempt to define religion will be inadequate, since such a definition cannot take sufficient account of the complexities of the numerous contexts and ways in which the word religion is used. Nevertheless, attempts to define religion are more than semantic games. Our definition of religion will influence what we choose to include when we discuss religion and what we are able to learn about and, perhaps more importantly, what we are able to learn *from* religion.

Defining Religions

The exercise of defining religion will reveal our perceptions of the phenomena which are labeled as religion and perhaps enable us to see the connections between these perceptions and our own past experiences and attitudes. For example, does a definition confine religion to what might be considered an accident of birth or socialization? Does a definition represent a bias, either positive or negative, towards religion as a whole or even, perhaps, towards particular religious traditions or certain phenomena? Does a definition include emerging forms of religion throughout the world, or is it related to religious traditions and what has formed part of your own experience in the past? Does a definition help you to feel confident about what counts as religion and what does not? This chapter therefore has the aim both of encouraging greater precision in terms of our thinking about religion and ensuring that our perceptions of religion reflect the multi-faceted nature of religion.

One place we could begin is with the etymology of the word "religion" (i.e., the history of a word). The word comes from the Latin *religio*. It is not a neutral, descriptive term, but has strong overtones of a political and moral nature. Cicero derived *religio* from *relegere*, to "re-read" ("that which is re-read," i.e., passed on along chains of tradition). Alternatively, Lactantius traces religion to *religare*, "to bind fast" (that which binds men and women to one another and to the gods). Etymologically then, "religion" has a strong emphasis on community, which is ironic given the tendency in the modern world to think of religion as something private and personal.

Linked to this etymological debate, it is important to note that not all religions have a word for "religion." So a Hindu who is writing in English may be happy enough to use the western convention of using the word "religion." However, when a Hindu is writing in a vernacular such as Hindi or Tamil, then the words used to describe the traditions of "Hinduism" (which is another word which is not found in the tradition itself) will have different connotations. As John Hinnells has shown, the Sanskrit word dharma, coming as it does from the root *dhr-*, has a variety of meanings. The primary sense however is that of "self-subsistence." Dharma is thus "that which maintains" all other entities and is used to refer to the "totality" of what is otherwise called "religion." "The characteristic term for what in the West is called 'Hinduism', from a metaphysical point of view at least, is 'sanatana (eternal) dharma'."[1]

For these reasons, if we are going to make sense of modern usage, then we need to think much more broadly about the meaning of the word. To provide some limits for our discussion, we shall in what follows examine only three different approaches to the definition of religion. The first is the traditional approach; it is the one taken in most dictionaries. This stresses the supernatural elements in religion. The second, exploiting the work of Ninian Smart, suggests that religion is best defined (or to be more accurate "understood") in terms of seven "dimensions." And the third approach defines religion in terms of "function." This is the approach often taken by the various disciplines, for example, sociology and psychology. We shall take these various models in turn.

Defining religion in terms of the supernatural

A feature of religion which is generally considered to be an important part of any understanding of the word religion is the dimension of the supernatural. This can be particularly well illustrated in the case of most dictionary definitions. The *Oxford English Dictionary*, for example, has defined religion as "recognition of superhuman controlling power, and especially of a personal God, entitled to obedience." The advantage of including belief in God is that it then excludes what are generally considered to be secular alternatives to religion, such as secular humanism and dialectical materialism, or even an everyday activity such as football. (The example of football is actually given as part of the definition of religion in the *Collins English Dictionary*.) If any consuming interest can be referred to as a person's religion, then the definition becomes so broad that the word religion loses any useful meaning for constructive discourse.

One problem with this stress on the supernatural, however, is that not all religious traditions make the supernatural dimension central. For example, in certain forms of Theravada Buddhism, God or the gods are not important in its theory or practice. Siddhartha Gautama, traditionally the name of the man who later became the Buddha, or "Enlightened One," discounted the importance of worshipping the gods. He suggested that gods are not helpful in the path of finding harmony and eliminating sorrow – the goal of "Enlightenment." The way of life which he taught was aimed at the much more practical goals of living in peace and contentment with all other creatures.

Another example is Confucianism. This "religion" began in China with Confucius, who taught very little about God or gods, although he did believe that ancestors live on in a "heaven." Again, what Confucius emphasized was the importance of achieving harmony. The form of harmony which he taught has a very practical expression in that it can be seen to be achieved within families, then within the wider community, the nation, and only then, maybe, with heaven itself. Gautama and Confucius both taught that, as a matter of priority, their followers should work towards the welfare of people rather than the appeasement of God or towards an afterlife.

It is true that belief in God is important in many religions. But it is wrong to assume it is central to all religions. For this reason, Ninian Smart has suggested that it might be more helpful to talk about different dimensions of religion. Beliefs (which for many religions have taken the form of belief in God) and the doctrines which convey these beliefs, are viewed together as only one of several other dimensions. Christianity is unique in the emphasis it places on a set of beliefs in terms of its own self-definition. It is to this dimensional approach that we turn next.

The "dimensional approach"

If we turn to the *Collins English Dictionary*, we find the following definition of religion: "belief in, worship of, or obedience to, a supernatural power or powers considered to be divine or to have control of human destiny." It then goes on to state: "any formal or institutionalised expression of such belief; the attitude and feeling of one who believes in a transcendent controlling power or powers; the way of life determined by the vows of poverty, chastity, and obedience." In addition it is "something of overwhelming importance to a person" and this is where the example is given of football being a person's "religion." And finally the dictionary suggests religion is, "Either 'the practice of sacred ritual observances' or the 'sacred rites and ceremonies' themselves."

In a single, short, dictionary entry under the term religion, we thus find the various dimensions of religion listed, including: belief, worship, obedience, social organization, attitudes and feelings, a way of life, overwhelming importance, ritual, rites, and ceremonies. These dimensions in fact provide the basis for the well-known six-dimensional (later seven-dimensional) classification of the characteristics of religion provided by Ninian Smart. Smart suggested that there are certain dimensions, or recurring motifs, to be found in all religions. The identification of these enables progress to be made with the study of religion. This dimensional model has proved influential in the field of religious studies, certainly in Britain where it was used in developing national curricula of religious education, but also in Scandinavia and more broadly.

Smart's framework consisted, first, of the *doctrinal* dimension, which may also include creed, if appropriate. Examples might be the Christian doctrine of the Trinity, or the Four Noble Truths of Buddhism. The second dimension is the *mythological* and examples given include the stories of creation which exist in so many cultures and traditions as well as in the Jewish and the Christian traditions, or the Ramayana epic in Hinduism. The *ethical* dimension may be illustrated by Torah, or the Sermon on the Mount. The *ritual* dimension includes, for example, ways of praying, such as the importance for Muslims of turning towards Mecca. The *experiential* dimension represents the feelings of the followers of a living faith, feelings which must be reborn in each generation, either gradually or in a dramatic conversion experience. The last of the original six dimensions, the *social*, refers to the whole way of life that results from being a follower of a faith tradition, exemplified by communities and institutions formed by believers, such as temples and monasteries. Ninian Smart later added the dimension of the *symbolic* to incorporate those "physical" means by which humanity has achieved proximity to the "holy" or the "Beyond" in whatever sense these are perceived. Such means often involve the elements, especially water and fire, and also the results of human interaction with the physical world in the form of food and drink.

In practice, these dimensions are very closely interwoven. Often, for example, the myth and the symbol are inextricably linked and together comprise the ritual and thus contribute to the social cohesion of a group. The dimensional approach is very helpful in that the dimensions capture the multi-faceted nature of religion, but as a definition it too has its limitations, as Smart would acknowledge. Religions participate in or reflect these dimensions in very uneven ways. As already mentioned, Christianity is more preoccupied with right beliefs; Buddhism, for example, stresses right practices. For people who accept Christian assumptions about the nature of religion, Smart intended his dimensional approach at least to challenge those assumptions and broaden the range of perspectives upon the phenomenon of religion.

Exercise   1   Imagine you have been commissioned to study religious life forms on planet Earth. You have never visited Earth before and know nothing about its religious customs and institutions. Where would you start looking for data? What sort of data might count as admissible evidence?

For example: What about the phenomena of football stadiums, Rock concerts, the "sun-worship" which appears to take place on beaches in every part of the world? How far can we tell what people are doing by observing their actions? Can religion be defined in terms of the function it is performing?

We turn now to the third approach to the definition of religion. This approach stresses the roles religion plays in our private and public lives.

The functional approach

What are commonly referred to as the "sciences" of religion often make use of what is called a *functional* approach to the definition of religion. Different disciplines define religion in different ways. So Karl Marx suggested that "Religion is the sigh of the oppressed creature, the feeling of a heartless world, and the soul of soulless circumstances. Religion is the opiate of the people."[2] This definition has often been understood to underline the oppressive role religion can play in certain cultures and circumstances. As we review the twentieth century there is no doubt that the world continues to be a harsh environment in which to live and people do crave relief. [Sigmund Freud] talked about religion in a rather different way but maybe not in such a different way from Marx as has sometimes been assumed. Freud claimed that "the benevolent rule of a divine Providence allays our fear of the dangers of life."[3] He is stressing the psychological role religion can play. However, perhaps these rather negative accounts of religion need to be supplemented by more positive images. So Walter Houston Clark suggested that "religion can be most characteristically described as the inner experience of the individual when he senses a Beyond, especially as evidenced by the effect of this experience on his behavior when he actively attempts to harmonize his life with the Beyond."[4] Again sociologists have a different perspective on religion. In *Religion and Ideology: A Reader*, the editors write as follows:

> A religion is a complex mixture of beliefs, values, symbols and rituals. Most major religions, such as Christianity, Islam, Hinduism and Buddhism, contain beliefs and values about this world, whatever they may say about another, super-empirical one. It is the influence of the empirical and super-empirical beliefs and values of a religion upon the social, economic, political and cultural activities of various groups of people, especially classes and ethnic groups, which is of concern to sociologists and social theorists . . . the issue of central concern to sociologists is not whether a particular religious claim is true or false, but what consequences believing it has for particular groups in specific circumstances.[5]

So we can see how the approach to the study of religion significantly affects one's definition of religion. Each approach has its own insights, but it would be a diminishment of the richness of religion to treat any particular approach as absolute.

The Study of Religion

The whole issue of definition has now flowed into the issues surrounding the study of religion. This is an endeavor which, again, is both elusive and multi-faceted. We have seen already the difficulties in coming up with a conclusive definition of religion. Much seems to depend on which approach to religion one takes. Ian Markham notes the positive character of religion, its distinctive Otherness in his "negative" definition:

> Religion is a way of life (one which embraces a total world view, certain ethical demands, and certain social practices) that refuses to accept the secular view that sees human life as nothing more than complex bundles of atoms in an ultimately meaningless universe.[6]

It is the task of the rest of this chapter to look at the various approaches and tools for studying religion. Studying religion, for most people, is a discipline which carries with it a personal element which is not found when studying other areas of academia. It is thus important to think about our commitments and biases when studying religions, as they will likely come to the fore quite quickly. A central question in this regard is whether one must be a follower of a tradition, that is a believer, in order to properly understand that tradition, or whether a more detached approach is necessary. We will return to this question later.

We will begin our look at the study of religion with a brief historical survey of the study of comparative religions. We will then consider three approaches to the study of religion, namely the phenomenological, the confessional and finally the empathetic.

History of comparative religions

The history of the tree of religion with its many branches, as Mahatma Gandhi would describe the world's religions, has been long and varied. People have been examining how their beliefs differ ever since they realized that their neighbor worshiped another God or practiced different rituals. Unfortunately, people have not always been open-minded when comparing their own religious practices with those of others. People often wanted others to conform to their own beliefs and sometimes resorted to force in order to make them do so. As a consequence, much of the history of inter-religious interaction has been hostile or patronizing.

The 1996 film *The English Patient* portrayed the tales of Herodotus being told around the campfire, and the main character could always be seen clutching his well-worn copy of *The Histories*. Herodotus was a Greek historian who traveled extensively in the fifth century BCE (before the common era) and wrote, significantly, about the religious practices of different cultures. Herodotus was one of the first scholars to write down his findings in a comparative form and he highlights his own Greek culture against the others. The **Stoics** also provide an important contribution to the history of the study of comparative religions. The Stoics were a Greco-Roman school of philosophy founded in Athens around 300 BCE. They are credited with classifying certain familiar traits of different religions into what has come to be referred to as "natural religion." Natural religion is commonly understood as comprised of those fundamental truths common to all religions which are knowable through sense experience and rationality. The Stoics believed in a single all-encompassing God (*logos* – Greek for word) whose mind or spirit was thought to be the creative power or reason behind the universe. Each human being contained a part of this *logos*, as did the rest of creation. At death, matter disintegrated and the "smaller" spirit returned to the universal, eternal spirit. Stoic natural religion claimed that all religions are, ultimately, part of this universal *logos*. We get our modern usage of the characteristic "stoic" from the idea that the greatest virtue a follower of Stoicism could have was to resist the senses and the passions in order to have "insight" into the eternal *logos*. A person thus resisted temptation by sensory excesses since it was detrimental to knowledge of the eternal spirit.

In the Greco-Roman world, the great classical novels and epic poems telling of the battles between nations and gods, combined with Stoicism's dualistic understanding of mind and matter, provided the contexts within which "other" religious traditions were understood. In general this context tolerated a great deal of pluralism – though of course not always a benign one. Against this background, the Judeo-Christian attitude of exclusivity towards other religions stands in sharp contrast. Much of this attitude may be attributed to the nature of Judaism and Christianity as monotheistic cultures, as well as the severe persecution followers of these traditions suffered at particular places and times. Judaism has always been a small minority tradition and Christianity, particularly at its inception, attracted considerable negative attention. Both groups have thus felt vulnerable to outside forces. Christianity even went so far as to assert that its adherents should not associate with non-Christians, except to convert them. The threat these traditions felt led them to consolidate and protect themselves through exclusivity. Some of the early Church Fathers emphasized this attitude by perpetuating the idea that other religions were the work of "fallen angels" or "evil spirits." Ironically, this exclusivity may well have allowed these traditions to survive through hostile circumstances and one of these traditions, Christianity, eventually became the dominant tradition of the western world. While we cannot discuss here the history and circumstances of this ascendancy, as western students it is important to take into consideration the historic bias in favor of Christianity and Judaism intrinsic to modern English-speaking societies.

While the current era in the West is dominated by Judeo-Christian culture, the other world religions have contributed a great deal throughout history to the comparative study of religions. A Muslim, Shahrastani (d. 1153 CE), is credited with writing a definitive survey of the world's religions in the twelfth century which far outshone any concurrent Christian study, and in the thirteenth century the *Examination of the Three Faiths* acknowledged the familial resemblance of Judaism, Christianity, and Islam and their common ancestor in the figure of the patriarch Abraham.[7]

The explorations of the so-called "new worlds" which began in the fifteenth century brought Christendom into contact with ancient and highly developed cultures. Ironically, a degree of religious tolerance grew out of western imperialism and Christianity. Tragically, however, despite the efforts of certain Christian explorers who through their travels gained increased awareness and knowledge, there was little sympathy for the indigenous religions, and oppression, persecution and forced conversions were all too common, and usually with the blessing of the explorer's church and state. The film *The Mission* illustrates quite profoundly one such occurrence between the Spanish Roman Catholic Church and Brazil, though a contrary picture is offered by Matteo Ricci (1552–1610). His life and exploits offer a more tolerant model of a Christian explorer and missionary. Ricci was a Jesuit missionary who went to China and found great wisdom and morality in the Chinese religion of Confucianism. Ricci's writings provided valuable information for subsequent scholars of comparative religion and gave fuel to the **Deists** who claimed that all religions, such as Confucianism, were essentially rational.

Deism, a version of Natural Theology, developed in response to the scientific arguments of the seventeenth and early eighteenth century. Many scientists during this period saw the complexity and order of the world as requiring a designer. Both cosmological arguments (where God is inferred from the existence of the world) and teleological arguments (where the order of the world is credited to an intelligent designer) were put forward as purely rational explanations of the world, crucially without interspersing supernatural elements. However, the aim of the Deists was to provide an explanation of all forms of religion and this led them to disregard the unique historical and cultural contexts which gave each religion its own distinctive character. Deists believed in a universal power which might be considered the ultimate reality or the supreme being, but which does not actively participate in world affairs or provide the means for salvation (that is, they did not believe in **providence** or the possibility of the **atonement**).

In the eighteenth and nineteenth centuries, a few scholars began to examine the factors identified as rational and irrational in religion. This subsequently developed into the study of the phenomenon of religion. These factors consisted of what could be discerned about religious experience by human reason and the emotional factors or feelings. The hypothesis emerged that religion was not static, as the Deists imagined (that is, a universal set of ideas which could be fathomed by reason and a strict and immutable moral code), but was dynamic, progressive, and included a dimension of uniquely religious phenomena. Religion was individualized in the sense that individual experience was taken into account when considering religion as a whole. This was an important step in the study of comparative religions in that it recognized the value of comparing and describing individual experience when attempting to explain the motive or inspiration behind the experience. The main proponents of this view were the German liberal theologian **Friedrich Schleiermacher** (1768–1834) and to a lesser extent the eminent German philosopher **Georg Friedrich Hegel** (1770–1831).[8] We will discuss further the way in which this attitude affected the practice of the study of religion in the section on the phenomenology of religion.

A growing sensitivity in the nineteenth century to the need to acquire different languages was an important component in the study of religions. The discipline of learning language skills and the systematic translation of holy books also meant that religious studies contained a clear "scientific" methodology and served to protect the study of religion from attacks by scientists. Such critical scientists thought that all study of religion was bound to involve superstition and uncritical reflection. In response to this, concentration on the critical translation of the Scriptures of the world's religions gave the study of religion the air and sometimes the substance of (social-) scientific endeavor. A person would undertake to decipher the language, culture, history and religion of a particular community or country and then attempt to discover what links there were between the results of the study and that of one's own culture. In this way linguistic analysis provided a connection between scientific method and comparative religion. While there were important scholarly benefits arising from the practice of translation, the personal benefits may have been even greater. When one becomes intimate with another language, an individual gains a special window into that particular culture. Armed with this greater appreciation, many western linguists in the nineteenth century helped to create a more open atmosphere to the rest of the world's religions and cultures, especially those of the East. For example, there were many British scholars during the nineteenth century who believed that in order for a British citizen to be involved in the empire (for example, India), he or she had to be well-versed in India's history and religions, which included the study of one or more of the indigenous languages. Some of the results of this attitude of the "British Raj" remain definitive works in "oriental studies."

One of the most important events of the nineteenth century was the publication of Charles Darwin's *Origin of the Species* (1859). For the West, the hypothesis of evolution set out by Darwin changed forever the way western culture looked at religion and science as may be seen in the following quotation: "The whole of human culture was examined afresh on new principles, with a view to discerning the origins, development and goals of each separate manifestation of the human spirit."[9] Evolution seemed to provide a framework from which all of the various approaches to the study of religion (for example, philosophical, historical, and sociological) could develop. With attitudes opening up to the study of religions, **Friedrich Max Müller** was the first to attempt to systematize the study of comparative religions with a consciously evolutionary theme. In his *Introduction to the Science of Religion* (1873) Müller called for people to compile "a Science of Religion, based on an impartial and truly scientific comparison of all, or at all events, of the most important, religions of mankind."[10] The significance of this statement lies not in that there was an interest in the study of other religions, but that it marked the beginning of a systematic approach to the study of comparative religions. From Müller's time the study of religions became diversified and subsets of the various approaches to the study of comparative religions were formed.

At the beginning of the twenty-first century, our interest in other faiths remains strong. Our world shrinks ever further due to advances in technology and communication. We are able to watch history in the making and view other cultures much more easily through travel and the media. When we study comparative religions we are able to conceptualize other cultures much better than in the past. While there are more opportunities for expanding our own knowledge and self-fulfillment, there is an even greater responsibility to care for our world and to respect our religious neighbors.

Exercises

2   Discuss some of the ways in which religion may be a difficult subject to discuss and why in certain circumstances conversation may have profound effects on currently held beliefs?
3   How did the modern period create the subject of "comparative religion"?
4   Traditionally, Judaism and Christianity viewed other religions with suspicion. Name some ways in which suspicions have been eased historically and explore some ways in which the world's religions may live peaceably in the future

Approaches to the Study of Religion

If you read the Quran, you must read it with the eye of the Muslim; if you read the Bible, you must read it with the eye of the Christian; if you read the Gita you must read it with the eye of a Hindu.[11]

Probably the most important decision we will make when we begin to study other religions is to determine the approach we will take and, consequently, to be aware of the difficulties and issues surrounding this approach. Crucially we must ask ourselves what preconceived notions, prejudices and understandings of religions we begin with. We may be coming from a particular religious framework or none at all and it is important to spend a bit of time thinking about how we want to approach the study of religion. The following sections contain brief discussions of three significant approaches in the study of religion (there are, of course, others): the phenomenological, the confessional, and the empathetic.

The phenomenological approach

The phenomenological approach aims at objectivity through the use of putatively neutral criteria which transcend the personal and cultural. We are said to obtain objectivity when we look at religion in an entirely detached manner. Many people feel that this is the only way for teachers or professors of religious studies to operate. After all, this approach maintains, we cannot have the professor trying to persuade the class of his or her beliefs . . . any other approach would be an abuse of power! "Objective" approaches are popular because they have the appearance of being the fairest. However, as we shall see, appearances can be deceiving. The weakness of such an approach is that no one can, in fact, be completely free from cultural/linguistic bias; the data one collects and the way in which it is interpreted will never be entirely value-free. But before we take this point any further, let us consider phenomenology in greater detail.

Phenomenology was originally conceived of by the philosopher **Edmund Husserl** (1859–1938) as an attempt to appreciate the pure structures of consciousness without the intrusion of preconceptions or cultural conditioning. Phenomenology, in a general and simplified sense, is a complex philosophical process of looking at the interaction of our minds with our environments (both seen and unseen) while filtering out everything that is extraneous to the "object" the mind is perceiving. Phenomenology is then relevant to the way in which we perceive our own religion as well as the way we look at other religions in that it allows us to approach religious **phenomena** in a putatively more objective manner. Moreover, and perhaps more importantly, it may give us the opportunity to critique a much wider range of phenomena with a wider openness. The phenomenology of religion provides a complementary philosophical method to the history-critical model. While history strives to recount the data, facts and events of religion, phenomenology attempts to probe the deeper meanings and intent of religion.

How did phenomenology achieve objectivity? Husserl's primary concern was to excavate the structures of pure consciousness and pure phenomena, that is, to get below all of the cultural biases and preconceptions overlaying the mind in order to discover how the mind perceived the phenomena – by which he meant the actual content of the ideas before it. Husserl's idea of *bracketing* or holding back the vast accumulation of judgments and assumptions about our outer reality (that is, everything outside of our consciousness) is the central tenet of phenomenology. It is important to note that Husserl's view of phenomena differs from **Immanuel Kant's** (1724–1804) conception of this term. Kant understood there to be a kind of wall between what he called the phenomenal (the objects or appearances of things as we actually perceive them), and the noumenal (those objects as they are in themselves, independent of our knowledge). For Kant, this distinction was a technical one serving to delimit the boundaries of our knowledge. Kant's distinction implied that there was no way we could know the noumenal, the things in themselves, but rather we could only know the phenomena. Husserl, on the other hand, asserted that the wall between noumena and phenomena was simply made up of all of the preconceptions our consciousness had built up, and hence it could be broken down provided one had the right skills. Phenomenology as a method of philosophizing meant to equip one with these skills.

So Husserl claimed, perhaps idealistically, that in order to find the pure meaning of a particular phenomenon one had to rid oneself of all presuppositions. This was done through "bracketing" off all of one's preconceptions and judgments and turning the gaze of one's consciousness inward on itself. This, it was claimed, would reveal the essential content of our consciousness – the phenomena – without subjective bias. A student of Husserl's, **Martin Heidegger** (1889–1976), took the claim further, positing the argument that one begins to intuit in the phenomenological process not just the essential meaning, but also hidden meanings.

Up to this point we have been discussing phenomenology in a purely philosophical sense. How is this approach used in the study of religion in a more practical way? **Max Scheler** (1874–1928) used phenomenology to analyze spiritual experience. Scheler believed that human beings contained an eternal element which implied two distinct human characteristics. First, the eternal showed the permanent possibility for religious experience. Second, the eternal indicates that humans are more than simply natural beings. Scheler's ideas of the eternal are related to Husserl's concept of *lebenswelt* or the "world of lived experience." Another broadly phenomenological treatment of religion is that of **Rudolf Otto** (1869–1937), whose book *The Idea of the Holy* (1923) set out an argument for the **numinous** as the central element of all religion. Otto emphasized the importance of the mysterious Other which gives religion its unique quality. "There is no religion in which it [the Other] does not live as the real innermost core, and without it no religion would be worthy of the name."[12] Otto's work is important because it paved the way for a renewal of research into personal religious experience which included mystical experience.

Phenomenological approaches to the study of religion gained popularity in recent times through departments of Religious Studies. These academic, interdisciplinary departments are a relatively recent development in the academy and are, in some instances, conscious responses to confessionally-based schools of theology. **Phenomenology**, with its bracketing off of subjective biases such as faith commitment, was seen to be the most appropriate model for the study of religion in these departments – though this has of late come under considerable criticism. The most significant critique highlights the fact that to be completely objective is impossible. Strict detachment from everything that is integral to our being, elements which religion often provides, simply cannot happen. Our prejudices and assumptions are part of what makes us who we are and we are bound to bring them with us to our studies. Also, an objective approach or one which attempts to "bracket" away all of the cultural and historical attributes that accompany a religious event or experience often fails to do justice to the felt experience of being part of a religious tradition. A cold and detached examination which provides the bare facts of a religion does not always appreciate the subtle beauty and wonder which a believer might feel as a committed follower of his or her tradition. In turn, this can leave a student puzzled as to why anyone would defend religion to the death or enter into a monastery in order to dedicate the whole of one's life to a particular religious tradition. Such fervor and commitment is partially explained in the confessional approach to the study of religion to which we now turn.

The confessional approach

Imagine that we are sitting at a table next to two people who are having a heated conversation. One person is a member of the "Christian Fellowship" who takes the Christian message of "go out into all the world and preach the Gospel" seriously. The other person is a traditional Muslim, equally committed to his or her own faith. Each person is confessing their own beliefs, but as we listen we are able to discern that each of these individuals is unwilling to accept any portion of the other's argument. There appears to be a lack of risk-taking by the two people which, were it present, would allow each of the disputants to both teach and learn from the other. This illustration of the confessional approach is a simple one, but is an example of how this approach often looks in practice.

But there may be more to the situation than meets the eye. Perhaps each of the hypothetical evangelists above is committed to the belief that their religion alone offers mankind the solution to its ills. In this case, is it not rational to want to share this cure with all and sundry? Furthermore, what if they believe that most people they meet are not even aware that there is a problem? Again, it is entirely rational that our evangelists, as caring people, would wish to help others by alerting their neighbors to the dangers surrounding them and showing them the way out. The point here is that strongly committed religious believers are, most often, doing what for them is the only rational, right thing to do. We must bear this in mind when we study religion since strong confessionalism can sometimes cause us to discount the claims of believers as "fundamentalism" or zealotry.

A stronger claim is that we cannot actually understand a religion unless we are members of that faith community; to know what a religious belief or practice means, we must know how it *feels* to be committed to that belief or practice *from the inside*. We are reminded of the old adage to "walk a mile in my shoes if you would truly know me," and the Christian theologian St. Anselm's formula, "faith seeking under-standing." There appears to be a great deal of sense in this approach. We might know all about how to make a cake through reading numerous recipes for cakes, and yet have no real idea of what a cake, or perhaps a good cake, is if we had never tasted one. But while there is some sense to the claim that experience adds an important element to our understanding of religion, it can by no means be essential.

To maintain that experience is essential to real knowledge is to deny the ability of language to communicate knowledge, and indeed it is a roadblock to the study of religion. While it might be difficult to explain what a particular religious belief or practice really means, it can usually be communicated sufficiently through the use of metaphors, analogies, symbols and images, so that we are satisfied that we have done the belief or practice justice. A more serious criticism of the confes-sional standpoint would be that it undermines conversion, so that, ironically, our disputants above, if they were fully confessionalist, could not hope to convince the other to their view because to understand the view one must already be a part of the community that holds it.

Clearly the confessionalist approach to the study of religion is seriously flawed, as is the phenomenological approach delineated above. A third way, perhaps be-tween the supposed "objectivity" of phenomenology and the unabashed subjectivity of confessionalism, must be found. This third way, the approach taken throughout this text, is the "empathetic" approach, which we will now consider.

Empathetic approach

Imagine yourself looking at a house at night. There are lights on inside the house which allow you to look inside at the people walking around. The house is built in a style with which you are unfamiliar and the people are sitting in a circle eating on the floor with many bowls in the middle of the circle. **Epoche**, or the shedding of preconceptions when engaged in the phenomenological study of religion, asks that as you stand outside the house observing the family, you should not bring with you any ideas of how one should eat or what kind of house people are supposed to live in. Instead, you are to take the experience at face value as an outsider, making no judgments at all. The confessional approach, on the other hand, would have you either shun the house and its occupants entirely since they might be committed to, in your view, the eating of the wrong foods or perhaps living in unsafe houses, or march in and try to convince them of their wrong ways of eating and the faulty nature of their house and then show them how to eat "real" food and live in "real" houses. The empathetic approach which we will be taking in this book provides a third option. It asks that you knock on the door and, with the great politeness and humility of a revered guest, be a part of that meal and be inside the house for a while. This approach requires that we take seriously the beliefs and practices of our hosts, for it is their homes in which we are temporarily guests. It does not mean that we should divorce ourselves from our own beliefs, that is impossible, but it does ask for an openness to learn and a willingness to converse. The empathetic approach relies, for better or worse, on the shared humanity of all, believers and unbelievers, and this includes an acceptance of all of the frailties and powers which human beings own. It requires diligent study and the full use of our imaginations. Its reward is a greater understanding of the faith and lives of our fellow human beings, an appreciation for the richness of other religious traditions as well as their shortcomings, and possibly a greater glimpse of the truths which drive the majority of people on the earth. While there are difficulties with the empathetic approach, some of which we will describe later and others which will become clear through the following chapters, its strength lies in its being a "middle path" through the sometimes difficult passage which is the study of religion, guiding us between the Scylla of phenomenological "objectivity" and the Charybdis of confessionalist subjectivity.

Exercises

5   Divide into two groups, the confessionalists and the phenomenologists, and debate the question: "In order to understand a religion, one must believe its tenets."

6   Reflect on the arguments given by both sides and consider how the empathetic approach might respond to both of them.

Academic Disciplines and the Study of Religions

We will consider very briefly, below, the contributions made to the study of religion from various academic disciplines. I refer the reader to other chapters in this text for further discussion of these areas.

History

Mircea Eliade (1907–86) is considered to be the most substantial contributor to the historical study of religions. Eliade sought to better understand religion through historical circumstances and endeavored to determine how history explained religious phenomena, or, how the "idea of the holy" manifested itself in a historical occurrence. Eliade coined a word to describe this process, "**hierophanies**," which is the manifestation of the sacred in creation. Hierophanies may occur as sacred places and people as well, such as the **Dome of the Rock** or **Jesus Christ**. For Eliade, Jesus Christ was the supreme example of a hierophany in that he represented the whole of the transcendent as well as the whole of human history within a single being.

Sociology/culture

Emile Durkheim (1858–1917) is considered to be one of the most important sociologists of religion. Durkheim was one of the first to discuss the significance of social groups in the perpetuation of religion. He claimed that there is a distinct difference between an individual seeking to make sense of religion and the group. Durkheim claims that religion needs a social group to give it life. Society is what an individual is born into and gives that individual the language, moral code and cultural attitudes which make him or her into the unique person they are. This hypothesis includes the religion one is born into. Societies continue after people die and religion is perpetuated by the group's continued practice of the tradition. Durkheim did not believe in the transcendent, but he did acknowledge that the ideas of religion which people perpetuated were true in that they gave people a sense of worth, and substance to their life in the world. Although modernity has seen a much greater number of people moving from one country or culture to another, it is still rare for an individual to convert to a different faith from the one he or she is born into. Faith traditions tend to carry cultural attributes as well as religious ones.

    Max Weber (1864–1920), another significant sociologist, was interested in the ways in which religion influenced society. His book, *The Protestant Ethic and the Spirit of Capitalism*, aims to show how the Lutheran and Calvinist idea of work (the Protestant work ethic) contributed to the modern nation-state and capitalist society.

Psychology

When we look at the psychological aspects of religion it gives us an insight into the behavioral and ritualistic aspects of religion which are an integral part of the experience as a whole. As we delve into the feelings and thoughts behind those actions and behavioral patterns, we gain knowledge of the psychological source and function of those feelings. Sigmund Freud and Carl Jung develop contrary views of the genesis and function of religion. It was William James, on the other hand, who provided perhaps the best typography and compendium of the variety of religious experience in his book of the same name.

Linguistics

We have already mentioned the important role language has played in the study of religion and the fact that language has helped to contribute to a formal "scientific" method for the study of religion. There are two important elements to the use of language in the study of religion. First, the one which we have already discussed, that the deciphering of different languages helps us to delve into deeper meanings of the words. For example, Friedrich Max Müller, who formulated the first systematic study of religions, began his interest with the study of Sanskrit and the holy books of the Indian religions. This led to Müller eventually becoming fascinated with mythology and, finally, led him to devise a "science of religion." Müller's science of religion was a system whereby he looked up the derivation of all of the words for gods in order to discover their similarities (i.e., the Latin *deus*, the Sanskrit *deva* and the Greek *theos* all refer to brightness).[13]

The second reason language is so important in the study of religion is that it provides access to a religion in a deeper way than with secondary texts and translations. The primary texts are those written in the original language and allow us to get underneath most of the layers of interpretation which accompany religious texts. An example of this emphasis on original texts is Islam. The Qur'an was originally revealed to the prophet Muhammad in a classical form of Arabic. Not only was this particular Arabic for the use of intellectuals, but it was also confined to a particular city in the sixth century CE (Common Era). Muslim scholars believe that the Qur'an is only to be read in Arabic and in order to truly comprehend the essence of Islam, the Holy book should really only be read in the dialect originally revealed to Muhammad. Now of course this is impossible or impractical for many students, so we must rely on the integrity and accuracy of the linguists – which is the reason this skill is so vital for the study of religion.

Of course, a major criticism with linguistics is that any translation is subject to the bias and subjectivity of the translator. If we cannot master the languages necessary to read the original texts of a tradition, then we must be aware of the possible biases of the translators on whom we rely. Clearly the area is complex and we must bear this in mind when we deal with the texts of a tradition.

Exercises   7   The setting is a TV talk show. The panel of guests have been labeled "Academics who won't work together." This is a classic case of the left hand not knowing what the right hand is doing. Each of the four academics has just published "the definitive book" on religion using only his or her discipline.

Choose a host.

Choose the panel: historian, psychologist, sociologist, linguist.

The rest of the class will be the audience who will be trying to get the panellists to work together in their studies of religion.

The presenter will bring out the guests one by one, who will explain who they are and the approach his or her respective discipline utilizes. He or she will try to convince the audience that religion should be seen only through their particular discipline's eyes and why they don't need to consult with their colleagues.

Hint: collaboration means they won't sell as many of their books.

8   Keep in mind Karl Marx's assertion that religion is an "opiate for the masses" and provides relief from our everyday activities. Or, is religion itself the motivation for how we live and conduct our societies. How would your attitude to these two approaches affect the way we study religion and relate to other disciplines?

9   Is the true motivation economics (the selling of books) or is there a convincing argument for keeping the disciplines separate?

10   Would collaboration weaken the stand of the individual disciplines?

11   Is religion a collective experience or is faith merely a personal experience where outside influences or phenomena are incidental?

GLOSSARY

Atonement   To be at-one with after a period of separation and/or the means by which one restores relationship (i.e., Jesus Christ is believed by Christians to be the atoner for the sins of humanity through the act of the crucifixion).

Deism   Refers to the belief in a supreme being who is the ultimate source of being, yet does not intervene in natural or historical phenomena through revelation, action, or salvation. Deists are most frequently associated with those who adhere to enlightenment principles.

Dome of the Rock   An Islamic holy site located in Jerusalem. Used as an example of an hierophany as coined by Mircea Eliade.

Durkheim, Emile (1858–1917)   A French sociologist of religion who contributed greatly to our understanding of how religion interacts with culture. He was particularly influential in his explanation of religion and ritual as the symbolic representation of societal bonds. His major work in this area was, *The Elementary Forms of the Religious Life* (1912).

Eliade, Mircea (1907–86)   A Romanian phenomenologist and historian who was primarily concerned with the place of myth and symbol. One of his major works is a three-volume *History of Religious Ideas* (1979–86).

Epoche The primary method for "doing" phenomenology for Edmund Husserl. Epoche consists of bracketing a particular object and then focusing on the actual structure of consciousness which makes us aware of that object, thereby capturing the essence of the object. The technical term for this process is transcendental reduction and refers to getting rid of all of the layers (i.e., prejudices, preconceptions, cultural conditioning) that separate the pure essence of an object and the pure structure of our mind which is responsible for being aware of that object.

Heidegger, Martin (1889–1976) A German philosopher who was concerned with "*Dasein*" or human existence in the world. Heidegger wanted to unravel the complexities of how human beings interacted with everyday things such as hammering, through their essential rationality. Heidegger critiqued Edmund Husserl's idea that there was only one essential nature of a phenomenon, but that that essential nature was capable of pointing to many hidden natures.

Hegel, Georg Friedrich (1770–1831) A German philosopher known in part for developing the dialectical process which included a thesis followed by an antithesis and in which, through the process of struggling with both of these opposing ideas, a synthesis was arrived at. In this way Hegel believed that one was able to comprehend more of the whole rather than just a portion and that this was truth as opposed to partial truths.

Hierophanies Mircea Eliade coined this term to refer to "the idea of the holy" as it manifested itself as historical occurrence or in historical places.

Husserl, Edmund (1859–1938) A German philosopher who is credited with the conception of phenomenology. He was primarily concerned with "essences" and his major works are *Investigations in Logic* (1900) and *Experience and Judgement*, which was published posthumously.

Jesus Christ Mircea Eliade cited Jesus Christ as the ultimate hierophany.

Kant, Immanuel (1724–1804) Prussian philosopher born in Königsberg who is regarded as one of the greatest modern philosophers. His most famous works are: *Critique of Pure Reason* (1781), *Critique of Practical Reason* (1788), and *Critique of Judgement* (1790). One of Kant's contributions is his idea of the "noumenal." Noumena for Kant is the thing in itself as it is independent of human knowledge – apart from its appearance or phenomena. Kant believed that noumena was inaccessible to human knowledge, unlike Edmund Husserl who believed that the barriers could be broken down with the right tools.

Müller, Friedrich Max A German philologist who is perhaps best known for his work *Introduction to the Study of Religions* (1873). In this book Müller attempted to systematize the study of all of the world's religions thereby initiating the discipline of the study of comparative religions.

Numinous The idea of the numinous was conceived by Rudolph Otto and refers to that which cannot be apprehended by human rationality. However, the numinous can be felt and experienced and is indicative of what makes religion unique.

Otto, Rudolph (1869–1937) A German theologian whose most influential work, *The Idea of the Holy* (1917), emphasized the importance of the feeling of the "mysterious" other and was responsible for a renewed interest in mystical religious experience.

Phenomenology Devised by Edmund Husserl as a branch of philosophy which was concerned with "the things themselves." It is a process of bracketing or *epoche* of all preconceptions or cultural attributes towards an object in order to be able to describe the object or experience accurately.

Phenomenon Phenomena (pl.). An observable act, object or occurrence. A religious phenomenon is that which has spiritual connotations.

Providence The belief that God directly acts in the affairs of the world. There are five primary characteristics of providence: First, creativity in the form of God's created order; second, sustenance in the way that God sustains the world; three, "general providence" which refers to God working in and through the natural order; four, the idea of "special providence" which refers to a specific action of God's; five, miracle or that occurrence which defies explanation.

Scheler, Max (1874–1928) A German phenomenologist who wanted to emphasize the eternal and spiritual in human nature through the phenomena of religious experience. His ideas of

phenomena pointing to a larger world than is immediately known are related to Husserl's concept of the lifeworld or *lebenswelt*. Scheler's major work is *On the Eternal in Man* (1921).

Schleiermacher, Friedrich (1768–1834) A German theologian, his major works were, *On Religion: Speeches to its Cultured Despisers* (1799) and *The Christian Faith* (1821–2). Schleiermacher is most famous for his definition of religion as "the feeling of absolute dependence." He is influential for including experience in an understanding of religion and is credited with being the father of "liberal" theology.

Stoic Stoicism was founded by Zeno (335–263 BCE) in Athens, Greece. The name derives from the Greek *stoa* meaning "porch", which was where Zeno used to teach from. There are two main contributions of Stoicism: first, the idea of the *Logos* which refers to the world-soul of which every human being is part. Second, the critical idea of the association between nature and reason claimed that reason was interconnected with nature. The doctrine of natural law was derived from this second attribute. One of the most famous Stoics was Cicero and two of his most important works for Christianity were, *De Officiis*, which was a handbook for his son on moral conduct, and *De Officiis Ministrorum*, which was devoted to the ethics of reason.

Weber, Max (1864–1920) A German Sociologist who was most influential in his work on the influences of religion on Capitalism. His major work is, *The Protestant Work Ethic and the Spirit of Capitalism* (1904–5).

Notes and References

1 John Hinnells, Raymond Turvey, and Reginald Piggott, *Penguin Dictionary of Religions*, p. 106.
2 Karl Marx. From the introduction to "Towards a critique of Hegel's Philosophy of Right," in David McLellan, *Karl Marx: Selected Writings* (Oxford: Oxford University Press, 1977), pp. 63–4.
3 Sigmund Freud, James Strachey (ed.), *The Future of an Illusion*.
4 Walter Houston Clark described religion from a psychologist's perspective in *The Psychology of Religion* (p. 22), where he makes a link between beliefs and behavior, e.g., by your fruits shall you be known.
5 *Religion and Ideology*, a reader, ed. Robert Bocock and Kenneth Thomson, p. 207. See also R. Bocock, "Religion in Modern Britain," ch. 15.
6 Ian Markham, *A World Religions Reader*, second edition (Oxford: Blackwell Publishers, 2000), p. 6.
7 Eric J. Sharpe, *Comparative Religion*, p. 11.
8 Ibid., p. 20.
9 Ibid., p. 25.
10 Max Müller, *Introduction to the Science of Religion*, 1873, found in Eric J. Sharpe, *Comparative Religion*, p. xi.
11 Mahatma Gandhi, *What is Hinduism* (New Delhi: National Book Trust, India, 1995), p. 112.
12 Rudolf Otto, *The Idea of the Holy* (Oxford: Oxford University Press, 1969), p. 6.
13 Douglas Davies, "The Study of Religions," in *The World's Religions* (Oxford: Lion Publishing, 1982), p. 18.

Chapter 2

Religion and Sociology

Julie F. Scott and Irene Hall

The Sociological Perspective

The Development of the Sociology of Religion

Researching Religion

The Main Interests of the Sociology of Religion

The Sociology of Religion Today

Sociology is, literally, concerned with the study of human society in all of its many forms. Sociologists are interested in the structures, patterns, and motivations underpinning our social lives. Sociologists study all areas of society from important social institutions such as the family, school, and government, to social phenomena like crime, poverty, and unemployment. Anything that affects our social lives will eventually fall under the gaze of the sociologist.

It is estimated that approximately 90 percent of the world's population adhere to a set of beliefs or ideas that could be loosely labeled as religious. These beliefs range from the old established traditions of Christianity and Hinduism to relatively new ones like Ufology and New Ageism. Given that so many of us profess to hold religious beliefs, it can be assumed that religion, in its many varieties, has some social relevance. Indeed in many parts of the world where religion permeates social life to a large degree, such as the Middle East, it would be impossible to fully understand society without looking at religion. It is for this reason that sociologists have always held an interest in studying religion.

The Sociological Perspective

We may take the world around us for granted and give little thought to how our society is organized or ordered. Indeed we may feel that there is little order or pattern to our and others' social behavior. Sociology seeks to demystify social life and demonstrate that behind often seemingly arbitrary actions are sets of rules, conventions and patterns upon which societies are organized. A sociological perspective also maintains that every society is different, albeit often in very subtle ways. We cannot assume that people everywhere do as we do. If we look, for example, at marriage in the West, it is based upon notions of romantic love, that is, we fall in love with our future spouse. Yet the majority of cultures in the world do not have such a form of marriage and instead practice arranged marriages where alliances are made between not just the couple but also their families, based on principles such as inheritance, social standing, political influence and so forth. To these societies the notion of meeting and falling in love with a future spouse seems haphazard and arbitrary, while we may view such arranged marriages as being too business-like and cold.

The sociology of religion focuses on the role religion plays for society as a whole and also at the level of the individual believer. Typically sociologists approach the study of religion in one of two ways. The first is the **macro** or **structural** approach, which focuses on structures and patterns. This approach focuses on questions such as: "What is the social significance of religion?", "What is the role of religion in today's society?", "How many people still go to church?" and "In what ways have beliefs changed over time?" It seeks to analyze the impact and significance of religion on society as a whole. The work of the famous French sociologist Emile Durkheim is a good example of this approach. Durkheim was one of the first to study religion sociologically. In *The Elementary Structures of the Religious Life* (1915) Durkheim sought to explain the role religion played in all human societies. His view was that religion served to reinforce social solidarity and communal spirit. The second approach that sociologists take in studying religion is termed the **micro** or **interpretative** perspective. In this mode the focus is less on society as a whole and more on the individual believer (or non-believer). Here the sociologist wishes to understand the motivations and ideas behind the individual's beliefs and actions, asking questions such as "Why do you go to church?" or "What did that prayer mean to you?" This approach seeks to study the social relevance of religion to the individual and was pioneered by the German sociologist Max Weber. It is best illustrated in his study *The Protestant Ethic and the Spirit of Capitalism* (1904–5). In this work, Weber wished to understand what role religious ideas and motives played in the growth of modern capitalism in western society. He concluded that certain religious ideals helped fuel early western capitalism before they became secularized.

The sociology of religion, by its very nature, is broad and can encompass both the structural view of Emile Durkheim, which can allow us to look at religion's wide social relevance, and the in-depth study of a researcher such as (for example) the American sociologist Nancy Ammerman. In her insightful book *Bible Believers* (1987) she takes us into the closed world of a fundamentalist Baptist group in Chicago. Sociologists also have no limit on the religious phenomena that they study. Work on established religions, such as Ammerman's on Christianity, sits alongside work on newer forms, such as the British sociologist Eileen Barker's *The Making of a Moonie* (1984), which focuses on the Unification Church.

The Development of the Sociology of Religion

Scholars have always been interested in studying religion: from the Ancient Greek philosopher Aristotle, who suggested that religion was a mirror for society, to the endless theological debates of the Middle Ages. However, the systematic study of religion in a sociological sense did not begin until the late eighteenth century. It was at this time of great social and intellectual change that sociology itself was born.

Classical sociology

Sociology was one of a number of academic disciplines, along with social anthropology, psychology, and economics, which emerged in the late eighteenth/early nineteenth centuries. It is no accident that these subjects which focus so greatly on our social lives should appear at this time. During this period western Europe and the USA were moving, often at a rapid pace, from traditional societies which had been relatively unchanged for hundreds of years to the modern forms we recognize today. Industrialization and urbanization took place alongside the ascendancy of science and technology as sources of information about our world. Science was seen as the means for future human progress. Old ways of living and believing began to decline. Academics of the time looked around and saw a new social world which could not be understood or studied using old established means, thus new disciplines which specifically focused on these new social worlds emerged. At this same period the spread of western imperialism in Asia, Africa, and South America brought the West into contact with new social forms which often radically differed from western practices – importantly, religious beliefs. These new forms meant that academics had to look again at how they interpreted their own as well as others' social worlds.

Classical, that is early, sociology focused on social order, social change, and the potential crisis of meaning in modern life. It sought to demonstrate that the often chaotic and meaningless modern social world that was developing was in fact understandable and ordered by rules and patterns. Religion was always a much studied social phenomenon within classical sociology. Indeed the majority of the leading sociologists of the nineteenth and early twentieth centuries all included studies of religion within their work. Early sociologists, such as Herbert Spencer, were fascinated by how societies evolved. Their work could be labeled **Social Evolutionism** and was directly influenced by the biological evolutionary theory of Charles Darwin. They wished to understand the origins of different social practices, such as religion, as well as their uses, before charting their evolution from "simple" forms to "complex" ones. Spencer "explained" the origins of religion as lying in the worship of inanimate objects, like rocks or places. Such concrete things were used to embody God(s) because "primitive" people did not have minds developed enough to comprehend an abstract God. Spencer believed that as societies evolve they move their image of the divine from the inanimate to a more detached abstract figure. The Social Evolutionists had many different explanations for the origins and development of religion but most were based on mistaken interpretations of religious practices found among non-western cultures as well as the assumption that such cultures were less developed than the West. However, one feature of these theories was the view that religion itself was not compatible with modern living. Religion was viewed as "primitive" and "irrational" and that it was thought it would die out as societies evolved into science-dominated rational forms. This view that religion was at odds with modern living and would eventually disappear dominated the sociological view of religion from sociology's foundation in the nineteenth century until it began to be challenged in the 1960s.

The three key sociologists of the classical period were the Germans Karl Marx (1818–83) and Max Weber (1881–1961), and the Frenchman Emile Durkheim (1858–1917). Two characteristics set these three apart from the other writers, such as Spencer. First, each tried to locate and identify social processes based on empirical evidence rather than focus exclusively on origins and often wild speculation. Secondly, the fact that each is still regarded as important and relevant within the discipline unlike so many of their contemporaries demonstrates the strength of their work. All three could be loosely labeled social evolutionists in that they too were interested in how modern society had developed from more traditional forms. Each focused on identifying the processes that had facilitated this transformation from the traditional to the modern.

Karl Marx, of course, wrote on topics other than religion. He was most interested in the wider structure and operation of capitalism within society. His view of religion is outlined in *On Religion* (1857) where he identifies it as a social institution which perpetuates the ideology of capitalism, along with the justice system, government, schools system, and the media. Religion is a force which helps to reinforce the capitalist system through alienating the working classes (proletariat) from the rewards of their labour. Religion does this by mystifying the world and preventing the working classes from protesting about the harshness of their lives by offering rewards in an afterlife (heaven). Marx described religion as "the sigh of the oppressed creature, the heart of a heartless world, just as it is the spirit of a spiritless situation. It is the opium of the people."[1]

Marx's view of religion is negative and he claims that "the abolition of religion as the illusory happiness of the people is required for their real happiness."[2] Communist countries who have founded themselves on Marx's theories have sought to eradicate religion and most prohibited religious practice and expression. Critics of Marx's analysis have focused on his inability to view religion as a force for social change as well as on the fact that no communist country, past or present, has managed to completely eradicate religion. Marx's work is still relevant in that it offers a useful analysis of how religion can operate as a system of oppression (see chapter 7, pp. 144–5, in this text for a further discussion of Marx).

Emile Durkheim viewed religion in a more positive way as a force for good in society. While Marx's sociology focuses on social conflict, Durkheim's is characterized by consensus. Durkheim wished to study the basic structures of society and how each worked. To do this he focused on the functions of different social institutions, for example, the family and religion. In Durkheim's view all social institutions work together to maintain the stability of society – rather like the different parts of a car allow it to function properly. If one part breaks down, the car may still operate but it will not be as efficient as before; but if several parts or a major part broke down, the car would not be able to function at all. In the same way each social institution works together. If one breaks down society may still function but if too many are affected society begins to descend into anarchy. This theory of society is called **Functionalism** since society is defined through the functions which its parts perform. Durkheim identifies religion as an important social institution. In the *Elementary Structures of the Religious Life* (1915) he theorized that all religion is *in effect* worship of the most sacred notion underpinning society – social solidarity. In essence, religion, according to Durkheim, is worship of the social group. He came to this conclusion through studying accounts of totemism among the Australian aboriginal peoples. **Totemism** is a practice whereby certain animals, plants, objects or places are held to be sacred or at least given special status. Totems are treated reverentially and taboos surround them, for example, a totemic animal may not be eaten. Totemism is found throughout the world. Durkheim found that aboriginal society was divided into clan groups each with its own totem. The totem was a mascot or badge for each clan. Because early studies of totemism mistakenly thought that totems were actually worshiped, Durkheim theorized that in worshiping their totems each clan is in fact worshiping itself. Durkheim, being a social evolutionist, saw aboriginal society as the most "primitive" and therefore saw totemism as the most basic form of religion. If all other religions evolved from totemism then all religion, including Christianity, was really about worshiping and holding sacred the social group. Durkheim stated that "it is unquestionable that a society has all that is necessary to arouse the sensation of the divine in minds, merely by the power that it has over them; for to its members it is what a god is to his worshippers" (*Elementary Structures of the Religious Life*, p. 206).

So Durkheim teaches us that Religion has a crucial role in emphasizing social solidarity. More contemporary studies of totemism have shown that Durkheim and others of his time were mistaken, and that a totem is not something to be worshiped but rather is more akin to a mascot or flag. A totem sets a group aside and marks them out in the same way that a country's flag or a baseball team's mascot do. Durkheim, like Marx, saw modern society as eventually becoming non-religious. He believed that as society developed into a complex structure the role of religion would be taken over by other more secular institutions as rational thinking became ascendant.

Max Weber, the last of the three great classical sociologists, shared this evolutionary view of society. He also saw modern society as being characterized by **rationalization**, that is, scientific thinking would dominate all social processes and "irrational" forms, such as religion, would whither away. Weber agreed with Durkheim and Marx that religion was a human construction with a specific role to play in society. Weber wrote more extensively on religion than either Marx or

Durkheim. He saw religion less negatively than Marx but did not subscribe to the positive role given to it by Durkheim; rather Weber saw religion as one of many social forces at play with both positive and negative qualities. His most significant work on religion, *The Protestant Work Ethic and the Spirit of Capitalism* (1904–5 in German; first published in English in 1930), sought to explain how society developed into its modern form ruled by capitalism and rationalism when traditional society had been dominated by religion and irrationality. Weber's hypothesis focused on how Protestant (particularly Calvinist) ideas concerning salvation gave rise to a certain ethic (the Protestant Work Ethic) which held hard work, frugality, charity and a strong morality in high esteem. These essentially religious ideas helped early capitalism to expand and eventually were absorbed into wider business practice until they were completely secularized. In this way Weber was able to demonstrate the specific process whereby society transformed itself through rationalization to its modern form. He helped explain why religion declines as society develops into a more complex form.

Sociology and religious belief

Marx, Durkheim, and Weber were particularly radical in viewing religion as a human construction which served a social purpose. A great majority of academics of this period viewed religion as a social force but not all were prepared to go so far as Marx or Durkheim. In the nineteenth century religion, particularly Christianity, was still a significant social force. The strength of reaction to Charles Darwin's work showed how very radical his ideas were concerning the origins of humanity and Darwin's implicit challenge to the role of a divine creator came under intense criticism. This view of religion as something created by humans with a specific social purpose led to a view, particularly within theology, that sociology was atheistic. Such a view was amplified by the fact that several key sociologists, for example, Marx and Durkheim, were themselves professed atheists. This stereotype of the sociology of religion has remained prevalent in the twentieth century and has prevented much collaborative work between sociology and other disciplines, in particular theology. It has also led religious leaders and believers to be wary of the subject as they often have felt that it has diminished the mystery and potency of their beliefs. This view was given weight by the tendency of nineteenth-century and early twentieth-century social scientists to pass value judgments on different types of belief. The overwhelming view of religion was that it was something "irrational" which had no significant place in modern society. Such a view of religion developed due to the dominance of scientific ways of thinking about the world which stressed logic and the evidence of the senses as the sole means by which to reinforce theories or test hypotheses. In philosophy, this view was held by the school of **logical positivism**. Because no concrete evidence can be found to prove that witchcraft or prayer work, then both practices were deemed irrational and false. Religious beliefs were not taken seriously but instead judged along scientific-rational criteria. This approach meant that the significance and power of such beliefs to their believers was often diminished and trivialized.

However, while many classical sociologists were atheists, many others were not. The often negative approach to religion that has characterized the classical period of sociology has probably more to do with the focus on structure than the personal beliefs (or non-beliefs) of individual theorists. Contemporary sociology of religion hence includes many who have open religious beliefs while others are atheistic. However, modern sociology takes a more interpretative approach which emphasizes sensitivity towards people's beliefs and which focuses less on structure and more on meanings and motivations. Most contemporary sociologists of religion attempt to portray religion in a way that emphasizes both its positive and negative elements. One strategy for doing this has been the rise in **relativism** within the subject. Relativism maintains that all cultural and social practices and beliefs can only be understood within their particular cultural context. If one removes a specific belief or practice, such as witchcraft, from its context and studies it in an abstract manner one loses an important element of its wider meaning and significance. Relativism, at least in its strongest forms, also affords equality to (almost) all social practices and beliefs; none are morally superior or inferior to others. A relativistic stance goes hand-in-hand with an interpretative approach where the researcher is trying to ascertain the significance of a practice to the group or individual. Relativism allows for a more sympathetic approach to religions and their followers. The rise of cross-disciplinary collaboration, particularly with theology, has also led to sociology having a more balanced view of religion which tries to abandon notions of religion being "irrational" or passing judgments on specific cultural practices. The philosopher Alasdair MacIntyre stressed the useful point that there is a difference between believing in a religion and understanding that belief. The former is an act of faith, the latter is an act of scholarship. Too often in the past sociologists have confused the two by failing to understand because they have been preoccupied with what they believe or do not believe. The role of the believer is to believe while the role of the sociologist is to try to understand that belief.

---

1   What do you think "irrational" means? Is this a relative term?   **Exercises**
2   Is "relativism" consistent? Are there beliefs or practices even strong rel-
    ativists must hold as absolute?
3   How do you think classical sociology's atheism affected the way we look at
    religion today?

The modern period

The work of Marx, Durkheim and Weber helped establish the sociology of religion founded on the basic tenet that religion is a human construction with a specific set of roles and functions in any given society. The influence of these writers on the subsequent development of the subject was profound. As sociology became a more widespread subject in the first half of the twentieth century the sociology of religion declined. This decline was due to the belief by sociologists that religion was becoming an increasingly irrelevant force in modern society and therefore not one worth studying. Such a view arose from the work of Weber and Durkheim, which had become hugely influential in European and American sociology. Sociologists of religion devoted most of their energies to charting this decline through statistical evidence as well as locating those social processes which had encouraged this decline. This focus was also due to a widespread adoption within the subject of the macro perspective with its focus on social patterns and trends.

It was not until the 1960s that the sociology of religion became popular and relevant to modern sociology. This occurred due to three factors. The first two of these factors relate to the subject itself. Sociology in the 1960s began to incorporate work from other disciplines, such as social anthropology, which had continued to produce insightful work on religion, and this sparked new interest in looking at religion. Relating to this was the popularity of the micro and interpretative approach which allowed sociologists to focus more on the individual's beliefs and actions. However, the most important spark for this revitalized sociology of religion was the postwar boom in religion in the West. The classical sociologists, such as Weber, had predicted that religion would decline as society modernized and rationalized. This view was adopted throughout sociology. Yet from the 1960s to the 1990s there has been growth in fundamentalism, cults, New Religious Movements (NRMs) including those labeled "New Age," as well as changing expressions of traditional beliefs. None of this was anticipated and it has forced the sociology of religion to look again at its theoretical perspectives, resulting in the study of religion becoming more central within mainstream sociology. Today's sociology of religion is far more dynamic in its operation and has a far greater breadth of topics than ever before.

Researching Religion

The early sociologists of religion, such as Herbert Spencer, formulated their theories by gathering together information from a wide range of sources. These sources included travelers, civil servants, missionaries, and others who came into contact with a wide variety of religious practices. Typically, the information was collected in an unsystematic way. Theorists like Spencer would then apply this information in often uncritical ways with data being used out of its cultural context. This piecemeal approach to research data eventually gave way to a more scientific and systematic approach.

Today sociologists base their investigations of religion on two key factors: empirical evidence and methodological concerns. Sociological theories of religion are always based on empirical evidence collected through a variety of research methods. Researchers strive to collect data in the most systematic ways with as little room for error as possible. The specific method used depends on the subject matter. Large-scale surveys of populations, through questionnaires and interviews, can provide useful statistical evidence on patterns of church attendance and religious belief, but such surveys would not be useful in trying to ascertain what attendance at a baptism means to a particular individual. In this case observation or an in-depth interview would be more appropriate.

Choice of research method also depends upon the researcher's methodological concerns. A **methodology** is the philosophy behind the researcher's methods of data collection and analysis. In other words the methods a researcher chooses depends how he or she views the whole process of collecting data. If we consider that a theory is an explanatory statement which a researcher presents to the world as accurate or "true to the data" then considering the methodology used will raise questions concerning what is true, what is false, and how we know which is which? Methodological debates within sociology have raged for over a century and are effectively divided into two competing perspectives: **positivist** and **interpretative**.

The positivist approach

Classical sociology was dominated by the positivist approach. Positivism was developed by the French sociologist Auguste Comte (1798–1857). This approach maintains that knowledge about the world can only be gathered through strict scientific investigation and observation. Something is true if it can be proven through empirical observation. This approach demands that the researcher remain "objective" meaning he or she must always be emotionally, socially, and perhaps physically distant from the research subject(s). Such **objectivity** prevents the researcher becoming too involved with the research subject, which would taint the research data produced. Objectivity allows for a purity of research material. This approach tends to focus on the macro level of society, such as social structure and patterns of the social group. Such an approach would use systematic and objective methods, such as surveys and questionnaires, in gathering material.

The interpretative approach

The interpretative approach challenges the positivists. This approach was pioneered by Max Weber. Weber introduced the phrase *verstehen* into sociology. It is a German word which literally translates as meaning "understanding." Weber maintained that the central methodological orientation of any researcher should be to seek a means of creating "understanding" of any given social phenomenon. *Verstehen* or "understanding" is about trying to create a framework which allows access to the **worldview** of a social group or an individual. A worldview is literally the way in which a given group/individual sees and interprets the world. The American social anthropologist Clifford Geertz likens the process to "catching a joke." We do not fully enter another's world but rather gain some insight into it. The interpretative approach focuses on the meaning behind behavior rather than on social structures. It is less focused on objectivity and rather tends to emphasize the **subjectivity** of the researcher. The interpretivist believes that there is value to subjective knowledge and to lived experience and that each provides insight into social action. This perspective acknowledges that the researcher affects the research situation and the resultant interpretation – the two cannot remain distant. Part of this process is to reflect on how the researcher relates to and affects the research environment. Interpretivists are very sensitive to issues of ethics and tend to stress very people-centered methods, such as participant observation and unstructured interviews.

Both perspectives are still widespread in modern sociology and most social researchers fall into one of the two types of researcher. However, the interpretivist approach has greatly influenced how contemporary research is carried out, with heightened sensitivity to issues of ethics, subjectivity, the nature of the research environment, and so forth.

Exercises

4   Can one be entirely objective in studying another culture or religion? If not, why not?

5   How much can a researcher really understand the "verstehen" of someone very different from themselves? Is it really possible to "walk a mile in their shoes"?

Words, definitions, and meanings

A further research problem facing sociologists, particularly in the past, has been in trying to define their subject area. What exactly does the term "religion" mean? In investigating any social phenomenon researchers need to have some idea as to what it is that they are trying to study. It is evident from the discussion in chapter 1 that the word "religion" is not as clear in its meaning as first assumed. Some sociologists wish to include under the label "religion" a wide range of phenomena including soccer, pop music, and Communism. Others would view such inclusions as inappropriate, feeling that on an intuitive level they are not "religious" phenomena. To rectify this problem sociologists have attempted to formulate definitions of what is and what is not meant by the word "religion." A universally applicable definition was also attempted. Such a definition could be adopted across the subject and applied to all cultures.

Sociological definitions fall broadly into two types: **Functionalist** and **Substantive**. Functionalist definitions define religion by what social function it fulfills, that is, what religion does. Such definitions can incorporate a wide range of phenomena and are particularly useful for studying changing societies because they are broad and flexible. Clifford Geertz offers such a definition when he defines religion as "a system of symbols which acts to establish powerful pervasive, and long-lasting moods and motivations in men by formulating conceptions of a general order of existence and clothing these conceptions with such an aura of factuality that moods and motivations seem uniquely unrealistic."[3] Substantive definitions are more limited in range, and focus on the content of religious beliefs, i.e., what religion is.

They are best used in studying stable societies and large established religious groups. An example would be the following: "An institution consisting of culturally patterned interaction with culturally postulated superhuman beings", which was formulated by Melford Spiro.[4] Attempts to find a universally applicable definition have been fruitless, probably due to differing views of what is religion coupled with the sheer diversity of beliefs and practices around the world. Contemporary sociologists are less preoccupied with absolute definitions as past experience has shown the difficulties in developing such a definition. Today most researchers use working sets of criteria with which to orient their studies and allow them to create a framework for research without having to waste time on developing an absolute definition. Perhaps more important than worrying about universally applicable definitions, sociologists today are concerned about the very words and terms that they use in talking about religion. Since the 1960s researchers have become more aware of the dangers of using culturally specific words, and translating words and meanings across language and cultural boundaries. The consequences that result are not just mistaken or lost meanings but relate to cultural prejudices and changed meanings.

This can be best illustrated in relation to the word "religion" itself. Wilfred Cantwell Smith in *The Meaning and End of Religion*[5] showed how the word "religion" has its roots in European and specifically Christian worship. Originally Latin for "a ritual behavior" it became transformed through its use across medieval Europe to refer to specifically Christian forms of worship and belief. The word "religion" therefore is Eurocentric and Christian-centered. Can we appropriately use it to refer to Islam or Buddhism? Similar work has been done with other commonly used words such as "believe." Contemporary sociologists continue to use such words but are careful to reflect on the meanings and implications of using them.

A final semantic consideration is translation of meaning, particularly across language and/or cultural boundaries. If you are a researcher investigating views of God among English-speaking Christians in America you will probably share a common language but even they may find that your view of what God means is different from theirs. Imagine how complicated this would be in researching the same topic among non-English speakers. This is compounded by the use of culture-specific terms and jargon for religious belief and practice which may be hard to translate. An illustration of this problem can be seen in the experiences of Christian missionaries in the non-European world. In northern Canada missionaries attempted to translate Christian concepts to the indigenous Inuit populations. This task was far from easy. How do you translate the idea of a concept such as "the Lord is my shepherd," to people who have never seen a sheep? To bridge this semantic gap some missionaries substituted seals for sheep but does this provide a suitable translation of meaning? Researchers must always try to be sensitive to such issues in their own work and not assume that their own meanings are universally shared or understood. Now that we have looked at how sociologists conduct their research into religion we are ready to look at what exactly they have been interested in studying.

The Main Interests of the Sociology of Religion

The sociology of religion is a vast subject and encompasses a wide variety of topics and issues. However, there are five key areas which have dominated research in the subject over the past one hundred years.

The Secularization Thesis

Probably the most important, and certainly the most debated, topic within the sociology of religion has been the **Secularization Thesis** (henceforth ST) or as it is sometimes know the Secularization Debate. The ST has had a profound influence on how sociology, as a whole, has viewed religion. The ST is not a unified theory but rather a collection of related ideas and studies which have a basic principle. This foundation lies, in the words of Bryan Wilson in *Religion in a Secular Society*,[6] in the assumption that religion will "lose its social significance." The ST formalized the view held by early sociologists, such as Marx and Weber, that as society progressed religion would lose social importance and influence. Weber was the first to explain how this process occurred in his idea of the "Protestant Work Ethic," which was discussed earlier in this chapter. Weber demonstrated how religious ideas and principles became rationalized and then secularized over time until their religious roots were forgotten or lost. Weber's model was widely applied in classical and later sociology. Bryan Wilson, the British sociologist, is perhaps the most important writer on the ST and certainly its more influential supporter. He took Weber's model and developed it further. Wilson maintains that religion loses social significance through the combined forces of **modernization** (society becomes modern and scientific, abandoning traditional ways), **rationalization** (society becomes dominated by rational principles), and **societalization** (society grows and different institutions control different areas of our lives. We become less connected to our local groups and more tied to national concerns). Wilson sees this process as inevitable and intrinsically linked to the very nature of modern society.

Theorists like Wilson maintain Durkheim's view that pre-modern traditional society was small and uncomplex. People shared similar social roles and beliefs. Communities were united by religion and ritual. Religion helped to educate, socialize, legislate and ritualize such communities as well as provide a moral code. But as society grows into a modern form it abandons old ways because they are incompatible with modern living. Modern society is urban, large and complex. The former unity of traditional life breaks down, as does the unity of cultural beliefs and ideas. This and the sheer size of modern society requires the development of specialized institutions, such as schools, hospitals, courts, governments and so forth, to take over the roles once provided within small groups by specific individuals and beliefs. Religion cannot compete with such institutions and so changes and begins to lose its traditional social roles. As modern society is also dominated by science and rational thought, religion also begins to be identified with the traditional and the irrational. The American sociologist Robert Bellah suggested that religion's ability to unify social groups through shared meanings had been taken over in modern society by what he called "civil religion," that is, symbols of nation or city were treated in a religious way, for example, the celebration of Independence Day in the USA.

The ST does not suggest that religion completely dies out in modern society but rather it becomes a marginal force. The British sociologist Steve Bruce, in *Religion in the Modern World*,[7] sees the continued use of religion within society as being among culturally marginalized groups, such as immigrants or minority ethnic groups. In these communities religion maintains cultural values and social cohesion. Religious centers, such as churches and mosques, become community resources in such marginalized communities and provide not only worship but often advice, education, basic health care and a sense of belonging. In Bruce's view religion flares up in situations where cultures feel threatened or oppressed, such as in the former Yugoslavia.

Supporters of the ST do not see the postwar boom in some forms of religion as proof that the ST is wrong. The rise in fundamentalism, for example, is viewed as merely a reaction against modern life, with this form of belief being prevalent in marginal or isolated communities. Similarly the cult way of life is seen as a form of escapism.

The evidence for the ST has been mainly statistical. Religious statistics for the USA and western Europe are surprisingly similar. They show that attendance at organized worship has dramatically decreased over the past one hundred years. In the UK less than one in ten attend weekly worship; while in the USA less than half the population do. Statistics for religious membership and the demand for ceremonials (baptisms, weddings and funerals) also show decline. The statistical evidence would seem conclusive except that there are problems with it. Religious statistics focus on large established groups, such as the Catholic Church, rather than newer but smaller groups. They also have quite a rigid view of religion which cannot incorporate new ideas such as New Ageism. Finally, the statistics relating to belief in God and other religious ideas are still high. Around 90 percent of Americans believe in God. This continued level of belief, along with the postwar growth in some religious forms, has led many sociologists of religion to challenge the ST. The ST is a good example of macro sociology with its focus on structure and function. Many of the challenges to the ST have come from interpretivist sociologists whose view of social action and meaning have allowed them to go beyond structure to look at what the individual is doing.

That is not to say that the ST has been abandoned but rather that some seek to modify it and to offer alternative models of religion. Postwar religion is characterized by two quite contrastive trends. The first is a shift toward fundamentalism and a "back to basics" approach to religious doctrine and belief. Fundamentalism has been a rising trend in all of the main world religions but particularly in Christianity and Islam. The ST would view this shift toward fundamentalism as further proof that secularization has occurred. Fundamentalism is most popular in isolated or marginalized communities as it offers a message of empowerment. Supporters of the ST see the fundamentalist as a reactionary trying to fight the forces of modern life. However, this view has been challenged by more recent research, particularly the ambitious *Fundamentalism Project*,[8] into this global phenomenon. This research has shown that fundamentalism exhibits a great diversity of types with different consequences in different societies. Given the influence and dynamism of fundamentalism across the world it would seem that to dismiss it as merely a reaction to modernity is too limited a view.

The second trend in postwar religion is the shift toward "privatized" and eclectic religion. The American sociologists Peter Berger and Thomas Luckmann popularized the phrase "Privatized" religion and used it to refer to the shift in modern society of religious expression from being a communal activity to being a highly personalized one. This is coupled with the prevalence of what has been called "**pick and mix**" religion where the individual literally picks and chooses those beliefs and practices that he or she likes the most. This approach sees the individual mixing and matching between different religions and beliefs, for example, a person could be nominally a Catholic, believe in reincarnation, practice Buddhist chanting and use holistic healing. Again supporters of the ST would dismiss this form of contemporary religious practice as being insignificant to society, as it is so individualized. They would view such eclecticism as further evidence of the breakdown in mainstream religion. However, other sociologists maintain that the ST does not fully explain such contemporary trends and that we must try to develop new ways of researching (i.e., privatized religion is by its nature hard to study) and understanding (i.e., do our old models of religion still work?) religion. The British sociologist Grace Davie suggests that we can locate privatized religion in the popular media and at national events, such as the funeral of Diana Princess of Wales, rather than by visiting churches or mosques.

The debate over the extent of secularization in the West continues but has been revitalized over the past thirty years by new research interests and methods. Many in the discipline feel that the ST is, in its present forms, too limited a model when applied to contemporary religious expression and belief.

Exercises

6   The ST states that religion will lose its social significance, do you think this has been the case for secular societies?

7   Discuss how Rationalization, Modernization, and Societalization all encourage the spread of secularization.

8   Has secularism been challenged? If so, how?

Worldview and meaning

If secularization theory has been dominated by macro sociologists preoccupied with social structures then interpretative sociologists, with their micro-level approach, have been more interested in looking at religious meanings and how actions and meanings interact. Their insights have allowed us to see more clearly how the believer interprets his or her world. Early work on religion by Max Weber, Emile Durkheim, and the social anthropologist Bronislaw Malinowski demonstrated that all religions have two components: belief and ritual. Religious beliefs are the cognitive aspect of religion which provides knowledge and explanation to the believer.

Ritual is the active and physical aspect of religion. Rituals allow individuals and groups to express and understand beliefs. Chapter 5 discusses religious ritual at greater length. For the benefit of this discussion, rituals are actions which involve the manipulation of people, objects, and space in a symbolic way that communicates meaning, at a symbolic level, to those taking part in the ritual. Holy Communion, prayer, baptisms, and celebrating holy festivals are all types of ritual.

Sociological analysis of religious belief has shown that beliefs are not mere opinions but are collections of "knowledge." This knowledge helps orient individuals or groups of believers in their world. The American social anthropologist Clifford Geertz demonstrated that beliefs help shape and define the world for the believer. Geertz proposes that individuals actively engage with their belief system through the use of rituals and other symbols in order to create a world which is meaningful to them.

Beliefs create what Max Weber called a **worldview**. Peter Berger defines a worldview as a "comprehensive" explanatory meaning system. The later chapters of this book outline the varied worldviews of the majority of the world's religions.

Worldviews can provide meaning both in the form of complex theology or philosophy and also in a more "folk" way such as in parables or fables. For example the opening chapters of the Book of Genesis, in the Christian Bible, provide an explanation for the creation of the world and everything in it. The work of Weber and also Peter Berger has shown that religious meaning is highly efficient in its use. A worldview contains both world-encompassing and contradictory elements. Contradiction is central to many worldviews and some life events particularly throw up contradictions for the believer. The unexpected death of a child may contradict the portrayal of a benevolent God. If God is so kind why has this child died?

Such contradictions are threatening to a religious worldview as they create a crisis of meaning because the strength of a worldview lies in its all-encompassing nature. A worldview has to be able to explain everything in the world as well as cover all eventualities. Weber, Berger, and Geertz suggest that religions overcome such contradictions by constructing **theodicies**, which are explanations for suffering. In the case of the child's death a typical theodicy might be that God works in mysterious ways or that the parents' sinful actions were being punished.

By studying how believers construct their worldviews and then use them to orient themselves in their social worlds, we can gain insight into how religions work. Consequently we can better understand the dynamics of different societies and cultures, particularly those that may baffle or confuse us with what seem like extreme beliefs.

Religion and power

Perhaps the greatest influence that Karl Marx has had on the sociology of religion is his work on religion and power. His analysis of religious power remains probably the most influential piece of work on this subject. One of the negative aspects of Marx's work on religion has been that he has influenced others to take a very limited and detrimental view of religion. Earlier in this chapter Marx's view of religion was discussed. Marx saw religion as a tool used by the ruling class (the bourgoisie) in capitalist society to oppress and suppress the working class (the proletariat). It helps ensure that the workers will not liberate themselves and their labour from the system through revolution. For Marx religion is a drug ("the opium of the people") which dulls the sense of the workers through promises and visions of an afterlife and therefore distances them from the reality of their everyday lives. Marx did not fully explain how this process worked. Later work on worldviews has allowed us to view how religion can become a force for wielding power in society.

In discussing worldviews it was shown that they explain the world through often elaborate meaning systems which are reinforced through ritual action. Weber discussed how all religions develop theodicies to explain suffering to believers. Effective theodicies prevent believers experiencing a crisis of meaning. The power of worldviews lie not only in their ability to completely explain the world but also in their ability to wrap this explanation in mystery. Religious worldviews are portrayed as being the work of God(s) or similar spiritual beings. However, worldviews are human constructions and so must hide the hand of humanity through obscuring the origins of beliefs. This process is called **mystification**. Rituals, symbols, and the lack of accurate dates or times can mystify historical events, scriptures, and other sources of beliefs. Marxist sociologists have shown that as religions grow they become distant from their founding principles and instead focus more on enforcing conformity in doctrine and practice. Worldviews become codified and inflexible. This stress on conformity and the power of worldviews gives religions the potential for tremendous influence and power over people's lives.

A social order dominated by religion would be hard to challenge. The individual would be challenging not only the inequalities of the social order but also the legitimacy of the religious worldview on which it was constructed. The challenge would be ultimately against whichever divine creator was behind the worldview in question. Such challenges are typically labeled **heresies**. Societies where religion is a political force have always brought particularly harsh punishments to bear on those that commit heresy. However, many heretics have been punished not for theological reasons but typically social and political ones. The many Inquisitions of medieval Europe, a society dominated by the Christian church, were conducted under the guise of expanding faith and creating a unity of belief. Most were actually conducted to suppress social protest movements, persecute certain religious and ethnic minority groups, annexe land and property, and wield political power across the continent. In Spain the largest Inquisition allowed the church to expel the Islamic Moors and the Spanish Jewish population who had occupied the territory for

several hundred years. The Inquisitions used torture and death as a way of persecuting minorities and spreading fear among local communities, which in turn ensured
that conformity of belief would ensue.

Religions often use the strength of their worldviews to control the lives of their
followers and to justify inequality in societies. The unequal treatment of women
in many Middle Eastern countries is justified through Islam. Yet many of the restrictions on women's lives are not actually prohibited by Islam but rather are desired
by the religious and secular authorities in those states. Religious leaderships may
also use their power to encourage their followers to persecute other groups in the
name of religion. In pre-revolutionary Russia the Russian Orthodox Church
whipped up anti-Semitism among its followers, which resulted in regular organized
attacks on Jewish communities, called pogroms. The Marxist analysis of religion is
insightful but it only provides half the story. Just as religions can control the lives
of their followers they can also empower them.

Religion and social change

In response to criticism of Marx's analysis of religion many neo-Marxian sociologists looked again at the relationship between religion, power, and social change.
They proposed that religion need not be a passive tool of oppression and that religion might, in some situations, be a force for positive change in society. This work
was prompted by the success of many social protest and revolutionary movements
which had strong religious elements, for example the American Civil Rights movement of the 1950s and 1960s. Ironically, the features which allow religion to be an
oppressive force, such as the presence of powerful worldviews, strong leaders, and
the use of ritual, are also potential sources for motivating groups and individuals
towards social change. Religious worldviews can lead groups to seek the prohibition of acts that they consider morally wrong, such as homosexuality. Yet others
may apply the same beliefs to justify the abolition of inequalities, such as laws which
outlaw homosexuality, on the grounds that such inequality goes against religious
views of justice and respect for humanity in all its diversity. Reforms against the
slave trade, child labor, and poverty in the USA and UK are just a few examples
of reform movements which originated among reformers influenced or directed
towards action by their religious beliefs. Often religious leaders can act as effective
leaders of mass movements as they can have wide appeal, not only due to their
often presumed political neutrality, but also because they have specific skills which
can energize others into socio-political action. Weber identified **charisma** as a
key feature of religious leaders through history. A charismatic leader is one who
through sheer force of personality can bring people to action. Such leaders are
often enigmatic individuals with gifts of oration who have or are imbued with
the power to attract mass numbers of followers. A good example of a charismatic
religious leader who used his religious beliefs to energize his supporters to socio-
political action is the Reverend Martin Luther King Jr., the American Civil Rights
leader.

Religious symbols and rituals can provide sources around which to rally and motivate followers. Examples of this would be the singing of hymns, the recitation of extracts from sacred scriptures, and the wearing of insignia such as crucifixes.

One final element of religion which can bring forth social change lies in the legitimate authority of many of the large religious groups, for example, the Catholic Church. Such weight of legitimacy can often add strength to public pressure. For example, in the UK the established state church, the Church of England, has used its traditional role to become an advocate for the unemployed and to speak out against poverty in modern Britain. It is listened to because it is identified as a member of the Establishment. The Catholic Church in Poland, as well as in some parts of South America, has used its traditional authority in a similar way to press for social reforms.

Religion and the social group

A final interest of the sociology of religion has been in looking at the social group itself and how religion "works" in communities. The focus on the collective nature of religion came to prominence in the work of Emile Durkheim. It remains a major interest in sociological and anthropological studies of religion, providing the researcher with a better understanding of specific societies and cultures.

Religion provides the social group with its essential quality – cohesion. The work of Durkheim and others has shown that religion is a key source of social solidarity. Every society requires some level of social cohesion in order to successfully function. In small groups cohesion is easier to establish due to size and, typically, uniformity of beliefs and values. Durkheim believed that religion was a **collective representation**, or in other words when the group assembled for worship they were in fact expressing their belief in the values of themselves as a collective. A worldview provides a group with its own specific way of explaining the world. Rituals provide active participation and expression of group values. Most cultures whatever their size have their own rituals, such as initiation ceremonies and festivals. Such activities highlight the group and its distinctiveness, as well as marking seasonal changes (for example Harvest Festivals and New Year's Eve celebrations) and the passage of time for individuals (confirmations, baptisms and weddings all mark the changes in an individual's status). The legitimacy of worldviews provides a strong cohesive factor for communities. When ethnic identity is linked to a particular set of religious beliefs it adds particular weight to community cohesion. The recent conflicts in the former Yugoslavia were exacerbated by the ethnic-religious divisions of the Christian Serbs and the Muslim Bosnians. These divisions helped to produce a strong sense of what it was to be Serbian and Bosnian and offered a clear set of criteria which differentiated between the two groups. Religious belief is typically strongest among communities that feel isolated or marginalized in a wider society. In Scotland there are higher levels of church attendance than elsewhere in the UK due to an association of Scottishness with being a member of the Church of Scotland.

Similarly, immigrant and ethnic minority populations tend to be more religious than more mainstream groups. For these communities, religion offers a strong identity and sense of meaning within a society in which they may feel dislocated. This phenomenon has been labeled the **Herberg Thesis** after it was first proposed by the American sociologist Will Herberg in *Protestant–Catholic–Jew*,[9] his study of immigrant populations in America. Herberg found that the religiosity of immigrant groups lessened as they became assimilated into mainstream society.

Larger groups, like nation-states, face a greater problem in creating cohesion. In the modern world most nation-states are run along secular political lines. Robert Bellah suggests that cohesion is maintained in these states through what he calls "**civil religion**" in which secular symbols of nation are held in a sort of religious awe. Such secular symbols, like national holidays, flags, and historical artefacts, create a sense of national identity and bring the often diverse communities present in modern nation states together. This is particularly found in nations where no one religion dominates or that have no national church, for example the USA. Nations with one dominant religion or a state church often have stronger identities and cohesion levels than those that do not. Bellah found that "civil religion" was less common in such nations. This is because homogeneity is created through common religious symbols and beliefs. Often new nations use religion to legitimize their sense of identity and uniqueness. Israel emphasized its Jewishness during its early years before becoming more secular. Similarly Pakistan was established as a Muslim state in contrast to its neighbour India's Hinduism. Pakistan's foundation was based upon its sense of being Islamic, which remains a strong source of national identity today.

Religion provides communal identity at a group level but also adds to the individual's sense of who he or she is. A Muslim woman's sense of her gender identity and role is informed by her religion. A Jewish boy learns about his place in his community and its related responsibilities when he turns thirteen and has his Bar Mitzvah. Religious worldviews teach us about the world and also about the rules and obligations of the communities to which we belong.

Unfortunately the powerful sense of identity and communal solidarity that religion can provide can also be the source and focus of social conflict, as is all too evident at the beginning of the twenty-first century. The secular nature of modern western society often results in conflicts between religious communities and secular authorities. Often this focuses on children and education. In the USA fundamentalist Christian parents remove their children from sex education and science classes because of conflict between secular education and religious beliefs. In France Muslim girls have been banned from school because they refuse to remove their head-scarves. French law prohibits religion in schools. In the UK many parents belonging to particular religions try to enrol their children in religious schools or at least agitate for the right to remove their children from classes which they deem inappropriate. In a similar way religious groups can organize protests against secular laws, such as abortion rights, which conflict with their religious beliefs. Typically such protests are defeated by the weight of secular authority.

More serious are the conflicts between communities based on religious divisions. The power of worldviews and the legitimacy they provide make them powerful agents for collective action. Added to this is the strength of identity and solidarity provided by religion. This can provide a potent force for conflict. This is best illustrated in the situation between Israel and the Palestinians. Israel's identity is entwined with Judaism and the weight of the Jews' historical struggle. Palestinians similarly have an identity wrapped up with Islam and a sense of historical struggle. The inability for either side, in this long conflict over land and nationhood, to compromise is partly due to the strength of the communal solidarity and sense of legitimacy provided by their respective religions. To seek compromise would not only affect political ambitions but would challenge the legitimacy of their respective belief systems. Similar religion-fueled conflicts can be seen in the former Yugoslavia, Northern Ireland, and between India and Pakistan to name but a few. It is easy to dismiss such conflicts as the actions of extremists but we should remember that we all have a strong sense of who we are and to which groups we belong. Our collective identities infuse our sense of our own selves and are easily affected, whether through supporting national sports teams or in challenging attacks on our cultural distinctiveness.

The Sociology of Religion Today

The sociology of religion has never been more dynamic and as important as it is today as we enter the twenty-first century. Secularization may have pushed some mainstream religions to the margins but it has also aided the transformation of religious expression and belief. Some sociologists, particularly Rodney Stark and William Bainbridge, maintain that religion is an essential social institution and can never fully disappear but merely transforms itself. Such essentialist debates are not particularly fruitful. More important a task is to try and follow the progress of religion in the contemporary world. As we enter the next millennium we are in the middle of a boom in religion. Partly this is a consequence of the time in which we live. Turns of century and millennia always produce a rise in religious belief due to people's apocalyptic fears, that is, they fear that the end of the century will also mark the end of the world. However, the growth of religion is also a consequence of the globalized nature of the world today and the greater knowledge we have of different beliefs and practices. Individuals have greater choices as to what to believe and are not as constrained as they once were. "Pick and mix" religion, and "privatized beliefs" all demonstrate this. On the other hand some people seek support from strong belief systems, like fundamentalism, as a source of power and strength in a world which can often make them feel marginalized and insignificant. The debates over whether such religious changes are beneficial or detrimental for the societies and cultures of the world have only just begun and will be carried into the twenty-first century. Sociologists of religion will remain important researchers of this often important aspect of our social lives.

9 (a) In a group, conduct a quick survey of your classmates' religious beliefs and practices, for example, how often do they attend church. How do your results correspond to the wider social patterns discussed on p. 33.

   (b) Still in a group, discuss which areas of social life still show religion to be socially significant. How would you account for its persistence in these areas?

   (c) Consider your own local community. How visible and socially relevant is religion to your community?

10 (a) In pairs try and explain key concepts and beliefs from your own religion or one with which you are familiar. Reflect on how easy it was to do this and consider how much harder this task would have been in a language foreign to you.

   (b) Still in pairs, reflect on the worldview of your respective religions. How easy is it to understand and empathize with each other's views?

   (c) How would you study the worldview of a large community. Consider which methods of research and methodological perspective you would employ. What problems would you encounter in this research?

Exercises

GLOSSARY

Charisma A special quality with which many religious leaders are perceived to be imbued.

Civil Religion Secular institutions, artefacts, and events are imbued with awe and are revered in a religious fashion in order to unite large and diverse nations.

Collective Representation An act in which the values of the group are expressed in a symbolic way.

Functionalism Sociological theory popular from the 1920s to the 1940s which saw society functioning as one unified body comprised of social institutions that all work together in harmony. Stressed cohesion and function of social institutions.

Functionalist Definition One which tries to define religion by what it does.

Herberg Thesis Immigrant communities and other marginalized and isolated groups always have high levels of religion as it acts to keep communities together and also provides a strong communal identity.

Heresies Crimes that involve breaching, challenging, or rejecting the legitimacy of religious worldviews.

Interpretative A methodological perspective which stresses subjectivity, experience, and the need to interpret action.

Logical positivism A methodological perspective which stresses a scientific approach emphasizing objectivity and the empirical method.

Macro or Structural Sociological approach which focuses on society-wide patterns and structures.

Methodology The philosophy underpinning a researcher's research process.

Micro or Interpretative Sociological approach which focuses on the individual and the meanings and motives behind his or her social actions and beliefs.

Modernization The process by which a society moves from being simple and traditional to complex and modern.

Mystification The process whereby religion hides the reality of the lives of believers through use of worldview and ritual.

Objectivity A viewpoint which stresses researcher distance from field subjects.

Pick and mix religion A style of religion characteristic of contemporary western society whereby the individual freely decides which beliefs to accept and which to reject.

Positivist A methodological perspective which stresses a scientific approach emphasizing objectivity and the empirical method.

Privatized Religion A form of religion characteristic of contemporary western society, in which religion moves from being a group or community act to being essentially a private and highly individualized act.

Rationalization A process identified by Max Weber. Characteristic of modern

society, it is where scientific and rational thoughts, concepts, and actions dominate social life.

Relativism A methodological perspective which stresses that all social practices and beliefs are unique to their particular contexts and can only be understood in context. It also views all social forms as being equal.

Secularization Thesis A theory which states that religion will lose its social significance and decline as society becomes modernized.

Social Evolutionism Sociological theory popular in the nineteenth century which viewed all societies as being on an evolutionary scale. Stressed origins.

Societalization The process by which the individual's loyalties and identification with his/her local community becomes lessened as he or she begins to view himself/herself as a member of a nation state.

Subjectivity A viewpoint which stresses the relationship between researcher and subject as well as the research experience itself.

Substantivist Definition One which tries to define religion by what it is.

Theodicies The defense of God's goodness and justice in response to the existence of evil.

Totemism A practice whereby certain animals, plants, objects, or places are held to be sacred or at least given special status.

Verstehen Max Weber's concept which demands that the researcher attempt to create a framework with which to understand field subjects through accessing their social world.

Worldview The way an individual or social group views and explains the world.

Notes and References

1 Karl Marx and Friedrich Engels, *On Religions* (Moscow: Progress Press, 1957), p. 37.
2 Ibid., pp. 37–8.
3 Clifford Geertz, "Religion as a Cultural System," in M. Banton, ed., *Anthropological Approaches to the Study of Religion* (London: Tavistock, 1966), p. 4.
4 Melford Spiro in M. Banton, ed., *Anthropological Approaches to the Study of Religion* (London: Tavistock, 1966), p. 8.
5 Wilfred Cantwell Smith, *The Meaning and End of Religion* (New York: Macmillan, 1962).
6 Bryan Wilson, *Religion in a Secular Society* (London: Watts, 1966).
7 Steve Bruce, *Religion in the Modern World: from cathedrals to cults* (Oxford: Oxford University Press, 1996).
8 See Martin E. Marty and R. Scott Appleby (eds.), *Fundamentalisms Observed* (Chicago: University of Chicago Press, 1991).
9 Will Herberg, *Protestant–Catholic–Jew: an essay in American religious sociology* (Garden City, NY: Anchor books, 1960).

Chapter 3

Religion and Psychology

CARL WILLIAMS

A Psychological Approach to Religion

The Beginnings of a Psychology of Religion

Psychoanalytic Approaches to the Psychology of Religion

The Objectivist Approach to the Psychology of Religion

Transpersonal Approaches to the Psychology of Religion

Conclusions

A Psychological Approach to Religion

There is a well-known story about a psychology tutor who planned to spend the first few minutes of his first lecture defining psychology. This task proved to be so mammoth that months later, at the end of the whole course, he and his employer were shocked to find that he was still defining psychology! With this in mind the definition of psychology presented here will be as succinct as possible. "Psychologists are concerned with understanding thought and behavior." It is thankfully short but inevitably this definition cannot do justice to the breadth of methods and approaches used in the discipline of psychology. It is reasonable to say that psychology is not really a unitary discipline at all, but instead is multidisciplinary in nature. In the very early days of psychology, the subject was characterized by a number of different schools of thought and even though the schools themselves have perished, the tendency for many different approaches has remained and possibly multiplied. The difficulty of providing a good definition of psychology probably arises because of the multidisciplinary nature of the subject.

Psychologists seek to explain thought and behavior, adopting in the process a range of explanatory levels. Some psychologists take an **objectivist** standpoint, measuring objective biological, **cognitive** or social behavior; still others adopt a **psychoanalytic** approach where subjective interpretation is very important. **Transpersonal** psychologists may try to explore the transcendent experiences themselves, sometimes using experiments but often relying on the stories or narratives provided by the person reporting the experience.

Table 3.1 Showing the different approaches taken to studying religious behaviors/ experiences by different orientations in psychology

	Objectivist	*Psychoanalytic*	*Transpersonal*
Mode of research	Experimental Correlational	Interpretative Phenomenological	Experimental Interpretative Phenomenological
Method of analysis	Quantitative Qualitative	Qualitative	Qualitative Quantitative
Level of explanation	Personality, Social Behavioral, Physiological	Personality Unconscious needs and motivations	Extended abilities Alternate realities Spirituality

The choices of which levels of explanation and particular research approaches to adopt are influenced by the paradigms or worldviews which inform the researchers' work. The objectivist paradigm is usually characterized by a belief in a materialistic universe where reality is single and is best understood by reducing it to its basic components. From this perspective science is value-free and knowledge is context-free. On the other hand, a transpersonal paradigm is more likely to be holistic, with different, multiple, interacting levels of reality which require sensitive, participatory forms of investigation that are inevitably context- and value-bound. Psychologists will necessarily adopt different approaches to studying religion depending upon their worldview and the research methods which are seen as appropriate within that paradigm (see table 3.1 for a summary and examples).

If a psychologist is concerned with a biological level of explanation then it is likely that she will devise experiments to gather data; for instance, she might record brain activity during meditation or prayer. If, on the other hand, the preferred level of explanation is social then she may conduct and analyze interviews, for example comparing people's experiences during prayer. If she wishes to examine differences in personality between religious believers and agnostics it is likely that she will use survey methodology and questionnaire measures. The type of investigation and the type of data gathered will inform the analysis process. Statistics are commonly used to analyze data from experiments and correlational studies employing questionnaires. Where the data was obtained from interviews or has a narrative form, interpretative or qualitative methods will probably be used. The empirical method is usually associated with experiments and quantitative assessment, while a more interpretative or phenomenological approach is associated with interviews and qualitative assessment.

The early approaches to a psychology of religion were interpretative but as the decades went by and psychology became gripped by the positivism of behaviorism, many psychologists turned their attention to the study of religious behavior rather than religious experience. The early books on the psychology of religion such as William James' *The Varieties of Religious Experience* were more concerned

with the interpretation and understanding of the experience itself (the phenomenological), whereas later studies focused upon the observable and ultimately
quantifiable nature of religious behavior (the empirical). There are signs that this
strict division between research approaches is no longer tenable and that the
phenomenology–empiricism debate can be transcended with both methods contributing to a psychology of religion.[1] The emergence of transpersonal psychology
since the 1960s has indicated that different research methods which have usually
been thought of as mutually exclusive, can actually be used in a complementary
way. Furthermore, this combination of methods is necessary in order to fully understand the richness and complexity of a subject, such as religious or spiritual experience and behavior.[2]

The methods of investigation and analysis used in psychology have also seen great
changes in recent decades, as psychology, like many of the social sciences, has
been strongly influenced by postmodern perspectives. Postmodernism argues that
a pluralistic view of the world is a more appropriate and realistic aim than the
ambitious grasping of singular truth that is the objective of positivist science. A
postmodern approach in psychology recognizes that the time and culture in which
we live help to construct our understanding of mind and behavior, and that our
knowledge about them do not constitute absolute facts. Within psychology, the objectivist position is most closely allied with the modernist way of thinking (which places
great faith in rationality, logic and a uniformity of truth which transcends culture)
and perhaps the transpersonal position is nearest to a postmodern paradigm.

In this chapter some of the main psychological approaches to religion will be
introduced along with their different perspectives, concerns, theories, methods and
conclusions. After providing a brief account of the early days of the psychology of
religion, the major contributions of some of the best known thinkers in psychoanalysis will be examined. Following this the objectivist approach will be examined.
Psychologists working within this paradigm have adopted a skeptical view of
religion and have aimed to account for religious experience, behavior and belief
in terms of physical, personality or social explanations. Finally, the transpersonal
psychological approach will be explored, in which researchers consider religious and
spiritual experience as an important and fundamental human experience and, more
importantly, accept that it may have some basis in reality.

The Beginnings of a Psychology of Religion

At the beginning of the twentieth century there was a growing interest in the application of psychology to religious behavior, experience and beliefs. Psychology at this
time was just a couple of decades old and still to find its feet, the discipline being
characterized by a range of competing schools of thought. Some of the very early
books on the psychology of religion were in fact written by scholars outside of the
field of psychology. By the turn of the century, however, a number of psychologists were turning their attention to the subject of religion.

In 1902, one of the earliest, and probably the most famous books in this area was published; it was by William James (1842–1910) and was called *The Varieties of Religious Experience*. James' arrival in psychology was circuitous. As a young man he had intended to study art; he later obtained a medical degree and went on to teach physiology at Harvard. He was strongly influenced by his father who was intensely interested in philosophy and religion. The young James was brought up in a lively intellectual atmosphere and was able to listen and participate in the many religious and philosophical discussions between his father and visitors to the house. From his childhood right through to old age, James suffered regular bouts of physical as well as psychological illness including dark periods of despair and depression. Some writers have argued that these factors were instrumental in his portrayal of religion in the *Varieties*. In his book, James attempted to explore the factors influencing religious belief and experience, such as the role of personality and the conscious and unconscious mind. Like many of the early writers he was concerned with religious experience and consciousness rather than religious behavior. Not all the works at this time were interpretative however; there were also some early efforts to gather quantitative data. Edwin Starbuck, for example, published his *Psychology of Religion* in 1899 and in it made extensive use of numerical data such as the frequencies of conversion, by age, sex and theological background.

James' approach involved submitting the experiences to a sensitive and penetrating analysis based on empathizing with the people who had experienced them.[3] This approach can be seen as both interpretative and phenomenological. James' approach is unsurprising considering that he felt that the essence of religion was to be found in the deep and moving personal experience of the individual. In accord with this he collected a range of experiences and instead of generalizing from these, as is usually the aim in such research, he chose instead to focus on the more unusual and extreme cases of religious experience. The experiences were taken from biographies, confessions and inspirational works. Some were obtained from the earlier survey research by Starbuck.

James examined religious experience in relation to the factors of health and sickness, and he explored the processes behind religious conversion, saintliness, and mysticism. One of the main themes he developed was that of the sick and healthy-minded soul. He used this to characterize two different personality orientations in experiencing the world; the sick soul always sees the darker side of nature, including its own sinfulness, and this plays a fundamental role in one's experience. The healthy-minded soul concentrates on the importance of good and yearning for union with the divine, almost entirely neglecting the negative aspects of life.

Another important aspect of James' work is the importance that he attributes to subliminal or subconscious dimensions of the mind. He asserts that there is "more" to the human personality or the self than that which is expressed through the physical form. The farther reaches of the personality stretch into the subconscious and it is here that religious experience has its origins. He saw this subliminal region as "the fountain-head of much that feeds our religion."[4] He proposed that religious impulses and experience begin in this unseen and uncharted territory, but that in spite of this, they have very real effects in this world, and if they have an effect then they must be classed as real. This approach is fundamentally a pragmatic one and entirely in agreement with James' own pragmatic philosophy.

James' book was undoubtedly influenced by his own experiences. His critics argue that he took a very individualistic position on religious experience, ignoring both historical and cultural factors. For all intents and purposes, the *Varieties* is about Christian religiosity. It also emphasizes the strong link between pathology and religiousness, and by adopting the subconscious as the center for this he anticipated the development of psychoanalysis.

Psychoanalytic Approaches to the Psychology of Religion

The publication of books with titles relating to psychology and religion increased in the years leading up to and immediately following World War One. Many of these began to respond to the growing impetus of the "new psychology" of Psychoanalysis. Sigmund Freud (1856–1939) provided the basis for a therapeutic psychology which recognized that health required a free flow of psychic energy between conscious and unconscious aspects of the personality. The Freudian unconscious was a repository for all those experiences and ideas which were unacceptable to the conscious self and which, as such, had been repressed. Therapy consisted largely of identifying these contents through accessing the client's unconscious: initially through hypnosis and later through dreams, then engaging the symbolism of the unconscious mind and isolating the underlying cause of the problem. The cause was usually some form of trauma experienced early in life. In examining the unconscious, Freud was directly concerned with the symbolism of the human mind. He had recognized that this symbolism could also be seen in the myths and stories of antiquity and could be interpreted, with the right keys, to illuminate the human personality. Religion was an example of this symbolic attitude; charged by a childlike need for security it involved the projection of these needs onto mythological deities. From a psychoanalytic perspective God shares the same function as a parent for a child. In essence, God is set in the role of supreme parent.[5]

Freud had read many of the anthropological works of his time and noted that in "primitive" populations there were similarities between those objects and areas of life designated as taboo (out of bounds within tribal life) and the phobias associated with neuroticism (associated with nervousness, hysteria, and other mild forms of mental instability). Magic and religious ritualistic practices share a similar sense of the omnipotence of thought characteristic of the childhood mind and offer, according to Freud, an illusory sense of control. Freud saw the possibility of tracing religion back to its roots. These roots existed, according to Freud, in the prehistory of humankind. Drawing upon the accounts published early in the twentieth century by anthropologists, he imagined early human communities to have a patriarchal structure, with a primeval father leader who headed the community and fought off challenges to his position of authority from the other young men in the tribe. The only way in which these young men could rise to a position of power was through killing this father figure. Freud used the Oedipus myth to structure his ideas here. In Greek legend, Oedipus killed his father and married his mother. This story played a fundamental role in Freud's thoughts about the critical developmental stages of childhood and the feelings associated with these that led to the development of religious belief.

For Freud, religion and ritual serve the same purpose as the obsessional acts of the neurotic, primarily the reduction of anxiety and the sublimation of harmful social, egoistic and sexual impulses. Freud considered the obsessional neurosis as being equivalent to a private religious system and religion as a universal obsessional neurosis. In his book *Totem and Taboo* (1913) he drew parallels between the prohibitions (taboos) attached to killing certain sacred animals (totems), those which prevented sexual relations between members of the same clan, and the submission to prohibitions in obsessional neurosis. According to Freud, these features of tribal life support the application of the Oedipal myth in relation to religion. The totem represents the common origins of a tribal group – it is in a sense the original parent – and in tribal life it is unlawful to kill the totem animal or to have sexual intercourse with members of the same tribe (descendants of the same totem). These are the two main features of the Oedipal myth: the fear associated with wishing to kill the father and the adoption of his role.

Religious experience, in common with many other pathologies, was located by Freud in primary rather than secondary processes. Primary processes refer to those subconscious activities such as dreaming; while secondary processes refer to the more conscious volitional activities such as problem solving. Primary processes are activities associated with a level of the personality Freud called the id; the other parts of Freudian personality include the ego and the superego. The id relates to the passions, desires and subconscious activities, the ego to the normal level of consciousness, and the superego to the conscience and the incorporation of a parent-like image into consciousness. So for Freud, religious experiences and beliefs derive from the irrational regions of the mind. These kinds of experiences should be subjugated to the higher will and aims of the ego.

Roberto Assagioli (1888–1974) is one psychoanalyst who interpreted religious experiences in a very different way from Freud. Whereas Freud saw himself as a "God forsaken 'incredulous Jew'" who was "profoundly irreligious,"[6] Assagioli was centrally concerned with the spiritual. He developed the psychic structure of the personality even further, subdividing the unconscious into different domains, and adding structures such as "the transpersonal self" which participates directly in a spiritual reality. Assagioli's psychosynthesis is concerned with personal development, employing visualization and interaction with the subconscious mind in order to reach self-realization. Assagioli has moved a long way from the beginnings of psychoanalysis and would now be more appropriately seen as a member of the transpersonal psychology movement.

A more mainstream development of Freud's work can be seen in the writings of Erik H. Erikson (1902–94). Erikson's work centered around the principle of "epigenesis." This term relates to the process of psychological growth and development of the individual. The term was borrowed from embryology where it referred to the development process of foetal organs. In both senses, the term describes the developmental process and the requirement for the proper and timely appearance of certain functions. Any developmental problems can adversely affect the overall functioning and health of the individual. This psychological process, unlike its biological equivalent, stretches over the entire lifespan from infancy to old age, and is condensed into seven stages. At the various stages in this developmental process, the individual has to overcome certain tensions described in bipolar terms. For instance, the first stage, occurring in infancy, is that of "basic trust versus mistrust" and requires the child to feel comfortable and trusting of the world, others and self. This process mainly occurs during the feeding and nursing of the child and any division between the mother and the child, such as the mother returning to work, or another pregnancy, can lead to division and mistrust.[7] The resolution of these feelings and the development of trust occurs through a strong satisfying sense of unity in the relationships, and by a gentle and gradual separation.

Another example of one of these important stages in Erikson's theory is that of "intimacy versus isolation" experienced in young adulthood. Having attained a sense of identity the individual is now adequately prepared to enter into intimate relationships where that identity can be combined with another's. Again it is important to recognize that the trust, sense of self, and confidence that were achieved in earlier stages are necessary to be able to enter fully into these intimate relationships successfully. If this stage does not proceed normally the individual may fail to enjoy successful relationships and become isolated and self absorbed.

The final stage, in old age, is one where the opposites of integrity and despair are pitched against each other. Assuming the individual has developed positively and fully there should be a sense of integrity, of coherence, order and spiritual meaning. Where the individual has failed to incorporate the qualities from the experience of the previous stages, he feels that time has passed too quickly, and is unable to accept closing of the life-cycle. This stage leads to a spiritual or religious awareness in which the wisdom of the experience of life brings the cycle to completion, resulting in a sense of hope. The qualities and issues associated with this final stage of life are traditionally linked with the role of religion. The same can be said of some of the earlier stages; for instance the development of a trusting relationship, the care and rearing of children, which are both events which are celebrated within religion and are often marked by ceremony and ritual.

Ritual and ceremony take on a particular meaning in Erikson's theory of development. He uses the term "ritualization" to describe a regular and repeated agreed-upon interplay between individuals which fosters the growth of the individual ego. These ritual elements occur again at different stages of life from infancy to old age, providing positive or negative outcomes contingent upon the success of the individual in developing the right relations between self, others and environment.

Erikson took aspects of psychoanalysis and placed them in an interpersonal developmental context, one which centers upon the resolution of life challenges in order to live as fully as possible. The psychology of religion in Erikson's view is placed firmly in the realm of day-to-day living.

Like Freud, Carl Jung (1875–1961) came from a medical background and specialized in psychiatry. He was an early ally of Freud's but eventually abandoned Freud's ideas as he became more and more dissatisfied with Freud's unidimensional and positivistic interpretation of the psychological. He redefined Freud's term "libido," extending it to cover psychic energy in general rather than the specific definition of sexual energy which Freud had supplied. Jung initially agreed with Freud's position on religion but he eventually took a much more sympathetic view than Freud; he saw religious experience as playing the most important role in the development of human consciousness. Jung also took the concept of the unconscious much further than Freud. He saw the unconscious less as a closet in which the skeletons of the past were kept and more as a dynamic and interactive guide for each individual's development – which Jung called "individuation." This development responds to the influence of archetypes, which are the constituents of a collective level of the unconscious. Archetypes are very difficult to conceptualize and define; however, they may be seen as preformed patterns and images which exist in potential for all humans (and probably other organisms). These preformed patterns and images are inherited in a similar way to instincts but, to be more accurate, in the case of archetypes we inherit the possibility of ideas. Archetypes include among others: the mother archetype (encompassing both the human and goddess mother and representing all those ideal characteristics such as nurturance, sustenance and fertility), the wise old man archetype (which represents wisdom and insight) and, perhaps the most important archetype for Jung, "the self" – the core of the personality which balances the unconscious and the conscious mind – representing the totality or whole. Jung was firmly convinced that archetypes existed and that these included images of God; however, he was reluctant to take these as proof of God. He did argue, however, that they are proof of a psychological representation of God.

As Jung's upbringing was religious and his father was a minister it is perhaps not surprising that much of his work was concerned with exploring religious experience. Jung's ideas were guided by his own personal experiences and he remarked that all of his work was really an outgrowth of the religious experiences he had in his adolescence. Although, like many of the early psychologists, his work was largely interpretative he considered himself an empiricist, remarking that he could only comment on the psychological aspects of the spiritual. However, in one of his final interviews when asked if he believed in God, Jung replied that he did not believe, rather, he knew that God existed.

For Jung, it was entirely natural and functional to turn towards religious concerns when the middle of life is reached. Jung saw this as a process much like the rising and setting of the sun. During the early part of life the individual establishes a career and family and develops their place in society, but after these have been consolidated inner concerns and spirituality should dominate. These inner concerns sometimes make themselves known of their own accord without any attempt to seek communion, since in Jung's view the psyche is a dynamic self-organizing system. These intrusions of the self might even involve images, events and forms far beyond normal religious imagery; they may, for instance, allude to the old alchemical processes of the transmutation of base metal into precious gold. In Jung's view, the religious rituals and ceremonies of different institutionalized religions all draw their life from these deep unconscious representations.

Jung placed great emphasis upon the importance of spiritual experience:

> No matter what the world thinks about religious experience, the one who has it possesses a great treasure, a thing that has become for him a source of life, meaning, and beauty, and that has given him a new splendour to the world and mankind. . . . Is there, as a matter of fact, any better truth about the ultimate things than the one that helps you to live?[8]

James Hillman (1926–) who became Jung's successor in terms of archetypal psychology, went so far as to say that Jung's archetypes, the patterns or metaphors in our imagination, are the primary reality and that there is a pandemonium of such images and a plurality of gods. These images are the source of religion and morality. As long as we are still in touch with these images we have a true religious response, but once we lose these images we become moralistic. According to Hillman, it is religious faith which endows these contents of the imagination with life. Like Jung, he sees religious orientation as extremely important for grasping and understanding the world.

The psychoanalytic view of religion clearly focuses on the internal world of the individual as he or she learns to live with him/herself and develop relationships with others. Most psychoanalytic theories incorporate a sense of development and inevitably identify psychopathology as the consequence of the failure to live appropriately. Religion for these psychologists is either an indication of pathology (Freud) or a central aspect of development (Assagioli, Erikson, Jung, and Hillman); either way, it plays an important role in the psychological health of the individual. Whereas psychoanalysis intended to be an empirical science, its theories derived partly from the preferences of individual theorists and drew support from subjective interpretation of the phenomena concerned. Most academic psychologists who take an empirical approach to the study of mind and behavior reject the claims of psychoanalysis to objectivity and empirical rigor. These psychologists, wherever possible, set their research in the laboratory or aim at least to quantify religious belief, experience and behavior. This movement is termed here the "objectivist approach" because of its strict concern for the empirical facts.

The Objectivist Approach to the Psychology of Religion

It has already been mentioned that psychologists occupy a wide range of philosophical and theoretical positions and may approach the same phenomenon in a number of ways. In this section we will examine some of the objectivist or empirical approaches taken in relation to religious phenomena. In the very early years psychology was influenced by the physical sciences like biology, which meant that many psychologists saw experiments as the natural way to investigate mind and behavior. It was this approach above all others which prevailed during the period from the 1920s through to the early 1950s when psychology was dominated by the strong positivistic approach of behaviorism. Proponents of behaviorism, such as J. B. Watson and B. F. Skinner, saw religious behavior as existing on the same level as any other behavior; it was learnt through association and had little reality beyond this. In a sense, for the behaviorists, religion and religious thinking is simply a matter of superstition and social control because it supports and encourages dogmas which are beyond rational verification.

The behaviorists adhered strongly to the philosophy of positivism, that is, the belief that only those facets of the world which yield to the senses can have any place in science. Unobservables such as the mind and thought cannot be discussed consensually and therefore should be left out of a truly "scientific" psychology, instead the behaviorists' aim was to fully describe and understand the observable aspects – behavior. They developed relatively simple models of behavior which consisted of chains of stimulus and response events (S–R). The co-occurrence of two events (a stimulus event and a response event) can become associated. We and other animals (most research in this paradigm was conducted on animals and the findings generalized to humans) learn to respond to situations by trial and error, eventually finding a response which resolves the situation. In some situations responses may be adopted which seem to provide solutions but which are in fact totally unrelated to the original event; these irrational associations, according to the behaviorists, are the origins of religious and superstitious behavior.

To give a specific example seen from this perspective, prayer is a behavior learned in childhood and often encouraged ("reinforced" and "rewarded" in behaviorist terms) by parents. Over time it also becomes associated with the relief of hunger (for example prayers are often said before meals), relaxation and the reduction of worry (prayers may also be said before sleep). Eventually, through association, the act of prayer by itself may bring about feelings of relaxation, satisfaction and the reduction of worry in the absence of those original conditions (relief of hunger and sleep) which previously preceded prayer.

Although the accounts of behaviorism must inevitably be seen as a simplification of psychological processes, it dictated the path that academic psychology took during the decades between the 1920s and the 1950s. Mainstream academic psychology has kept close to the ideals of complete objectivity, dealing only with behaviors that can be measured and avoiding discussion of anything subjective. Inevitably with this shift in philosophy from the more subjective efforts of the early psychologists and the psychoanalysts, the approach to religious phenomena also changed. Religious beliefs are beliefs about phenomena which do not exist for objectivist psychology, since the philosophy that underpins the discipline is one of reductionistic materialism – the same philosophy that motivates most contemporary science. This means that rather than looking at the spiritual issues themselves, the objectivist psychologists have turned their attention to how people practice their religiousness, what might motivate this, what everyday benefits they obtain from religiousness and so on.

Different ways of being religious

Researchers have found that there seems to be good evidence for people having different ways of being religious. For some people, religion is very closely related to their own personal subjective experience and belief; for others, it is more related to creating an impression and acquiring social acceptance and support. A range of researchers have proposed similar categorizations: for instance, Gordon Allport[9] explored religion in terms of an "extrinsic" and "intrinsic" division. From the intrinsic position, religious faith is important in itself, but from the extrinsic position the religious practices are utilitarian, they grant safety and social standing. A third orientation has since been added to Allport's intrinsic and extrinsic division by Batson and Ventis (1982): they call this the "quest" orientation. The quest orientation is characterized by an individual who constantly relates his or her beliefs to the physical and social environment, confronting difficult existential questions that ensue but without necessarily expecting to obtain absolute answers.

Other psychologists have offered similar categories of religious behavior. For instance, "primary" religious behavior is directed by personal inner experience of the divine. "Secondary" behavior may have had a primary source but has become a routine and uninspired obligation. "Tertiary" religious experience is used to describe religious routine which is accepted entirely on the basis of the authority of someone else.[10] Another similar formulation distinguished between "committed" and "consensual" religion: the former refers to a set of religious beliefs which relate to daily activities while the latter refers to a simplified and personally convenient view of religion.[11] Each of these dimensions relates to the degree to which religion is informed by personal experience or adopted from an external source, the degree to which they are actually "lived" rather than simply "acted" and the degree to which the consequences and implications have been explored by the individual.

Allport suggested that the extrinsically motivated individual "uses" his religion, and the person motivated from an intrinsic point of view "lives" his. This division between these two main characteristic religious behaviors has been further explored in terms of personality of the religious individual. The authoritarian personality research project[12] identified the authoritarian personality as having very orthodox religious beliefs. This relationship is a little clearer when we consider some of the underlying traits of the authoritarian personality, which include a low tolerance of ambiguity (a preference for clear and distinct concepts and instant solutions) and tendencies toward ethnocentrism, dogmatism, rigidity and prejudice. These tendencies suggest that religiousness in this respect serves a protective function by providing a formal framework for the interpretation of personal and social experience. There is evidence that both the intrinsic and the extrinsic orientation is related to these kinds of traits. The quest orientation seems the least likely to be involved in such relationships.

It can be seen from this work that different people become involved in religion for different reasons. It is likely that personality and social situation play a role in influencing the kind of religious orientation taken. It is also likely that religiousness has other adaptive functions, especially in terms of providing a belief structure which provides protection for the individual against the unknown.

Exercises

1   Discuss the three orientations and use these to describe the personality of three people, where each is led by an intrinsic, extrinsic, or quest orientation.

2   Having discussed the features of these three orientations, identify three public figures who perhaps exemplify these three orientations to religion.

Religious belief

In the Aristotelian view of the world – the philosophy which sustained the western world up to the Enlightenment – everything had its place; the world was like an organism, each part related to the whole, to God. Following the writings of Galileo, Descartes and Newton, a new view of the world as a machine became increasingly popular. At first this machine provided evidence of a grand architect, but as science developed there was less and less reason for including God in the equation. As the direct link with religion and spirituality had been severed, another reason for religious behavior had to be found. The interpretations offered by some anthropologists are valuable here; they saw religion as functional, offering social cohesion and control. Psychologists soon followed and saw religion as offering personal psychological benefits as well.

Religious beliefs can be seen as helping to reduce anxiety and fear; probably the greatest anxiety that anyone experiences is the anxiety related to thoughts of their eventual demise, the fear of death. The main contributor in this area was perhaps Ernest Becker,[13] who thought that if humans attained a full awareness of their condition they would be driven insane. So from this perspective, religious beliefs are like lies which act as a buffer against the otherwise paralyzing reality of impending death. According to Jack Schumaker:

> Magic, religion, and all forms of reality distortion are simply species-specific responses unique to the human animal. These act in our service. Paranormal belief did a great deal for us: it did nothing less than save us from extinction.[14]

According to Schumaker the oceanic feelings associated with mystical and religious experience are no more than a rush of endorphins (the body's natural opiates). Not only is religious belief a necessary cognitive deception, but he presumes we also evolved a biologically-based mechanism for deception.

Death and religiousness have also been associated in a much more positive sense. People who have had near-death experiences (NDEs) often report sudden and significant life changes which often include a new or renewed sense of religiousness and spirituality, although this will not necessarily mean a new commitment to a religious institution such as a church. The NDE seems to have a reasonably robust set of characteristics with strong similarities across individual cases. The experience is often marked by an out-of-body-experience and continues with the experience of traveling down a tunnel, a sense of transition, the acquaintance with an all-loving entity of light and perhaps the meeting of deceased family and friends. Many people who report NDEs report religious feelings and content, although this is not always the case. From a transpersonal psychological view this might be seen as evidence for a spiritual reality. From an objectivist position they are explained to a large extent through biological processes such as the increased production of endorphins, which account for the feelings of peacefulness and euphoria, and oxygen starvation which creates the tunnel effect as the outer areas of the brain die before the central regions.

Mental health and religious experience

As we have already seen, the psychoanalytic view of religion is closely tied up with mental health. From the perspective of objectivist psychology spiritual experience can have nothing to do with reality, so it is often interpreted as an indication of mental illness. These comparisons between mental health or illness and religious experience are an important and recurrent theme in the psychology of religion.

William James noted that "mystical ideas are often cited as characteristic of symptoms of enfeebled or deluded states of mind. In delusional insanity, paranoia as they sometimes call it, we may have a kind of diabolical mysticism, a sort of religious mysticism turned upside down."[15] Freud considered religion as a mass neurosis. Religion was an obsession evidenced in ritual, which was very much like the compulsive and obsessional behavior of neurotics. For Jung, the religious outlook was the key to mental health. He noted that people often came to him for help because they had not found a religious outlook. Erikson similarly described the importance of developing spirituality and wisdom, especially in later life. Allport recognized that beliefs were extremely important in a healthy life and of these beliefs it was religious belief that was most essential. Even the origins of the term "mental illness" can be traced back to St. Teresa of Avila; there is good reason to believe that the term "mental illness" was introduced by her in order to redefine religious fervor, which may have otherwise been interpreted as possession and laid the subject open to investigation from the Inquisition.[16]

The empirical evidence for a relationship between mental health and religious involvement was summarized by Batson and Ventis (1982).[17] This relationship should be considered as correlational rather than causal; that is, it is not possible to say that religious involvement can bring about mental health or sickness, it can only be said that they are related. They reviewed 67 findings from 57 empirical studies of religion and various aspects of mental health. They found that the majority of the studies (37) showed a negative relationship, with higher levels of religious involvement associated with lower levels of mental health. There were 15 studies which showed a positive relationship, with higher levels of religious involvement associated with higher levels of mental health, and 15 that showed no marked direction of relationship. This would suggest that the overall pattern of relationship involves lower levels of mental health among those who reported higher levels of religious involvement. This provides evidence to support Freud's contention that religious involvement was related to mental illness.

Exploring the problem more closely, Batson and Ventis note that a finer level of detail can be obtained by examining seven particular conceptions of mental health. These conceptions include: absence of illness; appropriate social behavior; freedom from worry and guilt; personal competence and control; self acceptance and self actualization; unification and organization (linked by Allport to a mature personality); and open-mindedness and flexibility. The pattern suggested above is not always consistent for all the conceptions of mental health. They suggest that this is the reason why different researchers have held contradictory interpretations, with both positive and negative relationships being identified between religious involvement and mental health; this results from measuring different aspects of mental health, some of these being negative and some positive.

Clarifying these relationships, Batson and Ventis conclude that the relationship is largely positive with more religious involvement being associated with absence of mental illness. However, religious involvement is negatively related to personal competence and control, self actualization, open-mindedness and flexibility, and freedom from worry and guilt. This seems to oppose the view of religious involvement as beneficial to mental health. The relationship between mental health and religious involvement is also modified by the way in which the participants in the study express their religiousness, with the extrinsic orientation being the one that generally involves the negative relationship with mental health. The intrinsic and quest orientations are positively related to mental health, although for different reasons; in the intrinsic orientation a sense of competence and control is based on a reliance on God, while the quest orientation seems to derive control from a sense of self-reliance. Although the links between mental health and religious involvement do seem to exist, they are not as simple as previously thought.

Religious concerns and ideas often play a large part in the symptoms of mental illness. This is not too surprising if we assume that there is an increased openness or sensitivity to material from the unconscious mind – a common characteristic of both religious and psychopathological experience. Often the experiences associated with psychotic breakdown are accompanied by delusions of a religious or mythical character. It may be that these religious interpretations, which even include the patient having delusions of being Jesus Christ or the Son of God, have a therapeutic value. One study of these kinds of delusions suggested that they were essential to a meaningful and valued view of life.[18]

Julian Jaynes in his book *The Origin of Consciousness in the Breakdown of the Bicameral Mind*[19] draws parallels between the auditory hallucinations of schizophrenics and the voices of the gods as mentioned in the ancient Greek myths. He proposed that the Greeks as represented in Homer's classic *The Iliad* experienced their own thoughts as a divine presence, as conversations with the gods. According to Jaynes, the modern mind evolved only recently and the consequence of its development was that it distanced the gods from us. Jaynes views the "voices" heard by schizophrenics as historic remnants of another time and another form of mind. It is interesting to note that a large number of the people who hear voices in this context have at one time or another interpreted the voices as having a supernatural origin, identifying them as gods, angels, or spirits.

Psychologists who adopt the psychoanalytic and objectivist approaches to the psychology of religion have regularly drawn parallels between religious experience and psychological illness. Some of the psychoanalytic and most of the objectivist psychologists assume there is no spiritual reality. Religious experiences and beliefs are at best adaptive illusions, at worst they are superstitious and irrational and perhaps indicative of mental illness. There are, however, dissenters to these views who champion the possibility of a psychological understanding and exploration of the spiritual. The humanistic movement, which began in the 1960s and which has since developed into transpersonal psychology, has challenged orthodox views of human psychological nature and has called for an expanded view of the psyche which can incorporate many of the attributes of spiritual or religious experience and belief.

Transpersonal Approaches to the Psychology of Religion

As we have already seen, the early psychologists of religion were predominantly concerned with the spiritual experience itself. After a period of concentrating on the behavior associated with religion it seems likely that transpersonal psychologists are taking the psychology of religion full circle, back to the experience itself. As with most interesting and complex phenomena, religious experience is not easy to define or operationalize. William James saw religious experience as a solitary venture where the individual confronts God. Drawing together an overall pattern for these experiences, James suggests that they represent an initial discontent and a favorable resolution and that without regard to their truth they are amongst the most important functions of humans. Jung also saw religious or spiritual experience as an important opportunity for the holistic development of the self. During the 1960s there were moves in psychology to try and move beyond the reductive methods of behavioristic psychology and the newer but equally limited perspective of cognitive psychology. Humanistic psychology and its eventual development into transpersonal psychology attempted to take the first few brave steps into what Abraham Maslow called "the farther reaches of human nature."[20]

In Maslow's opinion, spiritual, religious or in his own terms "peak" experiences were not at all pathological, instead they occupied the upper regions of a needs hierarchy. This hierarchy is usually represented as a triangle with the basics of life such as food and shelter positioned toward the bottom, and with peak or spiritual experiences right at the very top, standing for something exceptional and life enhancing. This same view is echoed throughout the transpersonal psychology movement. Spiritual experiences have been classed as one example among many forms of exceptional human experience, which Rhea White has described as seeds leading to new ways of living and seeing the world.[21]

One of the most important attempts to catalog and explore religious experience has been undertaken at the Religious Experience Research Unit at Manchester College, Oxford University, England. Beginning in 1969, Alister Hardy began to collect accounts of religious experiences. These experiences came from ordinary people who responded to requests in newspapers and on radio and TV. The experiences initially consisted of informal accounts, only later were questionnaire methods used. He published a book in 1979, summarizing the findings of this venture for a pool of 3,000 experiences which had been gathered up to that date.[22] Hardy used a classificatory framework consistent with his background as a biologist and at odds with the early discussions of such experience, for example, the approach of William James who preferred to let the experiences speak for themselves.

The experiences are categorized according to the form of the experience, for instance, whether it was visual or auditory. Each experience is further categorized in terms of other characteristics, for instance, a visual experience may be further described as a vision, or illumination, or a transformation of surroundings. There are hundreds of combinations available and Hardy likens this categorization process to that which involves the combination of molecules in chemical compounds. According to Hardy, the main characteristics of religious and spiritual experiences revolve around the feelings of a transcendent reality where "something other" is longed for, sensed, or desired in a relationship. This feeling of "something other" can lead to a resolution of "uneasiness" as William James called it. Certainly some of the experiences recorded at the Manchester College testify that many people who have such experiences have been led to fresh, creative perceptions that replace old, stagnant viewpoints. According to Hardy, it is through this kind of research that the spiritual nature is shown to be a reality and he argues that we need a new philosophy which will address this by studying consciousness as the fundamental attribute of life.

In spite of the many different categories of experience provided by Hardy it seems likely that there are some core features of such experiences. These features include:

1   Unifying vision, all things are one, part of a whole.
2   Timeless and spaceless.
3   Sense of reality, not subjective but a valid source of knowledge.
4   Blessedness, joy, peace and happiness.
5   Feeling of the holy, sacred, divine.
6   Paradoxical, defies logic.
7   Ineffable, cannot be described in words.
8   Loss of sense of self.[23]

Most of these features point to a state of mind which is quite different from our normal one. It is the characteristics of this different state, one where logic and rationality have no place, which fuels the prejudice of some psychologists. It is, however, in the investigation of these altered states of consciousness that the transpersonal movement really came into its own.

Exploring the psychology of religious experience

Transpersonal psychologists have tried to map out religious experience by altering aspects of an individual's sensory, cognitive and physiological environment. Here the concept of physiological arousal has played an important role. A cartography of religious states was tentatively mapped out by Roland Fischer in 1975.[24] He found that low or high arousal could bring about unusual experiences which included hallucinations and delusions but also mystical feelings and insights.

It is well established that unusual visual and auditory experiences occur in response to changes in arousal. Sensory deprivation techniques were used extensively in the 1960s and 1970s to explore changes in arousal and consciousness. This "sensory deprivation" took place in rooms with no light or sound, and in conditions where reductions in tactile perception were possible. After relatively short periods of time most people perceive simple visual patterns, images, and sounds. More complex imagery is also experienced when the isolation conditions are longer in duration, or when a suggestion, or expectation, of such phenomena exists. Religious people have reported religious imagery and these seem more readily seen by those with an intrinsic rather than extrinsic orientation. Although this is a rather artificial way of inducing religious imagery it may tell us something about the conditions in which such experiences occur naturally. For instance, reduced social contact is often encouraged in the pursuit of religious experience; usually this is attained by retreating from the social group to a location which is low in sensory stimulation. These conditions make it more likely that spontaneous religious imagery will occur, especially when it is expected. Add to these conditions the tendency to engage in fasting and absorbed or repetitive acts and we have a good recipe for the occurrence of powerful inner experiences.

William James had noticed that substances available in his own time, such as Nitrous Oxide, induced experiences which were not unlike those termed as religious. He noted that there seem to be other potential states of awareness which are hidden by the film of our normal consciousness. These altered states of consciousness (ASCs) are characterized by a loosening of normal ways of thinking and social norms, an increase in associative thought, a blurring of boundaries between self and other, a sense of unity between subject and object, changes in the perception of time and space. As we can see, these have a good deal in common with the core features of mystical experience.

During the 1960s, a number of psychological studies were conducted using hallucinogenic drugs. These included drugs such as cannabis and LSD-25, which brought about changes in awareness which ranged from mild elevations of mood to intense visual and auditory sensation, depending upon the drug, its dosage, and the conditions under which it was administered. Psychoactive substances which occur naturally in the environment (two examples include hallucinogenic mushrooms and the peyote cactus) have played an important role in the religious ceremonies of many cultures. Studies indicate that the interpretations of the experiences arising from the use of such drugs were intimately related to the belief systems of the individuals involved. It seems that the drugs deepened the specific religious commitment of those involved.

Probably the most famous of these studies on psychedelic drugs and religious experience was that carried out by Walter Pahnke in 1964. Using a double-blind procedure (where neither experimenter nor subject know whether the subject has been given the drug or a placebo), twenty first-year theology students were given either psilocybin (a hallucinogenic mushroom) or nicotinic acid (a stimulant). The drugs were administered on Good Friday evening and the students went to a private chapel where they listened over loudspeakers to a religious service taking place in another part of the building. A good number of the psilocybin students reported the features of mystical experience while the students who received the nicotine reported significantly fewer of these features.

The Pahnke study indicated that drugs can help to generate experiences with features that correspond to some features of mystical experiences. For some religious groups their rituals are heavily dependent upon the use of such substances. For instance some Mexican Indian tribes used the peyote cactus in their religious ceremonies to seek visions and guidance. One well-known popular example of this practice is represented in the writings of Carlos Castaneda[25] who allegedly became the apprentice of a Yaqui Indian sorcerer. In the early days of his apprenticeship with don Juan, Castaneda was exposed to a range of hallucinogens, including jimson weed, mushrooms and peyote. These had the effect of confusing and loosening Castaneda's normal conceptions of the world. After a number of years of these experiences and other practices which did not involve the use of drugs, he became convinced of the existence of alternative realities. These alternative realities could be accessed through changing awareness or entering altered states of consciousness; in these altered states the mind seems to experience a world governed by different rules of nature.

Religious and mystical experience have also been facilitated by other practices such as meditation, which has played an important role in a wide range of western and eastern religious disciplines. Meditation typically involves the focusing and control of attention exclusively and tenaciously on one object, image, phrase or word. This focused activity is sometimes accompanied by dancing and chant in some traditions, or by the repetition of a simple prayer. These techniques, although all from different traditions, seem to share a complete directed absorption in the process, a one-pointedness which exhausts the usual perceptions of the object and opens up fresh insights. This is most readily seen in the Zen tradition where contemplation of a Koan (a logical or paradoxical puzzle such as: "what is the sound of one hand clapping?") can lead to a resolution involving a new understanding of the puzzle.

Batson and Ventis (1982) propose that religious experience is very much like creative experience, and that both experiences are reality transforming. They suggest a number of propositions which encapsulate the nature of both creativity and religious experience. The main proposals are: that reality is constructed, that is, humans only know the world through their own constructions and interpretations; that these interpretations depend upon the development of our cognitive structures (for example, very young children forget about an object when it is moved out of sight, indicating that a sense of "object permanence" has not yet been incorporated into the cognitive structures of the child); and that the organization of these cognitive structures is improved through creative acts. Creativity seems to be composed of identifiable stages, *preparation*, *incubation*, *illumination* and *verification*. This account of the creative process resonates with William James' formulation of religious experience as being composed of two parts: an uneasiness and its solution.

In terms of spiritual or religious experience this can be summarized as a sequence involving an *existential crisis*, *self-surrender*, and the perception of a *new vision* and *new life* which removes the old worries and concerns, replacing them with a sense of assurance. However, not all religious experience leads to a restructuring of cognition and provides the means to overcome the initial existential crisis. It is possible that the experience could lead to a "flight from reality" into personal fantasy, or to the development of rigid and dogmatic beliefs about conduct.

Exercises

3   In the light of these comments think about the various techniques which have been used in your culture to attain religious experience and discuss what kinds of effects they may incur.

4   Compare the following accounts. One is drug-induced, the other is the experience of a famous religious mystic.

> Suddenly I burst into a vast, new, indescribably wonderful universe. Although I am writing this over a year later, the thrill of the surprise and amazement, the awesomeness of the revelation, the engulfment in an overwhelming feeling-wave of gratitude and blessed wonderment, are as fresh, and the memory of the experience as vivid, as if it had happened five minutes ago.
>
> All at once, without warning of any kind, I found myself wrapped in a flame-colored cloud. For an instant I thought of fire . . . the next, I knew that the fire was within myself. Directly afterward there came upon me a sense of exultation of immense joyousness accompanied or immediately followed by an intellectual illumination impossible to describe.[26]

Parapsychological research and spirituality

Paranormal phenomena such as telepathy (thought transference) and psychokinesis (mind over matter) have been systematically studied since the late nineteenth century. These human abilities have been hotly debated and the area is not without controversy, because it seems to challenge the very essence of science by exploring conjectural immaterial processes which many see as related to magical, spiritual or religious thinking. In fact, Joseph Rhine, the founder of experimental parapsychology, firmly believed that parapsychology would allow the scientific investigation of religion. William Braud, a contemporary parapsychologist, provides a powerful poetic image of these abilities.[27] He likens them to flowers in a garden, the existence of which is in dispute, but over the years enough evidence of these flowers has been collected and examined by parapsychologists for them to assert that these flowers and the garden exist, although they were previously considered as mythical. If they exist, this opens up the possibility of finding other more fabulous flowers in the same garden.

The existence of flowers such as telepathy and psychokinesis could provide evidence for more miraculous phenomena such as the healings and powers described in spiritual traditions. Accounts of such experiences are frequently reported in the general population, but it is likely that many of these experiences are attributable to misinterpretation and coincidence and many fewer to fraud; only a minority of these reports would be considered as being due to ostensible paranormal causes. However, it is clear that these special phenomena could be used to argue for the existence of a spiritual dimension, one in which there may ultimately be an intangible connection between individuals and also one in which there is survival beyond physical death. The experimental evidence for extrasensory perception and mental influence seems to suggest this interconnectedness. A range of studies have revealed that concealed targets can be successfully guessed (without any sensory contact) at significantly higher than chance rates, and also that two individuals remote from each other can influence and respond to each other's emotional states. These results are difficult to explain in normal terms and seem to suggest something which has been overlooked in mainstream psychology and science in general.

Another central question for many parapsychologists has been that of the survival of death. Early parapsychology researchers investigated displays of mediumship in their efforts to identify evidence for survival. The findings were mixed; some of these investigations yielded evidence which seemed to suggest contact with someone who had died, many others offered nothing of interest. More recently, some researchers have explored the question of survival using a situation based on the ancient Greek "psychomanteum" – a chamber in which the spirits of the dead returned to speak and advise the living. A modern day psychomanteum involves the use of a dark room, and a mirror into which the percipient gazes. The mirror is angled to the dark ceiling and offers a sense of depth but no identifiable visual features. A relatively large proportion of the people who have taken part in these studies have reported experiences ranging from a sense of presence, visual and auditory perceptions in some cases, to specific encounters with deceased relatives. A recent attempt to conduct a psychomanteum session under experimental conditions revealed interesting correspondences in terms of changes in the temperature and background radiation in the physical environment at times when participants reported a sense of presence.[28] The evidence for these abilities is accumulating; it suggests that the world is more interconnected than was suggested in the mechanistic images of the modernist philosophers and scientists. This interconnectedness may suggest the basis for a recognition of wholeness and future spirituality.

Exercise   **5** How might society and different religions react to the news that parapsychologists had proved that a life after death exists? Discuss the initial reactions and the more long-term consequences of such a claim.

Conclusions

This discussion of psychology and religion has focused on three broad perspectives: psychoanalysis, objectivist psychology and transpersonal psychology, drawing out the differences in approaches, findings and interpretations of religious behavior, belief and experience. It has also exclusively focused on western psychology: nothing has been said about eastern approaches to psychology. A different set of historical and cultural antecedents have provided a context for Indian psychology for instance, which permits the concepts of spirituality and religious experience to be accepted as real in a literal rather than just a pragmatic sense. Although Indian psychology has borrowed the experimental and quantitative analysis techniques from the West, it accommodates in its tradition many phenomena which are less amenable to such modes of measurement. In its development of transpersonal research methods western psychology has begun to accommodate some of these phenomena which it could not submit to experimental methods.

Psychological interpretation of religion has not always been welcomed by psychologists or theologians, and the case of religion informing psychology is quite rare. Interestingly there is something of a recent trend for a reversal of this position, with psychology itself being influenced by Buddhist theories of mind. In modern cognitive psychology and philosophy, especially that deriving from computer models of mind, there has been some acceptance that self as we usually experience it does not exist, i.e., it is illusory. This is not unlike some of the central insights about the impermanence of self in Buddhism. This is a positive development, indicating that psychology and religion can learn from each other.

It is impossible to separate the methods of any discipline from the culture and time in which it exists. In fact, the time and the place in which a scientific practice developed can tell us a lot about the practice itself. Here we have briefly and selectively reviewed some of the ways in which psychologists have touched upon the subject of religious behavior, belief and experience. For psychology, religion is inevitably multi-faceted with many possible interpretations, and it often seems difficult to draw general conclusions from often opposing and contradictory evidence and theory; to choose one broad and central concept that frequently appears in direct religious or mystical experience and which may also lie behind religious affiliation and participation in worship – a feeling of connection and at-one-ment. This seems quite close to one interpretation of the origins of the term "religion" – "religion" comes from the Latin "religare", which means "to bind" – in this case to "bind to the whole." This binding to the whole can lead to surges of creativity and new perceptions, as William James writes:

> When we commune with it, work is actually done upon our finite personality, for we are turned into new men, and consequences in the way of conduct follow in the natural world upon our regenerative change.[29]

As Wulff suggests in his book,[30] a reconsideration of the meaning of religion is important at this time since we are currently experiencing an ecological crisis, one which institutional religion has contributed heavily to and which perhaps a new sense of spirituality must retrieve us from. It is likely that a psychology of spirituality will help to inform these efforts. There are signs that seeds for this psychology are already being sown; its roots lie in scientific endeavor but its concern will be with the soul.

GLOSSARY

Authoritarian personality A personality type with a cluster of personality traits which relate to closed and rigid thinking styles.

Behaviorism Movement in psychology which emphasized the understanding of behavior in strict empirical terms.

Cognitive Refers to mental aspects of the personality; thinking, memory, decision-making.

Interpretative An analysis based on personal or theory-guided interpretation of qualitative data.

Neurosis A common and mild form of mental instability involving recurrent self-referent ideas about guilt and self worth. Symptoms might include depression, compulsions and obsession.

Objectivist Scientists who are generally concerned only with objective "hard" data, usually in numerical form.

Paradigm An approach to science or particular scientific investigations which is informed by particular agreed or implicitly accepted work practices and assumptions.

Paranormal Ostensible phenomena such as telepathy and psychokinesis which are currently unexplained in terms of mechanism but which have experimental and statistical evidence strongly supporting their existence.

Parapsychology A multidisciplinary subject which explores the possibility of human abilities involving communication and influence outside of the currently understood normal channels.

Phenomenological Approach which is concerned with understanding and describing the features of personal experience.

Positivism The approach in science and philosophy which emphasizes that only directly testable phenomena can be examined by science.

Psyche Greek term for soul from which the term psychology derives.

Psychoanalytic/psychoanalysis The movement started by Sigmund Freud which assumes that mental illness derives from the resurgence of repressed material in the unconscious. Psychoanalysts treat such problems using the "talking cure" psychotherapy.

Qualitative/quantitative Refers to textual and numerical types of data and analysis.

Transpersonal Beyond the normal conception of self, perhaps including a spiritual self or soul, or the experience of some self-transcending state characterized by a sense of "otherness."

Notes and References

1   C. D. Batson and W. L. Ventis, *The Religious Experience* (Oxford: Oxford University Press, 1982).
2   W. Braud, and R. Anderson, *Transpersonal Research Methods for the Social Sciences: Honoring Human Experience* (London: Sage, 1998).
3   This approach is also advocated by Ian Markham in *A World Religions Reader*, second edition (Oxford: Blackwell Publishers, 2000), p. 110.
4   William James, *The Varieties of Religious Experience* (London: Penguin Books, 1902/ 1985), p. 484.
5   It is likely that Freud drew inspiration for his projection theories from the German philosopher Ludwig Feuerbach. See chapter 7 – Secular Humanism – in this volume.
6   D. Wulff, *Psychology of Religion: Classic and Contemporary*, second edition (London: Wiley, 1997), p. 276.
7   Erikson reveals his psychoanalytic origins by highlighting the mythological aspects of the development process, likening this parting to the original Fall from grace or the loss of Eden.
8   C. G. Jung, *Psychology and Religion*. In C. G. Jung, *The Collected Works 11. Psychology and Religion: West and East* (London: Routledge, 1969), p. 167.
9   G. Allport, "The religious context of prejudice," *Journal for the Scientific Study of Religion*, 5 (1966): 447–57.
10   W. H. Clark, *The Psychology of Religion: An Introduction to Religious Experience and Behavior* (New York: Macmillan, 1958).
11   R. O. Allen and B. Spilka, "Committed and consensual religion: A specification of religion–prejudice relationships," *Journal for the Scientific Study of Religion*, 6 (1967): 191–206.
12   T. W. Adorno, E. Frenkel-Brunswik, D. J. Levinson, and R. N. Sanford, *The Authoritarian Personality* (New York: Harper and Brothers, 1950).
13   E. Becker, *The Denial of Death* (New York: Free Press, 1973).
14   J. F. Schumaker, *Wings of Illusion: The Origin, Nature, and Future of Paranormal Beliefs* (Amherst, NY: Prometheus, 1987), p. 26.

15 W. James (1902), *The Varieties of Religious Experience* (London: Penguin Books, 1985), p. 426.

16 T. Sarbin, "Metaphors of unwanted conduct," in D. Leary (ed.), *Metaphors in the History of Psychology* (Cambridge: Cambridge University Press, 1990).

17 C. D. Batson, and W. L. Ventis, *The Religious Experience: A Social-Psychological Perspective* (Oxford: Oxford University Press, 1982).

18 G. Roberts, "Delusional belief systems and meaning in life: A preferred reality," *British Journal of Psychiatry*, 159 (Suppl. 14) (1991): 19–28.

19 J. Jaynes, *The Origin of Consciousness in the Breakdown of the Bicameral Mind* (Boston: Houghton Mifflin, 1976).

20 A. Maslow, *The Farther Reaches of Human Nature* (New York: Viking, 1971).

21 Rhea White had a near-death experience in 1952 which led her into parapsychology. In recent years she has developed a broader interest in exceptional human experiences. These include the psychic, the spiritual, mystical, and creative, among many others.

22 A. Hardy, *The Spiritual Nature of Man: A Study of Contemporary Religious Experience* (Oxford: Oxford University Press, 1979).

23 Stace (1960) lists these eight core features. Cited in B. Beit-Hallahmi and M. Argyle, *The Psychology of Religious Behaviour, Belief and Experience* (London: Routledge, 1997), p. 74.

24 R. Fischer, "A Cartography of inner space," in R. K. Siegel and L. J. West (eds.), *Hallucinations: Behaviour Experience and Theory* (London: John Wiley and Sons, 1975).

25 C. Castaneda, *The Teachings of Don Juan* (London: Penguin, 1970).

26 The first of the two descriptions refers to an experience facilitated by ingesting an hallucinogenic drug. See H. Smith, "Do Drugs have Religious Import?," *Journal of Philosophy*, 61 (1964): 517–30, 522 cited in Batson and Ventis (1982), see note 17.

27 W. G. Braud, "Parapsychology and Spirituality: Intimations and Implications," in C. T. Tart (ed.), *Body, Mind, Spirit: Exploring the Parapsychology of Spirituality* (Charlottesville, VA: Hampton Roads Publishing Company, 1997).

28 D. I. Radin and J. M. Rebman, "Are phantasms fact or fantasy? A preliminary investigation of apparitions evoked in the laboratory." *Journal of the Society for Psychical Research*, 61 (1996): 65–87.

29 William James (1902), *The Varieties of Religious Experience* (London: Penguin Books, 1985), p. 516.

30 D. Wulff, *Psychology of Religion: Contemporary and Classic* (London: Wiley, 1997).

Chapter 4

Religion and Scripture: The Function of the Special Books of Religion

ALEX SMITH

Key Questions Regarding Scripture's Characterization

Judaism

Christianity

Islam

Hinduism

Buddhism

Sikhism

All religions have their special books. These books are considered important for the life of those religions, and are consequently invested with great authority. Christianity has its special books and the collection is called the Bible. The word Bible means simply *book*. To show that it is special and to be revered, the very descriptive adjective "holy" is often placed before it. Holy Bible however is a very Christian, and western, way of describing special books and it might carry the wrong messages if it were applied to the special texts of other faiths – Christians might think that the status and use of their special books are carried over into other faiths. Consequently, the word generally employed is Scripture.

If we are to use this word two points must be made in connection with it at the start. The first is that some people regard the term *Sacred Scripture* as implying something more than *Bible* or even *Holy Bible*. For such people *Bible*, and even *Holy Bible*, just refers to the collection of books which a particular faith community possesses but says nothing about the proper attitude to and use of those books; they are books like any other book. *Scripture*, and especially *Sacred Scripture*, says much more, ratcheting the status of the texts to a proper authoritative position. It may be that at the close of this chapter we will want to find a word which describes an attitude to, and an expectation of, a piece of writing that is uniquely different, but until that time the use of the term Scripture will carry no such nuance. Scripture will mean exactly what Bible means – something written. Neither Holy nor Sacred will be attached, and if they are it will mean the same thing at this stage. At the end we may have cause to change our minds and make a distinction.

The second point is that Scripture does imply something written, and as such might be taken to mean that it should be treated like any other written material – as something meant to be read. Most reading in the West however is done silently and in an interior fashion, and much Christian reading of their Scripture follows this fashion. This is not how Scripture is encountered in many of the world's faiths. There it is something principally heard. If it is read, it is read aloud; often the reading can be likened to a performance.

These two points, and especially the second, demonstrate an inherent difficulty in approaching any group of texts that are considered sufficiently similar to be termed generic. It is too easily assumed that the way in which a text is regarded and used among one's own people will be duplicated in other groups. When a Christian turns to the sacred texts of other faiths it is all too easy to take it for granted that how the Bible functions in Christianity will be how those texts will be treated. This is not just western insensitivity, for the approach is likely to be the same should an adherent of another faith come into contact with the Christian Bible.

The second point could perhaps be expanded. A great variety of approaches to and uses of a sacred text can be observed in one's own religion. There is a temptation however to squeeze the function of Scripture in another faith into a uniformity which, if applied to one's own faith, would be held to be a distortion. This should be borne in mind, and excuses made, if in the brief space of this chapter an insufficient variety of attitude and approach seems to be presented.

The approach to encountering Scripture in religion must beware of pouring what is considered generic into the same identical mold. Consequently in this chapter the very question of the generic nature of Scripture will be left open till the writings have been sufficiently explored. The first task must be to discover how exactly the texts are regarded, experienced and used. In order that the exploration might be adequately mapped, six questions will be put to the Scriptures of the religions encountered. They, and the reasons for putting them, are as follows:

Key Questions Regarding Scripture's Characterization

1   Can the Scriptures be translated into another language without ceasing to be what they are in the original language?
    How does the original language work in a modern setting?
    Does the adherent have to fully understand the contents of Scripture?
2   What part does Scripture play in public gatherings and how is it encountered?
    Where is it to be found in public worship?
3   What part does Scripture play in private life and how is it used?
    Where is it to be found in the spirituality of the individual adherent?
4   Where in the acknowledged authorities is Scripture placed?
    Does it play a central part in forming the particular identity of the religion?

5   What views are held about the origin and status of Scripture?
     What kind of language is used to undergird Scripture's authority?
     Is Scripture fixed and final, or can it be added to?
     Are some bits considered more important than others?
6   How is the past, represented by Scripture, brought into the present?
     To what extent is there a need to relate Scripture to present culture?

This chapter examines the use of Scripture in six religions. Three of these are associated with the Middle East; Judaism, Christianity and Islam. Three of them have their origin in India: Hinduism, Buddhism, and Sikhism.

Each section will gain from being read against the corresponding account of the religion which appears later in this book and in *A World Religions Reader*.[1]

Judaism

The quest begins with the first of the religions that started in the Middle East and remains a world faith.

The Jewish Scriptures are commonly taken to be the Christian Old Testament, or, more correctly, the Old Testament of Protestant Christians because it consists of those 39 books. (Roman Catholic and Orthodox Old Testaments contain more than 39 books: see below.) It should, however, be noted that Jews do not usually call their Scriptures the Old Testament, simply because for them there is nothing new in relation to which their Bible should be called old, and they would deny that it was not forever new and fresh. Furthermore, the word "testament" has so changed its meaning that it retains little if anything of the meaning to which it once pointed; that the books of the first part of the Christian Bible represent those writings which arose out of the covenant that existed between God and the People of Israel.

It should also be noted that Jews traditionally consider their Scriptures to consist of 24 books and not 39. The reason for this is the way in which they have been preserved and transmitted: what Christians call the books of Samuel, Kings and Chronicles are counted as one each, as are the books Ezra and Nehemiah, and the prophets Hosea to Malachi are counted as one. These last are sometimes referred to as the Minor Prophets, not because they are of lesser importance but because they are short enough to all be included on one scroll. One further point: a lot of misunderstanding could be avoided if we were to refer to these texts as the Hebrew Scriptures or Bible, for this focuses on what is important: it is written, with the exception of a couple of passages that appear in **Aramaic**, in the language that Judaism holds to be special.

These books are also ordered and arranged differently in the Hebrew Bible. They are arranged in three collections: the Law (five books), the Prophets (eight books) and the Writings, sometimes called the Hagiographa (eleven books). The last book is not the prophet Malachi, which ends looking forward to a messianic appearance, but Chronicles, the last verse of which records the order of the Persian king Cyrus to go up to Jerusalem.

A name often given in recent years to the Jewish Scriptures is coined from the first letters of the Hebrew words used to describe these three sections. The acronym is TNKH and, because it is composed only of consonants, to enable it to be pronounced vowels are added; it is often found as TaNaKH. The "T" stands for **Torah** which has been poorly translated as Law, the "N" stands for Nevi'im (Prophets) and the "KH" for Khetuvim (Writings). The reason why Law is not the best way to render Torah is that the word Law carries with it incorrect pointers to meaning. Torah would be better rendered by words such as "instruction" or "direction."

It is not without significance that "T" is the first letter, for Torah is not by chance found at the beginning of the Jewish Scriptures; it is there for a purpose and should be seen as being in a real sense *The* Scriptures, with all else acting as a commentary on these first five books, often termed the **Pentateuch.** For this reason the term has expanded to include all that relates to it and contributes to making it the center of Judaism.

The questions put to the Jewish Scriptures

1   There has always been a strong sense in Judaism that a translation would only serve to distort what had been originally written. There is a saying in the **Mishnah** that runs: "He who translates word for word is a liar and he who changes the meaning of any word is a heretic." There would be many who would agree with that judgment. The original revelation was delivered in Hebrew and even a most accurate translation would to some extent distort.

The legend concerning the translation of the **Septuagint** illustrates this general attitude. The Septuagint was the most famous translation of the Jewish Scriptures into Greek. The translation occurred at a time when Greek had become the common language of the eastern Mediterranean following the conquests of Alexander the Great, and fewer and fewer Jews of the **Diaspora** (those Jews who were "dispersed" in lands outside Judea) retained any knowledge of Hebrew, which had, in any case, ceased to be a living commercial everyday language after the Babylonian destruction of Jerusalem in 586 BCE. The legend tells of a mysteriously accurate translation accomplished by some 70 (or so) men in 70 (or so) days: this explains the name by which it is known, for it means "seventy" and is conventionally termed by the Roman numerals LXX. The legend concludes by recounting the dire punishments that were visited upon those who questioned the extreme value of the translation. Such a legend would not have been necessary had there not existed a prejudice about the value of translations.

Biblical Hebrew works, although it exists only as an ecclesiastical language. This is because young people, and especially young males, are sufficiently exposed to the language to be able to read it, and are sufficiently knowledgeable about the Torah to know what is being read. Translations are used but it is recognized that they are not "the real thing." It is, however, important to recognize that modern Hebrew represents the unique attempt to resurrect a language into a successful living and commercial means of communication, after centuries of being only used and heard in worship and study – think of trying to do the same with Latin! Undoubtedly, it succeeded only because it was generally known and understood.

2   The Torah occupies a central position in the corporate gatherings in the synagogue. The moment that the Torah scroll is taken from the **ark** and carried to the podium for the reading is the most solemn and sacred moment. Everybody stands and as it passes by, the prayer shawls (**tallits**) are placed so that they might touch the coverings of the scroll. To be asked to read the selected Sabbath portion is an honour shared in a regular way by all adult males in **Orthodox** congregations. A sign that Torah is generally well known is the practice of informing the reader(s) of any accompanying portion from the prophets well in advance, so that they might familiarize themselves with the reading; no such preparation is generally needed in respect of Torah. But this only goes to show that the Scriptures, and in particular Torah, are supposed to be read aloud. A name often applied to the sacred books testifies to this. It is **miqra**, and means *reading* or *proclamation*.

On special dates in the calendar five books from the Writings are read: they are called the **megilloth** which means *scrolls*. For this reason they tend to be the best known and most popular of the books to be found outside the Torah.

3   It is impossible for the practicing Jew not to be confronted by Torah every day. There is the obligation to recite the **Shema** twice daily; it begins and ends the day. This cannot but instill the content of the three passages which comprise this great declaration (Deut. 6: 4–9, Deut. 11: 13–21, and Numbers 15: 37–41). The Shema of course proclaims that there is only one God, but it helps to explain in a powerful way why for most Jews their religion is principally one of grateful doing rather than one of belief. The passage talks of hearing, and this is more than an injunction to receive it orally, for paying attention to a voice means to obey. The Shema is a reminder of the form that obedience takes. The love of God will take the form of total obedience. The verses of the first section, Deut. 6: 4–9, are to be found fixed to the entrance of the house in a **mezuzah**, which is a reminder as one goes in and out to talk of them while sitting in the house, especially to the children. They are also to be found bound to the head and the upper left arm in the **tefillin** during prayers, as a reminder that the love of God requires the total application of mental powers and bodily strength.

There is a suggestion in the **Talmud** (see below) that the weekly Torah portion should be read twice in Hebrew and once in the common vernacular. Even if this were not followed it is plain that Scripture in the form of Torah envelops the everyday life of the practicing Jew.

It will be noted that the Pentateuch contains a lot more than rules, statutes and ordinances. There are the sagas, like those depicting the obedience of Abraham and the steadfastness of Joseph. This has given rise to the practice of dividing the material into **Halakah** and **Aggadah**. Halakah means *walking* and refers to the rules and regulations for walking on the prescribed path, whereas Aggadah means *telling* and describes the ethical, homiletical and generally edifying material, often by way of anecdote, that accompanies and undergirds the more legal writings. These stories and dramas are well known on the popular level.

4   Torah, in the narrow sense of the five books of Moses, does not *in practice* represent the supreme authority in Judaism, nor does it form the particular identity that is associated with that faith. In order to understand this odd statement it is necessary to appreciate that in orthodox Jewish belief Moses received from God on Mount Sinai many more toroth (the plural of torah) than what is found in the Pentateuch. There is then the written Torah found in the five books of Moses, and the oral Torah which has been passed on from the time of the great lawgiver. This oral Torah is regarded to be as important as the written Torah, for they both were given to Moses by God. The oral Torah is a complement in that it explains what exactly is meant by the written injunctions. For example, the Pentateuch states that no work must be done on the Sabbath, but it does not state what exactly would constitute "work": the oral Torah deals with such problems. Finally, about 200 CE, it was committed to writing and is called the **Mishnah**, which means *repetition*, and by extension *teaching*.

But the Mishnah does not stand by itself, for following its written form succeeding rabbis subjected it to close study and discussed in minute detail every aspect of it. This too was written down and is called the **Gemara**, which means *completion*. The Mishnah and the Gemara together make up the **Talmud**, which means *learning*. There are really two Talmuds, one written in Palestine and the other in Babylon. The latter is the more extensive and authoritative, and is considered to have been completed by the mid-sixth century CE.

It is probably more accurate to say that it is Torah in this wider sense which is supremely authoritative in Judaism for, as the names of the supporting Torah suggest, it represents the complete teaching, and it is as the Jews seek to shape their lives by this complete teaching that their unique identity emerges.

5   The essence of Judaism is obedience and the shape of that obedience is found in the Torah both written and oral. Orthodox Jews believe that the essence emerges from the Torah and the Torah was given in its entirety to Moses directly from God. This confirms its supreme position.

Reformed and **Liberal** Jews are more open to the suggestions arising from the literary criticism associated with the **Historical Critical Method**, which sees in the Pentateuch a composite work reflecting a variety of interests and historical periods. Consequently these Jews might acknowledge that the Hebrew Bible in general, and the Torah in particular, is the work of human hands and minds. Its importance lies in the understanding that the community, with which they see themselves in continuity, has seen fit to endue these writings, and in particular the Torah, with authority. This authority, however, tends to be relativized in the light of new knowledge and fuller understanding, which means that these Jews sit somewhat lightly on some of the ritual observations.

Since there appears to be a tendency in Judaism to expand the supporting Torah as interpretation of Torah continues, there has arisen a vast body of writings which are all concerned with the study of Torah. This, very loosely, can be called Torah, but the devotion paid daily and weekly to the written Torah, in which it has become the supreme holy object, means that in the hearts and minds of Jews it is this and none other that is the true Scripture.

Enough has been written to make it obvious that the Torah is the most important part of the Hebrew Bible. There are naturally parts of the Torah that are more valued than others, such as the Ten Commandments, but they are never said to be more important. Even the material that deals with Israel's apostasy is important, though it is read publicly in a hushed voice.

6   The extensive literature which has grown up around Torah witnesses to the continual attempt to apply it in changing situations. Apart from the Mishnah and Gemara which make up the Talmud, mention should be briefly made of **midrash** (which means *searching* and then *exposition*) and commentary. In the searching and exposition of Scripture the midrashic material developed the Halakah and Aggadah quality found in the Torah itself. The commentaries for the most part are concerned with legal, literal and grammatical points, but contain much about practice and custom at the time of writing. One of the most famous was by Rashi who lived at Worms in northern France in the eleventh century, and his commentary on the Torah is considered so indispensable that no study edition appears without it.

There is never any attempt among the Orthodox to relativize any of the demands of Torah, as their co-religionists do. Questions of relevance to particular situations never arise. Obedience is central to what it means to be a Jew. The acid test of the religious person is obedience to something for which there appears, if only at the beginning, little rhyme or reason.

Christianity

The next religion to be visited is one which also started in the Middle East and could be described in one sense as a daughter of Judaism, in that it started as a Jewish sect and shaped its early identity and understanding of itself in reaction to Judaism. Certainly the Jewish Scriptures make up a large part of the Christian Bible.

The Jewish Bible is called by Christians the Old Testament, whereas the particularly Christian part is termed the New Testament. The terms can be understood in two ways; new can be seen as that which is merely later in time, or it can be viewed as something better in that it fulfills and completes, and therefore replaces, the old. Most Christians tend to view the relationship between the two testaments in the latter light, though there are some who would say that two covenants have been established and the first has not been replaced.

It should be recognized that although all Christians have the same New Testament consisting of 27 books, they do not all have the same Old Testament. Protestant Christians have an Old Testament of the 39 (24) books of the Hebrew Bible but Catholic Christians have one with seven extra books and additions to some of the others. Orthodox Christians have an Old Testament that is further expanded. The additional books are those that are found in the **Septuagint**, the Greek Bible, that attracted to itself books which were later excluded from the Hebrew Bible. Protestant Christians follow the choice reflected in the Hebrew Bible and consign the extra books to the **Apocrypha**. Another name given to these books is **deutero–canonical**, but this term can be confusing. Catholics interpret "deutero" as meaning second in time but sharing the same canonical status as the rest, whereas Protestants interpret it as denoting books with secondary importance.

The questions put to the Christian Bible

1   While some scholars still think that the full and true sense of the sacred text can only be appreciated through knowledge of the original languages of Hebrew (Aramaic) and Greek, the majority of Christians today are unique in valuing the access to their Bible through the vernacular and do not consider that any great loss occurs in the translation process. There are now on sale a bewildering assortment of translations, which has resulted in the production of books advising about the best translations.

For the Christian the original languages were merely the "common tongue" of the day, a vehicle for carrying the message. The message is what matters, and it is of paramount importance that nothing impedes the intelligent hearing of Scripture.

2   Scripture plays a prominent part in the public worship of all Christian traditions. Some follow a **lectionary** in which is laid out a plan for a regular and extensive reading of the Bible, while others leave the choice of readings to the judgment of the worship leader. If it has become traditional to see Christian worship as the meeting of **Word** and **Sacrament**, the former is seen to be comprised of the reading and expounding of the Bible. Moreover, the readings are usually introduced in words such as "This is the Word of the Lord," and concluded in a similar formula, such as "May God add his blessing to this reading from his Holy Word." (Older formulae such as "Here begins/ends the reading from the Old/New Testament" seem to many to imply that the books are merely useful and are different from others not by nature but only by degree.) A different outlook will sometimes be encountered when the text is kissed, especially if it's a **Gospel** reading, to indicate its supreme importance. In some forms of Christian corporate worship,

the Bible is met in a variety of ways other than by set lections: many hymns elaborate on Bible passages, while those services which are drawn from the monastic round of worship contain many **canticles** drawn directly from Scripture, and innumerable echoes from the Bible are found in such things as the **versicles and responses**.

3　In some Christian traditions it is considered a duty to read the Bible daily, and engagement in corporate Bible study is highly commended. Notice boards outside the churches of such traditions will announce the times for Bible study. There are also a great many aids to private Bible reading and these are graded to suit the age and maturity of the Christian reader. Bookshops sell devotional books arranged to provide a daily meditation on some Bible text. Calendars can be purchased with a Biblical text for each day, which calls to mind not only the day but a Christian duty. Some Christian homes will be found with Biblical texts hanging on their walls, which can be seen to have a similar intention and effect to the sacred pictures and statues found in other Christian homes. Obviously, this individual and private use speaks powerfully of the way these texts are regarded.

4　In some Christian circles there can often be heard an appeal to **Sola Scriptura** (Scripture alone). Here Scripture is held to be the determining factor in all Christian faith and practice and this takes two forms, at least in theory. For some, nothing is to be believed and done that does not have the support of Scripture; the other form does not demand the direct support of Scripture, but still believes that the Christian religion should have nothing repugnant to the scriptural witness. It is here that the idea of Biblical Christianity has a powerful appeal. For these groups, Scripture seems to occupy a very central and authoritative position.

There are other Christians who believe that the Christian texts were not written as Scripture, for that already existed in the form of what is now called the Old Testament. Rather, the books and letters of the New Testament were written against a backdrop of developing Christian identity. This identity, however, related to only a minority of the nascent "Christians." Consequently the Christian Scriptures lack the necessary comprehensiveness and coherence to be the sole guide for Christian faith and practice. These latter believe that the tradition of the Church (and some among them would give tradition an upper case T to show its importance) has equal status, and without tradition Scripture cannot, by itself, produce a single understanding of Christianity. This group likes to think that Scripture and tradition represent two strands of a single enablement, not in competition but complementary to each other.

There are others for whom human reason is the touchstone by which all else must be tested, and for whom, therefore, the Christian Bible represents ideas that are relativized because they emerge out of a primitive way of thinking which was naive and unscientific. The moral ideas and their challenge might still be attractive, but the **Biblical mind-set** can no longer be credibly adopted in this modern world. Beliefs about Jesus, who was called Christ, are presented in such mythological imagery that they can no longer be entertained as they are Biblically presented, but must be "translated" into what is acceptable to the modern mind. Such people are called **Radicals**, and for these the Bible is indeed like any other book.

5   All Christians would afford a high status to the Bible and would explain this status with words like "inspiration" and phrases like "Word of God." The inspiration of the Bible has been claimed not only for the individual books but also for the way in which they were brought together; it is widely held that the Church was itself inspired in its choice of the books. It should be noted that the Bible as the "Word of God" must be understood in the light of the conviction that, for all Christians, the paramount Word of God is Jesus Christ. This means that for a great many the Bible is the Word of God only in so far as it bears witness to the principal Word of God. There are consequently many who have great difficulty with parts of the Old Testament such as 1 Chronicles 1–9, which consists of nothing but genealogies that give an endless list of names.

Traditionally **canon** of Christian Scripture is fixed and final. This strengthens the belief that the faith to which it bears witness is also fixed and cannot be added to. It is the faith once and for all time delivered to the Saints (Jude 3).

There is little doubt that, for Christians, the most important part of the Bible is the New Testament. While in theory it is all thought to be inspired, in practice the conviction that Jesus is the long-expected **Messiah** (Christ) means that the Old Testament is relativized in its relationship with the New. The Old is read, as it were, through Christian eyes and judged accordingly. Christian lectionaries are witness to this practice, for not only is there more read from the shorter New Testament but large sections of the longer Old Testament are seldom if ever read. Most Christians would agree with the medieval slogan, "The New is in the Old hidden; the Old is in the New disclosed."

There are also interesting distinctions made between the books of the New Testament. Some traditions stand for the Gospel readings out of respect for the words of Jesus, and for these the Gospels are the most important books, but for others like the Lutherans, the Epistles of Paul are undoubtedly the favored part.

6   Scripture was never just read and left to have its own effect. It has always been expounded and its message made relevant to contemporary situations. In some Christian traditions the sermon is still expected to be an exposition on the Bible reading(s). It is still possible to find books of such sermons, famous and popular in their day, in second-hand bookshops.

In the last 200 years there has been an interest in the message that the original speakers, authors, or editors intended, or the meaning that the original readers or hearers obtained which so impressed them that they wished to preserve these writings and transmit them over the centuries. This search, usually called the **Historical Critical Method**, was the result of a suspicion that the meanings the official churches were reading from the Bible were the ones that served their dogmatic interests, and there were good reasons therefore to let the Bible speak for itself.

The consequence of this has been the rise of dictionaries, encyclopaedias, and commentaries, all helping to place the books, and the smaller **exegetical units** from which they are formed, in their historical and cultural setting. And they help to answer the historical questions: When was it written? Why was this written? To whom was it written? What did it mean to those who received it?

In its turn, this has produced a reaction which believes that this method has "atomized" the Bible and destroyed what is held to have been its essential unity and that in turn makes it impossible to read it in the way former Christians did. It is also believed that as a result of this historical scholarship there has arisen the conviction that it is impossible to read the Bible correctly without the aid of these experts. There is the suspicion that the message otherwise received is not the proper one.

What lies at the heart of this reaction is not predominantly any anti-intellectualism, but a fear that Biblical scholarship is producing a rationalism, in respect of the material, that encourages it to be read like any other book and at the same time makes it a **closed book**. It should be an open book, open to all, and it is not like any other book. How do these words sound today?

"Our gracious Queen: to keep your majesty ever mindful of the Law and the Gospel of God as the Rule for the whole life and government of Christian Princes, we present you with this Book, the most valuable thing that this world affords." To these words were then added: "Here is Wisdom; This is the royal Law; These are the lively Oracles of God." These were the words said as Queen Elizabeth II was presented with a copy of the Bible at the occasion of her coronation.

Islam

The third World Religion to emerge from the Middle East will now be explored. Islam was the last of the three to emerge and it sees itself as the correction to, and the fulfillment of, the first two.

The sacred book of Muslims is the Qur'an, and it is looked upon as the final book of guidance, sent down by Allah to the Prophet Muhammad through the agency of the angel Jibra'il (Gabriel). Every word is the Word of Allah.

The Qur'an contains 114 **surahs** (chapters) and 6,616 **ayahs** (verses). The revelation began in the cave of Hira in the Mountain of Light where Muhammad had gone to meditate. It continued, a few ayahs at a time, over a period of 23 years. The Prophet was an *ummi* (unable to read or write) and it was therefore his custom to dictate the revealed ayahs to a scribe who would write them on any available suitable material. The dictation would be checked for errors, but the Prophet and his more dedicated Companions would commit the ayahs to memory. In this way the whole Qur'an was committed to writing and memory.

Of the 114 surahs, 87 were received during the 13 years Muhammad lived in Mecca following the Night of Power which began the whole movement. The remaining 27 were sent down in the 10 years he spent at Medina following the migration from Mecca. The Meccan surahs are the shorter; they explain and build up faith, and lay bare the heart of the religion, while those of Medina expound upon the duties, and contain **shari'ah** law, with its guidance upon all aspects of social, economic, and political life. It is held that these ayahs of the Qur'an were given in particular situations as they emerged, some in answer to direct questions, and some to supplement previous revelations.

Much is made of the fact that the Muslim holy book was given to only one person and preserved over a short period. Muslims compare this with the Jewish and Christian holy books which became corrupted in their transmission. After the death of the Prophet, the first Caliph Abu Bakr, conscious that those who had followed Muhammad's practice of learning the whole Qur'an would in time be all dead, arranged that the ayahs, existing in their written form on a multitude of bits and pieces, be written into a single book. The whole process was meticulously checked; the written record had to be approved by at least two of those who had memorized the material after hearing the Prophet recite it.

The questions put to the Qur'an

1   There is a strongly held conviction that the Qur'an cannot be translated into another language without loss. It was delivered in the Quraysh dialect of Arabic, and is the Word of Allah, and is unalterable. But the loss would be not only to the meaning, but also to the hearing. The very word Qur'an means *proclaiming*, and it should be experienced aurally in the original language to achieve its fullest effect. A translation will not supply the same aesthetic pleasure; it cannot give the same "taste." There is no doubt about the attraction of the harmony of the words and the beauty of the sound, which is considered to be an intrinsic part of the text. This is particularly encountered in the chanting, whereby the voice is considered to be made sweeter. So important is the sound of the text that a special science called *tajwid* (perfection of recitation) has been developed, and Qur'an reading competitions are regularly held all over the Muslim world.

The beauty of the open text is also worth noting. The traditional formation of the letters makes the Qur'an a joy to the eyes also.

All this explains the amount of time given to learning the Arabic of the Qur'an. The young are taught how best to read it, and converts like Yusuf Islam (formerly Cat Stevens) know that their experience of their new religion will be incomplete until they understand the Book (see *World Religions Reader*, p. 325).

In a way that cannot be said of another religion's holy book, the Qur'an is Islam. It has been observed that what Jesus Christ is for Christians, the Qur'an is for Muslims, It is the visible manifestation of God's word.

2   The Qur'an is unavoidable in public gatherings. All prayers must proceed from its verses, for not even the most hallowed **hadith** (see below) is allowed in addresses to Allah. Moreover, the text is recited by Qurra' (reciters) who are versed in the science of tajwid (see above). The sermon, which deals with points of faith, is given

against a backcloth of Islamic scholarship based on the Qur'an. Everything is drawn out of it. Sometimes, as an act of Thanksgiving or in response to a vow, the complete Qur'an will be recited in one sitting, usually during the night. A favored time for this devotion is **Ramadan**.

3   It is said that to read and contemplate a letter of the Qur'an is equivalent to 10 good deeds. Recitation of the book is consequently not just a preferred, but the one essential, element in Islamic daily devotion. In addition to the sentences with which the Qur'an opens, it is normal for some of the shorter suras to be recited. There is much encouragement to memorize portions of it, and this learning continues to be the basis of education in the Muslim world. To become a **hafiz** (someone who has learned the entire Qur'an) is to be both honored and accomplished. A Muslim cannot be overexposed to this sacred text: something of what it means will be clearer to a Christian if the memorizing of the Qur'an were to be compared to partaking of the Eucharist. It is not therefore surprising that a copy of this sacred book is found in every Muslim house.

What the Qur'an means in the everyday life of a Muslim can be observed in the reverence given to the text itself. It is never placed on the floor but will be cradled on decorated book-stands; it is stored on top of all other books to demonstrate that it is never less important than any other; it is always held above the waist as a mark of respect.

4   The Qur'an brooks no rival when it come to authorities in Islam. It stands supreme and unchallenged. However, there remains the question of the ways in which what is contained in that book is understood and applied to the lives of Muslims removed by distance and culture from the time of the Prophet. Even within the sacred text there are supplements which were supplied in answer to Muhammad's requests for further enlightenment. There remain, however, certainly to western observers, some passages which are either difficult to understand or yield ambiguous meaning. It is at this point that a parting of the ways occurs, which is manifested in the **Sunni** and **Shi'ite** ways of understanding the use of the Qur'an in everyday life.

Both groups agree that Muhammad was the true interpreter of what is in the Qur'an, and that all authentic interpretation must be traced back to him. But the Shi'ites maintain that the Qur'an has two levels of meaning, one open to all and one safeguarded by God. This second is made known to those whom Allah has specially chosen, that is, the imams who, following the Prophet, stood in a family relationship with him, Ali (cousin and son-in-law of Muhammad), and the eleven imams who followed him. It is these who have inherited the special inner knowledge (called **ta'wil**) so obviously displayed by Muhammad. This knowledge enables the Qur'an to be forever relevant to contemporary situations, but it means that the true meaning of the Qur'an can only reach Islam and the rest of the world through the imams.

The Sunni think otherwise. The Qur'an is approached through the **Sunnah** (the customs of Muhammad and therefore precedents) which are found in the **Hadiths** (collections of his personal sayings and doings, and those which are known to have had his approval).

5   The origin of the Qur'an has already been described. No higher status can be claimed for any writing than to say that it was given to an unlettered man straight from God. Muslims can find all other explanations completely unconvincing, for the depth, complexity, and comprehensiveness of the material cannot be attributed to an *ummi*. His own condition suggests that he had no part to play in its composition save to be a channel for the divine Word, which is the true calling of a prophet.

With the death of the Prophet the Qur'an was complete. Nothing further was needed. The last ayah is reputed to be: "This day I have perfected your religion and completed my favour to you, and have chosen for you Islam as (your) religion" (Qur'an 5: 3). Although, as the direct Word of Allah, all of the Qur'an is important, there remain those verses which individuals may find most useful.

There will be, for example, a tendency to treasure those verses which speak of *tawhid* (the oneness of God), which most Muslims believe to be the greatest gift of the Qur'an to humankind. In this respect the short surah called "the Unity" (112) speaks as follows: "He is Allah, the Unique; Allah, The Source of everything; He does not father nor is He fathered; there is nothing to which he can be compared."

There will be the verses that appear in their prayers, chief among which is The Opening, the first verses of the Qur'an. Another favorite is the second sura, usually referred to as "The Cow" and sometimes called the Qur'an in miniature, because it makes mention of all the essential points found elsewhere. Because it also contains prayers for forgiveness it is frequently recited before going to sleep.

6   It is commonly taught that the Qur'an is the best explanation of itself. One section can therefore be used to shed light on any other (this method is also used extensively in Judaism, and to a lesser degree in Christian exegesis). If the Sunnah (see above) is, after the Qur'an, an acknowledged authority, it is followed by the Opinions of the Companions, for they were involved in many of the events which are mentioned there. After these comes the view of the majority of the Scholars. As the Qur'an has been commented upon there has never been any suggestion that something was being added as if the revelation lacked anything. Rather it was a question of laying bare what was implicit in it.

Nevertheless, there is an extremely extensive and rich body of *tafsir* (commentary) reflecting the wide variety of Muslim thought. It has taken two forms, exegesis based on tradition and exegesis based on reason. Many of the commentaries seek to show that modern developments in arts and science are not at odds with what is found in the Qur'an. On the contrary, for Muslim scholars the Qur'an has always urged advance in learning and discovery in science, and indeed has even hinted at what would be arrived at.

Hinduism

With Hinduism we leave the cradle of the first three religions we have looked at and move east to India, where the final three in our investigation emerged and continue to be the religions of millions to this day.

The six questions might seem to some a little odd in an eastern setting. However, the aim is, in part, to see what degree of commonality these sacred books possess, and if the questions seem more appropriate for the first three, that in itself is a discovery.

At the very beginning it should be noted that, in this setting, the very word "Scripture" might be misleading. It suggests that the sacred word is written. But in Hinduism the sacred word is spoken and heard; it loses something of its life and power if it remains simply written. The difference might be expressed by saying that if for Christians it is a matter of "In the beginning was the Word . . . ," for Hindus it is more a matter of "In the beginning was the Spoken Word or (better still) the Sound . . ." However, in time these holy words were written down, though their vitality is only fully realized when the words are sounded.

It is traditional to divide Hindu sacred books into two classes, **Shruti** and **Smriti**:

(a) Shruti, which literally means *heard*, represents what was heard by the sensitive ones, called the **rishis** (the seers), and passed on by them through spoken words in the form of the **Veda** (knowledge that liberates), for the enrichment of all. It is not something which they had composed, for it has come to them like a flash of lightning, vibrating with eternal rhythm out of the sustaining power of the Infinite. It is author-less, for it has no natural beginning.

The Veda is divided into four "layers," the first of which is the Samhitas (the Vedic hymns) and the last the Upanishads (the inner meaning of the Samhita). The earliest and latest Vedic material is usually dated about 1500 and 500 BCE. It should be recognized that the Samhitas are cultic liturgical texts, which were performed in the context of sacrifice. This explains the hymnic and incantational quality of the material.

The language of the Veda is Sanskrit, which is itself judged to be divine, and the material is passed on in the schools orally, and so in a very literal sense it is shruti, in that it is heard. These are the primary and authoritative texts for Hindus.

(b) Smriti, which literally means *remembered*, is considered to be of secondary importance to Shruti, but, because of its popularity, devotees will call their own favorite part the fifth Veda. It becomes a catch-all for all other sacred literature. It never claims to add anything new to the Veda but only to present the teaching in a way that can be more easily understood, to make obvious the hidden treasures of Shruti. It does this in a variety of forms, though it finds its most prominent expression in the great epic poems of the Mahabharata and the Ramayana. These took shape sometime after the Veda, and are considered to have been written down not earlier than 400 CE. The Ramayana is thought to have a single author, unlike the Mahabharata which is a collection to which new material was added over many years. The Mahabharata is huge; its extent can be gauged by comparing it with the Christian Bible, of which it is about seven times the size. One of its most popular parts is the Bhagavad-Gita. This tells of the incarnation of the god Vishnu in the human form of Krishna. In the Bhagavad-Gita Krishna teaches the divine truths through discussions with the warrior Arjuna, whose chariot Krishna drives. Written in Sanskrit, the popularity of these epics has meant that they have been translated into the regional languages of India.

In addition to the Epics, under the heading of Smriti can be listed **puranas**, **tantras**, and other more recent writings.

The puranas, which literally means *old tales*, contain myths and legends of gods, heroes, and holy people. They can be grouped by means of the god whose devotion they promote; the gods are Brahma, Vishnu and Shiva. They are usually dated 300–1600 CE.

The tantras, which literally means *looms*, are texts of popular Hinduism. They have to do with ritual technique and encourage the right actions at right times. Prominent among the tantric material is the **mantra**, which is a chant believed to empower and enhance (*mantra* is often used in a broader sense of any chanted material). These writings are dated between 500 and 1800 CE.

The Hindu sacred texts are not controlled by any strict concept of canon and consequently many writings, and especially devotional poems, over the years, and in particular districts, are added to Smriti as they perform its traditional role of making the religion contained in the original revelation meaningful and effective in new situations. Smriti continues to expand.

It is helpful to remember that the whole ceremony connected with the hearing of Shruti is a fairly exclusive affair. Traditionally it includes only males, and upper class ones at that. The attractiveness of Smriti is that it is essentially democratic in that it involves all classes and both genders. What is of interest is that some parts of it, for instance the puranas, while referring to the Veda are critical of it; it even goes as far as attributing to itself the same liberating power.

The questions put to the Hindu writings

1   The efficacy of the primary texts lies in their sound, for that is what was originally heard. Therefore, the very writing down of what was originally heard was for a long time resisted and a curse was invoked upon the man who would write down the Veda. Elsewhere scribes are honored people, but in Hinduism they were placed in a poor caste and writing was considered at one time to be polluting. The text was only finally committed to writing in this era (the Buddhist scriptures, some 1,000 years younger, found written form before the Veda). In this situation our first question is indeed odd. Even now, when there is a text, a translation would accomplish nothing, for the efficacy lies not in its meaning but in its original sound. The Veda is still passed down orally among the Brahmins in a language understood by relatively few, which has produced a very strange situation. The ordinary

person cannot personally access this power that liberates, and most Hindus are exposed habitually not to the Veda but to the other texts to which the access is more "user friendly," in that, with the exception of the mantras, the attraction lies in the meaning.

2   There is only limited regular corporate worship compared with the three Middle East religions. In fact there is nothing that corresponds to the church as institution. Hindus do however resort to the temple, especially at festivals, and it is here that vedic texts will be heard at the formal rituals presided over by the Brahmins. Other texts might also be encountered through the reciters, who tell in their own words from Smriti that particular part which deals with the object of their devotion.

An interesting part of communal devotion is the singing of **bhajans** (devotional hymns). This occurs quite regularly and often in the home. In a sense, they carry Hindu teaching in a way similar to the way that Christian, and especially Wesleyan, hymns summarize Christian teaching, but like many things Hindu the appeal is not principally to the head but to the effect of binding together the worshipers in a common fervor of devotion.

3   It is in the home that Hinduism finds its center. Household shrines are commonplace, some a complete room and others no more than a niche in the wall. It is here that morning and evening prayers are said through the chanting of mantras that accompany the daily offerings.

Shruti as something read is not a common feature of Hindu homes, but the edifying tales of Smriti are encountered through the stories told to children at home and school, and in the pictures or statues that adorn the household shrines.

4   On one level Shruti must be the supreme authority, for what the rishis have received, having removed all obstruction to the divine sound, is nothing less than eternal power. This eternal power is inherently present to everyone, and the spoken words of the Veda contain cosmic efficacy which is able to purify the consciousness, itself a salvific process, to the point where enlightenment happens. That is the purpose of Shruti. Westerners ought to note that it does not entail any mystical experience.

But, as has been previously observed, the average Hindu has recourse not to Shruti but to Smriti. And that is a difficulty and perplexity for most western, and particularly Christian, observers for whom Heaven (the final goal) is the hoped-for end of religious observance. The point, not hitherto mentioned, is that the average Hindu is less goal orientated.

Enlightenment and escape might be the final goal; meanwhile there is a life to be lived. For this **dharma** is needed. Dharma is everyday religion as it expresses itself in an ordered virtuous life. This is in the main now achieved through **bhakti**, an attachment and, in particular, a devotion to a particular god. And this is where Smriti is located. How successfully these duties are carried out determines the level of a future rebirth, though a life of immense devotion might even break the bonds of karma (the outcome of past action which determined the future) and lead to *moksha* (liberation). An alternative, parallel way is through the discipline of yoga. There is always time in a future incarnation to experience liberation. In general liberation is not a reward for a good religious life; liberation is something above and beyond mere morality.

5   This question has already been answered. Shruti is fixed while Smriti has no firm boundaries. (It might be truer to say that Samhita is fixed, for the other layers are somewhat vague.) Shruti is eternally and intrinsically powerful and is therefore forever authoritative, but Smriti is that which encourages and promotes devotion (bhakti), and this devotionalism is central to everyday Hinduism. There is consequently no unambiguous answer to the question about which parts are the most important, for it all depends upon the further question, "Important for what?"

6   Hindu sacred writings do not speak of the past but of that which is eternally present. It is available to all and, through the purifying disciplines such as yoga, can be entered into. Shruti puts one in touch with it. In the meantime Smriti continues to carry out its role of making present, through easily accessible means, in changing situations, what is believed to be the original teaching. In this way it encourages bhakti in the service of dharma.

Buddhism

When we turn to the Buddhist scriptures the first thing that strikes us is its great variety and quantity. There are distinct canons, but perhaps a better word might be collections, of which even the smallest would be something like a thousand times more extensive than the Christian Bible. No one has ever read the full extent of Buddhist scriptures. The diversity of its writing mirrors the diversity of the religion.

The Buddha had established his followers in monastic communities and it was within these communities that the Buddhist scriptures took shape. Following his death, controversy developed over the character and extent of the collection. Although the Buddha had taught for some 40 years nothing had been written down during his lifetime. Some wished to limit the collection to the words of the Buddha remembered by Ananda, a relative who had also been his closest follower. This school was formed around the monks who called themselves the School of Elders (**Theravada**). Ananda is said to have passed on all that he remembered of the Buddha's teaching, which was accepted by the community (**sangha**), and this was transmitted orally for several centuries until it was finally arranged and committed to writing. The teaching proper is contained in the **sutras**. In addition there was **vinaya** (the rules for living together as a monastic community), which were also considered to be his words. There was also the expansion of what was called the "seeds" contained in the sutras, which became the **abhidharma**; although they were not by the Buddha, they were set alongside the sutras and vinaya because the collection was considered necessary for a thorough understanding of the **dharma** (Buddhist teaching). These are the "three baskets" or **Tripitaka**, getting its name from the practice of writing on palm leaves and keeping the writings in baskets.

In Theravada the Tripitaka was written in Pali, and this represents the oldest Buddhist scriptures. The monks of this school considered themselves an elite, as the sole possessors of the true dharma. Opponents to this view claimed that anyone might become an **arhant** (Buddhist seeker) and were in general more accommodating to popular religion. In this the critics were being truer to the spirit of the Buddha whose teaching, in the context of sixth-century BCE Hinduism of his day, was a protest against hierarchical ritualism. This opposition soon became the larger movement and gave the smaller more conservative Theravadans the name **Hinayana**, the "Lesser Vehicle," thereby soon becoming the **Mahayana**, "The Greater Vehicle." The Mahayana Buddhists were great missionaries and took their teaching eastwards to China and Japan, and northwards to Tibet and Mongolia, translating and adding to the writings. Not only did the abhidharma part grow into a large **shastra** (philosophic) literature, but they were not adverse to composing new sutras, such as the Lotus Sutra. The claim was that as the real nature of dharma became clearer, so it was important to share this added clarity with others. Some would go so far as to claim that the traditional sutras were the more elementary and consequently of lesser importance. The important thing is dharma.

Perhaps it should be noted that Buddhism in its missionary enterprise did not seek to supplant or replace other religions. As a result it is not unknown for people to observe one religion at one level, and Buddhism at another.

The questions put to Buddhist scriptures

1   Buddhists have always been great translators, and it was the teaching in the vernacular that led to the rapid spread of Buddhism. The original language, Pali, is now dead and only understood by scholars.

2   Sangha may be one of the three succours in a Buddhist's life, and vinaya one of the three baskets, but Buddhism is basically a solitary pursuit. Certainly scripture is not read publicly, in the sense that it is read and proclaimed in the three Middle East religions. A verse or two from a well know sutra may however form the basis of a chant, but even here chanting is not about meaning but rather losing oneself in sound. The entertainer Leonard Cohen, who now spends a portion of his year in a Zen monastery in Mount Baldy, California, describes his time in the chanting hall in this way: "You really don't know what you are chanting because it isn't about meaning, but about manifesting yourself as sound. It's a good feeling."

3   There is no tradition of devotional reading. The devotional approach is meditation. Favorite sutras will be studied but only to be better able to travel the Buddhist path. Scripture is not something that in itself contains any value; it is not reified

into a holy thing. The importance of scripture for the Buddhist lies in the degree to which it is instrumentally helpful in moving the individual from this ordinary existence (samsara), full of suffering and frustration (dukkha), to enlightenment (Nirvana).

4   Scripture in its totality plays no part in shaping the Buddhist identity. The mind and outlook is formed by dharma and by the pursuit of the Four Noble Truths through the Eightfold Path. Certainly, dharma will be learned through the particular sutras which are thought to encapsulate the best "seeds" of the Buddha's teaching in any particular group or sect.

5   Scripture in Buddhism is not special in the way it is in the Middle East religions. They are not divine words but human words, and this, in large part, explains the vast extent of their writings – for there have been many additions. Words exist to point the way to something more important. They have been described as "fingers pointing to the Moon," and should never obscure that to which they point.

There is a branch of Buddhism that is so concerned at the way that even the best of words get in the way and become a distraction that a non-scriptural approach is advocated. This branch was only perpetuating that which the Buddha himself had set in motion, an ongoing dissatisfaction with the way in which traditions can become shallow and formalized, no longer promoting that to which they point. Yet even in Zen a bizarre paradox has occurred. The non-scriptural way has, over the passage of time, been itself written down, has, as it were, become scripture, and has become the very influential "Platform Sutra." It is interesting that it has even taken to itself the very term "sutra," which this particular system seeks to avoid.

6   The Buddhist scripture is not seen as emerging from some enclosed holy past. The Buddha's words are not considered unique in the sense that once spoken they can never be repeated. Gautama was but one in a line that could be repeated over and over again as enlightenment was experienced and shared. This is a very practical attitude to scripture in that it judges a text by whether it advances one along the path to Nirvana. Scripture is always related to the present. Should it be found to lose its relevance, it will soon be de-emphasized.

It is one of the interesting things about Buddhism that, of all religions, it possesses the greatest amount of holy writing, and yet seems to pay the least attention to it.

Sikhism

With this third religion to arise from India we arrive at the most recent, for its founder, Guru Nanak, was only born in 1469.

Sikhism can best be understood when it is recognized that it emerged in the context of Hinduism and Islam. The essential equality of Sikhism, where all men are the same and women are on an equal standing with men, is generally taken to be a revolt against caste and purdah. The daily careful combing of the hair is seen by many to be in direct contrast to the image of the Hindu holy man, a person who has withdrawn from everyday life with unkempt hair; all are called to the holy life and the holy life is possible wherever you find yourself. Similarly, it is hard to see the position given to the Sikhs' holy writings arising from Hinduism; the place of the Qur'an in Islam has been very influential in this respect. Sikhism, however, considers itself not as another religion among many, but as a witness to the truth, transcending all religions by drawing them together, especially Hinduism and Islam. In this there are similarities to Islam's view of itself as completing Judaism and Christianity.

It was after the nine gurus and their teaching that the Guru Granth was established as the continuing, living tenth guru. The fourth guru began the collection and the tenth finalized and established the writings, declaring them, as he was dying, to be the final guru. As a guru is seen to be only the mouthpiece of God, and, as such, to be separated from the Word of God which he uttered, so it was not ten different gurus giving different words, but ten gurus giving the same message. This same message was always suited to the needs of **karma**, the proper action for the follower in his particular time, situation and condition. This collected message now rests in the Guru Granth.

The Granth however is both guru and Word of God, and so great care is taken to keep the two apart to prevent the text becoming an idol. Yet the ceremony surrounding this text demonstrates the esteem in which it is held. It occupies its own house, the Gurdwara, in which it has the best room; it is covered with richly embroidered cloths, placed on a special cushion, located on a dais so that no one can be higher than it, and above is a canopy; in constant attendance is someone waving a *chowri* (a special fan), a reminder of its sovereignty and pre-eminence; before entry one must have bathed and be suitably clean, and shoes must be removed and head covered; on entry one bows to it and is careful never to turn one's back to it; it is ritually put to bed and woken up; offerings, usually of money, are placed before it. These ceremonies reflect and show that in the Granth Sahib it is believed that the living voice of God himself is encountered.

The questions put to Sikhism

1   The Sikhs' holy book was originally written in old Punjabi in the Gurmukhi script, which has passed out of common use. This presents no problems for the Sikh because the fifth guru, Arjan, left instructions that the holy book should be translated into many foreign languages in order that the Sikh faith should be known throughout the world.

For Sikhs themselves, however, the real value of their scriptures lies in knowing them in the original tongue, and singing them as such, which is proving a problem for expatriate Sikhs of the second and third generation.

2   The Granth lies at the heart of Sikh devotion. The hymns (**kirtans**) for congregational singing are drawn from it, but the significance of these hymns lies not so much in the words as in their sound. In the kirtan the individual is in tune and vibrates with the divine Word, just as a musical instrument might become aligned with a tuning fork. The spiritual power of the Granth only reaches its full potential when it is sung. In fact, above the hymns in the text are the instructions for their singing; they are like a musical score that only comes alive when it is performed. The learning of this singing is considered one of the most important items in a child's religious upbringing.

But a guru is expected to give advice, and advice to suit the karmic condition of the moment, and so the Guru Granth is looked to for that advice. In congregational worship there is surprisingly no set lections; rather, the Granth is opened at random and the reading begins at the top of the left page. Just as a living guru would know what was appropriate at any given time, this random selection is thought to deliver the right word at the right time. This taking of God's Word (**Vak Lao**) occurs in every act of worship, corporate and private, and once received is acted upon as God's guidance for that day.

3   The Vak Lao is taken every morning before the business of the day is started, and will be there to be meditated upon as the day progresses. Similarly, Vak Lao will be taken at the end of the day before retiring to bed.

In addition to this daily advice that the living Guru continually provides, it also is present in the required daily prayers (banis). These five daily prayers are drawn from the Granth, and like the kirtans, are generally sung. They have been likened to the comb that is used night and morning: as the wooden comb removes dead and broken hair, so the comb of God's Word removes from the heart all negative and evil thoughts.

It will come as no surprise that, in this setting, the most significant part of the marriage ceremony is when the bride and groom take Vak Lao as they walk around the Granth Sahib four times, singing the four verses of the marriage hymn.

4   There is no higher authority than the Guru Granth. The Vak Lao is taken at all key points in life: it is taken at Amrit (the initiation ceremony that has been likened to a Christian Confirmation in that it marks full membership in the faith); it is taken on the occasion of marriage, when a child is named, and when a death has happened. Moreover, when there is a problem about which there is no obvious answer, once again the Word of God is taken, and it is considered to provide the solution. Numerous accounts tell of the way in which this procedure has worked for the edifying benefit of the community.

5   The account already given indicates that, for the Sikhs, their holy book is nothing if not the Word of God. Whereas other religions use words to undergird their scripture's origin and status, the Guru Granth's supreme position is heralded by the Sikh's every action. Words can add nothing more.

6   In the Sikh consciousness their holy book comes to them from the past but
still remains the living Guru. It speaks and the words are found relevant. What has
happened more recently is the appearance of commentaries trying to relate the text
to the complexities of modern life, but, useful as they are, the knowledge and understanding provided is considered inferior to the real wisdom imbibed through the
devotional use of the Granth Sahib in Vak Lao and kirtan.

Exercises

At this point you might like to construct a grid, placing on the horizontal plane
the six questions put to the religions investigated, and on the vertical the six
religions so investigated. Then add what you have discovered are the religions'
answers to the questions. In this way you will be able at a glance to compare the answers, and arrive at some understanding of how Scripture works in
religion.

And here are further points to ponder:

1   The first concerns the way in which Scripture is appropriated; it is about
the tension between aural hearing and internal understanding. It is interesting that it was only in the fourth century CE that Christian scripture
was accessed by internal reading. When Augustine visited Ambrose in his
cell he was confronted with a new thing: Ambrose was reading from a book,
but Augustine was astonished that he heard not a sound.

Is poetry best received silently or aloud?
Is the West the poorer for losing the concept of holy sound?

2   Some brides on their wedding day carry a Bible in preference to flowers, and
it is a pious Muslim practice, especially during Ramadan, to write down verses
from the Qur'an and then swallow them.

What has happened to the Bible and the Qur'an?
What happens to Scripture when it becomes a holy thing in itself?

3   In the Buddhist section we came across the principle that scriptures
should be "fingers pointing at the Moon." When the moon is hidden something is wrong, and when the fingers no longer point it is time to amputate.

Should Scripture be pruned?

4   The Gideon Bible in a hotel bedroom does not become scripture to each
person who comes into contact with it. Scripture then appears to be a human
construct.

How is this construct affected by the postenlightenment mind-set?

5   Wilfred Cantwell Smith has written: "people in their diversity have poured into whatever text played that role (the scripture role) for them — people have imposed on the text, if you will — much of their deepest concerns, aspirations, fears, hopes, outlooks, feelings. Yet it would be a blunder to note this without recognizing further — and this is what cries out for understanding — that even in these cases, having poured these in they have received them back profoundly fortified and strikingly enhanced: their hopes activated, their fears assuaged, their choices strengthened with courage, their feelings enriched and deepened."

Does the human condition need a Scripture?
What else can perform the Scripture task?

6   The hi-tech world has already begun to affect Scripture, and is likely to continue and increase its effect.

Is a bhajan still a bhajan when it is listened to on a cassette on the way to work, or when it hits the Top Ten in India? Does the Gospel or Soul song lose or gain something when listened to in the same way?
Do the Scriptural epics on the big screen, be it the Mahabharata from the Hindu Smriti or the Exodus from the Jewish and Christian Bible, perform the Scriptural task?
Is the Bible still the Bible now that it surfs the internet?

GLOSSARY

Abhidharma   The expansion of the Buddha's teaching, considered to be growth from the "seeds" he had sown.

Aggadah   The word means telling, and refers to the edifying material which accompanies and undergirds **Halakah**.

Apocrypha   A name Protestant Christians give to those books in the **Septuagint** that did not find their way into the Jewish Scriptures. The term **deutero-canonical** is commonly used, especially among Catholic Christians, as an alternative, though not all the books in the Septuagint found their way into the Catholic Bible.

Aramaic   The replacement for Hebrew as the everyday language of the market place when Hebrew became in the main an ecclesiastical language.

Arhant   Buddhist seeker.

Ark   The elaborate housing for the **Torah** in the synagogue. It should be noted that the word was also used in the Jewish Scriptures for the housing of the stone tablets on which the Ten Commandments were written.

Ayah   A verse of the Qur'an.

Bhajans   Devotional hymns.

Bhakti   Religious devotion, usually to one particular god.

Biblical mind-set   The view about the explanation for the phenomena that existed at the time to which the Bible testifies, and the hopes and expectations that accompanied it.

Canon   When used in the context of Scripture this word refers to those books that are considered special and consequently authoritative.

Canticles   The Christian song drawn directly from their Scripture.

Closed book   The attitude that considers the Bible to be so difficult to understand properly that it results in the book never being read.

Deutero-canonical   A term commonly used by Catholic Christians to refer to those books from the **Septuagint** which they include in their Bible.

Dharma   Buddhist teaching.

Dharma   The material and moral foundation of the universe, which finds expression in everyday religion through the ordered virtuous life.

Diaspora   A Greek term meaning *scattered abroad* which is applied to Jews living outside of Palestine.

Exegetical   A term meaning the drawing out, as opposed to the putting in, of the meaning of a portion of text. The meaning of a section of text might well be distorted should it be conjoined with another; hence the importance of observing what is called the exegetical unit.

Gemara   The word means *completion*. Together with the **Mishnah** it makes up the **Talmud**, and is a commentary on the former.

Gospel   In upper case it generally indicates the Christian message, but can, in a liturgical setting, mean the reading from one of the gospels in the Christian Bible.

Hadith   The collections of Muhammad's personal sayings and doings which have become determinative of what ought to be said and done.

Hafiz   A person who has learned the entire Qur'an.

Halakah   The word means *walking*, and refers to the rules and regulations contained in the **Torah**. It highlights the importance in Judaism of walking in the prescribed way.

Hinayana   The "Lesser Vehicle," the name given to the Theravada, the smaller division in Buddhism.

Historical Critical Method   The application of contemporary literary and historical approaches to the text of Scripture.

Karma   The proper action for a particular time, condition and situation.

Kirtan   Praise to God, usually in the form of a hymn.

Lectionary   The regular reading of the Bible which includes most, if not all, of it.

Liberal Judaism   Sometimes called **Reformed Judaism**. It represents a section of Judaism that responds to secularism and modern criticism. It tends to emphasize the ethical ideals of Judaism and seeks to give a relevant meaning to the outward observances of the Faith.

Mahayana The "Greater Vehicle," the name given to the larger division in Buddhism.

Mantra Part of the **tantric** material; it is a chant believed to empower and enhance.

Megilloth It means *scrolls*. It refers to the five scrolls from the portion of Jewish Scripture called the Writings read at the major festivals. They are probably the best known and most popular writings outside the **Torah**.

Messiah See glossary in the chapter on Christianity.

Mezuzah Found in the entrance of houses, and containing the first part of the Shema, i.e., Deuteromony 6: 4–9.

Midrash The word means *searching*, and then, by extension, exposition and commentary. The exposition and commentary are on Scripture and Torah, and continue the process, witnessed to in Mishnah and Gemara, of making them of contemporary importance and significance.

Miqra A word attached to Scriptures, but especially the **Torah**, which means *reading* or *proclamation*. It suggests that Torah should be heard, and, of course, listened to.

Mishnah The codification in about 200 CE of what was the Jewish oral law.

The word means *repetition*, and by extension, *teaching*.

Orthodox In a Jewish context this refers to the group within Judaism which resists change and seeks to preserve the old customs and practices.

Pentateuch The term commonly used to refer to the first five books of the Hebrew Bible.

Purana Part of the **Smriti** collection: it means *old tale*, and contains myths and legends of gods, heroes and holy people.

Radical Those who cannot accept the **Biblical mind-set**, or indeed anything in the religious situation that seems contrary to human reason.

Ramadan The ninth month of the Muslim calendar, based on a lunar calculation, during which fasting is required.

Reformed Judaism Sometimes called **Liberal Judaism**. It represents a section of Judaism that responds to secularism and modern criticism. It tends to emphasize the ethical ideals of Judaism and seeks to give a relevant meaning to the outward observances of the Faith.

Rishis The sensitive ones who heard/ saw the **Shruti**.

Sacrament See glossary in the chapter on Christianity.

Sangha The Buddhist community.

Shastra Buddhist philosophical material.

Septuagint The translation of the Jewish Scriptures into Greek. It is often found in the form LXX.

Shari'ah The guidance or law which covers all aspects of social, economic and political life.

Shema The opening word of the Jewish confession of faith, drawn from Deuteronomy and Numbers, repeated twice daily, meaning *hear*: this highlights the importance in Judaism of obedience.

Shi'ites Those who believe that the special inner knowledge (**Ta'wil**) displayed by Muhammad continued after his death, especially in the imams which followed him. They are opposed by the **Sunni**.

Shruti The first rank of Hindu scripture; it means *that which is seen/heard* by the **rishis**, the sensitive ones.

Smriti The second rank of Hindu scripture; it means *that which has been remembered*, and is largely in story form.

Sola Scriptura The term, stemming from the time of the Reformation, suggests that the determining factor of what should be believed and practiced should be Scripture rather than the **Magisterium** (see glossary in the chapter on Christianity) of the Church.

Sunnah The customs set by Muhammad which have become precedents.

Sunni The majority group within Islam. They believe that the customs and precedents attributed to Muhammad should be the sole guidance in the Faith. They are opposed by the **Shi'ites**.

Surah A chapter of the Qur'an.

Sutra The Buddha's teaching.

Ta'wil The special inner knowledge or insight displayed by Muhammad, believed by the **Shi'ites** to have been passed on after his death.

Tallit A shawl, made of silk, worn by male Jews when praying.

Talmud The word means *learning*, and is the great collection of the **Mishnah** and the **Gemara**.

Tantra Part of the **Smriti** collection: it means *a loom*, upon which is woven what is correct in ritual technique and everyday action.

Tefillin Small boxes, bound to the head and the upper left arm, containing the first part of the Shema, i.e., Deuteronomy 6: 4–9. They are worn during morning prayers.

Theravada The School of the elders; it is the smaller division of Buddhism, and was named by the larger part **Hinayana**, i.e., the Lesser Vehicle.

Torah The *pointing* or *direction* for living the Jewish life, often poorly translated as *Law*. The Pentateuch is an important part of Torah but does not exhaust its meaning.

Tripitaka The "three baskets" of Buddhist teaching, viz, **sutra**, **vinaya** and **abhidharma**.

Vak Lao God's Word, taken from the Granth Sahib.

Veda The written form of **Shruti**: it carries the meaning of *knowledge which comes from the seeing/hearing*.

Versicles and Responses The term used for what the leader says and what the worshipers reply in some forms of Christian worship.

Vinaya The rules for living in a community.

Word The part of Christian worship that focuses on the reading and expounding of the Scriptures.

Note and Reference

1 Ian Markham, *A World Religions Reader*, second edition (Oxford: Blackwell Publishers, 2000).

Chapter 5

Religion, Ritual, and Culture

Seán McLoughlin

From Beliefs to Practices

Some General Approaches to Ritual

Durkheim and the Function of Ritual

Rites of Passage

Secular Rituals?

Culture

Religion and Culture

Ritual, Symbols, and Power

Conclusion

From Beliefs to Practices

In the previous chapter we examined the scriptural dimension of religion and focused on the importance of religious beliefs as expressed in sacred texts. As we have seen, scriptures are routinely understood – whether literally or symbolically – to constitute a body of revelation. They generally provide the main sources for theological reflection and legal authority within the world religions. However, it must also be appreciated that religious **communities** have existed, and continue to grow, in a variety of ever-changing historical and cultural contexts. Accordingly, such communities, which are the bearers of revelation, have had to address the ongoing problem of how to keep the spark of revelation alive in the minds, bodies and souls of their members.

For this reason, the ultimate realities – **theistic** and non-theistic – which believers perceive in scripture have been subject to interpretation and reinterpretation through time and across geographical space. However, elaboration of the basic religious ideas expressed in scripture has not been confined to intellectual statements of faith or opinions regarding sacred law. Rather, the development of religious traditions has also included the gradual formation of religious practices, most especially the various **rituals** which continually maintain and reinforce the **worldview** and **ethos** of a religion for its adherents. As William Paden argues, ritual "is the deliberate structuring of action and time to give focus, expression and sacredness to what would otherwise be diffuse, unexpressed or profane."[1]

So it is then that nearly all the world religions seem to have a cognitive aspect (belief) and an active component (practice). It is through the latter, the performance of ritual, that religions are made real for ordinary people. As the American anthropologist Clifford Geertz notes:

> The main context, though not the only one, in which religious symbols work to create and sustain belief, is of course ritual. It is the prayers and festivals around a saint's tomb, the exaltation and bead-telling in a brotherhood lodge, and the obsessive submissiveness surrounding the Sultanate that keep maraboutism [Moroccan Islam] going; private meditation, etherialized art and state ceremonialism that nourish illuminationism [Indonesian Islam]. Individuals can, and in Indonesia and Morocco a few do, attain a concept of cosmic order out-side of these institutions specifically dedicated to inculcating such a concept (though even in such cases there must be support from cultural symbols in some form or other). For the overwhelming majority of the religious in any population, however, engagement in some form of ritualized traffic with sacred symbols is the major mechanism by means of which they come not only to encounter a world view but actually to adopt it, to internalize it as part of their personality.[2]

Exercise

1 Draw up a list of some religious rituals that are familiar to you. How do these practices "continually maintain and reinforce the worldview and ethos" of a particular religion? Here is an example to start you off: the word Islam means "submission" and Muslims symbolically submit to God (Allah) by bowing and prostrating in the act of prayer.

As ritual is such a tangible aspect of social life, something we do, can see, hear and participate in, it reinforces the reality of more abstract religious creeds, commitments and values. Bodily actions – everything from eating, washing, kneeling, parading, chanting and so on – can be used to make statements about an equally wide range of ideas including submission, sharing, obedience, celebration, purification, and ecstasy. Sometimes, especially at formal religious gatherings, rites are led by a ritual specialist and there may be special places, objects or languages which are used. At other times, persons of a certain social status might be excluded from a ritual. For example, those deemed to be ritually unpure such as menstruating women or low status groups can be excluded from religious rites. This should alert us to the ideological dimensions of ritual. It can send all sorts of messages from the group to the individual, including the reaffirmation of hierarchy in society.

The key function of ritual would therefore seem to be communication and this operates on two key levels: (i) between people and their particular idea of the transcendent which may have some controlling power over the cosmos, and (ii) between the group and the individual, sometimes encouraging unity but at the same time very often legitimating the status quo. While routinely finding their origin, and then later the legitimation for their elaboration and continuance, in the revelations of scripture, the practices of the world religions must essentially be seen as a human response to that revelation. They are an attempt to express the inexpressible and in all their cultural diversity are a testament to human creativity and ingenuity.

Taking the time to recollect some of the many rituals discussed in *A World Religions Reader* reinforces this idea that the nature and function of religious practice is very diverse and linked to a variety of cultural contexts. For example, the Rig Veda, one of Hinduism's earliest sacred texts, informs us that the Aryan Indians offered *sacrifices* to their gods in an attempt to *control the forces of nature* and the world around them. Amongst the Buddhist *sangha* or community, especially the monastic orders, the ritual of choice has been *meditation*. For Confucians, the *habitual and repetitive* nature of rituals encourages right behavior whereas in Taoism, which is not much associated with ritual, there is nevertheless a strong *magical* strand with an emphasis on the *healing possibilities* of *ceremonies* which ensure one is in harmony with the universe. Most Shintoists will have a *kami-dana* or small *shrine* in their homes or businesses in order to reverence ancestors and *honor the gods*. In Judaism, all the great occasions of life are marked with an appropriate *rite of passage* and there are *guidelines for behavior* at the time of circumcision, Barmitzvah, marriage and death. For Christians, baptism is a sacramental *initiation into the community* of the church after Christ's example. Similarly the Eucharist is a symbolic *re-enactment* of the Last Supper. In Islam, washing is a sign of *respect* before undertaking the five times daily *prayer*. The ablution is an act of *purification* which marks a movement from profane space into the realm of the sacred. Like *festivals* during the year, the *regularity* of the prescribed prayers ritualizes the day and helps to overcome the human tendency to shut God out of busy everyday lives so preoccupied with time-management. Sikhs meet in a *gurdwara*, a special *building* where readings of the *Adi Granth* are *performed* and hymns are sung as a part of their worship.

Many of the key dimensions, and some of the examples, of ritual underlined in the previous paragraph will come up for discussion as this chapter unfolds. In the main, I shall be trying to interweave an account of the different approaches to ritual common in the western **social sciences** with some more detailed descriptions and case studies of specific rites. I should mention however that most, but not all, the cultural contexts I draw upon for illustration will be from Muslim societies. It is they that I know best of all but you should always be trying to relate what I am going to say to religions, rituals and cultures that you are most familiar with. In the next section I want to begin my survey of approaches to ritual, focusing on those which seem to have predominated in western societies.

Some General Approaches to Ritual

One of the main purposes of this chapter is to emphasize the fact that religion is something that people "practice" as well as "believe in." This statement sounds rather unremarkable but, in fact, it is quite important. Religious scholars have, throughout the ages and in many different traditions, concerned themselves with defining and prescribing the standards of **orthoprax** ritual just as much as orthodox belief. They have advised ordinary believers, to a greater or lesser extent, of their religious duties during rituals in terms of what they should eat, where they should parade, when they should kneel, how they should chant and why they should wash. (You can find out more about these prescriptions for ritual by referring to the chapters on individual religious traditions in this book.) Nevertheless, it is also fair to say that – perhaps in the modern West especially – many would argue that religion is in essence an existential and intellectual act of belief and faith. As such, matters of ritual practice are often seen as rather secondary.

Whether reference is being made to the Jewish, Christian or Muslim God, or indeed the Hindu Brahman, most believers and many theologians emphasize that the eternal and transcendent in religion is very much beyond the cultural particularities of specific rituals. From this perspective then, it might well be admitted that certain ritual practices – everything from pilgrimage or sacrificial rites to the veneration of icons or listening to devotional music – are attempts to point humanity in the direction of ultimate reality. However, these tend to be seen as "imperfect" "man-made" creations, being the husks and not the kernels of a given religion. For example, Nanak, the first of the ten Sikh gurus, who rejected the need for outward expressions of institutional religion, expressed this very notion in his *Mool Mantra*: "God is neither Hindu or Musalman [Muslim] so whose path shall I follow? The path I shall follow is God's." Against this position, it could be argued that it is only because religion is given a vehicle by different cultures that the world's faiths have spread around the globe.[3] But more of this in a later section.

In Europe, such commonplace attitudes were powerfully reinforced by the Protestant Reformation of the sixteenth century. From the Protestant perspective, the overt emphasis on ritual in the medieval Roman Catholic Church had compromised, indeed corrupted, the spiritual truths at the center of Christianity. The reformers wanted to clear away as much institutionalized formalism from religion as possible, taking scripture as their only guide. Therefore, they insisted on *sola scriptura* (scripture alone), rejecting what they saw as the erroneous idea of salvation by external works. The emphasis on "man-made" attempts to mediate with God in Catholicism, for example through pilgrimages to the shrines of saints, were seen by the Protestants as proof of a superstitious system. Moreoever, much of the elaborate mystery and drama of medieval Catholicism was deliberately removed as the culture of Protestantism was rationalized. For example, vernacular languages were used increasingly instead of Latin, the structure of church hierarchies was simplified, fewer sacraments were accepted as legitimate, highly decorative religious iconography was removed from churches and plainer vestments were used by clergy. However, Protestants have not so easily escaped the need to ritualize their own religion with the text of scripture becoming ever more the focus of attention.

In many ways, contemporary western attitudes to religion have their roots in Protestantism, which, according to the sociologist Max Weber, represents an important stage in the modernization and indeed **secularization** of western culture. Indeed, by the nineteenth century it was rationalist and scientific perspectives on ritual which predominated. The nineteenth century, the age of Darwin's theory of **evolution**, was also an age of European **colonial** expansion and consolidation in the non-West. Both of these factors combined to make the possibility of new scientific approaches to the study of "other" cultures and religions a reality. The evolutionary method suggested the need to search for the origins of religion while the process of collecting data to that end was eased by European dominance in large parts of the world. It was in this context that the modern disciplines of **Anthropology** and **comparative religion** were born. As we shall see, they have left both positive and negative legacies for those who are keen to learn more about the importance of religious practices today.

Scholars interested in the origins of religion began with an attempt to determine from which simple forms the complex systems of the world's religions had evolved. In their investigations they fixed upon what were often indelicately identified as the "pagan" rites of "savages" – very often using Australian data on Aboriginal tribes – inspired by the false notion that what was, in their terms, "**primitive**," was also prehistoric. For example, Sir James Frazer, anthropologist and author of *The Golden Bough* (1890), which was one of the best-known early works of comparative religion, followed Auguste Comte in thinking that all humanity would pass through three stages of development from magic to religion, and from religion to science. *The Golden Bough* documents so-called "primitive superstitions," and ritual is seen as the acting out or mimicking of forces that the participant wishes to influence, as in pouring water to ensure rain. Such solemnly intentioned action is understood to generate its effects on the basic principle of *ex opere operato*, that is, by the very fact of its enactment.

Frazer and other evolutionists understood ritual to be a premodern "science" which ignorantly, if rather quaintly, sought to manipulate spiritual forces in an attempt to secure some desired goal. However, the efficacy of rituals in "primitive" societies was routinely contrasted unfavorably with the "obvious" benefits of science and technology in "advanced" western societies, where universal truths were established empirically and objectively in strictly causal ways. While the attitudes of the evolutionists to "primitive" societies today seem very patronizing and **eurocentric**, that is, they reflect the biases of contemporary European and western presuppositions about themselves and others, some enduring insights into the functions that religious rituals perform in society emerged during this period. The name most associated with such developments was of course Emile Durkheim (1858–1917), a French atheist of Jewish descent. It is to Durkheim, his contemporaries, and others that followed them that we must turn next.

Durkheim and the Function of Ritual

As will be clear from the chapter in this book on the Sociology of Religion, Durkheim understood religion to be a system of beliefs and practices which binds people together in social groups. The main vehicle for these ideas was *The Elementary Forms of the Religious Life* (1912). Like many evolutionist scholars of his day, Durkheim based his work on a study of Australian aboriginal tribes, particularly the Arunta. He argued that the religion which they practiced – known then as **totemism** – represented religion in its most elementary or simple form, hence the title of the book. A totem was an animal or plant which was sacred to a particular group. The Arunta reverenced it with various rituals and observed certain **taboos**. For example, it was not permissible to eat the totemic plant or animal, except on important occasions such as a communion feast, for the totem was believed to be imbued with special powers, powers which set it aside from ordinary animals that might be hunted or crops that were gathered and consumed.

So it is then that Durkheim defines religion in terms of a ritual distinction between the **sacred** and the **profane**. Sacred objects and symbols are those set apart from the everyday and commonplace. But why was the totem so sacred for the Arunta? According to Durkheim it was an emblem of the group; it represented the values the Arunta stood for. Therefore, the respect which they gave to the totem was identical to the respect they had for the core values of their society.

From this very narrow base of data, Durkheim generalized that the focus of all religious worship is actually society itself and that the heightened feelings normally attributed to a totem or "the gods" on ceremonial occasions are in fact a measure of the group's hold over the individual. Religious ritual, according to Durkheim, has a crucial role to play both in maintaining social order and in encouraging social integration.

Durkheim's theory of ritual has been very influential, although it has not gone without criticism. As well as fixing upon the limited range of his sample, and the fact that he reduced all rites to one basic function, some have challenged the way in which he represented the integration of a community as rather simplistic. For a more sophisticated account of the way in which ritual can bind a diverse group of individuals together we must wait until the final section of this chapter, when we examine the power of symbols. In the next couple of sections, however, we shall examine the way in which Durkheim's work can be related to two quite different, if related types, of ritual activity.

Rites of Passage

As we have seen, Durkheim understood that ritual was central to the binding together of religious communities. For this reason he felt that they were especially important at times of life-crisis and change, when people pass from one social status to another and are in need of meaning and order in their lives. For example, birth and death are experiences common to all human beings and can unsettle social relationships. For Durkheim then, **rites of passage** are a chance to reaffirm the group when its members are most in need of support and reassurance.

An exploration of life-cycle rituals was more fully elaborated in the work of Belgian anthropologist Arnold van Gennep. Like his contemporary Durkheim, he did not do any fieldwork himself but rather relied on data collected by others, as well as information on world religions such as Judaism and Christianity. Nevertheless, in 1909 he published an influential study entitled *The Rites of Passage*. As Davies notes in a useful survey of van Gennep's key ideas:

> In the simplest of analogies van Gennep compared human societies with those houses that would have been so familiar to his European readers – houses possessing numerous rooms, corridors, and doors in which people live an ordinary life, moving from room to room through passages and across thresholds. By analogy, society was composed of particular social statuses with individuals passing from one status to another by passing over thresholds and moving through passages. Rites of passage were organised events in which, as it were, society took individuals by the hand and led them from one social status to another, conducting them across thresholds and holding them for a moment in a position when they were neither in one status or another.[4]

In line with his comparison between rites of passage in terms of the Latin word *limen* (meaning threshold or doorstep), van Gennep spoke of three phases of passage: (i) the pre-liminal involving separation from ordinary life; (ii) the **liminal** involving a transition period apart from one's original status; and (iii) the post-liminal which conferred a new status on people. Of these three stages most interest has settled upon the liminal stage, notably in the work of Victor Turner who lived amongst the Ndembu people of present-day Zambia. In *The Ritual Process* (1969), Turner argued that there is a sort of egalitarian relationship called "**communitas**" that emerges amongst people who engage in the same ritual at the same time and in the same place. Participation in the ritual divests them of their profane (secular) statuses – including hierarchical distinctions of class, gender and race – if only temporarily.

One interesting and fairly contemporary example of communitas at work is the experience of Malik al-Shabazz or Malcolm X, the Black-Muslim leader of the 1960s. In April 1964, he wrote about his *hajj* or pilgrimage to Mecca in a letter to followers in America:

> I knew that when my letter became public knowledge back in America, many people would be astounded – loved ones, friends, and enemies alike. And no less astounded would be millions whom I did not know – who had gained during my twelve years with Elijah Muhammad a "hate" image of Malcolm X.
>
> Even I was myself astounded. But there was precedent in my life for this letter. My whole life had been a chronology of changes.
>
> Here is what I wrote . . . from my heart:
>
> Never have I witnessed such sincere hospitality and the over-whelming spirit of true brotherhood as is practiced by people of all colors and races here in this ancient Holy Land, the home of Abraham, Muhammad, and all the other prophets of the Holy Scriptures. For the past week, I have been utterly speechless and spellbound by the graciousness I see displayed all around me by people of *all colors*.
>
> I have been blessed to visit the Holy City of Mecca. I have made my seven circuits around the Ka'ba, led by a young *Mutawaf* named Muhammad. I drank water

from the well of Zem Zem. I ran seven times back and forth between the hills of Mt Al-Safa and Al-Marwah. I have prayed in the ancient city of Mina, and I have prayed on Mt Arafat. There were tens of thousands of pilgrims, from all over the world. They were of all colors, from blue-eyed blonds to black-skinned Africans. But we were all participating in the same ritual, displaying a spirit of unity and brotherhood that my experiences in America had led me to believe never could exist between the white and the non-white. During the past eleven days here in the Muslim world, I have eaten from the same plate, drunk from the same glass, and slept in the same bed (or on the same rug) – while praying to the *same God* – with fellow Muslims whose eyes were the bluest of blue, whose hair was the blondest of blond, and whose skin was the whitest of white. And in the *words* and in the *actions* and in the *deeds* of the "white" Muslims, I felt the same sincerity that I felt among the black African Muslims of Nigeria, Sudan and Ghana.[5]

> 2   Explain how and why the *hajj* seemed to transform Malcolm X's relationship   Exercise
>   with white people. How did the ritual contrast with his experience of racism
>   in America? Why might it be difficult to maintain the experience of equal-
>   ity during a ritual in sacred time and space when one returns to profane
>   time and space?

We shall hear more of Turner's work in a later section when we consider the crucial role of symbols in uniting people of often very different backgrounds during the ritual process. But now we must turn to another approach to ritual, which is a development of Durkheimian thinking on the subject.

Secular Rituals?

In traditional societies, Durkheim maintained that religion affected almost every aspect of life, including basic categories such as time. This is why we have so many religious festivals, such as Christmas and Easter in the Christian tradition, that coincide with important changes in the seasons. However, as an evolutionist, Durkheim was convinced that religion was on the decline in modern societies characterized by rational and scientific cultures. He expected that religious ritual would preoccupy people less and less. Nevertheless, Durkheim intimated that as societies seem to rely upon religion for their sense of order and integration, ritual would be likely to persist, but in what form he did not really specify. As we shall see in this section, some sociologists have picked up on Durkheim's musings and explored the extent to which the traditional integrating functions of religion are being performed by **civil religion**, that is, the secular rituals (and institutions) associated with the modern nation-state.

The sociologist perhaps most associated with the idea of civil religion is R. N. Bellah whose work focuses mainly on the USA. According to Abercrombie and others, Bellah saw American civil religion as comprising the following: "(1) elements of the Judaeo-Christian tradition which emphasize achievement, motivation and individualism; (2) events from the national drama (the death of Lincoln and the Civil War); (3) secular values from the Constitution; (4) secular rituals and symbols (the flag, Memorial-Day rites and the Fourth of July)."[6] Overall, Bellah argues that in modern-day, multicultural America, where racial and ethnic division can be a social problem, the function of civil religion is to integrate citizens with a variety of backgrounds through promoting an overarching attachment to the idea of one cohesive nation.

It could be argued that most contemporary nation-states have seen the development of some sort of secular rituals. For example, the former USSR, while openly hostile to religion, saw Marx, Engels and Lenin become powerful symbols of a state-sponsored civil religion. The May Day celebrations in Red Square and other rituals reinforced a commitment to the ideals of the Russian Revolution. In Britain, public rituals which have the Royal Family as their focus have also been seen as forming a key part of civil religion. The monarchy in Britain is still closely tied to the Church of England, Queen Elizabeth II being head of both church and state. In the second half of the twentieth century, the role of the media in helping to construct this civil religion has become ever more important. This was perhaps first noted at the coronation of Queen Elizabeth II in 1953 and has been a feature of royal weddings ever since.

There is something ritualistic about the way in which millions of people can witness key events through the common experience of watching television. It helps create a temporary sense of community amongst people who are too dispersed, either nationally or globally, to gather together in face-to-face relationships. This was demonstrated by the mourning of Diana, Princess of Wales, who was killed in a car accident during late August 1997. Why the millions that gathered in London, from all over Britain, and in some cases overseas, were so moved to share in the experience of queuing to sign books of condolence and "participate" in her funeral is far from clear. But television relayed the whole experience to the rest of the nation and beyond, so extending the scope of this imagined community.

Are secular rituals really the same as religious rituals? This is a debatable point. However, it is clear that civil religion seems to perform many of the same functions as more traditional forms of religion. At the time of Diana's funeral, some wrote in national newspapers about the modern-day deification of the Princess and the way in which a new generation of pilgrims would flock to worship at her shrine. More insightful were those who observed the desire for a sense of collective belonging in a society which is highly individualistic. Indeed, there can be no denying that, for a moment at least, the **polyvalent** symbol of Diana the everywoman – mother, AIDS worker, glamorous pin-up – brought together people of very different backgrounds, though she stood for quite different things for all of them. Amongst the many articles which touched upon the civil religious dimensions of the events was one by Paul Vallely writing in *The Independent* on Saturday, September 6, 1997. He argued that although religious observance has declined in countries like Britain, there remains a certain instinct for it. He also raised a number of interesting points about ritual and Protestantism which also relate to an earlier section. This is an extract from his article:

"Petals, poems and a sense of shrine"

But perhaps the most interesting of the templates laid upon her is the spectacular secular canonisation which a nation largely without religion has conferred upon her . . . The words "saint" and "martyr" have been common among the sea of flowers at the royal gates. The ritual of leaving wrapped-up flowers at the scene of a violent death has become commonplace over the past decade. It speaks of a need for ritual even among those with no religion and it creates a new sense of shrine.

Saints and shrines accumulate power and presence. Pilgrims travel, often in groups, to places where sacred power is found, to acquire something of it and take it back with them into their everyday lives. It is not something much approved of in Protestant theology which prefers to concentrate sacrality on people rather than places. That is why shrines and pilgrimages have not been a British phenomenon since the Reformation. But such dogma has evaporated along with the religion which spawned it, and the public have returned to pagan instincts which other religions never abandoned. Roman Catholics have always been keen (they have 6,000 shrines in western Europe, 65 per cent of them dedicated to the Virgin Mary). Buddhists make pilgrimages not to power, but to light. Even Zionism might be seen as a collective pilgrimage.

The more arduous the pilgrimage, of course, the greater the benefit derived. Which is why 750,000 people queued for more than eight hours to sign a book of condolence for Diana. It was the queuing that was important; that and being there with others, for pilgrimage is most often a shared experience. Pilgrims usually need to leave something behind. Some take things away, which explains the tacky religious souvenir shops in places like Lourdes. But most want to leave something. The instinct which prompts people to throw money onto pools (and which prompts the *non gettare monetta alla tomba* sign at the tomb of the Italian mystic Padre Pio) also inspires them to lay flowers, and with them, epithets or rhymes.

At the Western Wall in Jerusalem the faithful cram prayers on scraps of paper into the cracks between the stones. At St. Ninian's cave in Whithorn they do the same, or leave stones from the beach marked with crosses. In St. James's Palace they leave messages in condolence books so numerous that they will never be read. No matter. There is an act of healing in writing.

The full gamut of religious experience is reflected in this secular sainthood. As well as the quiet devotion, we have already had an apparition of Diana appearing on a portrait of Charles I in St. James's Palace and an appearance by Diana, through the mouth of a psychic, live on radio in North Carolina . . .

Is all this in any way a valid expression of religious feeling or is it a mere corruption?

3 Draw up one or two examples of so-called "pagan" rituals that any of the **Exercise** world religions might have accommodated during the expansion of their influence. Why might it have been in their interests to do this? Do you agree that there is a need for ritual even among those with secularized life-styles?

So what have we learned in the last few sections? Well, while early anthropologists may sometimes have been chauvinistic in their attitudes toward other religions and cultures, they did at least begin to realize that practices were just as important as beliefs, despite the still persistent attitude that ritual is secondary to intellectual and existential aspects of religion. Durkheim and others were able to show that rituals play a crucial role in bringing communities together and organizing cooperation between members, especially at key points in the life-cycle such as birth, marriage and death. Moreover, after the decolonization of the non-West from around 1960 onwards, when anthropologists were forced to turn their attention to the more complex societies of the West, they found that sociologists and others were investigating the persistence of ceremonial behavior in secular societies.

As the twentieth century developed, several important social scientists continued to make the study of ritual a priority in their work. For the moment I want to focus on one very influential anthropologist that we have heard from already in this chapter, Clifford Geertz. Geertz is a good example of an anthropologist who has both worked on world religions and contributed to the ever more sophisticated theory of ritual. In short, he sees religion as a cultural system of symbols and is much more interested in interpreting the meanings of ritual than analyzing its social function. As such, Geertz's work is just one example of the way in which social theory since the 1960s has moved away from **functionalism**, through **structuralism** and **Marxism**, towards an emphasis on the interpretation of culture and **postmodernism**. All this will become clearer in time. In the next couple of sections, I want to be sure that we understand, firstly, the importance of the concept of culture, and then secondly, its relationship to religion.

Culture

Like the word religion, culture is a term that is at once very familiar but really rather difficult to define precisely. In public life today, it commonly refers to a range of matters from the arts to questions of identity and belonging. Within the English language, the word culture can be traced back to the fifteenth century when it was tied to an agri*cultural* context. Culture meant the sort of cultivation associated with the tending of crops or animals.

By the sixteenth century, the meaning of culture had been extended to more abstract matters, being associated with the development and cultivation of the human mind – a refined appreciation of the arts for example. Indeed the phrase "being cultured" gradually became synonymous with a certain type of background and education. What became known as "The Grand Tour" gave English "gentlemen" of the eighteenth and nineteenth centuries the chance to become civilized connoisseurs of the classical art of ancient European (especially Italian) society.

Definitions of culture in terms of intellectual and social improvement have therefore tended to refer to the upper and middle classes of society and the western nations of the world. However, in the twentieth century especially this has begun to change. There is now an appreciation of the significance of popular (particularly working-class and lower middle-class) culture within both academia and the media. As such, the study of culture in many universities today is just as likely to examine the historical and contemporary development of "rock and roll" as classical music. Moreover, with the establishment of departments of Comparative Religion and Anthropology, universities have extended the study of culture to non-western societies although, as we have seen in a previous section, the ways in which such societies have been represented has not always done them justice.

A contemporary focus on the "popular" culture of the many, as opposed to the "high" culture of the privileged few, has not met with approval in all circles. Some argue that the term "popular culture" is a contradiction in terms and that its emergence is just one deplorable example of the current "post-modern" reluctance to make critical judgments. They say that standards have been dissolved by an extreme case of cultural **relativism**. Postmodernists and relativists, for their part, are wary of the idea that there is just one objective reality by which everything else should be judged and evaluated. They maintain that the way in which any one of us interprets the world is dependent on the overall cultural context in which we are socialized. So for relativists and postmodernists the notion of "high culture" simply reflects the privileged and prejudiced values of a particular group – routinely middle-class, white, western males – a group which has traditionally had the power to insist that, for the most part, they are in the right. We shall examine the significance of this debate for approaches to the study of "popular" religious practices and rituals in the next section.

Alongside a focus on aesthetics and the acquisition of "civilization," there have been alternative – rather functionalist and so Durkheimian – definitions of culture which center on the way in which tribes, or more commonly today, ethnic groups and communities, are bound together by common life-styles and values. Thus, it is quite usual to hear about local (for example, aboriginal) culture; national (for example, German) culture, and global (for example, western) culture. To a large extent, this "**ethnicity**" model assumes that culture is a "holdall," containing immutable characteristics that people belonging to a certain community carry with them from birth. Indeed, many tend to think about religious heritage in the same way. For example, it is common to hear comments such as the following: "Aborigines do such and such" and "Muslims tend to be like that." The generalizations abound.

The somewhat romantic but nevertheless tribalistic and nationalistic notion of culture as a "complete way of life" can be dangerous then as it presents cultures as pure, unchanging essences that are somehow "in the blood." This notion is, of course, one of the root "assumptions" behind many of the major conflicts, wars, and tragedies of the twentieth century. Moreover, many of these have seen religion – and ritual as its most observable expression – fix the boundaries of difference between particular groups in society.

Like other approaches to the definition of culture, this fixing on "ethnicity" or group belonging has also been challenged in recent times. Most recent work in the social sciences has tended to reject the notion of culture as a "thing" – certain norms of custom that determine how people will think and act – and replace it with the notion of culture as a "practice." In this latter view, which it should be clear by now is most closely associated with Geertz, culture is a system of symbols which allows for the constant construction and reconstruction of people's worlds of meaning, as they struggle to render their lives significant. Religion as a cultural practice is something that people do, something they take an active part in creating. Moreover, as with language so with culture, people can be multilingual and multicultural. So human creativity is by no means necessarily confined to one cultural or religious system.

Finally in this section, I want to draw our examination of the concept of culture to a close with a few remarks about the nature of the world we live in today. The term "**multiculturalism**" mentioned above refers to the fact that during the late twentieth century especially, most nations have become pluralized with peoples of sometimes very different cultural and religious life-styles coexisting together in one society. This situation is as a result of international migration, prompted by economic and political inequalities between the West and the rest of the world, and facilitated by relatively cheap air travel as well as other advances in communications technology. These developments are part of a bigger process known as "**globalization**" whereby both time and space are becoming much more compressed than they used to be. This means that the potential for both cooperation and conflict between cultural and religious systems is ever more intensified as people from different backgrounds interact on a more regular basis.

The multicultural cities of the world therefore provide new challenges for established religious traditions. For example, while many migrants settled in North America and Europe may stress the continuity of their religious practices with those "back home," it is undeniable that transformations of their traditions have taken place. For example, according to Herbert J. Gans:

> Jews have abstracted rites de passage and individual holidays out of the traditional religion and given them greater importance, such as the bar mitzvah and bas mitzvah (the parallel ceremony for 13-year-old girls that was actually invented in America). Similarly, Chanukah, a minor holiday in the religious calendar has become a major one in popular practice, partly since it lends itself to impressing Jewish identity on the children.[7]

Religions have, therefore, adapted in order to survive and prosper in the diaspora under new cultural conditions. But what sorts of strategies have generally been open to them? On the one hand, we might say that sometimes they become more **revivalist**, seeking to reassert the primacy of scripture and tradition for their community over and against outside, especially western or other powerful influences. Other times there is a more **universalistic** and open exchange of religious cultures which of course is why certain "**new religious movements**" with roots in the East have prospered in the West. The International Society for Krishna Consciousness (ISKCON), more commonly known as "the Hare Krishnas," is a good example. In either case, no study of religion and culture can afford to neglect they way in which the globalization of culture has affected the reproduction of the world's religions.

4   In the West today there are a number of examples of what might be called   Exercise
    the "trinketization" of eastern religions. It is quite fashionable to consume
    clothes, music and ideas from ethnic cultures. Can you think of any
    examples? Do you think that the commercialization of eastern religions in
    any way advances a knowledge of these traditions or combats prejudice
    against their adherents?

Religion and Culture

The contemporary debates about culture described in the previous section have had serious implications for the way in which many scholars have come to think about religion and also, but perhaps to a lesser extent, the way in which religious people think about themselves and their communities. We heard earlier that religious practices can often be seen as secondary to religious beliefs, not least because the former are understood to be cultural while the latter are in some sense eternal. It is now time to take a more positive view of religion as a cultural practice in line with the comments in the previous section.

It is the contention of this chapter that all human practices – including religious practices – are enacted in particular historical contexts which are always culturally conditioned. Religion actually relies on the vehicle of culture for its very transmission. As Eric Sharpe has observed of those who insist on the importance of religion's relationship with culture,

> nothing – or at least nothing that is observable – in religion can be separated from the cultural forms in which it expresses itself. Every last detail – every idea, every ritual, every need met, every controversy, every organisation – has arisen out of the needs and concerns of a specific culture and must be viewed in that light.[8]

Of course, it could be argued that the very act of talking about a supreme being in a specific human language points to the inescapable reality that all human understanding – including spiritual understanding – is culturally conditioned. After all, the scriptures of the world's religions are written in many different languages: Sanskrit, Pali, Avestan, Hebrew, Aramaic, Greek, Arabic and Punjabi.

When we consider the concept of culture, then, we are reminded that religious communities are living, breathing and developing human organisms that adapt quite differently in different circumstances. Indeed, for the ideals of religion to maintain their sense of reality in a sociological sense they must be capable of reformulation so as to enter meaningfully into the local value systems of changing social realities. Islam, for example, is a world religion and as such it is not confined to one society or cultural tradition. This is something that Geertz makes clear in the following quotation about Morocco and Indonesia, two predominantly Muslim countries:

> They are an odd pair . . . But . . . they are in some enlarged sense of the word Islamic
> – they make an instructive comparison. At once very alike and very different, they
> form a kind of commentary on one another's character. Their most obvious likeness
> is, as I say, their religious affiliation; but it is also, culturally speaking at least, their
> most obvious unlikeness. They stand at the eastern and western extremities of the
> narrow band of classical Islamic civilisation . . . they have participated in the history
> of that civilisation in quite different ways, to quite different degrees, and with quite
> different results. They both incline toward Mecca, but, the antipodes of the Muslim
> world, they bow in opposite directions.[9]

One of the reasons that Islam spread so widely throughout the world – from Morocco in the West to Indonesia in the East – was its ability to accommodate itself to local cultures. In this perspective, religious **syncretism** and innovation is part of the "natural" growth and development of a tradition. New religions have to adapt to local practices to take hold. Indeed, it is clear that most of the world religions, though now considered to represent discrete and bounded communities, developed the orthodoxy of their distinctiveness relatively late in their development. Most religions bear the traces of the many different religious systems, cultures and civilizations that have influenced them, although that **hybrid** heritage is usually denied today as heresy.

Maraboutism is the chief characteristic of Islam in Morocco. A marabout, or *murabit* in Arabic, is a man tied to God in a close relationship. For ordinary Muslims, a *murabit* or saint is a source of blessing who fills the gap between this world and the realm of the divine. Maraboutism is therefore a form of Sufism, the mystical strain of Islam. All over Morocco there are thousands of white domed tombs (*siyyid*) and religious lodges (*zawiyah*) which testify to the importance of religious practices associated with the saints, dead as well as alive. These institutions grew up around the petitioning of saints who are asked to intervene with Allah on behalf of supplicants. People ask for many things including general well-being, good luck, fertility and prosperity. The shrine complexes associated with the tombs of saints have traditionally been the main way that people – especially in rural areas – learn about Islam in Morocco and Muslim societies in general. They learn through the journeying of pilgrimage, the dancing and whirling of *dhikr* (remembrance of the name of Allah) perhaps set to entrancing rhythms or music, and other rituals including animal sacrifices, mutual flagellation, soothsaying, snake-charming and fancy displays of horsemanship.

Exercise 5 Try to identify some of the ways in which cultural diversity in your locality, region or country affects the style in which a particular religion is practiced.

To account for the cultural diversity very evident in the world's religions, anthropologists of the 1940s introduced the notion of the **Great traditions** and the **Little traditions**. Usually this was expressed in terms of a dichotomy between: (1) belief and ritual practice as expressed in the religious texts and exegetical comments of scholars; and (2) the actual beliefs and practices of specific Muslim communities such as those in Morocco. In many accounts of research on Muslim societies this meant that scholars simply noted what a specific community had accepted from the Great tradition – for example, the Five Pillars of Islam – and what they took from less orthodox and orthoprax traditions – for example, the pilgrimage to shrines of sufi saints outlined above.

Remembering the debates about "high" and "popular" culture that we encountered in the previous section, it soon becomes clear that there are problems with this formulation. If we simply reinforce the ideas of a religious scholarly elite – the understanding that religion is either orthodox, scriptural and true, or **heterodox**, popular, and false – we will fail to understand how Islam is interpreted by many ordinary, often illiterate, people, on an everyday basis. For the student who does not want to change, condemn, or justify existing beliefs and practices, but to understand what they mean to those who produce them, there is little point in classifying religion according to the scriptural ideals of urban intellectuals and other elites. If what the people believe and practice is the only ideal they themselves know, then in terms of their knowledge of the world, it is their only reality. Thus, we should use terms like orthodoxy and orthopraxy carefully, lest we privilege the definitions of the powerful over the relatively powerless in society.

As we heard in the previous section, religious revivalism with its emphasis on the purity of religions is on the increase throughout the modern world. Like the Protestant Reformation in Christianity, Islamic revivalists today take as one of their main enemies the popular Islam of the masses, which they regard as impure. An awareness of alternatives to local beliefs and practices is growing at an ever quicker rate even in the relatively isolated communities where popular religion traditionally thrived. One of the reasons for this is the emergence of modern nation-states and the effects of globalization. Religious orthodoxy and orthopraxy is linked to the state through a formal education system, which routinely disseminates the views of those professional religious who have the power to define "true" Islam and control the means of its reproduction. Moreover, the communications revolution beams revivalist ideas to televisions and radios in even the remotest areas.

Some scholars have suggested that, because of the variety of cultural forms that the world's religions take, we should cease to use labels such as "Islam" to describe the diverse beliefs and practices of Muslims. They argue that to reduce all that Muslims say and do to such a unified category gives the impression that the religion is monolithic and undifferentiated. It is with this critique in mind that the alternative of "islams" has been put forward. This term, which is of course in the plural and without capitalization, can be seen as a simple but helpful way of emphasizing that, from a scholarly perspective at least, there is no one way of being Muslim and no one interpretation of "islam" has more intrinsic value than another. However, while the notion of "islams", or indeed "hinduisms" or "christianities," usefully under-lines the cultural diversity within any particular faith grouping, such an approach can all too easily overstate the extent of disunity within a religious community. To be sure, there has always been an empirical diversity and disunity within Islam. Nevertheless, one must be wary of dissolving the ties that have symbolically bound many millions of believers together for nearly fourteen hundred years. Regardless of their cultural heritage, Muslims do routinely consider themselves to be a part of the same community that was first inspired by the revelation of the *Qur'an* through Allah's last prophet, Muhammad, in the seventh century CE. This shared set of religious symbols facilitates an imagined continuity of experience through time and across space. As the next section demonstrates then, diversity within a religious tradition is perhaps best understood in terms of the plurality of meanings that indi-vidual believers attribute to a common set of authoritative symbols.

Ritual, Symbols, and Power

In this chapter the symbolic nature of much religious ritual has been alluded to consistently but without much extended discussion. This is the task I want to take in hand during this, the last of our sections. A symbol is something that can be invested with certain meanings so that it can be made to stand for something else. As we have seen, these meanings can be conveyed in a number of ways, through the ritual use of bodies, music, and drama, to name but a few examples. Symbols bring the power of focus to ritual as they condense and concentrate meanings into tangible forms. They make it easier to discern what is sacred and what is profane. For example, the move into the ritual time and space of the sacred from the mun-dane time and space of the profane is often marked by purification rites involving the cleansing of the body. Catholics bless themselves with holy water before going in to Mass, and Muslims perform ablutions before entering the prayer hall of a mosque.

Attention to the symbolic dimension of ritual also demonstrates the way in which ritual – consciously and unconsciously – links individual experiences to the cosmos and the complexities of wider society. In an earlier section, we heard how Durkheim argued that participation in religious rituals is one of the best ways to bring a group of people together. However, as we have begun to see, one of the main problems with Durkheim's ideas is that he was not sufficiently attentive to issues of diversity and division within religious communities. If we have seen that ritual can unify individuals of quite different and opposed social statuses we also need to consider the fact that ritual can be used politically to maintain and manip-ulate the status quo.

The formality and prescribed rigidity of much ritual practice can have rather distancing effects upon participants. It has been argued that ritual prevents spon-taneity and smothers individuality. It can discourage critical thinking and mystify us, reducing participants to their mechanical public roles. Moreover, the conventions of ritual can be said to reflect the hierarchical relationships between participants.

Indeed, the cosmological and social positions given to participants in a ritual normally express the roles allotted to them in wider society. Recalling the discussion of civil religion in an earlier section, the following reflections included in a recent review of the literature on ritual seem an interesting way of illustrating its reproduction of hierarchy:

> As I was beginning to write this, one of my colleagues was simultaneously appearing on a local radio (NPR affiliate) talk show regarding a humorous article he wrote about the religion of football at universities like Florida's. One particularly astute caller offered a straightforward and unusually serious analysis of the way in which the physical arrangement of the stadium itself reinforced the local social hierarchy. High above the field in air-conditioned sky-boxes sit the president, the wealthy and powerful and especially the generous contributors. Next in the shaded west stands one has, say, the upper middle class. In the east stands, and particularly behind the north endzone (both subjected to the blazing Florida sun), we can find students and the lower classes, with the cream of each of these groups located closest to the 50 yard line. Communal cheers and songs serve to obscure this social hierarchy somewhat, giving a momentary sense of communitas, but nevertheless one's bodily location in the stadium carries with it an undeniable social message – one that is seldom recognised.[10]

So it is then that many scholars today find it necessary to at least consider that ritual may cause some participants to experience, as satisfactory, a social condition which can be shown to be both oppressive and exploitative. From certain perspectives then, ritual can operate as an effective strategy of power. It can suggest that more consensus exists in society than there really is. It can create the impression that participants are redeemed by presenting a protected cosmic order, a sacred canopy to shield them from **anomie**.

While issues of power are important, as the discussion about popular religion demonstrated, ritual can not be said to always and everywhere uphold the status quo. Rather than indoctrinating people, ritual symbols are better seen as offering a way to have a degree of unity within a religious community without subordinating the individual to the group. These ideas can be brought together with reference to Victor Turner's idea that symbols are **multivocal**. In short, Turner found that symbols were capable of meaning quite different things to different people. As there was no universal agreement amongst participants as to what any given ritual might mean, he argued that this elasticity of symbols keeps communities together. So people hold a symbol in common and not necessarily the interpretation of the meanings they give to it. Therefore, ritual is much more likely to aggregate people than integrate them into an homogenous unit.

6 Reflecting on a ritual that you have observed or participated in, discuss in groups how you interpreted the ritual as an individual and whether you felt in any way part of a group.

Exercise

Conclusion

In this chapter we have seen that ritual is a social and cultural aspect of religion, which gives concrete expression to notions of the transcendent. Rituals dramatize the rather abstract tenets of belief through regularized bodily actions – often employing special objects and spaces. As such, they are essential to the maintenance of both the worldview and the ethos of a religion. The symbolic meanings attached to particular rituals facilitate communication between groups, individuals, and their ultimate realities. They therefore fill the gap between the cosmos, the social, and individual experiences.

.... GLOSSARY ....

Anomie State of meaninglessness and crisis for the individual.

Anthropology Academic discipline which studies human (especially) non-western cultures.

Civil religion Secular rituals which seem to perform the same unifying functions as religion.

Colonialism Domination of one social, economic, political and cultural block by another; as in western colonial domination of the Muslim world during the nineteenth and early twentieth centuries.

Community A body of people united by some common interest.

Communitas Feelings of equality with others while participating in the same ritual.

Comparative religion Academic discipline which began as a scientific approach to the study of religion.

Culture A particular way of constructing and creating the worlds we inhabit.

Dhikr Ritual involving repetition of the name of God (Allah) in Islam.

Ethnicity A social group's characteristics; especially in relation to another group.

Ethos The characteristic spirit of a religion.

Eurocentric Reflecting the biases of European and western views of themselves and others.

Evolutionism Darwin's theory about the development of species from simple to complex forms; adapted to the social world to suggest that some cultures are more advanced than others.

Functionalism Sociological "school" interested mainly in how society works and how it is bound together.

Globalization The compression of time and space by communications technology such that the world feels smaller and more interrelated.

Great tradition Orthodox and universal religious beliefs and practices; usually with reference to scripture.

Hajj The Muslim pilgrimage to Mecca.

Heterodox Not orthodox.

Hybridity Cultural crossfertilization.

Liminal Transitional stage in van Gennep's rites of passage when one is between old and new statuses.

Little tradition Local religious beliefs and practices.

Marxism Sociological "school" mainly interested in conflict between capitalist and working classes.

Multiculturalism Describing both the emergence of plural societies due to international migration and the state policies organized to deal with cultural diversity.

Multivocal Many meanings.

Murabit One close to God (Allah) in Moroccan Islam; a saint.

New religious movements Movements which emerged in the 1960s which are characteristically charismatic, often espousing millennial or utopian beliefs, and often have roots in the East.

Orthoprax Correct practice of religious rituals.

Pagan Irreligious person; usually derogatory reference to non-Christians in western usage.

Polyvalent Having many meanings.

Postmodernism Movement which deconstructs the way we know things.

Primitive At an original or early stage in the development of civilization.

Profane Commonplace, mundane; opposite of sacred.

Qur'an The holy scripture of the Muslims.

Relativism The idea that there are no objective realities, just different culturally constructed knowledges.

Revivalism Renewal of religious fervour; in scriptural religions usually for a return to the texts of revelation.

Rite of Passage Ritual involving symbolic passage from one stage of life to another; e.g. initiation, involving the movement from childhood to adulthood.

Ritual Structured action which gives expression to the sacred.

Sacred Held especially holy; opposite of profane.

Secularization Gradual withdrawal of religion from social, especially public, significance; characteristic of modern western societies.

Siyyid A saint's tomb in Moroccan Islam.

Social science The scientific study of society, for example, sociology and anthropology.

Structuralism Sociological perspective emphasizing that underlying structures are prior to individuals.

Symbol Something that can be made to stand for something else.

Syncretism Merging of different ideas, cultures and so on.

Taboo Prohibited; set aside as sacred.

Theistic   Professing a belief in God or gods.

Totemism   Belief system whereby an animal or plant is adopted as the emblem of a tribe or clan.

Universalistic   Widespread applicability.

Worldview   A particular vision of or outlook on the world characteristic of a specific group.

Zawiyah   Sufi lodge in Islam.

Notes and References

1   William Paden, *Religious Worlds* (Boston, Massachusetts: Beacon Press, 1994), p. 95.
2   Clifford Geertz, *Islam Observed* (Chicago: The University of Chicago Press, 1968), p. 100.
3   Of course, while Nanak did not want to found a religious tradition, his successors gradually set about institutionalizing Sikhism and eventually gave it an identity distinctive from Hinduism. When Guru Gobind Singh established the elite of the *khalsa* (meaning the "pure"), with its distinctive uniform including *kesh* (uncut hair and beard, the former conventionally bound by a turban), the ritualization of Sikhism in culturally specific terms began. See chapter 10 on Sikhism in this book.
4   Douglas Davies, "Introduction," in Jean Holm with John Bowker (eds.), *Rites of Passage* (London: Pinter Publishers Ltd, 1994), p. 3.
5   Malcolm X with the assistance of Alex Haley, *The Autobiography of Malcolm X* (London: Penguin, 1968), pp. 454–5.
6   Nicholas Abercrombie, Stephen Hill, and Bryan S. Turner (eds.), *The Penguin Dictionary of Sociology*, second edition (London: Penguin, 1984), p. 33.
7   Herbert J. Gans, "Symbolic Ethnicity," in John Hutchinson and Anthony D. Smith (eds.), *Ethnicity* (Oxford: Oxford University Press, 1996), p. 147.
8   Eric J. Sharpe, *Understanding Religion* (London: Duckworth Press, 1987), p. 126.
9   Geertz, *Islam Observed*, p. 4.
10   Dennis E. Owen, "Ritual Studies as Ritual Practice," *Religious Studies Review*, 24, 1 (1988): 26.

Chapter 6

Religion and the Arts

SHANNON LEDBETTER

Platonic Opposition to Art

Medieval Use of Art as a Route to the Spiritual

Islamic Integration of the Rational with Art

Victorian Culture

Theological Perspectives on Art

The Modern Confusion

Case Studies

Introduction

The arts are part of our culture and they permeate all aspects of our lives. To speak of the arts in culture is to discuss society as a whole – not just what is commonly referred to as "high culture" such as painting, ballet or classical music. Furthermore culture, as we saw in chapter 5, is a global concept. It undergirds our lives and provides the context, and sometimes the content, for the way we behave towards each other, talk, eat, relax, and dress. The purpose of this chapter, then, is to explore the impact of religion within the arts, and through this, its dialectic with culture. It is clearly impossible, in a short chapter, to look at every part of the world, so to make the discussion manageable we shall confine our discussion to the Anglo-American–European dimension (that is, the western arts). It is important, however, to note the significant and rich traditions of eastern religious art – though I will not consider them closely here. In many ways the claims I will make here considering art and religion will also have some relevance to Indian, Chinese and Japanese artistic traditions. But of course there will also be much that is very different, and I am not here arguing for some universal principles of art and religion. With these caveats out of the way let us begin.

In this chapter we shall discover that, historically, western religion has inspired a particular way to view the arts: one which held that, whatever the medium, "Art" has intrinsic value. Hence, one of the main questions we shall consider in

James Abbott McNeill Whistler, *Nocturne in Black and Gold: The Falling Rocket*, 1875, oil on wood, 60.3 × 46.6 cm, Detroit Institute of Art, Gift of Dexter M. Ferry, Jr.

this chapter is whether this expectation is a fair requirement to make of the arts. And if art does have some essential value, have we in the West lost sight of it? Due to the limitations of space, I will concentrate primarily on the history of visual arts, although I will mention other areas as well. Parallel histories could be made for both music and literature that would illustrate the same tendency.

What is art? I will begin by examining the landmark trial between an art critic, **John Ruskin** (1819–1900), and an artist, **James McNeill Whistler** (1834–1903), which forever changed the way western society approaches "Art." In 1877, John Ruskin made the following statement regarding Whistler's painting, *Nocturne in Black and Gold*: "but [I] never expected a coxcomb ask two hundred guineas for flinging a pot of paint at the public's face." This provoked Whistler to sue Ruskin for libel. Ruskin's criticism reveals three important points for our discussion of religion and the arts. First, Ruskin accused Whistler of being a "coxcomb." The significance is not that Ruskin called him conceited, but the implication that the artist willfully presented to the public a canvas which was not edifying. Second, "flinging a pot of paint at the public's face" was a condemnation of the worst kind. Ruskin was saying that not only was the work painted in an unorthodox way, but the image on the canvas was not immediately recognizable as representing anything which would lend itself to contemplation. This brings us to the third point: the public. Ruskin expected the artist to perform a public service. Whistler had been selfish and painted a picture that did not inspire the public spiritually and did not teach a great moral lesson. The picture was merely meant to be "beautiful." The canvas was an arrangement of color (called a nocturne by Whistler), loosely inspired by fireworks over an amusement park outside London. It was this ambiguity between beauty and edification which the Victorian mind could not comprehend. The judge ruled in Whistler's favor. However, he ordered Ruskin to pay only one farthing in damages and no court costs.

The trial is significant in that Ruskin was considered to be one of the most influential art critics and writers about art history in England. He saw art in all of its diverse forms as being essentially revelatory: a bridge between nature or the thing represented, and the grandeur of God. In order to convey transcendence the artist needed to paint something recognizable. Abstraction could not be understood, and neither could "arrangements of color" be integrated into the conscience or into popular culture. While this was not the first time Ruskin encountered artistic challenges to the cultural norms, he was fighting a losing battle: as the industrial revolution began to develop and science became more prominent, the traditional, quasi-religious attitudes toward art were less and less tenable.

Ruskin saw Darwinism as posing a tremendous threat to his own traditional attitudes. He believed art was meant to portray the greatness and beauty of God and regarded the ethereal and sumptuous works of the **Pre-Raphaelite Brotherhood** (formed 1848, disbanded 1855) as a model. The brotherhood employed three main themes: **realism**, which consisted of historical and religious paintings; "truth to nature," which stressed contemporary scenes depicted in an almost hyper-real fashion; and a fascination with the Middle Ages, primarily the myths of the Arthurian legends. The world Darwin portrayed, on the other hand, was one of skeletons, leaf formations and macro- and micro-scopic biological patterns. Under Darwinianism's growing influence, landscape painting became less idealistic and more clinically realistic. Ruskin saw less and less of God in artists' renderings. When the Whistler trial was over, Ruskin stopped practicing art criticism, threw up his hands in despair and told the artists to paint as they wished – he would no longer take part. Ruskin retired to Cumbria in the north of England and eventually fell into obscurity, grieving the cultural shift which he had been responsible for naming.

Ruskin viewed Whistler's work as the final insult to civilized culture. If Whistler could get away with eliminating truth in the form of accurate representation from his paintings, then it would not be long before truth could be eliminated from public consciousness altogether. This interpretation is certainly open to debate, but it could be argued that the Ruskin–Whistler trial was indeed an important turning point in modern art culture. Perhaps the point we should draw, however, is not whether truth and, subsequently, God had been eliminated from artistic endeavor, but whether artists and their public were learning to see God and truth in new ways.

The twentieth century has seen monumental shifts in the classical arts, and the debate concerning what is art has never been stronger. The twentieth century has also seen the emergence of many different types of art that are all competing for our attention. They include film, television, photography, performance and video (which, for the first time, in 1997 won the prestigious London Royal Academy's Turner Prize). Simply speaking, there have been four historical western attitudes toward art: (1) Platonic opposition to art; (2) medieval use of art as a route to the spiritual; (3) the Victorian view of art as description of reality; (4) the modern plurality. Let us take these in turn, outlining the extent to which the arts and religion have been integrated and, in turn, how they have interacted with the particular prevailing culture.

Platonic Opposition to Art

Archaeologists and anthropologists have shown us that there has never been a time when human beings were not interested in representing in art the world around them. Ancient art is evidenced by the wealth of artefacts that have been found. They include cave paintings of rain dances in France, fertility goddess figurines in Africa and India, and great and little temples erected to gods and goddesses around the world. Although the artefacts come from all over the world and many different cultures, they all have one thing in common – they are all representational. The pieces are all meant to tell a story or represent an individual, god, or goddess. Even the architecture of the temples was meant to represent the grandeur of a particular deity. The idea that the figures or pictures had an intrinsic power was widespread. It was believed the images were able to illicit responses from the viewer or relay messages to the ancestors beyond our world. Ultimately though, the images were meant to inspire belief and "right" behavior. The ancient world also had its critics of this conception of art, of which **Plato** is particularly important.

Plato is arguably one of the greatest influences on western thought and, despite his negative attitude towards the arts, still shapes it today. Indeed one can see aspects of his arguments being discussed now. One of Plato's tasks in his *Republic*, was to outline the perfect education for the "philosopher king." To do this he discussed the role of the arts as it related to the state and included a consideration of the educational requirements of his day, including arts education. It was assumed that every child would be trained in three areas, physical education, reading and writing, and what was called secondary or literary education. We are concerned with the last category. In Plato's world the works of the great Greek poets, of which the most important was Homer, were used by the majority to learn about the lives of the gods and to receive moral insight. Plato's belief in earthly forms of perfect Ideas made him suspicious of art, literature and drama, from which he believed people received false ideas of reality and truth. An expansion of Plato's notion of Ideas or "Forms," will be helpful here. Plato believed every entity in the world is a mere shadow or image of the more perfect reality of that object in the world of Ideas, or more strictly a class of objects in the world of Ideas. Let us take a horse for example. An earthly horse is a horse, for Plato, precisely because it is a particular instance of the perfect Idea of a Horse, in the realm of Ideas. The Idea of a Horse represents the essential characteristics of all horses, and the horses one encounters in a field are mere examples. This is a "top–down" view where particular instances depend, for their characteristics or essences, on the universal objective Ideas to which they correspond. The implications for art are considerable. Plato argued that for an artist to create a picture, say of a tree, they would in fact be making a copy (the picture) of a copy (the tree) of the true Tree (the Idea). This imitation of an imitation would make it that much more difficult for someone to contemplate the actual reality. Furthermore, Plato posits, the pictures weren't really that good any-way. Plato disliked literature and drama even more since they were rather more ambiguous representations of the realities they were trying to copy.

Plato claimed that there were primarily two problems with the written word. First, the poets or dramatists themselves, including the great Homer, were basically misguided in truth and, subsequently, the people who heard them were misdirected. Homer's tales were comprised of stories of the gods engaged in treacherous and barbaric acts as well as noble ones. Plato considered the gods to be perfect and wholly good and any representation of them otherwise could not be allowed. To portray them otherwise encouraged, according to Plato, like behavior among individuals.

For example, you are invited to the Coliseum one evening to watch a perform-ance of the latest play. The story would probably get an R (US scheme for 18 years and over) rating for violence, language and, of course, sex. The plot revolves around the gods and their antics. The actors are some of the best in the area and you are involved in their every move and get caught up in each of their dilemmas. You find yourself sympathizing with their emotional conflicts as well. You come away at the end of the play exhilarated having just experienced all kinds of emotions both good and bad. You've struggled with moral questions and felt love. You have been the perfect spectator and taken it all in – all for a few coins. According to Plato, you've just been fooled in the most wicked manner. His first objection is that the writers have attempted to portray the activities of the gods, which can only be a gross distortion since the gods are perfectly good and cannot be represented by humans. Second, you as a participant have had feelings that were not based on a real experience, but in reality were mere shadows created by an image which in itself was just a representation of the truth. You yourself have not actually experi-enced pain, but an empathy that feels like pain. The play controls our emotions instead of us controlling our own emotions.

Plato's main objection to the arts then, it would seem, is that one is deluded into believing that the artist's rendition is as pure and good as the reality, even when those images are negative. In turn, the less than perfect imitations and negative interpretations of the gods' activities will influence beliefs and behavior. This mis-understanding, in turn, takes one's mind off contemplation of the Ideas that are real. Historically, the West has grappled with these issues most prominently as it sought to reconcile theodicy and art. How does one represent the reality of suffering along-side the glory and goodness of God? The answer, for the most part, has been to emphasize Christ's suffering and the cross, as can be seen most prominently in the medieval period.

Medieval Use of Art as a Route to the Spiritual

The Middle Ages saw the flowering of Christian art. In fact, when we speak of the Middle Ages historically we think of the age of Christendom. Cathedrals, spectacular paintings, choral music, mystery plays, and vestments all were examples of religion integrated into art with the hope of then merging into everyday life and individual psyches. Art became a primary means for teaching theology and to both give glory to God, and present God's glory to the public. It is important to also make mention of Eastern Orthodox art, which achieved prominence in the West with its rendering of biblical characters in icons. Eastern Orthodox icons have throughout Christian history played a prominent role in Christian religious art and continue to be a source of contemplation and theological vision. Attaching a precise date to the start of the Middle Ages ranges from 476 CE and the fall of the Roman Empire to the opinion of more modern scholars, who place the date around 1100 CE. For our purposes, it may be useful to consider the date of 312 CE, as the signal of the Emperor Constantine's patronage of Christian arts; 312 CE marked the beginning of Constantine's reign as senior emperor after defeating Maxentius at Milvian Bridge. Constantine marched into battle with a Christian monogram on his standard, the **labarum**, after he had seen the symbol in a dream and become the first Roman Christian emperor. Constantine was responsible for commissioning many great works of art – not least of which were the architectural masterpieces in **Constantinople**.

It is interesting to note that early Christians produced little art for the first few centuries for two main reasons. First, they were few in number and were struggling for survival. Art is a luxury for those who have the time and resources. Second, early Christians still adhered to their Jewish heritage of not creating representations of divinity as well as wanting to be different from the pagans who worshipped idols. It is also important to take note of the changes in the attitudes of the early Christian artists to the art of their Greek and Roman counterparts. The little art that was produced in those first few centuries was primarily funerary (i.e., pieces associated with death and funerals). The earliest extant pieces we have of Christian art were found in catacombs and include primarily cave paintings and sarcophagi. The Greco-Roman philosophy behind art was, as mentioned previously, that it was to be representational. However, idealized beauty of the human form, nature and architecture was its substance. Greco-Roman art was meant to be a re-creation of the perfection of form in and of itself. The object was meant to convey a rational understanding of itself. Christianity took the opposing view that the object was to point to a spirituality beyond itself and to invite the onlooker to project his or her own imagination onto the subject. For example, when an artist painted the Last Supper an attempt was made to convey the beliefs which went beyond the material elements of people, bread, and wine. The effect was accomplished through a variety of techniques such as shading, symbolism (the most famous being a fish), and allegory. The result was a much more impressionistic style, yet still very much representational.

Constantine's conversion meant that Christians were no longer widely perse-cuted, and they began to become integrated into society. The arts were allowed to flourish and although many artists attempted to capture Christian themes within traditional styles, the more abstract forms seemed to engage the mystique of the Christian message in a more profound way. This was the beginning of a unique medieval style. One example of this particular style was to depict a human figure two-dimensionally, enhancing her or his eyes and gestures. In this way, the artist was denying the physical world and pointing towards the spiritual. However, as Christianity gained in importance, the old influences of the Greek and Roman world were utilized in order to present the grandeur of God, especially in architecture. The doctrinal issues of Christianity that were discussed in the early Church Councils and involved such topics as the Holy Eucharist, the true nature of Christ, salvation, Trinitarian formulations, the Annunciation, and saints, all became prime subjects of medieval artistic endeavors.

In the eleventh and twelfth centuries, the papacy began to encourage and sup-port a uniform style that came to be known as **Romanesque** art. Although there was diversity in style within the realm, the overall impression was one of power, extreme beauty, symmetry, and order, as well as a desire to prepare people for the afterlife. Preparing individuals for the afterlife meant that art must be educational and used as a tool for instruction, especially in an age where literacy was low. The educational aspect of art also served to be a justification for what was a great expense and had the potential to distract people from their meditations. The Romanesque artists attempted to creatively express the concrete using a unique combination of eastern and western styles to expose a distinctive view of what humanity looks like in its earthly surroundings and its interaction with the divine.

While medieval artists emphasized the spiritual over the material and rendered their images more abstract or impressionistic than the classical artists, who wanted to present an idealized reality, the art remained representational. While the classical artist desired to represent the reasoned order of nature, the medieval artist wished to present the otherness of nature. The purpose of art in the Middle Ages was to teach and inspire people to envision the heavenly realm where God reigned triumphant, and, subsequently, was to present the church as supreme ruler on earth; this was most exemplified by the Romanesque style.

Islamic Integration of the Rational with Art

Of great importance to the medieval period was the emergence of Islam in the seventh century. It is not my purpose to discuss Islam in detail, but to briefly outline a few of Islam's great artistic offerings. Islam's artistic influence upon Chris-tianity was widespread, especially in Spain and Africa, through its architecture, textiles and metalwork. The Muslims had reconciled the significance of science and mathematics to the spiritual many centuries before the West even seriously grappled with these issues and nowhere is this more evident than in their art. Symmetry, geometrical patterns, and an attempt to synthesize the rational with the non-rational all characterize Islamic art. Islam's concentration on pattern in its art is due in part to its refusal to replicate the human form, in a similar way to Judaism, as signifying the divine. The great mosques exemplify this philosophy with their large open worship spaces surrounded by repeating columns and arches. These columns and arches were carefully built with different-colored stones in order to convey an optical illusion of infinite space. Patterns that allowed you to leave the space where you had knelt down to pray and enter into another realm.

One of Islam's main components is a belief in a detailed material heaven. This is in contrast to Christianity's emphasis on a spiritual afterlife. As a consequence, Islamic artists appear to concentrate more on items of physical comfort and the decorative arts, which became highly prized by the West. For example, highly-decorated eastern silks were used to wrap Christian relics, and the so-called "crusader canteen," based on an eastern style that depicted intricate decorations illustrating biblical themes, were considered treasures. Where Christian artists were concerned with the representational, Islamic artists were much more practical, yet they developed skills of patternwork which are unparalleled. Fine art and crafts merged into one, turning mundane objects into exquisite forms that transported the viewer to beyond the temporal. One can see the influence of pattern by eastern artists especially in the arts of the Romanesque period, which coincided with the beginning of the crusades in 1095. Architecture, illuminated manuscripts such as the Lindisfarne Gospels, sculpture, and painting all took on a decorative element.

Exercise   1   Divide into groups and design a cathedral. Keep in mind what the cathedral is meant to represent and to house (think of relics, Eucharist etc.). Who or what is a cathedral meant to attract? Remember what shape a cathedral is meant to be and why. What relevance does this shape have to the early church, and to Greco-Roman culture? You may wish to consult the chapter on Christianity in this volume.

Victorian Culture

We have already discussed Victorian culture briefly at the beginning of the chapter. The Victorians play a crucial role in modern art history. The traditional function of art in the West as a spiritual and political guide shows the first signs of fragmentation, and the future begins to appear hollow. The transformation to a more secular expectation of art will prove to be painful and Ruskin is to be one of tradition's primary martyrs. Three phenomena are crucial in understanding the climate of the nineteenth century. First, the industrial revolution and the extension of primary education served to alienate people from their environment. Second, the crusades of two men, John Ruskin and Henry Cole, created an historically unprecedented desire for widespread art education among the masses. Finally, the manufacturing of decorative arts (i.e., wallpaper, teapots etc.) was treated in the same manner as traditional artistic endeavors, which effectively served to place all arts onto the same platform.

The impact of the industrial revolution cannot be underestimated. Its chimneys and assembly lines entered into every aspect of people's lives, from politics and health to religion and art. For the first time in the history of the western world more people lived in cities than in the countryside and, as a consequence, saw more buildings and factories than trees and mountains. Widespread education meant that most people spent some time inside a classroom, and the nineteenth century saw people begin to leave their classrooms and factories to travel to the countryside as tourists. Along with this dramatic change in the landscape the very colors of life were changing. Painters enlisted darker colors and black became the predominant color for clothing. Writers such as the French poet Charles Baudelaire, and a German Professor of Aesthetics, Friedrich Theodor Vischer, both wrote of the retreat by society from color. Echoing St. Paul in 1 Cor. 13: 12, the literal "cloudiness" of the nineteenth-century skies infected the space between individuals and nature, so that a person was no longer capable of seeing clearly. However, cloudiness did not mean blindness, but to "see through a glass darkly" resulted in an impairment of vision, an estrangement from nature. Ruskin's philosophy purported that to "see clearly" was the greatest achievement of a soul. Not only to view the environment with clarity, but to discern the otherness of an object.

Imagine you are sitting in a garden in February. The garden has an assortment of trees, some are deciduous, some are evergreens. There are green shoots of crocuses and daffodils popping up and the hedgerows are just beginning to bud. Taken as it is the garden may be considered beautiful, frozen between the vivid colors of autumn and its future abundance. Ruskin believed not only that people were losing the skill to accurately depict the scenes around them, but that they also were losing the capability for memory or a vision of the future. This vision encompassed the spiritual, and without vision the object became dead, or a denial of the possession of a life beyond the present moment. Industrialization contributed to an attitude where we either take nature too seriously or not seriously enough. We have ceased to be truly comfortable with nature and our environment. There was one major exception to this deterioration of sight, the Pre-Raphaelites. The Brotherhood was compulsive about painting their subjects as they saw them in their natural environment. This meant that each component of a painting was real. This practice was a radical change from prior styles, where much of a painting's background and ornamental details might have come from a painter's imagination. What is the significance of this? For Ruskin, it meant that the truth of an object could be painted in its pure form. However, if a painter had clear vision, the object could take on its divine nature as well. In this way the object or person could be painted in its entirety. Only then could one discover the essence of a scene.

Our second consideration is the considerable interest in art education undertaken by the English. This was reflected by the way in which art education and drawing classes were being made available to everyone. While England was the world's leader in manufacturing goods, the country was lacking in the design skills to produce luxury items and determine fashion trends. The Victorian era saw perhaps a not so subtle shift in the necessity for the arts: the change from looking to art to teach and inspire, which began to give way to the commercial potential for the artistic product. A systematic approach to arts education in England was devised by Henry Cole, and was created between 1852 and 1873 when he retired. It was during this time that art education became compulsory in schools. Schools of design were set up all over the country and evening courses were designed to assist laborers. Also, a London headquarters was established which eventually became known as the Victoria and Albert museum.

Related to this second point is **Karl Marx**'s (1818–83) view of the marketability of artistic goods. Karl Marx, in the second chapter of *Capital*, discusses how the desirability of a good is solely related to the value and extent of its exchange. This attitude turned the traditional beliefs about art upside down. The truth of the form could not be blessed as real unless it could be reproduced into a saleable commodity. The question of the quality of an item was secondary to its marketability. Did this transformation spell the end of the creation of beauty, or was this metamorphosis a widening of the vision of beauty?

The third characteristic of the nineteenth century is the blurring of the distinction between the decorative arts and the high arts. With the increase in manufacturing came the ability to mass produce items for popular consumption. Just as the printing press caused books and prints of pictures to be in the general public's hands, manufacturing allowed an entire new population the opportunity to be involved in the creative process. Ironically, Ruskin's petition for comprehensive art education led to a diminishing appreciation and understanding of the higher arts, while at the same time involving the entire nation in a rudimentary knowledge of decoration. The full comprehension of art must come with "clear sight" and, as well intentioned as people may be, unless they were able to experience the truth of nature they would never be able to transfer the purity of form onto an object, utilitarian or otherwise. The nineteenth century saw urbanity encroaching on nature for which there was no replacement, and God as yet had not permeated the tenement block or dockland.

The Victorian era brings us full circle, back to the objections of Plato, with **Leo Tolstoy** (1828–1910). Tolstoy wrote a famous collection of essays called *What is Art?* (1898), in which he rejects the traditional definition of art as embodying beauty. Tolstoy disagrees with this conception because he says that beauty is not simply that which is pleasing and can be equated to the perfectly good, or God: "the good is that which no one can define, but which defines everything else." Tolstoy dismisses Plato's belief that art is divorced from the good (indistinguishable from the beautiful as Plato would define it), and advocates, rather, art as infectious. Tolstoy believes that the artist's feelings must be transferred to the listener or viewer in order for a work to be considered art. Tolstoy also claims that the artist must be overwhelmed with a particular feeling, which can only manifest itself in an original creation whether good or bad, positive or negative, beautiful or ugly. Tolstoy's criterion holds that an artist must experience a genuine feeling for which he or she creates an original piece of art. In turn, the person who comes in contact with the piece is then "infected" with that same feeling or feelings and may experience a recognition of him or herself in the work. Tolstoy goes on to condemn most art as counterfeit, including Shakespeare, Dante, and Beethoven. Most artists are merely creating commissioned or formula pieces dictated by demand, which are therefore not containing true feeling, but are imitations.

Tolstoy also condemns symbols, especially religious ones, because they have been reproduced so much as to be empty of meaning. In a sense, he wants to eliminate the symbol and experience the mystery alone. In this way experiences are not polluted with representations or imitations of what the numinous may look or feel like, but the chances of participating in true reality are greater. Tolstoy ultimately believed that "the task of Christian art is the realization of brotherly union." He believed that if art could be used to elicit reverence for the Eucharist, increase political fervor or create loyalties, then art should be used to create feelings of love for each other, to recognize the dignity of each human being as well as to joyfully submit to sacrificial behavior toward each other.

The Victorian period was a tumultuous time for culture as a whole. The clash of art and science caused artists, critics, and lay persons alike to think seriously about what they expected art to be as well as what they believed it should convey. It would seem that, up until the end of the nineteenth century, most people adhered to the belief that art should contain intrinsic value, from the relatively minor expectations of beauty to Tolstoy's radical political ideas that art could reform the world. The nineteenth century also saw people interacting with their environment in a new way. For the first time in history people were visiting the countryside rather than working in it. This led from an intimacy with the land to a kind of awe and distance. Despite compulsory art education in schools the familiarity we once instinctively enjoyed with nature may never be regained, which may be one major contributing factor to abstraction in the arts in the twentieth century.

1 In modern times "Art is a crime or only an absurdity" – John Ruskin.   Exercise
Discuss.

Theological Perspectives on Art

This next section will look at several different points of view about how art and religion intertwine, from a number of twentieth-century Christian theologians. Karl Barth (1886–1968), who has proven to be one of the most influential theologians of the twentieth century with his theology of neo-orthodoxy, believed the visual arts had no place in houses of worship. Barth contended that art distracted people from more authentic revelations of God, and was highly dubious of a medium which claimed to issue forth experiences of the divine. Paul Tillich (1886–1965) believed in a much more positive relationship between religion and art. In Tillich's influential *Systematic Theology*, he discusses how the visual arts are an integral part of the Spirit, just as music and the written word are also part of the complete experience of creation. Tillich wants to say that, in the act of expression, an artist influences what he or she is attempting to express. Therefore, for art to be religious in nature there needs to be what Tillich refers to as the two principles: the principle of consecration and the principle of honesty. The first indicates the intent to convey transcendence typically through religious symbols. The latter points to the commitment to producing images in a style which is both inspiring and culturally relevant. Conflict arises when new styles challenge the older, more traditional styles. Tillich, like Ruskin, feels strongly that religious art should express something of the transcendent, and that paintings which eliminate what Tillich believes to be an inherent part of creation fall outside the realm of religious art. Tillich's work has been greatly influential on the attitudes of theologians in the twentieth century.

Karl Rahner (1904–84), like Tillich, wants to affirm art's role in theology. In an essay entitled "Theology and the Arts," he insists that theology must encompass all of the arts and not just the verbal arts. To do so would beg the question "whether such a reduction of theology to verbal theology does justice to the value and uniqueness of these arts, and whether it does not unjustifiably limit the capacity of the arts to be used by God in this revelation." Hans Kung (1928–) sees art representing an eschatological function or one which points to the end times. The idealized beauty shown in a painting gives hope that "the world as it ought to be will at some time actually rise." Finally, Hans Urs von Balthasar (1905–87) developed an intricate Aesthetics in his seven-volume *The Glory of the Lord: A theological aesthetics*. Von Balthasar perceived art as being capable of inspiring the viewer beyond itself to contemplate the more profound glory the piece represents. As a result, von Balthasar saw theology and art as integrally related. Theologians need art to facilitate an expression of the inexpressible, and art needs theologians to attempt to articulate the divine.

The Modern Confusion

Our vision of God continues to be challenged within modern culture, and we are presented with more and more abstract images that are meant to inspire us to greater belief in God. However, for the first time in history art has ceased to be solely representational or religious. The entire theory of art has been turned upside down. Our ideas of truth, beauty, spirituality, inspiration, representation, and education are all in flux. The twentieth century has seen everything, from a smooth black, granite wall carved with the names of soldiers who died in the Vietnam war as representing one of the most emotional symbols of the latter half of the century (Maya Lin, dedicated 1982), to the debate over whether or not Damien Hirst's parts of cows in formaldehyde can even be considered art. We have had Fauvists, Futurists, Cubists, Cubofuturists, Pop, Dada, Productivism, Art Deco, Surrealism, Constuctivism, Deconstructionists, Bauhaus, Expressionism, as well as Abstract Expressionism, Modernism, Postmodernism, Neo-Romanticism, Op, Conceptualism and, of course, Kitsch. The last thirty years or so have seen feminists attempting to deconstruct art as it has been and to write, sculpt, and paint themselves into history, not willing to content themselves in the shadows of their male counterparts. No longer is there a fundamental theme for artists to refer to. Evolutionary progression is limited only by the artists' own circumstances and imagination.

Art in the twentieth century may perhaps be characterized as operating on the edges of society, rather than within the central tenets of belief and practice. Artists are continuously pushing to create new forms. **Pablo Picasso** (1881–1973) exemplified this inclination. Picasso was born in 1881 and by the beginning of the twentieth century was already establishing himself as a great artist. Tolstoy would have approved of Picasso. Tolstoy's antipathy for art schools was lived out by Picasso. On one occasion, at the School of Fine Art in Barcelona, when Picasso was asked to write "I will learn how to paint," he responded by writing "I will not learn how to paint." Both Tolstoy and Picasso believed that painting was a gift which came from within, not a skill to be learned and mimicked. However, Tolstoy also advocated the conviction that a painter be familiar with all of the previous styles in order to create an original form. Picasso proved to be a model student of this philosophy. Picasso spent his early years painting after the styles of the old masters and prominent artists of the past. He took these classic styles and painted them with élan. He grew bored and rearranged, toyed with, and left only an echo of these stylistic influences while Picasso himself dominated his canvasses. By the time he was 25 years old he had astonished his teachers, and had begun to show himself to the world as one of the world's most eminent painters. As he sought to establish

Pablo Picasso, *Guernica*, 1937, oil on canvas, 349.3 × 776.6 cm, Museo Nacional Centro de Arte Reina Sofia; copyright © Succession Picasso/DACS 2000.

his own style two prevailing themes emerged; those of color and of the manipulation of form.

A critic once said of Picasso, in a sentiment very different from traditional attitudes, "[He] has the power of divining the essence of things . . . Like all pure painters, he adores colour for its own sake." How different this sounds from only a few years previously when Whistler and Ruskin were in court. No longer is the subject the source of inspiration, but it is color that evokes the mood and spiritual truth. Picasso's "Blue Period", begun in 1901, was a prophetic start to the century. With their stark and sombre images, the paintings arouse feelings of melancholy and uncertainty. Only five years later, in 1906, Picasso was restructuring the way we look at art forever. In his portrait of Gertrude Stein, Picasso left behind purely representational art. The goal was no longer to accurately represent the figure, but to manipulate the structure. It was in this way that the technical aspects of a work of art became as important as its subject. Noses became triangular, eyes curvilinear hollows, and light and dark were made into solids. Picasso was to become the architect of Cubism, with its radical repositioning of forms and drastic abstraction. Before his death in 1973, Picasso would establish himself as the most important influence on western art culture in the twentieth century.

Picasso ideally sets the stage for modern culture and personifies the questions we have been asking throughout this chapter. Picasso is Picasso and his genius shines through all of his work. His exuberance is that of a creator whose vision exceeds any who have gone before. The value of his paintings and sculptures is not that they are representations of a religious theme meant to teach and inspire, but that they are forms born out of a mold no one had seen before. The miracle was that they had come into existence at all. **Dorothy Sayers** (1893–1957), an English writer, has written extensively on art, and talks of a distinctively Christian art that is characterized by its creative nature. She claims that the doctrine of creativity is a distinctly Christian offering. The creative act by humans is not only emulating the creator God, but is also a way in which that same God may continue to be present in the creation. Sayers postulates that the image is to the artist much as the Son is the express image of God. This in turn is linked to a Trinitarian unity of creativity. The artist, the subject, and the creative mind combine to portray experience, expression and recognition. While Sayers presents a helpful hypothesis for Christian art, what of the non-Christian, or non-religious for that matter? Is secular art, for instance, able to be considered art at all?

It may be argued that secular culture is exemplified by fashion. In 1913, Sonia Delaunay began to transpose her Cubist paintings into women's dresses. Women's bodies began to be draped with modernism. Delaunay's dresses were called "simultaneous" and, in the greatest cultural shift in history, women would spend the rest of the century in an attempt to be simultaneous to the current trends of fashion, liberation, and consumerism in all they did. However, access to these cultural markers has actually been achieved by a relatively small number of wealthy and privileged women, while the arts have retained their masculine basis despite a large female audience.

Throughout the century there have been a number of significant fashion trends that have corresponded with music. Music, it could be argued, has been equal to fashion in cultural importance in the twentieth century. Music has partnered with fashion in such trends as jazz and the flapper, the Beatles and Mary Quant's miniskirt, punk rock and the punk look – perhaps exemplified by Malcolm McLaren's "bondage trouser" – rap music and baggy trousers (rap may be considered an entire cultural phenomenon on its own), while the Seattle sound goes along with the Seattle look. Perhaps Andy Warhol spoke for all of us when he was asked if there was any special message to be gleaned from one of his exhibitions and Andy answered simply, "No." Maybe Andy Warhol was also right when he claimed that anyone could have their 15 minutes of fame. Is it possible twentieth-century culture has just been a series of 15-minute soundbites?

This, of course, would be glib. The African American experience alone has produced a wealth of literature, painting, jazz, and gospel music, deeply rooted in profound and spiritual experiences. The enormous scale of tragedy in this century has produced, ironically, some of the most excruciatingly beautiful works of art in all of the mediums. Perhaps it is precisely the horrors of our time which have rendered realistic forms obsolete. Artists have found it necessary to break the traditional molds and to reach beyond barriers in order to give voice to the age we live in.

Culture and art have become infinitely complex in the twentieth century. Up to and through the nineteenth century, people have looked to art to convey to them beauty and spirituality in its various guises. While tragedy, passion, and many other emotions have been portrayed in the past, it is only in the last 100 years that people have looked to art to mirror their lives as well as to splinter it into an intricate kaleidoscope of possibilities for them to contemplate. In this way people are able to experience a full range of emotions from a safe distance. They may glimpse the terror of insanity in Edvard Munch's "The Cry," or soar to the heavens with the sky scraper, without having to get too involved or to disrupt their usual routines. Architecture has provided us the opportunity for art to be integral to our lives with buildings such as Frank Lloyd Wright's Guggenheim Museum and the Sears Tower in Chicago. Although you will be reminded of Plato's arguments against empathy, even Plato could never have envisioned a world such as ours. Technological inventions and advances in film, photography, and television have taken the transformation begun with the industrial revolution to an extreme. The lines between good taste and bad taste, valuable and valueless, transcendence and emptiness, have all been blurred beyond recognition. Ultimately, though, is it Marx's criterion for art that we must accept as truth – will it sell? Is the highest bidder the one who is the most knowledgeable?

The innovation, which began with Picasso at the beginning of the century as a miraculous birth of a new form, may, at the millennium, have given way to emulation. With even more films being mere sequels and formulaic copies, and as virtual reality grows more indistinguishable from real life, the question "what is art?" has never been so important. Where do we go for authentic inspiration, to learn of truth and beauty? While we have never had more diversity of forms or stimulus for our senses, we must also be more discerning. The twentieth century may be characterized by its infinite possibilities and its endless tragedies, but it is important for us to habitually ask ourselves "what are we looking for and why?"

Christianity has ceased to exert the same influence over western culture in the twentieth century as it has enjoyed for some 1700 years. Christianity no longer dictates the subject matter of artistic pieces, nor is it able to insist upon the requirement of distinctly Christian values. This is not to say that religious art is no longer a viable entity. On the whole our society's conception of God and spirituality has increased, and our capability of seeing God in new ways has widened.

Exercises

2   "What was commercial was considered art" – Karl Lagerfeld. Discuss.

3   Do you consider great art to have a similar essence (i.e., must it be beautiful, spiritual, obviously involving extraordinary talent etc.) despite the medium?

4   If so, what is that essence? Up until the twentieth century that essence would have been the spiritual or what might be called a spiritual completeness.

5   In order for something to be considered art, must it have an essence apart from itself or may it be an ordinary object placed in an ordinary setting?

6   Using John Ruskin's idea of "clear sight," predict the future of art. You have learned a bit about the historical trends of the arts and glimpsed their present, now what do you think is in store for the future? Keep in mind what kind of future is likely and what kind of future you might like to see – are the conditions appropriate for your vision.

7   *For Discussion.* The Human Form and the way in which attitudes have changed toward it.

The human form has been regarded in a wide variety of ways throughout history. The Classical period sought to idealize the body as a god or goddess. Christianity's opinion of the body changed over time, with the earliest Christian artists depicting two-dimensional, crude figures, denying the physical and pointing toward the spiritual. The medieval artist looked to the body to represent either the iconographic, representing the Christ, or human beings being represented as the image of God. The purpose was to inspire the viewer to contemplation of spiritual matters, not to celebrate the human body as an entity worthy of painting or sculpting alone. Although the Romanesque and Gothic periods also portrayed the human form as two-dimensional, the artists sought to represent both the physical and the spiritual dimensions. The artists achieved this impression by painting minutely detailed features to portray the emotions and actions of the subjects, along with including sumptuous materials (i.e., gold paint, intricate decoration, ornate frames etc.) to suggest divinity. The late-Gothic period saw the emergence of a kind of hyper-realism, begun by Claus Sluter who sculpted life-size figures so skillfully that they seemed to take on a life of their own, and the painter Jan van Eyck, who is considered to be a pioneer in the medium of oil. This new style considered the physical to be equal to the spiritual and sought to record an accurate account of the complete image. Gutenberg's invention of the printing press in 1455 CE began to put into the hands of the common people sacred images they could relate to. For example, the idealized Christ child gave way to an ordinary toddler leaning on a walker.

The nineteenth century again sees the human form idealized, but in a realistic manner. Pre-Raphaelite women draped in Greek robes, with their flowing hair and intelligent eyes, pointed to a classical revival. The Victorian moral climate was such that women were portrayed either as coy angels or as repentant figures who had been cast out of society. While piano legs were being covered up because they were considered titillating, artists were painting voluptuous bodies.

With the turn of the century, the human body started to take on more concrete and abstract shapes. The advent of Cubism gave birth to a human body which was visualized as a series of shapes to be put together much like a puzzle. Colors and objects which formed the background were integrated as solids with the pieces of the body. Sculpture was created in the same way, with the materials being used as they were in themselves. A rusted metal was meant to look like rusted metal turned into the bust of a man, unlike classical marble statues which were carved so that the eye might be deceived into thinking it was looking at flesh (e.g., Michelangelo's David).

Most of the century has been spent in taking the glamor and idealization away from the body. Lucian Freud's work portrays overweight and rather unattractive nudes surrounded by mundane rooms. There seems to be a trend toward metarealism in painting the human form today, which encapsulates the uncertainty and plainness of average human existence. The only place western culture appears to idealize the human form today is on the catwalk. The supermodel has become the form we place on a pedestal, draped with exotic fabrics and captured on film. She has become modern culture's new muse.

Case Studies

Matthias Grunewald (ca. 1475–1528), Crucifixion (ca. 1510–15), from the Isenheim Altarpiece

Grunewald's *Crucifixion*, arguably one of theology's most profound artistic influences, was the only painting Karl Barth found inspirational in a positive way and he kept a copy of it over his desk. Grunewald was both an engineer and an architect as well as a painter, which may be seen in his meticulous arrangements. The Isenheim Altarpiece was rendered in a traditional northern European style, with many panels which could be folded over in various combinations to show different scenes depending on the liturgical year. The paintings were meant to be a teaching device, utilizing gospel messages as well as saints and symbols. Grunewald's hyperrealistic

Matthias Grunewald, 1515, *The Crucifixion*. Panel from the Isenheim Altarpiece,
oil on wood, 269 × 307 cm, Musée d'Unterlinden Colmar, photo, O. Zimmerman.

account of the pain and tortuous death Jesus experienced became a profound
inspiration rather than repelling those who prayed before it. Jesus' overwhelming
presence overtakes the smaller figures who look on from the foot of the cross. The
hands of Christ are horribly constricted and obviously in great pain. This truly is
the Man of Sorrows. John the Baptist is represented to one side of the cross holding the scriptures with the verse "he must increase, but I must decrease" (John 3:
30), inviting the viewer to meditate on this thought. Beside the Baptist is the
symbolic lamb with blood pouring out of its chest into a chalice. On the other
side of the cross stands the beloved disciple holding onto Jesus' mother, Mary.
Mary Magdalene kneels beside the cross in much the same way worshipers might
find themselves kneeling before the altarpiece: in agony and feeling the empathy
of their God.

Salvador Dali (1904–89), Crucifixion (Corpus Hypercubus) *(1954)*

"It is perhaps with Dali that the windows of the mind are opened fully wide for
the first time." This startling statement was issued by André Breton in the preface
to Dali's first Paris exhibition in 1929. Breton founded the surrealist movement,
which Dali joined, also in 1929. The surrealist movement was an endeavor to
unlock the confining structures of the mind through myth, to reveal the interior-
ity of the human psyche as advocated by Sigmund Freud. Freud, as the founder of
psychoanalysis, was a great influence on the surrealists, especially Dali. Dali, who

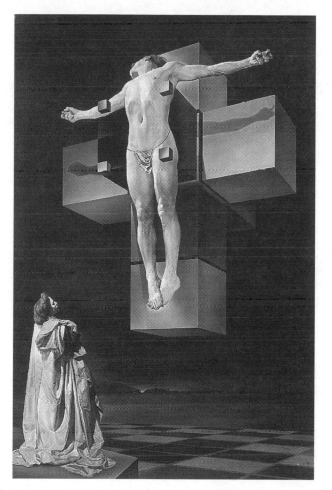

Salvador Dali ("Hypercubic body"), 1954, oil on canvas, 194.5 × 124 cm.
The Metropolitan Museum of Art, Gift of Chester Dale collection;
copyright © Salvador Dali – Foundation Gala – Salvador Dali/DACS 2000.

was fascinated by the study of paranoia and its characteristic of seeing what was not there, took on what he developed as his paranoiac-critical method. This was a process of disciplining his own vision to view objects or images in new or surrealist ways, in order to conceive their hidden meanings. Once the image is infused upon the mind then the mythic quality takes effect, and that same image may be transferred onto similar shaped objects or objects with the same feel. Dali's obsession with Millet's *Angelus* and its evolutionary role in Dali's paintings is a prime example.

Although Dali's *Crucifixion* is an example of his more conventional style, there remain many elements of Surrealism. Most obvious is the cross, which is three-dimensional and made up of cubes. The nails are blocks which seem to be floating

Edwina Sandys, *Christa*, 1975, bronze.

away from the body. The ground appears to be a floor and the landscape is reminiscent of the beach near Dali's home in Spain. Ironically, in its unreality, the crucifixion becomes not merely an event in the past, but an ever-present reality in our mind.

Edwina Sandys (1938–), Christa

On Maundy Thursday of Holy Week, 1984, Edwina Sandys unveiled her bronze statue of the female crucifix, *Christa*, at the Cathedral of St. John the Divine in New York City. The event caused an uproar. There were many who were outraged, repulsed and angered by such "sacrilege." Yet, as the Dean of the Cathedral wrote, "the artist gave sight to the blind." The statue is made of bronze and depicts a naked woman with outstretched arms wearing a crown of thorns on a cross. The sculpture drew strong reactions against feminists, but like the Grunewald painting, is capable of great healing among women who have been abused. The message of God's grace was made manifest in an unorthodox image, yet has become one of many powerful images which speak to a diverse humanity.

GLOSSARY

Constantinople A city in northern Turkey, founded by the Roman Emperor Constantine, which is called Istanbul today and is famous for its architectural masterpieces.

Labarum The name of the standard which was adopted by the emperor Constantine after seeing it in a vision. The symbol consisted of the Greek letters X and P which formed the first two letters of ΧΡΙΣΤΟΣ, meaning Christ.

Marx, Karl (1818–83) Within the realm of aesthetics, Karl Marx is influential for his belief that the value of a good is based solely on its marketability. The quality or look of an item is inconsequential.

Picasso, Pablo (1881–1973) Arguably, the most influential painter of the twentieth century. He invented the Cubist style and remained an innovator his entire life, constantly experimenting with color and manipulating form.

Plato (427 BCE–347 BCE) Plato, a Greek philosopher, was influential in the world of aesthetics through his discussion in *The Republic*, where he outlines his ideas regarding the arts. The arts comprised inadequate and imperfect representations of the more perfect reality in the world of forms. In dwelling on the arts instead of contemplating the perfect form an individual is likely to become misguided.

Pre-Raphaelite Brotherhood An English school of artists, founded in 1848, whose most notable member was Dante Gabriel Rossetti. The group disliked the current neo-classical trend, which they believed was begun by Raphael (1483–1520), and desired to paint in the style of the early renaissance which preceded Raphael. The Brotherhood's style is characterized by vibrant color and sumptuous depictions of classical and moral themes. The Brotherhood was a favorite of John Ruskin's due to the purity of their style.

Realism The movement in art which emphasizes the reflection of lived realities and an aspect of immediacy, often in order to act as a critique of them.

Romanesque A form of art which was patronized by the papacy in the eleventh and twelfth centuries. The papacy encouraged artists to present paintings that would be educational in nature and would prepare people for the afterlife. The art may be distinguished by its extreme beauty, symmetry, and power.

Ruskin, John (1819–1900) An influential English writer and critic about art in the nineteenth century. Was instrumental in encouraging the expansion of the practice of art to the masses, and providing profound insights into how painting was affected by and affected popular culture.

Sayers, Dorothy (1893–1957) An English writer and theologian, Dorothy Sayers advocated a distinctly Christian art. Sayers believed that art emulated the creator God of Christianity. Her distinctive offering to aesthetics is her idea of a Trinitarian unity of creativity.

Tolstoy, Leo (1828–1910) In his work, *What is Art?* (1898), Tolstoy discusses art as being that which is born of genuine and fresh feeling. In turn, the viewer must be "infected" with that same feeling. Tolstoy condemns most art as being "counterfeit," and counters the traditional arguments that art must be beautiful. He contends that art may be expressed through the complete range of emotions.

Whistler, James Abbott McNeill (1834–1903) Whistler was an important American painter who incurred the wrath of John Ruskin when he exhibited an impressionist painting, "Nocturne in Black and Gold." The painting sparked a pivotal legal trial that depicted the evolution from realist paintings which told a story, to more impressionist, stylized paintings.

Chapter 7

···

Secular Humanism

J'ANNINE JOBLING

Historical Survey

The Enlightenment

Worldviews

Case Study: Religion as Oppressive

Ethics

Modern Expressions

Conclusions

In the modern world, there is a sense that religion is in decline. Consider the following extract from a British nineteenth-century poem:

> The Sea of Faith
> Was once, too, at the full and round earth's shore
> Lay like the folds of a bright girdle furl'd.
> But now I only hear
> Its melancholy, long, withdrawing roar,
> Retreating, to the breath
> Of the night-wind, down the vast edges drear
> And naked shingles of the world.
> *(Extract from Matthew Arnold's "Dover Beach," 1867)*

This expresses the feeling that the sacred is becoming less and less important to human lives. The Sea of Faith is ebbing away. This shift in ideas and practice, away from God and religion, is known as **secularization**. The predominant understanding, until the seventeenth century, was that events were caused and guided by some higher power or powers. Increasingly, though, it seems that people look to science to explain the world: not to God. Fewer people participate in organized, institutional religion. Society seems to owe more to human policies and actions, rather than to divine providence.

Alongside the drift from institutional religion has gone an upsurge of interest in humanist ways of seeing the world. What is humanism? Basically, it is a tendency to stress human concerns. Cicero, a philosopher of ancient Greece, said that philosophy was called down from heaven to earth in the fifth century BCE. This was when social, political and moral questions appeared on the agenda and human concerns and interests became fit objects for reflection. Humanism is also associated with the **Renaissance** period of the fourteenth to sixteenth centuries, when interest in the classical learning of ancient Greece and Rome flourished. At this time, humanism went hand in hand with the Christian religion. It was, though, a move toward placing humanity rather than God at the center of attention and toward a stress on human ability to find out about the universe. By the nineteenth century, humanism had acquired an association with **atheism** and **agnosticism**. Atheists are those who deny the existence of God. Agnostics, more cautiously, claim that there is no basis on which to affirm the existence of God, without altogether discounting it as a theoretical possibility. Humanism in this tradition can be understood as a **secular** worldview, which places human concerns and interests at its center whilst making no reference to a deity, an afterlife, or to any supernatural forces.

The growth in non-theistic forms of humanism is intimately linked with that broader shift in social, political and philosophical thinking known as secularization. We see here an important change taking place as people move away from traditional religious beliefs and practices. For religions such as Christianity, freedom and joy, strength and salvation, are to be found in and through God. For the secular humanist, all these things can in fact only be found by *overthrowing* "God," who is really a myth created by human needs and desires. God and religion are seen to be not only false, but also undesirable. This attitude is very well expressed by Robert G. Ingersoll, a well-known American **freethinker** of the late nineteenth century:

> When I became convinced that the universe is natural, that all the ghosts and gods are myths, there entered into my brain, into my soul, into every drop of my blood the sense, the feeling, the joy of freedom. The walls of my prison crumbled and fell. The dungeon was flooded with light and all the bolts and bars and manacles became dust. I was no longer a servant, a serf, or a slave . . . I was free! I stood erect and fearlessly, joyously faced all worlds. (Cited in Frederick Edwords, "What is Humanism?", http://www.infidels.org/library/modern/fred_edwords/humanism.html)

Exercises   1   Why might deciding there is no God make somebody feel as if they had been freed from a prison?

2   (a)   What evidence might you look at if you are trying to decide whether religion is or is not in decline?

(b)   Prepare a presentation arguing either for or against the view that religion is in decline.

Historical Survey

What are the roots of secular humanism? In fact, the foundations of humanist thought can be discerned in ancient times and many different places. Philosophers of ancient Greece such as the **Stoics** and the **Epicureans** made an important contribution to the development of this tradition in the West. **Confucianism** is representative of early humanist thinking in ancient China. Humanist concerns and ideas were also very strongly present in the philosophies of ancient India. As we have seen, humanism surfaced strongly at the time of the Renaissance in western Europe, although predominantly within a Christian context. During the following centuries, now within the context of secularization, a humanist association with criticism of God and religions gathered momentum

The process of secularization is complex. Many trends have contributed to it over the last few hundred years. The rise of science, for example, produced not only new knowledge but also new ways of thinking about the world.[1] The world became something to be analyzed and scientifically explained. The clash between science and religion is most clearly apparent in the fate of Galileo (1564–1642), and in the reaction to Charles Darwin (1809–82). Galileo was an Italian mathematician and astronomer, who upheld the view that the earth revolves around the sun rather than vice versa. He was persecuted by the Church, and obliged to back down. ("And yet . . . it moves," he is reputed to have muttered even in the act of signing a statement to the contrary!)

Darwin was a British naturalist who suggested that the various living species, including humanity, had evolved from earlier forms: in the case of humanity, from apes. The radical aspect of Darwin's findings was not only the idea that higher life-forms developed from lower ones, which blew a hole through traditional notions of how God created the world and humanity. Just as theologically hard to swallow was the suggestion that this process was based on natural selection. According to this theory, the creature best adapted to its environment would survive and the weakest would fall by the wayside. So, for example, giraffes with the longest necks would be best able to reach food on trees; the longest-necked giraffes would therefore survive, and by the laws of inheritance their offspring would be more likely to have long necks. This "survival of the fittest" is logical but leaves little room for divine guidance, because it is based on random biological variations that then give rise to environmental advantage. Darwin met with ridicule from many religious quarters, although others found his observations too convincing to dismiss. The debate between religion and science over evolution continues to this day.

Alongside the rapid advancements in scientific knowledge, society was also altering dramatically. Political history made a significant contribution to this. For example, the old regimes of the West, dominated by the aristocracy and the Christian Church, increasingly gave way to more democratic forms of government and religious pluralism. The colonization of the Americas and Australia by Europeans had a very obvious impact on the development of those nations. The socio-economic background was also undergoing upheaval. Agricultural and industrial revolutions shook up the organization of traditional communities and led to a movement of population from countryside to towns. All of these processes had their part to play, as new patterns of religious beliefs and practices began to unfold.

It is, of course, important to bear in mind the social, economic and political backcloths to secular thinking. However, our analysis will not focus on these developments. Rather, we shall look at what was happening in philosophy. We are going to consider certain key thinkers of the nineteenth century, and see how their ideas promoted secular humanist worldviews. But first, let us set the philosophical scene.

The Enlightenment

Also known as the Age of Reason, the "**Enlightenment**" refers to a cluster of philosophical ideas concentrated in Europe in the seventeenth and eighteenth centuries. Its uniting theme was an emphasis on reason as the only reliable means through which to understand the world. As such, it presented a great challenge to the dominant religion, Christianity. For Christianity was not, of course, based on reason alone, but also on sources such as revelation by God, tradition, scripture, Church authority, and faith. The credibility of Christianity came under attack. It began to seem *unreasonable*: a religion for the simple-minded or the ignorant. People began to think that for a religion to be viable, it had to be possible to explain it in entirely rational terms. The disclosure of God's truths through divine revelation became, for some theologians, simply a supplement to what human reason could work out for itself. Revelation could even be done away with altogether. Matthew Tindal, in *Christianity as Old as Creation* (1730), argued that the Christian **gospel** was, essentially, a republication of the truths evident in nature. What the gospel said, people could have worked out for themselves by using their reason. Key Christian doctrines and traditions were reassessed.

One example of how important Christian ideas were reappraised is to be found in attitudes toward miracles. There was a move toward seeing the miraculous events recorded in the Christian Bible as impossible. David Hume, an important philosopher of the time, made an influential contribution to this debate with his *Essay on Miracles* (1748). The general argument was that miracles could not happen because, judged on the basis of contemporary experience, they were not feasible. The Bible itself also fell under critical scrutiny: German biblical scholars demonstrated its internal contradictions. The Bible, it seemed, could no longer be regarded as the direct Word of God. Instead, it was the product of many (human) hands. The Christ proclaimed by the Christian Church was, moreover, a myth. Behind this unlikely divine redeemer figure lurked a simple Galilean teacher, whose real significance could be found in his moral and spiritual teachings.

Thus, the Enlightenment established a spirit of critical inquiry from which Christian beliefs and theology were certainly not exempt. The critique of the Christian religion, if anything, intensified in the following centuries. Later criticism also included a devastating assault on whether Christianity was either desirable or relevant to modern life. Such criticisms have nourished modern, non-theistic forms of humanism. Of those involved in the assault on religion, most particularly on Christianity, we are now going to look at four major thinkers: Ludwig Feuerbach, Karl Marx, Auguste Comte and Friedrich Nietzsche.

Ludwig Feuerbach (1804–72)

Feuerbach was a German philosopher, whose major work was *The Essence of Christianity* (1841). He wrote at a time in the nineteenth century when the problem of God was the focus of heated debate. His aim was to account for what he termed the "religious illusion" on the basis of psychology. For Feuerbach, the traditional theological schema is reversed: it is not God who creates humanity, but humanity who creates God. Human consciousness expresses its own aspirations through the idea of God. "God," then, really represents human desires and wishes. Those who have no desires, wrote Feuerbach, have no gods either. God has no independent reality and does not exist, except as a human creation. God, in fact, is a myth. So according to Feuerbach, theology is anthropology: which is to say, to study God is really to study humanity. God is the projection of human ideals.

Furthermore, human creation of God actually works to the detriment of humanity. This is because humanity attributes its highest thoughts and values to God, and in doing so, humanity defrauds itself. The ideals of wisdom, justice and love are human properties. Yet humanity projects these ideals onto this mythical being, "God," whose only real existence is in the human imagination. Feuerbach calls religion a vampire. That is because, like a vampire, religion feeds on humanity and steals from it all that is great and wonderful.

At the same time, Feuerbach saw religion as what you might call a necessary evil for human development. Religion had served a purpose as the human race matured. But he thought the time had come for humanity to reclaim for itself what had been projected onto God. This was because, in the religious life, humanity is alienated from its true self and its own greatness. To be alienated from something is to be out of touch with it. Humanity, then, had lost touch with its own true nature, by not realizing that all the greatnesses attributed to God actually belonged to humanity itself.

We have seen that Feuerbach does not believe in the real existence of God, yet he disliked the title "atheist." He insisted that the true atheist was not the person who denied the existence of God, but the person who denied the worth of divine attributes such as love, wisdom and justice. These attributes humanity, at its best, could display. In this sense, Feuerbach did have a concept of the divine. It was simply that he did not think of the divine as a supreme being other than humanity, but rather as the highest qualities of which humanity is capable: again, for example, love, fellowship, mercy and so on. Thus, it is the essence of humanity which is supreme, not a God. Feuerbach is not suggesting here that individual human beings are supreme. Human "divinity" is not attached to particular persons, but achieved in fellowship with others; the essence of humanity is fulfilled through living out humanity's best qualities and ideals.

Thus Feuerbach, whose ideas exerted considerable influence upon his contemporaries, promoted a form of humanism based upon the illusory nature of God and the greatness of human nature. The psychological explanation for religion has continued to be influential, as could also be seen in the work of that other great psychological thinker Sigmund Freud (1856–1939).[2] Like Feuerbach, Freud argued that religion is projection, an illusion, derived from human wishes and needs.

Karl Marx (1818–83)[3]

Marx was a German philosopher and economist; the impact of his major works, *The Communist Manifesto* (1848), and *Das Kapital* (1867–94), has been profound. He came to prominence in the wake of Feuerbach, who has been called the "spiritual father" of **Marxism**. Marx, like Feuerbach, held the opinion that "man makes religion, religion does not make man. Religion is indeed the self-consciousness and self-awareness of man . . ." (Karl Marx, from the introduction to "Towards a critique of Hegel's Philosophy of Right," cited in *A World Religions Reader*, p. 23). However, Marx thought that Feuerbach's conception of humanity was too vague and too abstract, too removed from the concrete realities of human existence. Marx was very concerned with people's actual social and economic circumstances. He thought that in a **capitalist** society the majority of workers were in a state of alienation. To be alienated from something is to be separated from it, to see it as something external to you. You therefore have no personal connection to it nor power over it. Marx thought that this was how workers saw their work; Marx argued that, as workers felt no sense of ownership towards their work, they were alienated from it. The concept of alienation is the key to Marx's critique of capitalist society, which he considered to be oppressive.

Workers were alienated from their work because they did not work for themselves. They worked for others and did not own the product they made. The work did not fulfill the worker. Work provided no satisfaction beyond the means to make a living. Thus the worker had no connection to the product. Work was a stifling of the self, of creativity, of hopes, and dreams. This state of frustration and disconnection from work led to alienation also from self and others. Alienation, ultimately, prevents a person from self-realization; it means leading life in such a way that an individual's true nature cannot be fulfilled.

Marx considered that religion contributed to this state of alienation. Here, Marx's analysis differs from that of Feuerbach. As we have seen, Feuerbach also thought that religion alienated humanity from itself. But, for Feuerbach, this was because religion obscured the true greatness of human nature. People projected their ideals onto God when really these supreme values and attributes belonged to the essence of humanity. Marx thought the opposite: religion obscures, not the greatness of human nature, but its misery.

As we have seen above, Marx thought that workers were alienated from their work in an oppressive social and economic system. This social oppression encouraged people to turn to religion, for it provided consolation and a means to cope with the unpleasantness of existence. So religion is, then, the product of unhappiness and oppression: "Religion is the sigh of the oppressed creature, the feeling of a heartless world . . ." (Karl Marx, from the introduction to "Towards a critique of Hegel's Philosophy of Right," cited in *A World Religions Reader*, p. 23). Yet Marx thought that religion was false, an illusion created by humanity. Thus turning to religion to escape from social alienation only led to spiritual alienation also. Now, according to this analysis, humanity is in a state of both social and spiritual alienation, each helping to produce the other. Social alienation makes people turn to religion, which causes spiritual alienation. But religion enables people to carry on living with their social alienation, by blinding people to their true situation. Religion acts as "the opium of the people,"[4] closing people's eyes to the here and now and focusing them on a mythical afterlife. Religion meant people were less likely to do something about their current situation; it counteracted tendencies toward revolution. Thus, it prolonged the oppressive system which was causing human alienation.

This meant that, to overcome human alienation, a combined assault was needed. It was necessary to do away with both religion and the oppressive socio-economic regimes with which it was associated. Marx thought that once a just socio-economic system was established, people would feel no need to be religious. Religion would have ceased to perform any meaningful function. Marx thought that **communism** would provide a way of living which was both secular and non-oppressive: so communism would be the logical culmination of humanism.

What Marx has bequeathed as a humanist legacy is a stress on the materiality of human existence. He was concerned with actual social and economic conditions. It is not enough simply to theorize, to discuss the freeing of the human spirit. It is also necessary to liberate the poor from the concrete conditions of existence. Marx commented that philosophers interpret the world: the point is to change it.

Auguste Comte (1798–1857)

Comte is another influential thinker who rejected belief in the existence of God in favour of humanist ways of thinking. This French philosopher is also well known as the first person to use the term "sociology."

Comte turned away from traditional religion and developed his own particular philosophy of life, which is in the **positivist** tradition. Positivism is a philosophy that emphasizes scientific, physical laws as the basis for approaching the world and answering society's questions. It stresses logic and reason. Comte was convinced that just as laws were the key to studying the physical world, laws were also the key to studying society. Comte did make it clear that the laws by which the world works could not be absolute, for they are not fully known: they are subject to a continuing process of speculation and observation. Comte's positivism was to provide the foundations of society. He called it the secular "Religion of Humanity."

This positivism, the Religion of Humanity, was the culmination of human development. Comte suggested that humanity went through three stages of knowledge.

First, there was the theological or supernatural stage; secondly, the abstract or metaphysical stage; finally, the positive or scientific stage. The first stage, the theological, was a product of human immaturity; in this state, people turned to gods, spirits, and demons as explanations for the world and for guidance. In the metaphysical stage, with the rise of science, people referred to unseen forces and principles as the basis for explaining the world. However, these abstract forces were not understood or explained. In the third stage, the positive stage, we realize that we must confine our knowledge-claims to what we can demonstrate empirically – that is to say, what we can show on the basis of evidence. This becomes the guiding principle for all of life.

It is in this third and final stage of human development that the Religion of Humanity is established. Entirely secular, freed from theological immaturity, the Religion of Humanity is orderly and hierarchical. The positivist's enhanced knowledge of the laws governing social behavior enables societal evils to be eradicated. Just as the doctor uses medical knowledge to cure physical ills, so the sociologist could employ societal knowledge to cure social ills. Comte's Religion of Humanity placed stress on social love, brotherhood, and doing your duty by your fellows.

The Religion of Humanity was not merely an ethical philosophy. Comte actually founded a new Church. This Positive Church, as it was known, had a twofold motto: Order and Progress. It had its own religious calendar and rituals, its own sacraments. Comte declared himself the High Priest. It even had its own saints, amongst whom were Frederick the Great and the economist Adam Smith.

Comte's positivism is especially interesting for its explicit combining of religion with secularity. Comte's Religion of Humanity had all the things that we might associate with a religion – except God! With its church, sacraments, rituals and saints, the Positive Church raises probing questions about the nature of religion. Comte's Religion of Humanity is not a unique oddity in the history of religions. There are forms of non-theistic humanism today which, like Comte's humanism, have all the trappings of traditional religion: but are devoid of belief in God.

Friedrich Nietzsche (1844–1900)

Nietzsche is a complex and fascinating German thinker who wrote vehemently against religion. Amongst his many significant writings are *Thus Spoke Zarathustra* (1883–5), *Beyond Good and Evil* (1886), *The Gay Science* (1887), and *The AntiChrist* (1888). However, whilst Nietzsche has made a significant contribution to atheist philosophies, we must make it clear that Nietzsche did not share the same values as contemporary secular humanists. Yet he made an important contribution to human-centered philosophies, and inasmuch as his writings focus on the need for human potential to be realized, he has been labeled by some as a humanist. However, so different is his thought from other forms of humanism, he has also been described as an anti-humanist! Nazi Germany drew on aspects of Nietzsche's thought – although it is often considered that the Nazi use of his work was based on misinterpretation of it.

Nietzsche argues that religion is a process of human debasement. That which is best in human nature is allotted to the sphere of "God," and that which is worst to the sphere of "humanity." Humanity has therefore degraded itself. It has deprived itself of its own strengths. Humanity needs to take possession of what is rightfully its own. But it was Christianity as a religion which came in for the fullest measure of Nietzsche's contempt:

> Wherever there are walls I shall inscribe this eternal accusation against Christianity upon them – I can write in letters which make even the blind see . . . I call Christianity the *one* great curse, the *one* great intrinsic depravity . . . – I call it the *one* immortal blemish of mankind . . . (*The AntiChrist*, para 62)

Christianity is, for Nietzsche, the extreme form of human debasement and especially repellent. In Christianity everything that is good or true is seen as the product of God's grace, rather than simply as integral to being human. Another reason why Nietzsche deplored Christianity comes from its focus on the weak. Nietzsche uses the terms "weak" and "strong" quite broadly: he is not meaning simple physical fitness. Nietzsche thought that most people were weak in that they were content to be herd creatures, happy to be the same as everyone else. They would not understand someone who dared to rise above the common crowd and exercise their own strength and creativity – in Nietzsche's terms, a "Superman" or "Overman." Christianity was too focused on life's losers for Nietzsche's taste.

He also despised the way in which Christianity seemed to advocate toleration of present suffering. He thought that Christian virtues limit human potential. Notions of guilt and sin dragged people down and held them back. Furthermore, the promise of eternal and heavenly life made Christianity into a "poison," diminishing the grand tragedy of real life. Even worse, Christianity did not only corrupt the mediocre and the lower classes, in whom Nietzsche had little interest, but attracted to it men of strength.

God, to Nietzsche, exists only in the human mind, where his presence is both distorting and deplorable. It is necessary to proclaim the death of God, especially the Christian God, in order for humanity to achieve its fullest potential. So, says Nietzsche: God is dead! This is not simply a statement of fact; Nietzsche does not mean that there was a real divine being, who actually died; nor does he mean that God is dead in the sense that nobody believes in God anymore. Proclaiming the death of God is the expression of a choice, a rejection of God and the values associated with him. Indeed, in this sense, the death of God is actually the murder of God; as Nietzsche puts it, "We are the assassins of God." And yet, Nietzsche saw this choice yielding its results only slowly: "Lightning and thunder require time; the light of the stars requires time; deeds, though done, still require time to be seen and heard" (*The Gay Science*, para 125). The shadow of the dead God falls long.

Nietzsche understood that for those emerging from their theistic illusions, life could seem threatening. The void, he said, opens at their feet; they feel terribly insecure, as though they are falling, as though life has lost all value and meaning.

But then, a very few can manage to move beyond this. What had seemed a crime – a murder – becomes an act of triumphant conquest. God is dead! No longer need humanity stagnate, caught in its illusions of a world ordered by God. With the death of God, humanity can and must of its own energies go upwards, onwards: must, in fact, become the Superman. It is an occasion for rejoicing.

> Indeed, we philosophers and "free spirits" feel, when we hear the news that "the old god is dead," as if a new dawn shone on us; our hearts overflow with gratitude, surprise . . . the sea, *our* sea, lies open again; perhaps there has never yet been such an "open sea." (*The Gay Science*, para 343)

Atheism has then become the necessary condition for human greatness, freedom and responsibility. Through the death of God, human debasement can be overcome, human exaltation achieved. Yet Nietszche saw also a foreshadow of doom. He believed that along with the death of God went the collapse of traditional values and interpretations of the world. As we have seen, Nietzsche thought that to be a positive thing, and he sought vigorously to affirm human life through a revaluation and reinterpretation of the world. Yet he also saw that the disintegration of traditional values would spark off a deeply negative reaction, and that this would be the coming of **nihilism**. Nihilism is the view that there is no meaning or value in the world, and thus, it could be argued, no justification for morality. In Nietzsche's later works, written shortly before his descent into insanity, he saw himself as the herald of a tragic era. He foresaw that Europe would be enveloped in darkness and that a black tide was rising. Thanks to him, he thought, a catastrophe was at hand: it would be the coming of nihilism.

Exercises

3 List the main reasons for rejecting belief in God given by Feuerbach, Marx, Nietzsche, and Comte. What philosophies of life did they propose or advocate instead?

4 Consider the following passage by Robert G. Ingersoll, who has already been mentioned as an important advocate of "free thought" in nineteenth-century America:

> Secularism is the religion of humanity; it embraces the affairs of this world; it is interested in everything that touches the welfare of a sentient being; it advocates attention to the particular planet in which we happen to live; it means that each individual counts for something; it is a declaration of intellectual independence; it means that the pew is superior to the pulpit, that those who bear the burdens shall have the profits and that they who fill the purse shall hold the strings. It is a protest against theological oppression, against ecclesiastical tyranny, against being the serf, subject or slave of any phantom or of the priest of any phantom. It is a protest against wasting this life for the sake of one that we know not of. It proposes to let the gods take care of themselves. It is another name for common sense . . .

(Robert Green Ingersoll, "Secularism," The Independent Pulpit, Waco, Texas, 1887; http://www.infidels.org/library/historical/robert_ingersoll/secularism.html)

Why is Ingersoll in favor of secularism as the "Religion of Humanity"?
5   Express in your own words the feelings that Nietzsche is describing in the passage below:

> The madman jumped into their midst and pierced them with his eyes. "Whither is God?" he cried; "I will tell you. We have killed him – you and I. All of us are his murderers. But how did we do this? How could we drink up the sea? Who gave us the sponge to wipe away the entire horizon? . . . Whither are we going? . . . Are we not plunging continually? Backward, sideward, forward, in all directions? Is there still any up or down? Are we not straying as though an infinite nothing? Do we not feel the breath of empty space? Has it not become colder? (The Gay Science, para 125)

The four influential thinkers discussed so far – Feuerbach, Marx, Comte and Nietzsche – demonstrate different lines of humanist thinking. All four have different philosophies with which they propose to replace Christianity, but all four share a perspective which starts from the human, esteems the human, and is concerned to free human potential. We can see, then, that humanism may be identifiable by its focus on humanity, but otherwise covers a very diverse range of thinking. Having briefly examined some of the modern roots of humanist thinking, let us turn now to humanism in one of its twentieth-century guises: contemporary secular humanism.

Worldviews

As we have already noted, secular humanism is skeptical about the supernatural; secular humanists are atheist or agnostic and have chosen to reject worldviews based upon the existence of God or any other type of supernatural being or beings. This distinguishes secular humanism from theistic forms of humanism, such as Christian humanism. However, as the American Humanist Association's *Humanist Manifesto II* (1973; see Markham (ed.), *A World Religions Reader*, pp. 42–6) states: "views that merely reject theism are not equivalent to humanism. They lack commitment to the positive belief in the possibilities of human progress and to the values central to it." It is worth stressing this point. Non-theistic modern humanism does not only embody a rejection of God but is coupled to an affirmation of humanity and the potential for value in existence in a world quite stripped of belief in God. So according to this viewpoint, meaning and purpose in life do not in fact depend upon the existence of God. For secular humanists, life has whatever meaning and purpose we give it; we create our own. Matt Cherry (Executive Director of the

Council for Secular Humanism) and Molleen Matsumara put it this way: "Humanists believe the meaning of life is to live a life of meaning" (Cherry and Matsumara, "10 Myths About Secular Humanism", *Free Inquiry Magazine*, vol. 18 no. 1, http://www.SecularHumanism.org/library/fi/cherry_18_1.01.html).[5]

Let us return, however, to our earlier point, and explore in slightly more detail the reasons for modern humanist rejection of theism and traditional religions. Secular humanists identify several aspects of traditional religions which they hold to be actually harmful to the human race. They do, however, also recognize that religious experience is a significant dimension of human life and that, at its best, religion can inspire high ethical ideals. Why, then, do secular humanists support a nontheistic view of the world and what do they see to be negative about orthodox religious beliefs and practices? The following reasons are a sample of some commonly cited arguments. It is important to remember, though, that secular humanism is a philosophy of life but not a set of doctrines: secular humanists do not all believe exactly the same things. But typically, a secular humanist might argue in favor of atheism or agnosticism and reject traditional religions on the following grounds:

- There is simply not enough evidence to demonstrate the existence of any kind of God.[6] No divine purpose can be seen at work either in the universe at large or in human lives. Modern scientific knowledge allows us to see that the universe is not dependent on divine initiative and planning. There is no scientific basis for belief in life after bodily death. Richard Dawkins and Julian Huxley are well-known representatives of this type of thinking.[7] We might also quote here from *A Secular Humanist Declaration*, which was made in 1980 by the Council for Democratic and Secular Humanism (now the Council for Secular Humanism):

  > However, we find that traditional views of the existence of God either are meaningless, have not yet been demonstrated to be true, or are tyrannically exploitative. Secular humanists may be agnostics, atheists, rationalists, or skeptics, but they find insufficient evidence for the claim that some divine purpose exists for the universe.

  This emphasis on what can be demonstrated to be at least probably true is very typical of humanist outlooks. When it comes to understanding the world and solving human problems, humanists argue that we should look to reason and science as our most reliable tools – not to any hypothetical deity, nor to any supposedly divinely inspired books. There is no way to test the truth or validity of religious claims, and therefore the only knowledge we have is that coming from our own senses and reason. Humanists acknowledge that even this knowledge is imperfect and may be wrong; this does not mean that we should abandon reason and science as sources of knowledge, however. It means we should be aware that all our judgments, whether moral, social, or scientific, are

tentative and require constant critique. Furthermore, so there is no misunderstanding here, it should be understood that secular humanists do not see reason
as antithetically opposed to emotion or feeling, nor advocate science whilst despis-
ing the arts. Rather, reason and compassion, science and the arts, complement
each other in the development of a balanced and fulfilled human person.

This kind of argument is also very typical of modern humanism because it is
naturalistic. This is a feature common to the forms of humanism under discussion. Naturalism is the view that everything belongs to the world of nature
and makes sense within those boundaries. There is no need to call on hypothetical supernatural forces, or to attribute moral and spiritual purpose to the
universe independent of that which we choose to give it. In terms of method,
modern science is naturalistic: it seeks to explain its data with reference to natural laws and phenomena.

- Concepts such as "heaven" and "hell" are bad for the human race. According
  to the American Humanist Association's *Humanist Manifesto II* (1973): "Promises
  of immortal salvation and fear of eternal damnation are both illusory and harmful" (see *A World Religions Reader*, pp. 42–6). This is because "they distract humans
  from present concerns, from self-actualization and from rectifying social in-
  justices." Religions tend to deflect attention from humanity's own potential and
  responsibilities by encouraging dependence upon God and belief in an afterlife.
  This can make people more passive in their lives and less likely to strive for
  fulfillment and social change. This is a kind of argument that stems from the
  Marxist tradition, in which religion is seen as "the opium of the people." For
  secular humanists, no God will save us. We must save ourselves.
- Religions may lead to discrimination against other groups with different
  beliefs.[8] Religion sometimes plays a role in causing or exacerbating wars and
  conflicts. Religion can thus promote intolerance and violence, rather than harmony and peace. Generally, secular humanists advocate tolerance of other people's
  beliefs and practices as long as they do not cause damage to others. Ironically,
  this principle of tolerance actually includes other people's religions: secular humanists support the right to freedom of choice and expression in the religious sphere.
  So, whilst secular humanists maintain their right to be free from religion, they
  support other people's right to practice their religion. We might also point out
  here that toleration of others' perspectives does not mean believing that all points
  of view are equally valid. All ideas and beliefs are open to critical scrutiny, and
  it is possible to believe both that a person is wrong, but also that they have a
  right to their opinion, and that all parties can benefit from an exchange of ideas
  and arguments.
- Religions can act to legitimate oppression. For example, the Christian Bible has
  been used to justify anti-Semitism and persecution of Jewish people. Religion
  can also bolster up unfair social and political regimes, by encouraging those suffering under them to believe it is the will of God. One of the most pervasive
  forms of oppression throughout the world's religions is the roles historically allotted to women. This has been vigorously challenged, especially in the twentieth

century with the rise of feminist perspectives.[9] The increased awareness of how women have been discriminated against is demonstrated in this book itself, which identifies gender issues as a pressing contemporary problem and a central theme to be addressed. This being so, we are now going to turn to this theme as a case study for how religion can institute or encourage oppressive systems, ideas and attitudes. Since much of the critique of religion in the West has historically focused on Christianity as the prevailing religion, we shall continue this focus by looking primarily at feminist critique of Christianity. It is important to note, however, that feminist critique has been directed at all the world's religions and similar trends can be discerned.

Case Study: Religion as Oppressive

Feminists are those who perceive the relationship between the sexes as one of inequality at the expense of women, and who seek to alter that relationship. It can be demonstrated that women have been accorded fewer rights and privileges than men in spheres ranging from the social, economic and religious, to the legal and political. Women's roles have been both devalued and restricted. Society is seen to be **patriarchal**. Literally this means that society is ruled by men. More generally it refers to a whole system of structures which favor men over women, and to societies which are dominated by males.

Feminist opinion ranges from simply wanting women to have equal civil rights as men to more radical perspectives, which believe that men are oppressors by nature and only through separating from them can women be free. It is important to beware of generalizations when talking about feminism, because it covers a wide range of political and philosophical perspectives. Feminists of many different standpoints are, however, united in their perception of traditional religion as oppressive to women. However, the critiques differ in their intensity: some feminists believe their particular religious tradition can, after a measure of reinterpretation, be rescued. Others, with varying levels of regret, think that the tradition is irredeemably biased against women.

Where Christianity is concerned, the well-known critic Daphne Hampson argues that feminism puts forward such a devastating critique that it "represents the death-knell of Christianity as a viable religious option" [Daphne, Hampson, *Theology and Feminism* (Oxford: Blackwell, 1990, p. 1)]. Hampson also argues that the only logical and consistent reaction a feminist can have to the Church is to leave it.

By definition, feminism cannot accept a worldview that sees women as inferior or subordinate to men. That men and women are created equal in the world and in society, as well as equal in value before God, is the starting point of feminism. Most forms of Christianity, however, require taking the Bible and its claims seriously. The problem goes deeper than dealing with a stray text here or there in the Bible, such as the notorious 1 Corinthians 14: 34 and 1 Timothy 2: 12, which instruct women to keep silent. More profoundly, the image of God in the Bible is overwhelmingly male. Christ is the Son of God the Father, and God is presented as the God "of our fathers," that is, of Abraham, Isaac and Jacob. Christianity is a historical religion and cannot sidestep its historical reference – and that reference is to a history steeped in patriarchy.

A crucial theological point emerges from the overwhelming predominance of masculine language for God. According to the Christian tradition, humanity is created in the image of God. If a religion presents its God in predominantly male terms, how can a woman see herself and be seen as fully and equally in the image of God? Indeed, the conclusion that she cannot, in those circumstances, be seen as fully in the image of God has been reached not only by contemporary feminists but also throughout history, notably by the founding Fathers of the Christian faith.

The Fathers of the early Church understood that to be in the "image of God" could not be a physical image, for God does not have a body. Therefore, it was through the possession of rationality and the capacity for freedom and dominion that man was in God's image. Those, of course, are just the qualities that have historically been denied to women. According to Augustine (354–430), by virtue of what woman symbolizes in her bodily difference, she is only the image of God together with her husband, whilst man "is the image of God as fully and completely as when the woman too is joined with him in one" (*De Trinitate* 7.7.10). The point that women cannot be seen as fully in the image of a God spoken of in almost exclusively masculine terms can be taken even further. One of the leading lights of radical feminism, Mary Daly, pronounced that if God is male – then male is God.

Another feminist criticism is that divine–human relations have usually been pictured as hierarchical in nature, with the line of command being God–Christ–man–woman. Genesis is the biblical book which tells the story of how humanity and the world were created. Interpretations of Genesis have usually upheld this hierarchical view of relationships; woman, so the story goes, is derived from man and is therefore secondary in human creation. Moreover, woman was created not just *from* man, but *for* man. The first woman, Eve, was scapegoated as the cause of humanity's Fall and the introduction of sin and evil into the world. As the Church Father Tertullian (160–225) said of women: "*You* are the devil's gateway . . . *You* destroyed so easily God's image, man" (*de Cult. Fem.* 1.1). In the New Testament, 1 Timothy 2: 11–15, we find:

> Let a woman learn in silence with all submissiveness. I permit no woman to teach or to have authority over men; she is to keep silent. For Adam was formed first, then Eve; and Adam was not deceived, but the woman was deceived and became a transgressor. Yet woman will be saved through bearing children, if she continues in faith and love and holiness, with modesty.

Women in the Christian tradition have also been associated both with a sinful sexuality and with bodily impurity. Eve has been said to represent the body and bodily appetites, and Adam to represent the realm of spirit and intellect. *Male* and *female* were thus seen to represent a whole series of dualities: intellect/body, active/passive, rational/irrational, order/disorder. Menstruation has historically been seen as a form of pollution. When the sacramental priesthood of men developed in the sixth to ninth centuries, one of the reasons given for denying women contact with the "holy" was their bodily impurity. The influential Protestant theologian Luther (1483–1546) sums up this attitude rather well: "God has created man with broad chests and shoulders, not broad hips, so that men can understand wisdom. But the place where the filth flows out is small. With women it's the other way around. That's why they have lots of filth and little wisdom" (*D. Martin Luther's sämmtiliche Werke*. Erlangen and Frankfurt, 1826–57). The purity argument was voiced by some in the Anglican debate over the ordination of women, and in the Orthodox Church, technically speaking, women may still not take **communion** during menstruation or for a period of forty days after childbirth.

The Christian Bible tells us that man is the head of the woman. Luther described the life of the ideal woman: "It is the highest, most valuable treasure that a woman can have to be subject to a man and certain that her works are pleasing to him. What could be happier for her?" (*D. Martin Luther's sämmtiliche Werke*. Erlangen and Frankfurt, 1826–57). This reflects Luther's view that:

> Women are created for no other purpose than to serve men and be their helpers. If women grow weary or even die while bearing children, that doesn't harm anything. Let them bear children to death; they are created for that. Childbirth is the manner in which women perform God's will, by suffering and perhaps dying through these delicious pains. (*D. Martin Luther's sämmtiliche Werke*. Erlangen and Frankfurt, 1826–57)

So for those who take the equality of women seriously, the Christian Bible and tradition present something of a problem. Nor, for feminists, is the relationship between women and men the only problem with patriarchal religions. Underlying much of feminist theology is a definition of patriarchy implying considerably more than simply domination of women by men. It is not just that personal and institutional power is largely concentrated in the hands of men, but that the whole structure of relationships in the world is hierarchically ordered: "power" can often seem to boil down to "domination." Many scholars consider that at the root of this hierarchical ordering of the world are those dualities we talked about earlier, in which the universe is broken down into superior/inferior divisions. Dualism splits the world: the classical split is to set spirit over body.

Sexism has long operated as a symbol of this split universe – as God is spoken of in male terms, nature is spoken of in female terms. But this is not the only dualism. According to the feminist critique, the tendency to divide the world into superior/inferior is at the roots of patterns of domination and subordination. The issues of domination and oppression, not only in terms of male and female, but also in terms of race and class and geography, are powerfully raised by the feminist

critique. Feminist theology has itself been criticized – and justifiably – for replacing the white middle-class man as figure of true humanity with white middle-class
men and women. Patriarchy then is seen to be the cause not only of sexism, but
also of racism, classism, and environmental exploitation. This is not seen *with* that,
but this is seen *over* that. Associated with patriarchy is the ideal of aggressive com-
petitiveness, be it in politics, economics, or war. The triumph of patriarchal structures comes when they are accepted and recognized as *the* way to order society, not
just by the groups in positions of privilege but also by the groups at the bottom of
the patriarchal heap.

So, fundamentally, the feminist critique of patriarchy is a critique of power structures. From the Christian theological point of view, this critique highlights not just
that men and women are both in the image of God, but also that our image of
God is powerfully affected by our image of men. God is the Almighty Father, Lord
and King. Many feminists find the dominance of these metaphors unsatisfactory,
not just because they are couched in male terms but because they speak of God as
distant, controlling and transcendent. Thus, religion in a patriarchal society is for
many feminists inevitably bound up with patterns of oppression and used to reinforce them. This identification of religion as oppressive is a potent argument against
religion for the humanist, who usually places justice and individual rights and free-
doms high on the moral agenda.

Exercises

4   Woody Allen commented in 1973: "If only God would give me some clear sign!
    Like making a large deposit in my name at a Swiss bank." Reflect on the
    assertion by secular humanists that there is no evidence for belief in a deity
    or the supernatural. Do you agree?
5   What difficulties does modern science put in the way of religious belief?
6   Apply a feminist critique to any religion other than Christianity.
7   *For Discussion:* Can you identify ways in which religions either historically
    or at the present time may have contributed toward violence?

Ethics

By now it should be clear that humanism is a profoundly ethical philosophy of life.
It has already been mentioned that humanism is not a set of particular doctrines;
humanists may make quite divergent political and moral judgments. There are
certain principles which are common, though, to most forms of humanism. Most
of these principles are to do with human freedom and tolerance, qualified by the
proviso that no harm should be done to others. Free thought, for example, is very
much at the heart of humanism. There is nothing that, theoretically, people should
not be able to investigate, to challenge and to doubt. Thought should be free, critical and open to new evidence and new ideas. No political or religious institution

should attempt to shackle people's minds and restrict inquiry and ideas. Thus, the attempt by some Muslim groups to censor Salman Rushdie's *The Satanic Verses* (1988) goes quite against the spirit of humanism.[10]

This ideal of free inquiry, furthermore, "entails recognition of civil liberties as integral to its pursuit, that is, a free press, freedom of communication, the right to organize opposition parties and to join voluntary associations, and freedom to cultivate and publish the fruits of scientific, philosophical, artistic, literary, moral, and religious freedom" (*A Secular Humanist Declaration*, 1980). An insistence on civil and human rights means that most humanists are deeply opposed to totalitarian or oppressive systems, whether to the political left or right, whether religious or secular. Humanists support societies which are open and pluralistic; humanism there-fore has a natural affinity with democracy as a political system and usually advoc-ates the separation of Church and State. But humanism is not a political creed: humanists can be Republicans or Democrats, Labour or Conservative.

Secular humanists often contend that religions are morally authoritarian over issues which are far from clear-cut, and that religious factions try to impose their own ethical codes upon others as a legal requirement. For example, abortion, reproductive rights, sexual behavior, and voluntary euthanasia are all ethical "hot potatoes." Secular humanists believe in the right to self-determination in such matters, which means that it is up to the individual. So, for example, where sexual behavior is concerned, secular humanists argue that consenting adults should be free to choose their own mode of sexual expression if no harm to others is thereby caused.

In the moral arena, secular humanists begin with humanity, not God. Moral values and ideals come from human experience, and need no sanction from any supposedly higher power. Whether an action is right or wrong depends on its con-sequences, not on any divinely inspired moral code. People should be free to choose their own paths in life based on their own needs and desires – again subject to the proviso that this does not harm other people. Moral principles stem from the applica-tion of human reason, with the goal of seeking the common good of humanity. Such moral principles may be very difficult to decide in the complexities of real life; humanists are aware of the need to take responsibility for these hard moral choices.

Modern humanist stress on responsibility extends out beyond our own selves to the wider community across the globe, reaching to the environment. Thus whilst humanism strongly supports human freedom, this is not the freedom of anarchy. Individuals should be free to fulfill themselves, but allied to this is a sense of respon-sibility. Care, compassion, and respect for other people and the non-human world are important values.

The worldwide context of responsibility is also significant. Humanists generally promote international cooperation and dialogue, with the aim of building global peace and justice. Humanists often work to secure human rights in every country of the world. Humanists may also be interested not only in greater political free-doms across the world, but also in greater social and economic equality between and within the nations. The commitment is to all humankind; this is "the highest commitment of which we are capable; it transcends the narrow allegiances of church, state, party, class or race in moving toward a wider vision of human potentiality" (*Humanist Manifesto II*, 1973; see *A World Religions Reader*, pp. 42–6).

Exercises

8   Summarize the main ethical perspectives of modern humanism.

9   "When men can no longer be theists, they must, if they are civilized, become humanists" (Walter Lippmann, 1929). Discuss.

10   *For Discussion*: What justification might there be for acting morally in a world without God? Or does abandoning belief in God necessarily lead to nihilism?

Modern Expressions

Modern humanism now finds focus through a large number of organizations, with national bodies from New Zealand to Cuba and including groups such as the Society for Humanistic Judaism, and African Americans for Humanism. Nearly one hundred of these humanist organizations subscribe to the International Humanist and Ethical Union, formed in 1952. Places where humanist societies are particularly strong include North America, northwestern Europe, and India. Education, international development work, community work, publishing, and campaigning for human rights are amongst the activities of humanist societies. Humanism is not, however, one single philosophy or grouping. This is reflected in the variety of names by which humanism goes: amongst these, you may well see references to scientific humanism, democratic humanism, naturalistic humanism, religious humanism, or atheistic humanism – or, of course, to secular humanism! Generally, these forms of humanism can be distinguished from theistic types of humanism (such as Christian humanism). They would normally share the worldviews and ethical perspectives outlined above, which might be summarized as naturalistic, democratic, compassionate, and reliant on reason and science.

One of the most interesting paradoxes in the modern expression of humanism is the question of whether or not it is religious. We can see this quandary very clearly in the distinction made between religious humanism and secular humanism. Both share the same basic lifestances and ethical principles. Both signed the Humanist Manifestos of 1933 and 1973. The debate over whether or not humanism is a religion goes on both within the humanist movement and outside it.

This may seem confusing. If both religious and secular humanism share the same general views, then presumably that means religious humanism can also be described as non-theistic, and – like secular humanism – does not depend on beliefs in the supernatural, the afterlife or the divine. How can this be so? If modern humanism is non-theistic, then religious humanism may seem like a contradiction in terms. However, we must remember here what we learned of Auguste Comte's Religion of Humanity – which was entirely secular and entailed no belief in God or the supernatural. There are also two semantic points we may note about describing humanism as a non-theistic religion.

First, we must consider what we mean by the word "religion." Religion does not necessarily involve belief in God or other supernatural phenomena. Rather, religion can be functionally defined. According to this definition, what is important about religion is not the particular belief-system it involves, but its role and function in society. Religion serves the needs of particular social groups, offering the opportunity for shared rituals, meetings, and rationale for life. The social anthropologist Emile Durkheim[11] stressed the functional aspects of religion in the late nineteenth century. It would seem quite possible to affirm the value of religion for the role it plays in the lives of communities and individuals, without reference to the sacred, divine, or transcendent. This tends to be the case for religious humanists. Describing humanism as religious means seeing humanism as a worldview and ethical perspective that fulfills the same *functions* as theistic religions.

Secondly, if humanism can be described as a non-theistic religion, we may wish to give some more thought to what is meant by "non-theistic." And what is chiefly important here is that non-theistic does not equate to atheistic. Whilst all atheists are non-theists, not all non-theists are atheists. Agnosticism may also be described as non-theistic. So might any philosophy of life or perspective which is put forward without reference to God. Whether God does or does not exist is then beside the point. So a worldview might be described as non-theistic if it does not rely in any way upon the existence of God – but such a worldview does not *necessarily* preclude the existence of God. However, as a naturalistic philosophy, humanism is based only on what enters into our experience of the world, upon our own reason and feelings, and upon science. So whilst some religious humanists may remain open to the question of whether there is or is not a God, their vision of life is formulated on human experience and with no reference to religious dogma, creed, or authority.

Ethical Culture, the Ethical Union, or Ethical Humanism as it is also known, is an example of what can be called religious humanism. It entails no beliefs about the supernatural. Ethical living is at its heart; it is a religion centered on life and on this world only. It is the ordinary experience of this world, this life, that inspires reverence, devotion, and joy in the Ethical Humanist. Ethical Humanism stresses its spiritual dimension, which gives it an affinity with religious worldviews, whilst rejecting the creeds, authorities, metaphysics and supernaturalism that traditional religions usually entail. It neither affirms nor denies God, this being a matter for the individual; its philosophy of life is non-theistic and without reference to a divine being.

What Ethical Humanism offers is a religious community, serving social needs, as well as a philosophy of life and a sense of shared purpose. Social and cultural meetings, weddings, funerals, and child-welcoming ceremonies may form part of the religious fabric of an Ethical Humanist community. Their leaders are trained and in the USA are legally recognized as ministers of religion. Religious Humanists may also very often find a home in Unitarian Universalist congregations. Here too non-dogmatism allows for a wide range of stances with respect to "God."

Secular humanism is a term which has only come to general and widespread use in the last thirty or so years. It stands in contrast to religious humanism because it explicitly considers itself non-religious as well as non-theistic. Matt Cherry and Molleen Matsumara are firm about this: "Secular humanism is not a religion by any definition: There are no supernatural beliefs, no creeds that all humanists are required to accept, no sacred texts or required rituals. Humanists are not expected or required to have 'faith' in what is said by any authority, living or dead, human or 'supernatural'" (Cherry and Matsumara, "10 Myths About Secular Humanism," *Free Inquiry Magazine*, vol. 18 no. 1, http://www.SecularHumanism.org/library/fi/cherry_18_1.01.html)

It is sometimes claimed that secular humanism in the USA was declared to be a religion by the Supreme Court. This is a misunderstanding stemming from the *Torcaso* v. *Watkins* case of 1961. Torcaso, a humanist, refused to swear that he believed in the existence of God and was thus refused his commission as a notary public. When this was brought to a court of law, Torcaso won. The belief that the case had defined secular humanism as a religion came from a footnote which Justice Hugo Black added to his decision. The footnote stated: "Among religions in this country which do not teach what would generally be considered a belief in the existence of God are Buddhism, Taoism, Ethical Culture, Secular Humanism, and others." However, such footnotes do not have the force of law, but are simply commentary. Furthermore, in 1994 the Federal Circuit Court issued a ruling on the *Peloza* v. *Capistrano School District* case, which explicitly stated that secular humanism is not in fact a religion for legal purposes. This case came about when a science teacher argued that he was being obliged to teach the "religion" of secular humanism because the school district had put evolution on the science syllabus.

Conservative religious critics of secular humanism often contend that evolution is one of its central tenets. In fact, that is not quite the case. Contemporary science has presented considerable evidence to demonstrate evolution in the natural world, which is why secular humanists tend to support it as a theory. Secular humanists would argue that evolution should be on a science syllabus because it represents a dominant strand of scientific thinking and there could be no scientific reason for excluding it. However, that does not mean it is beyond critique. Most scientific theories are modified and improved over time as knowledge and understanding grows. Secular humanists are, though, as we have seen, committed to naturalistic accounts of human existence.

Of course, traditional religions also have groups whose ideas and viewpoints have humanist roots. Usually these find fullest expression in the liberal wings of particular religious traditions. It is ironic, but frequently a liberal Christian, say, would find more shared opinion and common ground with a secular humanist than with their fundamentalist counterpart. Both theistic and non-theistic members of the modern world share cultural heritages, which frequently include humanistic ideas. However, it is outside traditional religions that humanism in the modern sense flourishes, as a distinct philosophy of life which is thoroughly human-centered.

To be a secular humanist is, then, to start and end with humanity: not God. A suitable figurehead for secular humanism is Prometheus, who in Greek mythology stole fire from the gods to give to humankind. Thoroughly focused on this world, secular humanism is both naturalistic and non-theistic. Yet secular humanists do not find this world in consequence to be dreary and bleak. Wonder and joy are to be found here, along with suffering and pain. The argument is that waiting upon a world to follow diminishes human engagement with the here and now; the secular humanist aims to live life to the full. This is not merely a **hedonistic** philosophy, valuing pleasure above all. For humanists, the fullest life is to be lived in commitment to others. And for the secular humanist, God is a hypothesis we no longer require.

Exercises

11 Frederick Edwords is the Executive Director of the American Humanist Association. Comment on his assertion that: "Religious Humanism should not be seen as an alternative faith, but rather as an alternative way of being religious."

12 Is secular humanism a religion? Consider both sides of the argument and justify your conclusion.

13 Present the case either for or against secular humanism.

14 Consider the compatibility of humanism with a religious tradition of your choice. You might wish to consider issues such as:

- Are other religions tolerated?
- Do central ecclesiastical authorities regulate beliefs and worship?
- Are diverse theological opinions within the religion tolerated?
- What is the relationship to civil and political government?
- What ethical principles characterize it?
- What social structure is associated with it?

Conclusions

Secular humanism is a human-centered philosophy of life which emphasizes both reason and compassion. It is non-theistic and naturalistic. It is not a set of doctrines but more an attitude of mind. Ethically, secular humanists value freedom of thought and action, but this is coupled with a sense of responsibility toward one's fellows. Secular humanism is not simply equivalent to atheism or agnosticism, because it is a very positive philosophy which stresses human worth and potential in a global context. It is debated whether secular humanism can be called a religion.

GLOSSARY

Agnosticism The viewpoint that there is not sufficient evidence to assert that God exists although the possibility is not ruled out.

Atheism The denial of the existence of God.

Capitalism An economic system which is based on private ownership and a free market.

Communion Christian religious practice in which bread and wine are sanctified and consumed in remembrance of the death of Jesus.

Communism An economic system which is organized for the benefit of all members and in which property is collectively owned.

Confucianism Philosophies based on the teaching of Confucius (ca. 552–479 BCE).

Enlightenment A cluster of philosophical ideas in eighteenth-century Europe which emphasized the use of reason and critical assessment.

Epicureans A Greek school of philosophy stemming from the fourth century BCE, which emphasized pleasure as the greatest good for humanity.

Freethinker Somebody who embraces free rational inquiry and who rejects authority and dogma.

Gospel In Christianity, the "good news" about Jesus Christ. Four books of the Christian Bible are known as gospels (Matthew, Mark, Luke, and John).

Hedonism A devotion to pleasure.

Marxism Karl Marx's economic and political ideas; Marxism stresses the idea of a class struggle and sees communism as the logical development from an oppressive capitalist system.

Naturalism The viewpoint that everything belongs to the world of nature and can be studied on those terms.

Nihilism The view that there is no justification for values or purpose in life.

Patriarchy A male-dominated or male-ruled society.

Positivism A philosophy stressing what can be known through the senses and demonstrated to be true.

Renaissance A revival of classical art, literature, and philosophy, which began in Italy and spread across Europe during the fourteenth to sixteenth centuries.

Secular Not relating to religion or to a religious body; worldly.

Secularization A process by which society becomes less dependent on religious beliefs and practices.

Stoics A Greek school of philosophy stemming from the fourth century BCE which suggested that the goal for humanity was freedom from passions.

Notes and References

1   See *A World Religions Reader*, second edition, edited by Ian S. Markham (Oxford: Blackwell Publishers, 2000), pp. 19–22. Hereafter, *A World Religions Reader*.
2   Ibid., pp. 24–7.
3   Ibid., pp. 23–4.
4   Karl Marx, from the introduction to "Towards a critique of Hegel's Philosophy of Right," cited in Markham (ed.), *A World Religions Reader*, p. 23.
5   Markham (ed.), *A World Religions Reader*, pp. 37–40.
6   Ibid., pp. 29–31.
7   Ibid., pp. 21–2.
8   Ibid., pp. 31–5.
9   Ibid., pp. 40–2.
10   Ibid., pp. 35–7, 310.
11   Ibid., pp. 27–8.

Chapter 8

....

Hinduism

Tinu Ruparell

The "Hindu Mind"

Worldviews

Institutions and Rituals

Modern Expressions

Women in Hinduism

Introduction

To explain Hinduism in a relatively short chapter is, by some accounts, an impossible task. One of the most telling statements I have ever heard about all things
Indian – and of course this would include, perhaps paradigmatically so, that diverse
extended family of religious traditions falling under the umbrella term "Hinduism"
– is that in India, if anything can be said to be true, its opposite is also true. A
statement like that leaves one speechless, and perhaps rightly so. Nevertheless, I shall
try in this chapter to sketch out a reasonable map of this most slippery yet substantial religious tradition. To begin, let me offer three metaphors: the first concerns the diversity inherent in Hinduism and the second relates to the integrity of,
or similarities between, Hindu traditions. These two metaphors together fall under
the category of "The Hindu Mind," which for the purposes of this chapter will
serve to indicate the broad outlines of the tradition as well as some context for
what will follow. The third metaphor will give us a key for discussing some of the
main features of Hinduism through the rest of the chapter.

The "Hindu Mind"

So to our first metaphor. In Calcutta's botanical gardens is a tree: not just any tree,
but a great Banyan (*ficus Bengalhensis*). Banyan trees are notable in that they grow
and spread by sending down aerial shoots which take root, become thick and strong,
and eventually become indistinguishable from the original trunk or the many other

Sculpture of Shiva Nataraja from the Old Royal Palace, Patan, Nepal.
Photo: Corbis/Macduff Everton.

old aerial shoots. The Calcutta Banyan (well over 200 years old now and having a canopy of about 4 acres) resembles a veritable forest – a host of trees and branches without any apparent botanical center – yet it is a single growing organism, imbued throughout with the same life-sap. The spreading nature of Banyans has resulted in this tree becoming *polycentric* or "many centered" – macrocosmically one and microcosmically many. In other words, it is a network or web of particular "trees" integrally connected to one another. It is no longer possible to identify the original trunk, nor to fix the boundaries of one "tree" from its neighbors, since the edges of one part of the Banyan fuse and overlap with the others and create a single complex forest. The view of Hinduism I wish to describe is like this ancient Banyan. What appears to be a large, overgrown, and diverse forest of religious traditions is also the single growing tree of Hinduism. The original trunk of Hinduism is no longer identifiable and the tradition as a whole is now polycentric. Furthermore, the various Hindu traditions show immense diversity: just as not all parts of the forest look alike, not all of the Hindu traditions look alike – but there is an underlying integrity. And just as, over the centuries, some sections of the ancient Banyan have waned, died, resurrected in new forms, or vanished forever, Hindu traditions have come into being, flourished, changed, and sometimes died – the dead sections still exhibiting some influence on the survivors, if only by providing growing space for them. Hinduism has thus survived over the centuries as an integrated whole, though its form and content has changed. This holistic, integrated diversity is an important element of what we are calling the Hindu mind.

The ancient Banyan is an evocative image of the diversity of Hinduism, but the polycentricity I have just described is not merely a large-scale characteristic of the tradition as a whole, but also a process *within* Hindu traditions. On the largest scale, polycentrism implies a particular structural dynamic or process at work in Hinduism: one that permits Hinduism to exist as a single unity made up of diverse particularities. Polycentricity results in what might be seen as a "tensive equilibrium" where we have a balance of energies: *centripetal* or consolidating and unifying forces on the one hand, matched by *centrifugal* or separating and diversifying forces on the other. In other words, there is a process at work within the collection of Hindu traditions which balances the drive to diversify into ever more individual traditions and the opposite tendency toward unification and consolidation into fewer and larger traditions.

While driving the development of the wider tradition, this self-regulating, continually shifting process also has a pacifying effect, at least in theory, since when there are competing or dissonant voices within the religion, a potentially destructive competition between them may be averted or resolved if and when this balancing equilibrium is brought to bear on the situation. So for example, if some strands of Hinduism became dominant over others, one might expect that the "weaker," subordinate strands would be swallowed up by the "stronger," dominant forms. If such a process of homogenization continued, we could predict that eventually a single (or a few) dominant tradition(s) would emerge. Undoubtedly this homogenizing process has occurred in relatively local ways in the past, and perhaps it is still occurring, but when the tensive equilibrium of centripetal and centrifugal forces are brought to bear on the system, the equilibrating effect of Hindu polycentrism will work to counter it. The result is that a very large number and variety of religious traditions can coexist without large-scale subsuming and homogenization. Whenever a dominant tradition overreaches itself in attempting to subsume or swallow up others, the polycentric equilibrium will favor the many other smaller traditions and counteract the homogenization. If the number of Hindu factions becomes too large and threatens to dissolve the whole all together, the equilibrium ensures that the relatively stronger traditions begin to include the weaker ones, thus strengthening the coherence of "Hinduism." The result of the equilibrium will be a very broad plethora of religious traditions, all falling under the umbrella term

"Hinduism." Add to this a relative downplaying of dogmatic adherence to particular formulations of belief (for Hindus "what one believes" is secondary to "how one lives") and we get the situation of an almost infinitely adaptable and resilient religious tradition maintaining its integrity over the millennia.

Now this view of Hindu identity, or perhaps the Hindu Mind, as a process of diverse traditions within an integral whole makes a definition of "Hinduism" extremely difficult to sustain. In fact, the idea of "defining Hinduism" is on the edge of being meaningless: one can always respond "whose Hinduism?" since there are so many traditions. Any discussion of Hinduism must therefore acknowledge the great variety of "Hinduisms" existent, always maintaining the provisionality of what is put forward, aware of the centripetal and centrifugal forces at work in the tradition, and finally remembering the contextuality of what is then said.

This has been an outline of how the polycentrism of Hinduism sustains a kind of dynamic democracy of Indian religious traditions, but polycentricity also informs Hindu thought at a more fundamental level. By this I mean that it informs many typically Hindu ways of approaching the world. Here we are getting closer to a "Hindu Mind" since we can see what follows as descriptive of a "dominant mentalité," to borrow Julius Lipner's terms. Very briefly, one can observe a tendency in Hindu thought and attitude which allows for and even encourages, to some extent, an open-ended and shifting *perspectivalism*. This is well illustrated by many Hindu speculative texts. When reading Hindu philosophical analyses of a particular topic, one very often sees a continual displacement or shifting of perspectives. Just before a particular examination or train of thought reaches its conclusion, one is introduced to another way of seeing the issue – another way of speaking about the subject at hand. When one approaches, in turn, the end of a particular analysis, another one is introduced, and the process of analysis is temporarily deferred and extended. This deferral is continued until all the relevant or interesting positions have been exhausted, and it is done, moreover, in an open-ended way so that we are confronted not by myriad confusing alternatives from which we must choose, but rather by a collection of often complementary or mutually supportive perspectives. We are not given an *either-or* in Hindu thought but rather a *both-and* and this results, not in "a death by a thousand qualifications," but in "life by a thousand enrichments." To use another metaphor, Hindus characteristically examine a subject much as one might examine a large diamond or crystal – by holding it up to the light, turning it this way and that, and observing its changing appearance and rainbow of colors. This open-ended perspectivalism and the healthy relativism which it entails, might be seen as the mental counterpart to the polycentric structural equilibrium I described earlier. This characteristic mode of thinking and relating permeates Hindu social structures and a great deal of its philosophical and religious systems. Indeed it can result, again in Lipner's phrase, in a religion of seemingly

> *calculated paradoxicality* . . . where the cool detachment of shifting and pliable conceptual structures tempers the absolutist ardour of the quest for truth and value in a ceaseless and multifarious display of mutually corrective alternatives and possibilities;

where, in short, the so-called weakness of systematic tentativeness belies the mature strength of the capacity to tolerate and to endure.[1]

So now we have a metaphor for the Hindu Mind. Hinduism shows its multi-form nature structurally as well as at the deeper level of typical forms of thought, through a tensive equilibrium. The centripetal and centrifugal forces outlined above work at the intellectual or existential level as well as the social or cultural levels, and the result of the equilibrium is a "Hinduism" which is characterized by difference within unity. With this in the back of our minds, we must always, therefore, maintain the tentative nature of what we purport about Hinduism. But, while the diversity I have described is perhaps the most visible characteristic of Hinduism, if it is also the primary or essential characteristic, then we will soon find ourselves at a loss for words. Let us then move to a metaphor about Hinduism's integrity.

Contrapuntal to the variety of Hindu traditions is their overall integrity and inter-relatedness. If Hindu traditions are as diverse as I claim, then what is it that holds them together? Our second metaphor speaks to the holism of Hinduism and our ability to speak about it. What unites the various traditions of a religion, that is what allows us to legitimately include them under their "umbrella" names, is well expressed in terms of *family resemblances*. Just as the parents, children, uncles and aunts, cousins, and even more distant relatives of a particular clan can be seen to belong to a certain family through possessing some complement of a set of characteristic features, so too can the various historical traditions, each calling themselves, for example, Hindu, be seen to possess some members of a set of characteristic common traits. I am not suggesting that any particular Hindu tradition must have features in common with any other Hindu tradition – they may possess distinct subsets of a larger collection of Hindu characteristics. What I am arguing for, rather – and this is now generally accepted by scholars of religions – is the notion that Hindu traditions are usually recognizably Hindu, rather than say, Buddhist or Sikh, due to their sharing a family resemblance.

Now, of course, much in the idea of family resemblance depends on "recognition" and all that this entails. And without digressing too far, we should admit that recognition is often predicated on very subtle and difficult to define cues, and, also, that a great deal depends on the viewer. Obviously, some things are much easier to recognize than others and I am not here interested in the clear-cut cases. When it comes to the more difficult cases – recognizing "hindu-ness" within a number of diasporic Indian traditions (for example) – the notion of family resemblances is more useful. In these cases one must rely on appearances, hints and fragile similar-ities, acknowledging the shakiness of one's judgments, but also willing to argue for them. The art of perceiving resemblances is thus a skill acquired through much practice and thorough familiarity with the subject – a form of practical knowledge. So, when I suggest that Hindu traditions are connected through family resemblance, I am presupposing these caveats surrounding the process of recognition. The difficulties of recognition should not, however, dissuade us from positing certain characteristics which are central to the traditions. These characteristics will be elucidated under the next heading of "worldviews" – as well as, of course, the rest of the chapter.

Worldviews

We finally come to a discussion of the central tenets of "Hinduism." I have spent a fair bit of time on the introductory remarks so far because it is important to take heed of the difficulties of describing a radically pluralistic tradition, as well as to get an idea of the larger context. One must first see the forest into which one ventures and be aware of its dangers. But venture forth we will, and in order to make our way through the forest it will be useful to have a map – my third metaphor. Minimally, a good map should (among other things) help you find something and/or trace a route (one of many possible routes) from point A to point B. Both scale and detail are important considerations. If I wish to find my way to the nearest shops, a world atlas is unlikely to be of much use. Similarly, if I wish to find a route from my office to these shops, a geographical survey map showing each and every byway and pavement, the relative elevations of the hills and dales, as well as every lamp post and post box between the two points, will be needlessly detailed and probably confusing. In many ways, a quick sketch of the main arteries between the two points, drawn on the back of a handy envelope, will serve very well – it will be a good map for our purposes. It is this that I wish to provide in the following pages: a quick sketch of the major arteries of Hinduism and some routes between a few of the major points of interest. This will include a brief look at Hinduism's historical development, its institutions and rituals, ethical expressions (highlighting its attitudes toward women), and its modern expressions. Along the way I will, unfortunately, have to neglect a great many significant features, or at most merely indicate them as detours from the routes I am sketching – and for some this will be frustrating or misguided. If your house or favorite park is not indicated on a map of your home town, you might feel that the cartographer has neglected the best parts, and that the map this individual has created is consequently deficient in serious ways. As the cartographer for this chapter, all I can offer in response is that limitations in space compel me to present here only a quick outline of the major features of Hinduism. I will, for this reason, have to leave aside many of the details of folk religion, mythology, arts, and politics for instance, as well as most of the non-brahminical and heterodox movements – important though they are. What I will focus on are the seminal ideas of the Hindu traditions as they have been interpreted after the Hindu Renaissance in the Vedanta and the Bhakti traditions.[2] These central ideas will be the clearings in the Banyan forest, as it were, and our job will be to move between them.

Let us first endeavor to find a starting point. This is no mean feat when dealing with Hinduism, for most devout Hindus hold that Hinduism has to do with **dharma** or the "wisdom/law/teaching." Dharma is **apauruseya** or "without beginning . . . eternal," and is promulgated in every age to great **rishis** or "seers" who then teach it to their disciples and students. The fact that dharma is received by rishis does not mean that it is purely apophatic or mystical in nature; dharma, like natural law in the western traditions, is available (at least in theory) to all rational beings, and it must be implemented in one's life wisely and with due heed to the particulars of the situation at hand. These particulars include, importantly, all of one's various duties and responsibilities within all of one's various social contexts. Clearly dharma is "exceedingly subtle and difficult to know": it is the rule of right thought and action as well as the foundation for such − it thus both upholds and is reflected in the macrocosmic natural universe as well as at the microcosmic social and psychological level. The idea of "upholding" is key to understanding dharma: it is the foundation upon which all, both material and immaterial, is laid. We will further refine our understanding of dharma as we go, but let us here signpost it as the moral and natural foundation of the cosmos.

Dharma is clearly one of the central ideas of the Hindu traditions, and while it can be seen as a sort of superstructure into which other elements fit, it is not the only pivotal notion. There are four key concepts in Hinduism: **samsara**, **karma**, **moksha** and the already mentioned dharma. Underlying these are three basic presuppositions: first that the universe is governed by cyclic time, secondly that the individual is related to the cosmos as microcosm is to macrocosm, and thirdly that release from rebirth is possible for all. Of course these ideas and presuppositions are integrally related and mutually dependent. We have already introduced the notion of dharma; let us move to the others in turn.

Karma is perhaps the most recognizable Hindu idea. One often hears the term used in all kinds of non-Indian contexts. Literally, karma means "action" or "deed" but it also means "making," and by this it is understood that every action results in the production of something, be it available to the senses or not. This connotation of "making," which I will discuss shortly, is important because it underlies the moral working of the law of karma. The **law of karma** itself can be understood through the idea of cause and effect: every cause will result in an effect, regular in kind and magnitude. As the principle of causality, the law of karma is understood by Hindus to be a simple fact of the universe, applicable to all in it as well as to the universe itself as a whole. It is, moreover, the engine of existence, driving the cosmos forward in time, since every cause results in some effect which will itself be a cause resulting in another effect, which in turn will cause another effect, and so on. The law of karma thus gives a direction to the universe, ensuring that time ceaselessly moves forward until there is no impetus left, until the bond between cause and effect can be transcended. We will discuss how this can be brought about later. Let us now consider the moral implications of karma.

As mentioned above, karma connotes a "making," and if every action is at the same time a production, then the result of action is always a sort of "substance." This substance might be thought of as "karmic residue" and we can *imagine* it as a sticky kind of matter, adhering to the true self (the **atman**) and moving with it from birth to birth. The more one acts (and acting includes almost everything, such as simply existing, breathing, or thinking) the more karmic residue one collects. In this sense there is no such thing as "bad karma" versus "good karma" understood literally: all karmic residue is "bad" since all of it will produce some fruit, be it in this life or future lives. The only good achieved is to act in a ways which produces no karma at all (I will comment on this later) or in ways which reduce one's karmic debt. "Good karma," consequently, is really to act, or not act, such that one's karmic debt is reduced. The fact that almost all action produces karmic residue should not be taken to mean that therefore anything goes. Certain actions collect more karmic residue than others – wanton cruelty for instance will produce much more karmic residue than reading a newspaper, and there are some actions (devout prayer for example) which actually reduce, or "burn off," karmic residue. There are, thus, actions which are better and worse. The ethical implication of this, which I will discuss further below, is that one will wish to act in such a way as to reduce karmic debt. As one does so, one's rebirth will be more auspicious and one can thus "move up" the chain of being. Also, the higher up one moves in birth circumstances, the less likely one will be to cultivate karma-producing attitudes and behaviors – which would of course result in a lower rebirth. There is, in this sense, a natural disposition to move up the chain of being. If, however, one continues to collect karmic residue, then the only result will be to continue being reborn until all of one's karmic debt is paid off. The continuous cycle of rebirth that this entails brings us to our next central concept: *samsara*.

Samsara refers to the temporal wheel of rebirth. Most often symbolized as a circle of flame kept moving through the combined effect of divine action and natural law (including the law of karma), samsara connotes a cycle of coming to be and passing away. At the macrocosmic level this means that the created universe periodically comes in and out of being, emanating out of and receding back, accordion-like, into the ultimate transcendent Real.[3] These cycles of evolution and devolution stretch over immensely long periods (3.1536×10^{14} human years) and within these periods are subsidiary cycles – wheels within wheels – the felt experience of which is of being reborn into the flux of time and thus suffering the slings and arrows of this world. In essence, then, samsara is the never ending wheel of life.

Samsara is at once both tremendously positive and negative. On the positive side, it holds out the possibility of always getting a second chance. If this turn through existence does not work out well for us, there is always the promise of another birth to come since the eternal part of all living things, the **atman** or the true self, is neither born nor does it die, but is constantly shedding bodies at death only to take on new ones at rebirth (much like one changes clothes each day). There will, therefore, always be another chance to burn off accumulated karmic residue. The cycle of rebirth also means that one is free to pursue any of the legitimate goals of life (these are pleasure [**kama**], success [**artha**], moral perfection [**dharma**], and enlightenment/spiritual release [**moksha**]) within the boundaries of one's birth-context. Samsara thus implies that there will be more lives – countlessly more lives – in which to pursue all of these goals, and that one does not *necessarily* have to work at "spiritual" goals in this one – though of course one is recommended to do so. The Hindu view of existence is thus extremely optimistic. One is never completely lost since the universe will likely continue to exist until all are finally purified of their karma and thus debt-free. It may be a difficult journey, but all will make it in the end.

But this is not the whole story. The negative side of samsara means that, until one is completely free of karmic residue, one will be doomed to be reborn and reborn. Now if it could be ensured that all of one's existences would be full of bliss and joy, then this might not be so bad, but there is a price to pay. First, there is the actual pain of birth and death – often traumatic for the person coming into or departing the world, and most assuredly painful for mothers at the beginning of life and loved ones at the end. Secondly, there are the myriad miseries accompanying life's experiences: diseases, accidents, strife, poverty . . . surely no one is immune from at least a small amount of the world's pain and evil. As the Buddha said, life is characterized by **duhkha** or "unsatisfactoriness." Even if, by some great stroke of unimaginable luck, one could be guaranteed an endless succession of entirely pleasurable experiences, with not a single instance of pain at all, one would eventually grow weary of it. If the next billion trillion lives could be rigged so that no evil would intrude, would not one want a modicum of mild pain, if only to break the monotony? The upshot of this example is that samsara has, on balance, a rather unpleasant meaning. There may well be many positive aspects to it, and it does give us many tries at existence, but there is always a price to pay. In the end, the best course is simply to get off the merry-go-round of rebirth.

Is such a release possible? Can one stop from being reborn and thus escape from the realm of samsara? If, as I said earlier, all action causes karmic residue, and existence always results in actions, then how could one ever hope to get rid of all karma for good? The situation seems hopeless. Here we must introduce our third concept: **moksha**. The term moksha literally means "release" and this means escape from the endless cycle of birth and rebirth. We should be careful not to equate moksha with a pie-in-the-sky-when-you-die notion of paradise or heaven. There are heavenly realms within Hindu tradition (as there are hellish ones), but these abodes are themselves part of the created universe and therefore still within the samsaric merry-go-round. One might attain a heavenly abode and remain there for many many future lives, but in the end this can only be temporary existence, and final release must still be won. Speculation varies widely as to what happens at moksha, as well as whether one can attain such release while living or must wait until death. One thing is clear, however, and that is that moksha means not being reborn again. Normally moksha is only available to human beings in the three highest "castes" (they thus gain the appellation "twice-born"). This may seem unfair, but we must remember that, in the long time-scale of samsaric existence, it is entirely likely that all will be born into these groups at some point.

Moksha is often spoken of as a return to one's original state – or rather a realization of one's true nature. Escape from samsara thus does not necessarily mean a literal transport or removal, but more like a coming to an awareness. The notion of waking up after a dream is a good analogy. Waking from a dream, one realizes that the experiences one had while dreaming were not ultimately real, even though they seemed entirely real at the time. On waking, one realizes the true nature of the dream experiences, as well as the real relationship between your dreaming and waking self. This process of "waking up" is like the experience of moksha. Upon release, one "wakes up" from the delusion that samsaric existence is ultimately real, and that the self one imagines as real (the ego or subject) is the true self. One wakes up to the true nature of reality and oneself within that reality. The process of moksha can be as sudden as waking after sleep, but is more often thought of as a gradual process. Once one achieves moksha, no further rebirths are required and one escapes the samsaric cycle. But how is moksha achieved? How is one to come to this realization and thus break the bonds of karmic existence? The answer to this question brings us back to the broad notion of dharma.

As mentioned above, dharma is the material and moral foundation of the cosmos. This implies that it is an ontological principle (having to do with what basically is) as well as an ethical principle (having to do with right and wrong). Furthermore, on both of these modes, dharma functions at the macrocosmic and microcosmic levels. Let us now unpack how dharma is understood at each of these points.

At the macrocosmic end of the scale, dharma is the ontological or metaphysical "ground" of the cosmos. One can thus say that the existence of the universe depends on and is constrained by its natural dharma. The Hindu notion of "ground" includes within it the western ideas of material cause (what a thing is made of) as well as its *telos* or goal (a thing's purpose or sense). Dharma thus gives the universe its intrinsic makeup and sense, and the universe can therefore be said to be secondary and derivative in being to its dharma. This relationship is analogous to the characteristics of a thing depending on the nature of its underlying substance. A gold earring has particular properties (weight, shininess, malleability, and so on) which will depend on the gold from which it is made. The essential characteristics of that earring are thus grounded in the gold from which it is formed. The actual shape and form of the earring is similarly dependent on its purpose. An earring is "for something" and this comprises its sense. Similarly, the universe has its dharma – its purpose or sense – and must move toward satisfaction of this purpose. Again, much speculation exists regarding what the dharma of the universe might be. A consideration of this question will give us the moral sense of dharma.

The moral purpose of the universe is not an ethical judgment *per se*, but rather has to do with perfection. It cannot be said that the universe is good or bad, since these are judgments and on what basis would one judge the created universe? Rather, the moral dharma of the universe is a measure of its perfection. The universe is understood to evolve or emanate from **Brahman** – or the ultimate reality. In its perfected and primeval state, the universe is coterminous with Brahman, it is an undifferentiated unity. In this state it is also fully actual or perfected. At the moment of creation, Brahman self-evolves, becoming many from one. In this evolution, the universe becomes manifest. It emanates from Brahman, or more correctly, Brahman self-emanates as the manifest universe. In this manifest state, it has moved some "distance" from its origin, and thus has moved away from the primeval, static state. The distance it has moved out into, potentially, is a measure of the universe's imperfection, and thus one could say that the manifest cosmos is at a less perfect and thus worse state than at its terminus. It is only in this sense that the universe itself has an intrinsic moral nature.

The universe thus has a perfected state from which it has moved, and must eventually proceed back towards its goal, which is to achieve pure actuality again. The signs of the universe's dharma are to be found in the laws by which it functions, thus the natural laws of the universe reflect its relative perfection. When the universe was less evolved, the laws by which it was governed functioned more harmoniously. Fewer calamities and natural disasters took place, and relations between all living things were more balanced and concordant. As the universe grew farther away from its origin, its dharma also decayed so that the workings of creation went awry more frequently. Eventually the universe extends to its limit – bottoming-out so to speak – at which time it will be reabsorbed and a new cycle can begin. These evolutions and devolutions are understood by Hindus as a complex series of ages (yugas) within ages within ages. The names of the yugas come from the throws of the dice, perhaps implying that life is a big dice game. The first age is the *krita*, the second the *treta*, the third *dvapara*, and the fourth and final yuga (in which we are presently) the *kali* yuga. As one age follows the other, dharma decays and morality suffers. The dharma of the universe is tied, in these ages, to individual dharmas, and it is to the microcosmic or existential and social levels that we turn, after the following exercises.

Consider the following questions for discussion: Exercises

1   Does the doctrine of Karma undermine one's motivation for social action,
    that is, if someone is suffering due to their past karmic residue, should one
    help them, or let them get their just deserts?
2   "Hindu polycentricity enables it to absorb other religions." Do you agree with
    this statement? Discuss the positive and negative aspects of what it entails.

Institutions and Rituals

Each living thing has a dharma of its own to fulfill. Just as the universe has a purpose and sense, individual animate beings have their own intrinsic natures. The dharma of a plant will be different from the dharma of a dog or cat, and each will have their own dharmic duties. Just as the universe functions according to laws, individuals have laws by which they will, or ought to, work. These laws have been codified into duties and obligations, and so for individuals, fulfilling one's dharma translates to satisfying these duties and obligations. I will discuss the ethical implications of this below. Let me continue here on the social and natural part of individual dharma by pointing out that it is almost entirely linked to one's birth, and thus one's dharma is part and parcel of how one acts within the law of karma. One's intrinsic nature is partly governed by one's birth. If one is born as a tortoise, one will have a tortoise nature and consequently a tortoise's dharma. If one is born into a high caste human family, then to some extent, one's nature and dharma will be determined. While this might sound rather predestinarian, it is in fact not too far from the modern understanding of the role of genetics in constructing one's character. Moreover, the system does not actually eradicate free will, or the effects of nurture, but rather sets the broad parameters of one's intrinsic character. The way karma works in this context is to deal you a hand from which you are free to play in whichever way you wish. The hand one is given is one's dharma, within which one has free will to live, make choices, and pay the consequences. Now one's dharma is often subtle and difficult to know, but it is in principle always do-able. Moreover, and now we finally answer the question of moksha's possibility, broadly speaking it is in fulfilling one's dharma that moksha is finally won. The exact way one fulfills one's dharma is somewhat more complicated, and I will discuss this later. We should note here, however, that the context in which one works out one's dharma is delineated by the institutions and rituals of Hinduism, and it is to these that we must turn. But since we have covered a great deal of ground already, it would do well here to take stock of the journey so far.

We entered the forest of Hinduism with full acknowledgement that there are many centers to the tradition, and that there are many paths through the wood. The point of entry was the description of Hinduism as the **sanatana dharma**, or the eternal wisdom, law, or teaching. The key element of this description is the notion that Hinduism reflects that which undergirds the moral and physical universe, both at the cosmic and individual levels. From this point we ventured forth, making our way through a series of clearings which are the central concepts and presuppositions of orthodox Hinduism. As the discussion has progressed, we can see that there are a number of paths connecting these clearings, each intersecting with others and forming an interconnected web. Indeed, to get the full scope of each concept, we must refer to the other concepts. This preliminary foray has shown us some important paths through the forest, and we have thus mapped a significant part of the ancient Banyan. It is now necessary to follow some of the spokes radiating out from the central nexus. Here, too, we will find that the clearings we come to, in the form of institutions and rituals, will be connected to other new clearings.

The first clearing we come to on our second foray is surrounded by what looks like the oldest parts of the forest, such are the thick layers of leaves underfoot. This is the clearing of scripture, and the nourishing layers of foliage are the hundreds of generations of interpretation. The Hindu body of sacred scripture is called the **Vedas**. The term Vedas comes from the Sanskrit root *"vid,"* which refers to "knowing" or "knowledge," and is related to the English word "wit." The Vedas are a collection of texts of various genres, sizes, ages, and influence and are considered revealed wisdom or **shruti**, meaning "that which is heard." Most devout Hindus consider shruti to be **apauruseya**, that is beginningless, and therefore not attributed to human authorship, but it is thought by scholars that the texts were composed probably between 1700 BCE and 500 BCE. Of course pious Hindus are likely to admit these dates, perhaps, as only when they were codified or transcribed. The **rishis** (seers) of old received the hymns, which are the heart of the Vedas, and preserved them in their original form and order through oral recitation. This they passed down to their disciples and thus it has come to us.

The Vedas proper are divided into four collections, called the Rg (pronounced "rig"), Sama, Yajur and Atharva, each with four sections, called the **samhitas**, **Brahmanas, Aranyakas** and **Upanishads**. The Rg veda is composed of 1028 hymns containing the oldest part of the vedic corpus. The hymns or samhitas are mostly invocations, praises, and utterances to be used in sacrificial rituals. The hymns of the Sama and Yajur vedas repeat the Rg veda samhitas, but prescribe a different performance of them or add other information relating to the vedic sacrifice. The Atharva veda is somewhat different from the other three in that it does not pertain to the ritual sacrifice, but rather contains information, spells, incantations, and chants dealing with medical and other areas. The Atharva veda was for some time not considered sacred, but eventually was accepted into the vedic corpus. The four sections of the **Vedas** differ as follows: the samhitas, as mentioned, are hymnic chants used in ritual, the Brahmanas are treatises commenting on the ritual, the Aranyakas are more speculative "forest texts," meditating on the meaning of the samhitas, and the Upanishads, which literally means "sitting near the feet of [the teacher]," are the final part of the Aranyakas and are composed of speculative and philosophical analyses of the true meaning of the scriptures, the universe in general, and our place in it.

While the term "veda" is most accurately conferred on the **shruti** (or revelation) texts, and perhaps even more narrowly on the samhitas only, many Hindus extend the term to include the **smriti** texts. Smriti means "that which is remembered" and refers to the texts written after about 500 BCE. These texts are handed down through tradition (hence remembered) and, while not having the authority of real revelation, are considered to be in the same spirit of truth as shruti. The smriti texts are also quite broad in scope and kind, and unlike the shruti texts, which have always maintained a close connection to rituals and to the Brahmin priests who performed them, exercise a great influence on Hindus. Included in the smriti texts are the epic poems the *Mahabharata* (the great epic of India, or alternatively, the great epic of the sons of Bharat) and the *Ramayana* (the Story of Rama), as well as the **Dharmashastras** (codes of law and ethics, including the *Laws of Manu*) and **Puranas** (old tales). We will consider one part of the *Mahabharata*, that is the *Bhagavad Gita* (Song of the Divine) later when we discuss the **bhakti,** or devotion traditions.

At this point, we should outline the role and power of scripture as understood in the Hindu tradition. I mentioned above that shruti was closely connected to the ritual sacrifice. These sacrifices were primarily the responsibility of the brahmins, and the priests tended to guard access to the ritual scriptures quite closely. This was, undoubtedly, partly to ensure their role in society remained protected, but it is also due to the understanding of the power of the words of scripture. In the Hindu tradition, sacred speech is seen to have creative and sustaining power. The language of the Vedas (usually Sanskrit) is thus seen to have some degree of cosmic efficacy, and this meant both that scripture needed to be vocalized to have an effect, and that it should be performed in the proper context, that is the ritual setting. Such was the belief in the power of the word that the precise order and intonation of the verses needed to be exactly right or the ritual could turn out to be unsuccessful. An unsuccessful ritual did not merely bode badly for those participating in it, but because of the power of the holy mantras, could put the very cosmos at risk. The syllables of the Sanskrit texts thus gain an almost supreme importance, obviously increasing the weight of scripture, as well as going a long way to establishing and maintaining the power of the Brahmin guardians of scripture.

Scripture was indeed guarded. Access to it was tightly controlled and, as mentioned, only twice-born males were admitted to learn it. Brahmins controlled to whom, how, when, and where the holy knowledge was divulged and, like almost all aspects of Hinduism, there was a system involved. This brings us to the next "institutional clearing" in the Banyan forest, one called **varnashramadharma**.

Varnashramadharma is in fact a conjunction of three distinct words: **varna**, which literally means "color"; **ashrama** which referred to the stages of life; and of course the omnipresent and encompassing **dharma**. While the term "varna" reaches back perhaps to the supposed invasion of the Aryans into India around the eighteenth or nineteenth century BCE, and literally referred to the differences in skin color between the Aryans and the indigenous people, it is now generally understood to connote *classes*. Originally there were four classes of people in Indian society, corresponding solely to their roles in the culture. These were the **Brahmins** or priests, which I have mentioned already, the **Kshatriyas** or warriors and rulers, the **Vaishyas** or the mercantile class, and finally the **Shudras** or the laboring class. In one of the hymns in the Rg veda (called the "Hymn to the Supreme Person," see *A World Religions Reader*, p. 98) the class divisions are delineated and their roles defined. At this stage, the varnas were a purely descriptive record of the functioning of society. One could become a member of a class by taking on the roles corresponding to it, and similarly one could leave a class by shrugging off its role. It was only much later, around the time of the writing of the ***Laws of Manu*** (a dharmashastra of about the first century BCE), that the descriptive classes of society became more ossified into the rigid **castes** of today. We should note here that the Sanskrit term for "caste", **jati**, really refers to the particular birth station of one's parents – though in modern parlance, this distinction is rarely made. The "caste system," as it is known today, is repressive primarily because membership in one's caste depends entirely on birth, and thus it is no longer possible to change castes as it once was. This rigid caste system has been rightly condemned, and is officially banned by the Indian government. Unfortunately such repression dies hard, and signs of the importance of "caste" in Hindu society still abound, most blatantly in the marriage pages of some Indian newspapers. It should be noted that the *Laws of Manu*, while likely reflecting the social practices of its day, was probably taken with a generous pinch of salt in its own time, and that "caste" restrictions have always been the object of significant internal criticism.

In parallel to the varna system, are the **ashramas** or stages of life. Here again there are four, lasting for varying periods of time. The first stage is that of the student and is termed **brahmacharya**. In this stage one is to dedicate oneself to study and to remain celibate. Typically only males of the three highest castes were given the right to study, but there is evidence that in earlier times (that is before the first century BCE) girls were allowed education in the scriptures as well. The *brahmacharin* was to be supported by his or her family and was usually taken on by a personal guru. The second, usually longest, stage was that of the **grihastha** or householder. After the student stage, one was to marry, be employed, and raise a family. The householder was the economic backbone of the society and their work was considered to be for the support of their families, as well paying their debts to society, their parents, and gurus. Most men never went beyond these two stages and probably the brahmacharya stage was rather cursory. The third stage is one of semiretirement and is called **vanaprastha**. When a man sees his grey hair and wrinkled skin, when he sees his grandchildren, he is to retire to the forest with his wife to lead a simple life of prayer and solitude in order to study the scriptures. The final stage, one embarked on by very few, is that of **sannyasa**. Here the man renounces all in order to gain salvific knowledge and cultivate utter detachment. He gives up his home, possessions, status, name, spouse and family – even going as far as staging his own social death – in order to divest himself of all ties that might hinder his final journey to realization and moksha.

As we can see, Hindu life was ordered according to one's place in society and one's age. The activities of each stage were appropriate for that level. Not all activities were allowed however. There are, in Hindu thought, four broad categories of legitimate aims in life which, within the context of varna and ashrama, are to guide one's actions. I have alluded to some of these earlier in my discussion of samsara. The legitimate aims of life are **artha**, wealth and power or success in all its forms; **kama**, which might be translated as pleasure, including sexual pleasure as well as the appreciation of beauty; **dharma**, which as we have seen relates to the proper acquittal of one's duties and obligations in society; and **moksha**, striving for ultimate spiritual release. These goals are in themselves neither ethically good nor bad, but the timing and vigor with which one pursues these goals may or may not be appropriate. Furthermore, one may in all good conscience develop only one goal for all of one's life, provided one is willing to accept the karmic consequences. Within the context of samsara, there will undoubtedly be another turn of the wheel.

We have spent considerable time talking about Hinduism without much mention of Gods and deities. This has not been without some purpose. Perhaps the most common misconception about Hinduism is that it is entirely concerned with propitiation of the many thousands of gods which clutter the universe. This, along with the idea that Hinduism is thus polytheistic, is false, though it is easy to see how this misconception arose. The idea of divinities is a path running through almost all of the clearings in the Banyan forest. While it appears quite different within many of these crossroads, this path might be seen as a ring-road connecting most of the clearings. To discuss the gods of Hinduism we must begin even before the earliest texts of the Rg veda.

The indigenous people of the Indian subcontinent are called the Harappan civilization. Centered around the Indus River, they get their name from one of the great cities they built, Harappa, which is about 480 kilometers up river from another great city of the time, called Mohenjo-Daro. The archeological evidence from these city sites reveals what was likely a sophisticated and thriving society, flourishing around 2750 BCE, though some scholars date it earlier. While much remains mysterious about them (their script is still to be decoded) the religion of the Harappan people is believed to have been based largely in their agrarian society, with worship of mother goddesses being central. Several small statue figures of what appear to be mother deities have been found. These figures are dressed only in a short skirt, with a fan-like head-dress, and holding two cups which appear smoke stained, leading one to believe that the statue may have been used to hold incense. A large number of seals and amulets have also been found at the sites, some of which may have had a religious significance. Several of these seals portray a male figure, seated in what looks like a classic yoga posture, surrounded by a number of animals. This character may have been the precursor to the later Vedic god who was the lord of beasts. This god further developed into the classical Hindu deity **Shiva**. Similarly, the mother goddess might have been the progenitor of, for instance, the Hindu goddess **Parvati**. If these theories are correct, then the religion of the Harappan civilization may survive still in the gods and characters of what grew to be the Hindu tradition. The gods of the Aryan civilization, which is said to have invaded and taken over the Harappans, include several deities which share many characteristics with Harappan figures. The Aryan invasion theory suggests that the conquering peoples slowly and gradually infiltrated the indigenous peoples, and either adapted their own gods to take on the characteristics of the Harappans' or simply absorbed them into their own system or pantheon. In either case the similarities between the various deities is striking.

The Aryans, who are credited with the Vedas (a point of continuing debate), had a large number of gods whom they ritually worshiped. Similar to the pantheon of the classical Greek civilization, these gods had larger-than-life personalities and seemed to be heavily involved in various intrigues between themselves and with humans. In general, these gods were associated with some natural forces or phenomena, and with various social or religious practices. Hence we have **Indra**, the god of war, and **Varuna** the god of truth and justice, who are two of the most important gods; as well as **Agni**, the god of the (sacrificial) fire who thus made his home in every hearth, **Sarasvati**, the goddess of speech and learning, and **Parvati**, often conflated with **Durga** or **Kali**, who ruled over destruction and was the consort of **Pasupati**. Later Vedic gods include **Narayana** (**Vishnu**), **Shri** (**Lakshmi**), and **Shiva**.

The development of these deities as well as the modes of their proper worship illustrate Hinduism's skill at synthesis. Just as the invading Aryans are said to have incorporated the Harappan gods into their own system, with, of course, the requisite changes and adaptations, the later Vedic gods developed and changed too. These developments usually meant an increase in power and function, that is the gods became more universal, as well as greater abstraction, so that the gods became less anthropomorphic. So it is the case that a relatively minor god of early Hinduism, **Brahman**, who presided over the sacrifice, slowly grew in importance, so that he became not simply the chief among the gods, but even the power underlying all of divinity and reality. By the time of the composition of the Upanishadic texts, Brahman is seen to be the "One without a Second," the ground of Being transcending all and upholding dharma itself. This development surely followed the growth in importance of the role of sacrifice and ritual in Indian society, and the parallel growth in importance and stature of the priestly class of Brahmins. The strand of a Hinduism that centers around Brahman and the role of the Brahmin priests in society is consequently called "Brahminical Hinduism," and while there are sharp criticisms of the privileged position of Brahmin priests in this system, it is certainly not amiss to say that Brahminical Hinduism constitutes what is considered to be orthodox.

So we have a clear development of the concept of deity in Hindu tradition, from the pre-Vedic agrarian and fertility gods of the Harappan civilization, to the introduction and ascendancy of the Aryan or Vedic gods, and the slow coalescing and abstraction which led to Brahminical Hinduism. By the time of classical Hinduism, a period spanning from about 500 BCE to around the twelfth century CE, the major gods of the Hindu tradition were well ensconced, and Brahminical Hinduism was canonized to a great extent. Within this system what is sometimes referred to as the **Hindu Trinity** emerges. The trinity of deities is that of **Brahma**, the creator god, **Vishnu** the sustainer, and **Shiva** the destroyer, and while each of these gods is separate and they have distinct roles to play, they are also considered to be three versions, manifestations or faces of a single lord, often called **Ishvara**. Though this trinity has three faces and one "substance," in practice allegiance is usually given to either Vishnu or Shiva, perhaps reflecting a holdover from an earlier age when the gods were seen as utterly distinct competitors. In modern devotional Hinduism we find a great many followers of Vishnu (usually in the form of one of his ten earthly manifestations or **avatars**) who are known collectively as **Vaishnavites**, as well as the devotees of Shiva who are known as **Shaivites**.

The classical period is both the culmination of Brahmanical Hinduism well as a turning point in Hinduism's history. This period is also that of the great epic texts and before we consider their permeating influence on the whole tradition and history which followed, let us develop the Hindu understanding of the relationship between God and creation.

As just mentioned, the classical period saw the ascendancy of Brahman as the literal ground of being, supporting all of reality. During this time several schools of interpretation and philosophy arose, the traditional number being six (these are the **Nyaya**, **Vaisheshika**, **Samkhya**, **Yoga**, **Purva mimamsa**, and **Vedanta** schools), each developing their own systems of thought describing reality. Most of these schools took their cues from the Upanishads, though, significantly, other texts were used as well. In the Upanishads, Brahman is described as the One without a Second, that is, the Ultimate Reality Completely transcendent, there is no way in which our human languages can hope to have any meaning when used to refer to Brahman. Brahman is always *neti neti* or "not this, not this." What this means is that Brahman transcends all that we can refer to through our rationality and language. God is never what we can point to or hope to capture with our words or thoughts. The best that we can do, then, is to rely on revelation, remembering that this too is only provisional. The nature of Brahman, as given by revelation, is that the ultimate reality can be described as **saccidananda** – a term made up of **sat**, meaning truth or reality, **cit** which is consciousness, and **ananda**, or bliss. So even though little can be known of the transcendent reality, we can say that experience of it is real or truthful, conscious and blissful. One further characteristic of Brahman is crucial, that is that Brahman, the ultimate reality underlying all creation, is in fact identical to the true self (**atman**) within all living entities. This is indeed a radical proposition. It means no less than that every living being is ultimately, in reality, the same as Brahman. A famous phrase in the Upanishads encapsulates this truth: "*Tat tvam asi*" or "That [Brahman] Thou Art" and we ought to try to develop this notion now.

Earlier, in our philosophical ramblings through the Banyan forest I mentioned that moksha is achieved through fulfilling one's dharma. This was actually only part of the story, since fulfilling one's dharma in the sense of acquitting oneself of one's duties, is simply one way of achieving release from samsara, or even just the first step. There are in fact three ways, or **margas**, by which one can achieve liberation, two of which we will describe now leaving the third to when we speak of the *Bhagavad Gita*.

The first way is called the path or marga of action (karma). This path requires one to act dutifully and without any thought of selfish gain. This **yoga** or discipline is closest to what I described as fulfilling one's dharma. One does one's duty as prescribed by one's caste, stage in life, and circumstances. The second marga is that of knowledge or **jnana**. In this yoga, one tries to come to saving knowledge through the force of intellect, scriptural study, and meditation. The jnana marga presupposes, however, that one is morally pure. In this sense it encompasses the karma marga, since one cannot be morally upright without having done one's duties to family, society, and self. The exact nature of the saving knowledge is that of coming to the realization of the essential unity of the atman with Brahman. This realization is, moreover, much more than simply understanding the sentence "That thou art," since if that were the case most readers of this chapter would now be liberated. Rather, it is an existential experience of this truth at the deepest level of one's being. It is an entirely immediate perception, requiring no rational mediation, and might be something like the immediate knowledge of oneself as "a thinking thing," as Descartes put it. The realization of this unity is actually more like a remembering, or as I described it earlier, a "waking up to," since if atman is identical to Brahman, then there was never a time when this was not the case. Atman always was and always will be Brahman. Indeed time has no relevance to Atman-Brahman. The realization of the truth of this unity is thus, in a very real sense, a dissolution of error rather than a true discovery.

Jnana marga, or jnana yoga, is by all accounts extremely difficult, and very few are able to achieve liberation through this method. Karma yoga, while much more pedantic, is in some ways no less difficult a path, since it requires that one act solely for duty's sake, forgetting all selfish motive and acting with no regard for the fruit of one's actions. A little reflection will show that such action would have to be almost motive-less, and thus quite irrational. Karma yoga requires an almost impossible level of selflessness, and a single-minded adherence to the duty at hand. These two paths do not appear to give us much hope of attaining moksha. Fortunately there is one other path, that of devotion or **Bhakti**, and in order to understand this, it is necessary to return to the epics, which set the context for this teaching.

The two great epics of India, the *Mahabharata* and the *Ramayana*, undoubtedly arose from a long history of oral performance by bards and wandering story tellers. Each epic is lengthy. In fact, the *Mahabharata* holds the title of the longest poem ever "written" at over 100,000 verses. As part of the smriti texts, neither has the official status of Vedas, but as already mentioned, they are held to be very much in the same spirit of truth, and together are often referred to as "the fifth veda" – an honorific title indeed!

The epics have traditionally had a great deal more influence than the Vedas. While the vedic corpus *per se* is usually reserved for ritual purposes or philosophical study, almost every Hindu will, as a child, have heard stories from the epics, and many will have copies of the texts at home, at least in expurgated editions. Even today, formal readings or performances of the entire text of Ramayana (called **Rama Lila**) take place over a number of weeks, the readers/performers interjecting homilies at various points in the proceedings for the benefit of pious Hindu audiences. Furthermore, both epics have now been produced as television series and broadcast over many months. When the *Ramayana* and *Mahabharata* were shown to audiences over a period of sixty weeks, the Sunday morning broadcasts drew the highest ever audiences in Indian television history – sometimes quite literally driving the entire nation to a virtual halt.

The stories of the epics are long and complicated. Without going into detail, the *Ramayana* is the tale of the righteous king **Rama** and his queen **Sita**. During the course of events, Sita is kidnapped by an evil demon **Ravanna**, and Rama and his brother, along with a host of heavenly and mortal compatriots, endeavor to rescue her, showing bravery and righteous conduct along the way. Sita is eventually rescued and Rama returns triumphant to his kingdom. The return of Rama to his kingdom is today remembered in the Hindu festival of **Diwali**, known as the festival of lights, signifying the candles and fireworks lit to celebrate Rama's return. The *Mahabharata* is a much more complicated story revolving around a feud between relations. The *Pandavas* are at odds with their cousins the *Kauravas*, over ultimate control of the kingdom. Over the course of the epic, we discover that the

Pandavas are in fact the sons of gods on the earth, each manifesting the power of his divine parent. At the crux of the story, the armies of each side are arrayed against one another for the decisive battle. Seeing his cousins at the ready to fight him and his family to the death, one of the Pandavas, **Arjuna**, asks his charioteer to drive him out between the forces so that he can survey the situation. Little does Arjuna know that **Krishna**, his charioteer, is none other than the God Vishnu in earthly form. As he looks to the armies on each side, Arjuna suffers a loss of nerve, and Krishna instructs him to take up his bow and fight. What follows is a dialogue of eighteen chapters which are known as the *Bhagavad Gita* or the Song of the Divine (see *A World Religions Reader*, pp. 70–95). In the *Gita*, which some have called the "bible of the Hindus," Krishna teaches the true nature of reality to Arjuna as well as revealing himself to be Vishnu, the Lord of All and the Ground of Being – that is Brahman itself (the *Gita* is a Vaishnavite text). Krishna teaches the three ways of salvation – of which karma yoga and jnana yoga we have already considered. He then recommends that for this **kali** (age), given the difficulties of the jnana and karma paths, the third way of devotion is most appropriate. In the **bhakti** path, one devotes one's self, one's thoughts and actions, wholeheartedly to Krishna as lord. By his love for his devotees, Krishna ensures that all such devotion will be free from karmic residue and in fact will purify one from old karmic debt. This gift is given to all, regardless of sex, caste, stage of life, or circumstance, and moreover, devotion to Krishna will transform one so that fulfilling one's dharma becomes as natural as breathing. Bhakti thus satisfies all of the requirements for achieving moksha in this life, and thus is a sure method for breaking the bonds of karma which imprison one in samsara.

Clearly the development of bhakti is a pivotal point in the history of the Hindu tradition. So great was its influence that it ushered in a flowering of Hindu thought and culture, lasting from the Middle Ages through to the modern period, and it has, in the twentieth century, once again become the dominant expression of Hindu religion. This focus on devotion does not mean that the older brahminical and even pre-Vedic religions have died out. As I have said, in Hinduism nothing is thrown away, and much ritual, philosophical study, sacrifice, and meditation still takes place in the diverse forest of Hinduism. Just how these diverse elements appear today is what we will now consider.

Exercise   3   Compare and contrast the Hindu tradition with a western religion with respect to the question, "How does one gain the religious goal?"

Modern Expressions

The history of modern Hinduism begins at the turn of the nineteenth century in what is now known as the Hindu Renaissance. In response to the growing British

Empire on India's soil, Indian thinkers sought to translate and sometimes reinterpret Hinduism in order to challenge the largely false impressions of the religion they felt were being propagated by the colonialists. Hindu reformers and apologists such as Ram Mohan Roy (1772–1833), Dayananda Sarasvati (1824–83), Ramakrishna (1836–86), Keshab Chandra Sen (1838–84), and Vivekanda (1863–1902), tried to reassert the universality, breadth, sophistication, morality, and religious efficaciousness of Hinduism as the *sanatana dharma*. Ironically, the kind of Hinduism they propagated owes a great deal to their British disputants since they tended to rely on classical Hinduism and, in particular, the Vedanta philosophical school as sources for their views. These sources are quite philosophical and rationalistic in nature, and while it is understandable that the reformers relied on these texts in order to counter the rationalistic arguments of the British missionaries to India of the time, they have bequeathed to us a particular, rationalistic, view of Hinduism. This is important for contemporary Hinduism since we now have, particularly in the West, a significant bias in how the "orthodox" tradition is understood – one favoring the rationalism of Vedanta over the ritualism of the older parts of the Vedas. Thus it is not too much to say that for most of the Hindus one is likely to meet in the urban centers of India, for example, or in the diasporic Hindu communities around the world, Hinduism really means Vedanta.

That said, contemporary Hinduism is as much a diverse collection of traditions as it ever was. While, for lack of space, we cannot enter into a proper discussion of contemporary Hinduism, we should note that one can still encounter all the major (and many minor) forms of Hinduism in India. Hinduism is alive and well in its homeland; indeed there are a number of quite powerful Hindu nationalist groups working in India today – a situation not all are happy with. Hindus also now live in most of the countries of the world, and one can see that temples are being built, social rituals enacted, birth, initiation, marriage and death ceremonies observed, and a host of other elements kept alive throughout the world. The growth of a distinctive Hindus is interesting, for these Hindus are perhaps at the growing margins of the ancient Banyan. Hinduism's development in the West is producing many novel reinterpretations of ancient doctrines and practices and it might be argued that a new, syncretic form of "world Hinduism" is emerging. As second and third generation immigrant Hindus prosper in the West, they are reconstructing their tradition in the light of the break-neck pace of growth in information and communication technology and the phenomenal changes this is driving in society. Hinduism is becoming, for lack of better words, a postmodern religion: able to use its inherent flexibility to take on new guises and perform new roles for ever-choosier people. And this should not be limited to the diaspora; the same can be said, though for different reasons, of Hindus in India. Under the pressures of secularization, "open" markets, and cultural colonization, along with Hinduism's inherent "tensive equilibrium," contemporary Indian Hinduism continues to develop in new and surprising ways. By responding to pressures, both internal and external, and to change, the ancient Banyan continues to grow – its new forms adapting to their new climates and pressures, maintaining links to their historical expressions while at the same time developing fruit of different colors and tastes. One of the most important of these developments is the role of and attitude toward women in the tradition, and before finishing our discussion we must consider this important topic.

Women in Hinduism

The traditional view of Hindu women is that of the docile, oppressed woman born beholden to her father and brothers, married to serve her husband and to bear children, and dying under the roof and rule of her sons. Such is the life of Hindu women if they make it past childhood – the threat of infanticide being great for female babies – and are not forced onto their husband's funeral pyre as a **sati**. But this view, while perhaps in the past being, unfortunately, true to some extent, is extremely simplistic and is now little more than a caricature of reality. The truth about women in Hinduism is far more complex than the traditional view portrays. Although a full treatment of the topic is far beyond the limits of the present chapter, a few myths must here be dispelled.

Hindu literature has by and large been ambivalent on the subject of women's roles. Women are portrayed as saints and harlots, strong matriarchs and vulnerable girls, goddesses and demons – often in the same work. This ambivalence is by no means unique to Hinduism; Christianity has also had this bivalent view of women. Of course the truth is far more complex. Women in India, like women everywhere, have had a variety of roles within society and within the home. It is due mostly to a particular text, *The Laws of Manu* (see *A World Religions Reader*, pp. 99–103), that the negative view of Hindu women (above) has been propagated, and by various accidents of history, it is this text that has, in the past, guided much western scholarship and understanding of Hinduism. But it should be noted that the dictates of the *Manusmriti*, as it is often called, were not always followed, and even the *Laws of Manu* themselves are ambivalent (see *A World Religions Reader*, p. 102). What we now know to be true is that the ideal Hindu woman was to be pure, virtuous, righteous, and dutiful in fulfilling her dharma – as was the ideal Hindu man. Fulfilling her dharma, moreover, gave her great power and women have been poets, priests, teachers, counsellors, artists and patrons – a far cry from the docile wife/ mother/servant.

As a further counter to the view that the ideal of Hindu womanhood is that of the docile wife, serving at home, all one has to remember is the fact that the various divinities in the Hindu pantheon are always seen and understood as necessarily and essentially both female and male, and furthermore it is the female aspect of the gods in which power (**shakti**) resides. Now, this is not to say that all the gods are hermaphrodites – though in some instances some gods are so portrayed – but rather that each male god is balanced by a female goddess. So Vishnu is paired with Lakshmi, Shiva with Parvati, and Brahma with Sarasvati. In each case, it is the goddess that represents the energy – the raw power – of the divine. This fact means that, at least for traditional Hindu theology, the female is far from meek and mild! Of course the female ideal in the form of the goddess does not always, or usually, translate to the level of everyday life, but it is worth remembering this central theological point when we talk of women in Hinduism.

The other myth that I will consider, and that should be dissolved, is that of widow-burning or **sati**. Sati was vehemently condemned as evil by the Christian missionaries of the eighteenth and nineteenth centuries, and while I do not suggest that they were wrong to do so, the facts, as usual, make things rather more complex. First, it is unlikely that the practice of sati (pronounced "suttee" by the British of the time) was as prevalent as was claimed. Traditionally, a widow *might* retain the high honor paid to her as a dharmically righteous wife and mother (particularly of sons) by immolating herself on the flames of her husband's funeral pyre. The practice was thought honorable by wives of (kshatriya) warriors and kings after the fourteenth century and was originally practiced only by a queen, and was little practiced by other castes or at other times. The occasional, freely chosen suicide of a devout wife was seen, in these circumstances, to be a witness to dharma, and satis were often revered as saints, the sites of their suicides sometimes becoming centers of pilgrimage. But the practice became corrupted when members of lower castes, in trying to emulate the upper caste widows, used force or pressure to make their own community's widows commit sati. The case in 1987 of Roop Kanwar received a great deal of media attention for this reason, since it was alleged that she was coerced into committing sati in front of hundreds of witnesses. Overall, however, the practice is uncommon in modern times and should not be seen as a religiously sanctioned, normal expectation on widows.

We have now covered much ground. While there are many things I have left out among the diverse traditions of Hinduism, the ideas and texts I have brought attention to are, in a real way, the main thoroughfares through the religious life of almost one-fifth of the world's people. Hopefully, you as the reader are now equipped to make your own journeys of discovery in the Banyan forest. Through your travels you will no doubt come across parts of the tradition that seem very new, and perhaps have only a tenuous link to what we have discussed. But by the same token, you are bound to recognize the subtle cues and resemblances identifying traditions as part of the extended Hindu family.

4   Compare and contrast one of the Abrahamic religions with Hinduism on the   Exercise
     question of religious self-identity. That is, for each religion, consider what
     it is that determines whether a particular person is in fact part of that
     religion.

GLOSSARY

Agni The God of fire in the Hindu pantheon; fire.

Ananda "Bliss," "delight."

Apauruseya Impersonal; not the composition of any person; authorless.

Aranyakas A division of the Vedas composed of allegorical and meditative material on the ritual portion of the Vedas; meant for ascetics living in the forest, hence lit. "forest text."

Arjuna "Bright"; "white"; "clear"; one of the sons of Pandu in the Mahabharata; Krishna's conversant in the Bhagavad Gita.

Artha Wealth, prosperity.

Ashrama Stage of life – traditionally four in number; lit. "a halting place"; hermitage.

Atman The inner self (understood differently within different strands of Hinduism).

Avatar "Divine descent"; divine manifestation in physical form.

Bhakti Loving devotion; the path of devotion leading to union with God.

Brahma The creator of the universe; one of the Hindu Trinity composed of Brahma, Vishnu and Shiva.

Brahmacharya Student; the first stage of the Indian social order; lit. the path that leads to Brahman.

Brahman The ultimate reality; ground of the universe; the Absolute.

Brahmanas Liturgical texts providing commentary on and explanation of the Samhitas and rituals.

Brahmins Priests; members of the first (priestly) caste; those devoted to the study and perpetuation of the Vedas.

Castes Social economic divisions of society based on function – traditionally four in number: brahmins, kshatriyas, vaishyas, and shudras (see these individual entries); in modern times these have been linked to birth (see **Jati**).

Cit Consciousness; one of the three primary characteristics of Brahman according to Vedanta.

Dharma Literally means that which holds up or together; the moral and material foundation of the universe; righteousness; religious duty; law; goal of life.

Dharmashastras Law book; text codifying customary law.

Diwali Indian festival of lights; for Vaishnavites it commemorates the return of Rama as King of Ayodhya.

Duhkha Unsatisfactoriness; sorrow; pain.

Durga "The incomprehensible one"; "she who is hard to reach/conquer"; the Goddess.

Garhasthya Householder; the second stage of the Indian social order.

Hindu Trinity Traditionally the triumvirate of Brahma, Vishnu, and Shiva seen as a unity.

Indra "Rule"; "chief" (of the gods in the Vedic pantheon).

Ishvara "Lord"; "God"; "the great God."

Jati Birth; class; the station of one's birth.

Jnana "Knowledge"; "wisdom"; "comprehension."

kali "The black one"; the terrible form of the Goddess.

Kali The last of the four ages (yugas).

Kama Desire; pleasure; aesthetic enjoyment; lust; love.

Karma Lit. action; deed; event; a "making."

Krishna "Black"; "dark"; the ninth avatar of Vishnu; the Godhead in the *Bhagavad Gita*.

Kshatriyas Warriors; members of the warrior or second (ruler) caste; those whose duty is the protection of others.

Lakshmi The goddess of wealth and prosperity; the consort of Vishnu; good fortune.

Law of Karma The law which determines that every cause must have an effect (in this life or future lives).

Laws of Manu One of the law books; ostensibly the law book of the ancestor of humanity.

Mahabharata "The great epic of the Bharatas"; one of two Hindu epics, it consists of 220,000 lines in twelve books making it the world's longest poem. It tells the story of the struggle between the Pandava brothers and the Kaurava brothers and contains within it a wealth of secular and spiritual material, including the *Bhagavad Gita*.

Mantra Sacred word or phrase of special significance or power; sacred sound.

Marga "Path"; "way"; path of salvation.

Moksha Liberation, release, freedom, goal of human life.

Narayana "God in humanity"; "incarnate divinity."

Nyaya "Logic"; "axiom"; the orthodox Hindu philosophical school of logical realism; closely linked with the vaisheshika school.

Parvati "Daughter of the mountain"; Shiva's consort; divine mother.

Pasupati Lord of creatures; lord of becoming.

Puranas Ancient story; sacred book.

Purva mimamsa The orthodox Hindu philosophical school of the older or prior exegesis.

Rta Literally "truth"; "law"; "Right"; "Order"; connotes the true order or "way" of the cosmos. A precursor to the concept of dharma.

Rama "Pleasing"; "delight"; the seventh avatar of Vishnu; the hero of the *Ramayana*.

Rama Lila Performances of events from the *Ramayana*.

Ramayana "The vehicle of Rama"; the oldest known Sanskrit poem and one of the two Hindu epics. It tells the story of the abduction of Rama's wife Sita by the evil ten-headed demon Ravanna, her eventual rescue, and the triumphant return of Rama and Sita to the throne of Ayodhya.

Ravanna The evil ten-headed demon king of Lanka as told in the epic *Ramayana*.

Rishis Seers; a Vedic sage.

Saccidananda "Existence/know-ledge/bliss"; according to Vedanta (partic. advaita) these are the attributes of Brahman.

Samhitas A division of the Vedas composed of hymnic material; hymns particularly as they are used in ritual.

Samkhya The orthodox Hindu philo-sophical school of enumeration of dualistic realism; lit. refers to the enumeration or discrimination of the ultimate objects of knowledge; closely linked with the yoga school.

Samsara Empirical existence, the wheel of birth and rebirth.

Sanatana dharma The eternal dharma; the eternal, absolute religious law.

Sannyasa Renunciate; monk; lit. to throw down completely, i.e. to renounce utterly; the fourth stage of the Indian social order.

Sarasvati "She of the stream"; the Goddess of wisdom/learning; the con-sort of Brahma.

Sat Existence; reality; being.

Sati The burning of widows on their husband's funeral pyre.

Shakti "Power"; "energy"; "potency"; the power or force of the cosmos.

Shiva According to Shaivite schools he is the supreme Godhead; lit. "good" or "auspicious."

Shaivite A follower or devotee of Shiva.

Shri Goddess of prosperity, see Lakshmi.

Shruti Lit. "that which is heard" – revealed wisdom.

Shudras Servants; members of the fourth (serving or laboring) caste. Those who provide manual labor.

Sita "Furrow"; the heroine of the Ramayana.

Smriti Lit. "that which is remem-bered"; traditional wisdom or teachings.

Upanishads The last sections of the Aranyakas; philosophical and specula-tive material communicating the most esoteric, essential knowledge regarding the nature of Brahman and atman; lit. "to sit down near" connoting that which is imparted when sitting down close to one's guru.

Vaisheshika The orthodox Hindu philosophical school of particularity, closely linked with the nyaya school.

Vaishnavite A follower or devotee of Vishnu.

Vaishyas Businesspersons;   mer-chants; members of the third (mercantile) caste; those who provide goods and services.

Vanaprastha "Forest dweller"; the third stage of the Indian social order.

Varna Lit. color; refers to the four traditional classes of Hindu society.

Varnashramadharma Those dharmic duties particular to specified varnas and particular ashramas.

Varuna In the Samhitas he is lord of the sea, but more generally under-stood as lord of the cosmic order.

Vedanta The orthodox Hindu philosophical school founded on the teachings of the Upanishads; lit. the "end" (teleological, formal, chronological) of the Vedas.

Vedas Knowledge; wisdom; scripture — There are four collections of the Vedas: Rg, Sama, Yajur, and Atharva.

Vishnu According to Vaishnavite schools he is the supreme Godhead; lit. "the supreme lord, all pervading."

Yoga "Union"; "yoke"; the process or path of discipline leading to oneness with the divine or with one's self; the orthodox Hindu philosophical school of meditative union; closely linked with the samkhya school.

Notes and References

1   Julius Lipner, "Ancient Banyan: An Inquiry into the Meaning of 'Hinduness'," *Religious Studies* (March 1996), p. 28. The image of Hinduism as the great Banyan presented here is Lipner's.
2   This limitation is perhaps legitimized by the fact that these two traditions dominate modern understandings of Hinduism.
3   This model of the periodic creation and dissolution of the universe bears striking resemblance to the "rebound" theory in modern cosmology.

Chapter 9

Buddhism

David Torevell

Historical Survey

Worldviews

Institutions and Rituals

Ethical Expression

Role of Women

Modern Expression

The followers of the Buddha Gotama are awake and
forever watch; and ever by night and by day they
find joy in love for all beings.

(The *Dhammapada* 21: 300)

A world faith without a belief in God, Buddhism opens up new and interesting
ways of encountering religion focused on the Buddha's teaching that there exists
an important relationship between mindful awareness and spiritual awakening. The
word "Buddha" actually means "awakened one," and is used as a description of a
person who has been aroused from the harmful effects of spiritual ignorance which
had created obstacles to "seeing the way things really are" and to living in the truth.
The goal to be achieved is absolute awakening – the attainment of a state of perfect bliss called *Nirvana*. This is an immortal condition, only likely to be accomplished after numerous rebirths purifying the mind and heart. Such an apparently
simple way of defining this religion, however, should not prevent us from appreciating the demands of its spiritual practices or the complexity of its philosophies;
like all the great religions written about in this book, Buddhism is a profound faith
about ultimate concerns.

Buddhists strive to put into practice the teachings of the Buddha. A man called
Gotama, who became a perfect Buddha in the sixth century BCE, identified the
cause and cure of the unhappiness of the world. He then taught the fruits and implications of his findings in a series of sermons, given out of compassion for a world

A line of golden Buddhas in a wat in Bangkok, Thailand. Photo: Corbis/Jack Fields.

he claimed was still sunk in suffering (*dukkha*). The most famous of these sermons gives an account and explanation of "Four Noble Truths," identified by the Buddha himself after a period of homeless wandering, ascetical living, and meditation. These truths involve not only a way of seeing the world as it truly is, without distortion or error, but the advocacy of a spiritual path which leads to permanent happiness. In essence, Buddhism is a religion which centers around this revealed teaching of the Buddha, the *dhamma*, offering a path to followers out of the unsatisfactory nature and experience of existence.

Historical Survey

The Buddhist religion has its roots in the Hindu tradition. Buddhism emerged around the Ganges basin in the sixth century BCE, where the major religious influence at the time was Brahmanism, which had been established as early as 1500 BC. Many features of Buddhist spirituality can be traced back to some of the religious practices of the priests of this tradition known as *brahmins*, who regularly took part in meditational and ascetical practices in preparation for the ritual sacrifices they performed. The notions of reincarnation and *karma* were well established by the time of the Buddha's birth, although these were linked closely to involvement in sacrificial action and to the doing of duty according to one's *varna* or class, beliefs which the Buddha later rejected. Another important religious group at the time was the Jains, who believed that all things contained a *jiva* or "life-principle." They too engaged in ascetical practices, taught the importance of absolute non-violence toward all living beings, and shared the belief in rebirth and *karma*. Buddhism developed out of this northern Indian context, upholding some of these deeply embedded religious and cultural assumptions, while rejecting others, as we shall see.

Let us look at how the religion developed. Initially, to be identified as a Buddhist entailed "taking refuge" or comfort in the Buddha himself. Early adherents of the religion sought wisdom and insight from being in the presence of their *guru* (an important Indian word meaning teacher), by hearing and meditating on his words, and by trying to live in accordance with their demands. He might be regarded now as a perfect teacher since he had mastered the ability to attract his followers by use of "skillful means" (a Buddhist concept which refers to the skill to tailor thoughts precisely to the level and concerns of listeners). But such refuge in the Buddha sometimes took a spiritual form when physical proximity was impossible and is summed up for us in the following description by an elderly convert:

> With mind I see him as by eye,
> I brighten night in praising him;
> Hence not as absence deem I that.
> With faith and joy and heart alert
> Naught turneth me from his behest:
> Unto what realm the quickening sage
> Doth move, to that then I am drawn.
> Since I am frail and worn with age
> Thither my body goeth not,
> But with strong purpose e'er I move
> And so my heart is linked with him.
> (Extract taken from *Sutta Nipata 1142–4*,
> quoted in A. Skilton *A Concise History of Buddhism*
> (Birmingham: Windhorse Publications, 1994), p. 43.)

Shortly after the death of the Buddha the first Council was held at Rajagaha, where discussion and clarification took place about the contents of the Buddha's teaching, the *dhamma*, and the code of discipline, *vinaya*, his followers were to follow. Further Councils were to follow in which discussion about doctrines and practices occurred. The most influential figure of the early period was the emperor Asoka of India who lived ca. 268–239 BCE. He began to proclaim the ethical precepts of Buddhism as a basis for his rule and leadership, and during his reign Buddhism spread rapidly throughout the Indian subcontinent. He was also responsible for sending out missionaries to the Near East and Macedonia and accounts of these journeys are inscribed on the huge stone monuments Asoka left throughout his kingdom. Between the seventh and twelfth centuries CE, universities were established which taught Buddhist philosophy and prestigious Buddhist centers flourished in the south and northwest of India. But, by the end of the twelfth century, Buddhism had virtually disappeared from India due to repeated attacks on Buddhist monasteries, the most notable instigated by the Muslim Turks who regarded Buddhists as idolaters. Buddhism, however, was far from vanquished and soon started to flourish outside its place of origin.

Buddhists today would identify themselves as belonging to one of two central traditions, the Theravada or the Mahayana (see map in *A World Religions Reader*, p. 120, for geographical distribution). The Theravada is the earlier and literally means "abiding teaching," or "Doctrine of the Elders," and refers to those senior monks who preserve the tradition through their ongoing personal commitment to the way of the Buddha and by their teaching of the *dhamma*. Reaching Sri Lanka from India about 250 BCE, it was not until the eleventh century that the religion became rooted in Burma, followed by Thailand, Laos, and Cambodia over the next 200 years. Theravadins in Sri Lanka, Burma, and Thailand continue to enjoy Buddhism as the established religion of their country as a result of the prestigious support and patronage it receives.

Mahayana means "Great Vehicle" and is so named because it regards itself as the universal way to liberation. This phrase was used in opposition to those lesser Vehicles, *hinayana*, which adherents to Mahayana claimed offered an inferior path. Perceiving non-Mahayana groups as somewhat selfish (since they emphasized individual salvation), the tradition wished to develop what it considered to be the true spirit of Buddhism based on absolute altruism and a concept of "full awakening." This new approach became epitomized in the figure of the *bodhisattva*, a being of overwhelming compassion, who seeks Nirvana, not for him or herself, but in order to help others in their suffering. The tradition began in the first century CE and, unlike the Theravadins, who regarded the Buddha as being dead and no longer accessible, it acknowledged that various Buddhas could be experienced and contacted as spiritual aids toward salvation. Indeed, the tradition partly began because some practitioners had claimed mystical experiences of living Buddhas during their own lifetimes. The new Mahayana texts, which were produced from about the first century BCE to around 500 CE, show strong evidence of devotion to such archetypal Buddhas and *bodhisattvas*. Less emphasis was also placed by the Mahayanists on monasticism as an ideal, thereby encouraging more lay aspiration toward the highest spiritual goals possible.

The Mahayana Buddhist tradition is now a major religious force in Central Asia, China, Korea, Tibet, Japan, and Taiwan. From its earliest Indian roots, this form of Buddhism became established in China (where it made its mark from the first century CE), Korea (late fourth century CE), Tibet (about the seventh century CE), Japan (sixth century CE), and Taiwan (in the seventeenth century CE). One of the remarkable features of the Buddhist religion was that it existed happily alongside the indigenous religions with which it came into contact. For example, in China, the interplay between Buddhism, Confucianism, and Taoism is a distinctive feature of Chinese religious history (see chapter 11, on Chinese Religion), and traditionally, it was not unusual for some Japanese to be married with Shinto and buried with Buddhist rites (see chapter 13, on Shintoism). Indeed, one of the best-known forms of contemporary Buddhism, Ch'an (known as Zen in Japan), emerged precisely as a result of the creative interaction between Taoism and Buddhism.

As the religion grew and prospered, two further refuges were added to the first refuge of the Buddha. These were the *dhamma*, the teaching of the Buddha, and the *sangha*, the community of disciples. The phrase became recited in formal initiations into the Buddhist religion and involved a triple formulation:

> I take refuge in the Buddha,
> I take refuge in the *dhamma*.
> I take refuge in the *sangha*.

Still made today, the declaration is a public means of dedicating and renewing oneself to the Buddhist way of living.

At this stage it might be helpful to clarify some points about the word "Buddha" itself. Strictly speaking, the word should be used *descriptively*, not as a noun, since it may be applied to anyone who has become an "awakened" or "enlightened" One. The Buddha taught that there is a Buddha-nature within all of us, waiting to be perfected. The deepest and most profound layers of the mind and heart are essentially pure and bright, like clear pools of water. Such purity can be restored once the defilements and obstructions which have tainted them over time are substituted by compassion and loving kindness. The teaching is universal and may be applied to everyone; each person has the possibility of eradicating the harmful effects of *samsaric* conditioning which constantly invade and unsettle the stillness of the mind and heart. Once an unconditioned life is attained, happiness naturally occurs.

The Buddhist religion has always taught that other Buddhas lived before the historical figure Gotama, who lived in the sixth century BCE. Although he became a well-known Buddha and a perfectly "awakened one," he is simply the most recent in an infinite line of Buddhas. At important moments over time, spiritual *gurus* arise who are able to comprehend the eternal Truth and reveal it to others, out of wisdom and compassion. No doubt in the future, there will be other Buddhas. Later traditions also taught that perfect Buddhas exist in different parts of the universe, even if these might be rare. Such observations serve to remind us of the dangers of associating the "beginnings" of Buddhism too closely with the man Gotama.

Worldviews

Attempting to "see the way things really are" has always been a central aim of Buddhists. Two commonly used images will assist us to understand this important teaching. The first depicts a cock, a snake, and a pig chasing each others' tails. This image of the three animals symbolizing craving, hatred, and delusion captures the relentless grip they continue to have upon the world. Progression along the Buddhist path entails a process of sustained detachment from such harmful influences or defilements, achieved primarily through deliberate and conscientious efforts at "letting go," and the practice of mindful awareness in association with ethical living.

The second image is that of the lotus, a flower which rises above the defilements of the earth, symbolizing the possibility and potential of all sentient beings to escape the debilitating conditioning of the world. The Buddhist religion teaches that, just as a lotus flower lives in water and yet is able to raise itself to rest above it unsoiled, so too each person, although born into the world of *samsara*, can arise above it unsoiled. These two images, set starkly side by side, are helpful in highlighting the Buddha's teaching about the persuasiveness of "*dukkha*" combined with the hope of its eradication. Buddhists do not believe in a transcendent creator God to help them secure this release, but in the *dhamma* of the Buddha, which teaches that each individual can become enlightened and freed from the cycle of rebirth, *samsara*. Such a release comes about through the awakening and cultivation of mindfulness, virtue, and wisdom.

Gotama was born in approximately 563 BCE in a town called Lumbini near Kapilavastu, the capital of a region on the borders of Nepal and India. He was brought up in a well-known family of the Shakyas people, and is sometimes referred to as Shakyamuni, the "Sage of the Shakyas." Legend has it that he was conceived immaculately, and at birth took seven paces while stating that this was his last rebirth as he was destined for Enlightenment. His real spiritual quest began, however, after he came to realize that it was futile continuing to put trust in those things which are impermanent and transitory. This change of heart is encapsulated in a famous story about the four sights he witnessed on leaving his opulent palace: old age, sickness, death, and asceticism. Experiencing the implications of these for his own life led him initially into a state of depression as he reflected upon the notion that he, too, was subject to all the precarious conditions he had encountered; but the sadness also prompted him to engage in contemplative action and when he was 29 years old he left his wife and son to begin a "homeless" existence in order to find a solution to the problem of the transitoriness of the suffering world.

After six years of wandering, ascetical discipline, and trying out various meditative techniques (including an experience of near death due to starvation), he rejected the strict life-style of the ascetics, *samanas*, with whom he had been associating and sat under the Bodi tree at Bodh Gaya. Cross-legged in calm meditative posture, he battled against temptation, symbolized by Mara, the Evil One. Finally overcoming any weaknesses, and having experienced "the four watches of the night" (see *A World Religions Reader*, pp. 124–7), he discovered the nature of all conditioned phenomena – the way things really are. In other words, he discovered the Truth. The Buddhist Scriptures recall this momentous happening in poetic language:

> Mandarava flowers and lotus blossoms, and also water lilies made of gold and beryl, fell from the sky onto the ground near the Shakya sage, so that it looked like a place in the world of the gods. At that moment no one anywhere was angry, ill, or sad; no one did evil, none was proud; the world became quite quiet, as though it had reached full perfection. (*A World Religions Reader*, p. 126)

Gotama had now become a Buddha, a fully enlightened being who would no longer be troubled by any disturbing feelings of sorrow or unsatisfactoriness, or harmfully conditioned by the passing temptations of the world. He had entered a state of absolute mindfulness and bliss and the condition was permanent.

Having been persuaded by a celestial being that he should teach the world what he had discovered, the Buddha proclaimed his *dhamma*, heralding that the doors of the "deathless" (*Samyutta Nikaya*, V. 8) were now opened for those who wish to enter. His teaching stressed that there was a "Middle Way" toward happiness, located between the two extremes of ascetic stringency and sensual indulgence; such a route led to everlasting happiness, *Nirvana*. But the possibility of liberation entailed an appreciation and practice of Four Noble or Holy Truths. The first of these is that *dukkha* is inherent and constant in life. The English translation "suffering" does not do justice to the Buddhist word since it refers to any experience of unpleasantness, unsatisfactoriness, or pain which a sentient being might undergo. This may include physical and mental pain, suffering due to repeated rebirths, or simply feelings of frustration because things are unstable and constantly changing. As the British scholar Peter Harvey points out, it can sometimes even be "a vague unease at the fragility and transitoriness of life" (Harvey, 1993: 48).

The second truth points to the cause of suffering – craving or thirst, *tanha*. Three types are identified: thirst for pleasure, thirst for existence, and thirst for prosperity (see *A World Religions Reader*, p. 130). Craving for pleasure refers to the gratification of sensual desire, craving for existence to the enhancement of the ego, and craving for prosperity to the desire to destroy rather than create. Prosperity also refers to the denying or pushing aside of anything which causes unpleasantness. The third truth teaches that *dukkha* can cease. Once craving is eradicated, *Nirvana* can be experienced as a state which is "unconditioned" and "unconstructed." The fire imagery used by the Buddha in his depiction of craving draws attention to its nature as a destructive force, but the flames of desire can be reduced and eventually snuffed out or extinguished when thirsting is worked on and minimized. This description also helps us to understand *Nirvana*, not as a place, but as a condition of being that can be experienced fully in the present moment as well as in the future. A second-century BCE Indian Buddhist, Nagarjuna, emphasized this notion that *Nirvana* exists right here and now; it occurs gradually when we appreciate that all phenomena are conditioned and when we attempt to live an unconditioned life in the light of this truth. *Nirvana* and *samsara* are not separate at all – their difference lies only in our perception of them.

The fourth truth contains the actual moral path which leads to the cessation of *dukkha* and is eight-fold – right belief, right aspiration, right speech, right conduct, right means of livelihood, right endeavor, right memory, right meditation. The spiritual quest is to try and perfect each element simultaneously (not consecutively) and to allow each to impinge on and encourage the other. As the contemporary western Buddhist Kulananda writes: "One works in different ways on different aspects all the time" (Kulananda, 1996: 21). The path itself can be subdivided into three sections and includes different results:

Factors 1–2 refer to the cultivation of wisdom, *prajna*,
Factors 3–5 to moral virtue, *sila*, and
Factors 6–8 to mindfulness, *samadhi*.

The journey is both a meditative and an ethical one, accomplished within the wider context of the pursuit of wisdom and compassion gained through the attainment of mental equilibrium and purity.

"Seeing the way things really are" inevitably calls for an understanding of the nature of existence and how it operates. Buddhists are reminded in their Scriptures that the world of *samsara* is entirely made up of conditioned phenomena. Nothing exists independently except *Nirvana*. Consequently, any clinging or grasping onto those things which are impermanent (because of their dependency) is foolish and will cause further suffering. The roots of spiritual ignorance lie here. The process of awakening can only occur once one starts to live in accordance with the truth that all conditioned things are insubstantial and fleeting. To help his followers understand this more clearly, the Buddha set out three definitive features of existence. These are:

dukkha, suffering
anicca, impermanence, and
anatta, no-self.

Liberation happens when one comes to appreciate the importance of these doctrines and their crucial implications for developing the spiritual life.

Anicca refers specifically to the fact that all conditioned things are impermanent and will pass away: everything that comes into being arises and then falls. This includes states of mind as well as physical phenomena, like mountains and trees. Having come into being, they all eventually cease to exist. The Buddha's advice to his disciples was that by uprooting the defilements of pride and wrath the disquiet of the mind will eventually be erased; disciples shall then be able to live with joy and wisdom. But followers must be ever watchful and alert. It is only by such mindful concentration that they will come to realize that grasping onto fleeting phenomena is futile and always leads to further frustration and self-deception. Buddhist spirituality is about letting go rather than holding onto those things which are characterized by impermanence.

Anatta is related to this concept and refers to the fact that there is no permanent or immutable essence to anything, no underlying unchanging self, not even within the human person. What constitutes an individual is the combination of five *khandas* or groups of grasping: body, feeling, senses, constructing activities, and consciousness. During each lifetime these constituents interact dynamically with each other, making up what might be termed, for convenience sake, "the person." But there is no permanent essence or core to this process or "person." Over time, meditation helps the practitioner to delve deeper into the nature of this phenomenon and truth, and gradually the *khandas* come to be exposed as a bundle of shifting mental and physical processes, without any real substance. At each rebirth these are reconstituted in accordance with the working out of the law of *karma* (see chapter 8, on Hinduism), and in relation to the mind-set, *citta*, which has developed in each person. There might be distinctive personality traits which are passed over from one lifetime to the next, but these fluctuate and are never unchanging over successive rebirths.

This is not to say that the Buddha never used conventional ways of referring to the "self," as in "myself" or "yourself." But such labels are "mere names" and only refer to the empirical or conventional "self" and not to the notion of a metaphysical or immortal "self," as some might refer to the "soul" in Christianity as signifying the eternal or real "spiritual essence" or "core" of the person. The famous conversation between King Milinda and Nagasena about the analogy of the chariot illustrates this teaching succinctly:

> "If you have come on a chariot, then, please explain to me what a chariot is. Is the pole the chariot?"
> "No, reverent Sir!"
> "Is it then the wheels, or frame or the flag-staff, or the yoke, or the reins, or the goad stick?"
> "No, reverent Sir!"
> "Your Majesty has spoken a falsehood."
> "I have not, Nagasena. For it is in dependence on the pole, the axle, the wheels, framework, the flagstaff etc. that there takes place this denomination 'chariot,' this conceptual term, a current appellation and a mere name."
> (Extract from "The Questions of King Milinda," in E. Conze (ed.), *Buddhist Scriptures*, 1959: 148–9)

While it is true to say, then, that there is some degree of continuity from one existence to the next, any notion of a substantial entity being passed over or being transferred from one life to another is rejected in Buddhism. The Buddha opposed the Upanisadic theory of the soul, *atman*, as an unchanging essence, and argued that the person was more like a combination of rapidly changing phenomena, constantly shifting and moving: "Form is like a ball of foam, feeling is like a bubble of water, perception is like a mirage, volition is like the trunk of a banana tree (without a core, like an onion) and consciousness is like a ghost" (*Samyutta Nikaya*, III. 142).

Recent research about the doctrine of *anatta* has argued how the Buddha was more concerned about giving a *soteriological* rather than ontological account of the person. Clinging to the notion of a permanent self only enhances feelings of ego, literally "self"-ishness, and in turn leads to further suffering. Therefore, it is wiser for any teaching on the subject to concentrate on *how* a person functions, the causes of, and solutions to, the factors of ego enhancement, rather than on what a person actually is. As Susan Hamilton comments about the doctrine of *anatta*:

> when we try to understand the doctrine of anatta, I think we can take a cue from the Buddha's other teachings. They are all, without exception, concerned with the question of how things are, and not what they are. We need to put this together with the point that the Buddha never answered any ontological questions because they were not conducive to attaining liberating insight. . . . The implication of all this

is that it is virtually inconceivable that the doctrine of anatta is intended to be a straight-forward denial of being: that there is no self. . . . The doctrine of anatta simply states the manner in which human beings exist is not as independent selves. (Hamilton, 1995: 57)

We can claim, therefore, that the Buddha was keen to explain *how* a person operated so that *the way out* of suffering could be attained. He was not interested in a theory about what self is; in fact, attachment to such opinions and views is often detrimental to the attainment of wisdom and insight.

Attachment to things which do not endure leads us away from liberation. The Scriptures record how an enlightened monk neither agrees nor disagrees with anyone, but goes along with what is being said in the world, but without ever being attached to it. It was left to later Schools to set up "theories" about the nature of the self based upon the Buddha's teachings. For example, the Perfection of Wisdom literature of the first to the fourth century CE, instigated by the *Madhyamaka* School, developed the notion of no-self much more radically than any earlier texts had done, arguing that all things lack essence and that the world is simply a collection of empty phenomena, *sunyata*, in a constant state of flux.

The process of conditioning in Buddhism (see *A World Religions Reader*, pp. 131–2) is also a crucial one since it pinpoints how liberation is possible and actually occurs. It is summarized neatly in the Buddha's delineation of Twelve Links of Co-Origination, *paticcasamuppada*, and must be understood as a cyclical pattern of birth and rebirth. The links are: spiritual ignorance; constructing activities; consciousness; mind and body; the six sense-bases; sensory stimulation; feeling; craving; grasping; existence; birth; aging and death. Here we have a systematic account of the *reason why* suffering, *dukkha*, exists. Having as their origin spiritual ignorance, the links, *nidanas*, interact dynamically as part of a relentless cycle, like dominoes falling one against another in succession, causing further effects. The presence of spiritual ignorance is the first and root cause of this arising and interplay of the links and may be described as a *misunderstanding* of reality, of *not* seeing the way things really are, of still being in a state of spiritual slumber. The main aim, therefore, is to eradicate spiritual ignorance so that karmic results cannot be "constructed." The means by which a Buddhist may slice through such ignorance is by being alert to its causes; moral virtue, *sila*, and wisdom, *prajna*, awakened by meditation, investigate and work on the spiritual slumber and destroy its effects.

The doctrine of *annica* – that nothing exists independently – is reiterated here. All phenomena are dependent upon certain conditions for their existence and arise from spiritual ignorance. This formula also explains the origin and existence of *dukkha*, the operation and effects of the law of *karma* and the process of rebirth in relation to the emergence of the personality. Since there is no essential self which underlies the *nidanas*, what really matters is the manner in which a person's previous actions are still able to control and influence the kind of person an individual becomes, how they continue to affect a person's consciousness, identity, and psychology, and even the physical body. The doctrine can also be understood as working over three lives: spiritual ignorance and constructing activities (links one and two) are influential from one's past life, which in turn lead to links three to eleven in the present life, which then result in and determine one's future life – birth, aging, and death (link twelve).

Time is never understood in a linear way in Buddhism; the notion of history having a God-given purpose or direction (as in Judaism and Christianity) is absent. In contrast, cosmology is involved in a rhythmic and cyclic operation. The physical universe is made up of five elements – earth, water, fire, air, and space. World systems come into being through the interaction of these five constituents and are found throughout six directions of the universe. As the British scholar Damien Keown writes, "These world-systems are thought to undergo cycles of evolution and decline lasting billions of years" (Keown, 1996: 32). As such, they too are conditioned by *annica* and show signs of impermanence, since they come into and pass out of being and then others evolve again to be part of a cycle known as a "great eon." Within this Buddhist world-system there are six realms of rebirth. The three realms of ghosts, animals, and hell are depicted as being unfortunate, while the other three – humans, Titans, and gods – are seen as fortunate. The gods realm can then be divided into 26 other levels making a total of 31. What determines one's own place within the system is the extent to which actions and thoughts have been motivated by pure intentions and how the law of *karma* has operated in relation to them.

Institutions and Rituals

Within the Buddhist tradition, the *sangha* (the community of followers) is the institutional refuge for the aspiration and practice of spiritual awakening. So central is its role and importance, it could be argued that if this context for the attainment of enlightenment faded or died, then so would the religion itself. The contemporary British scholar Richard Gombrich suggests that the history of Theravada Buddhism, seen from the point of view taken by the tradition itself, *is* the history of the *sangha* (Gombrich, 1995: 87). Here we have a community of disciples, from the earliest days down to the present, who follow the most demanding rules, the *vinaya*, practice mindfulness and self-discipline with stringency and regularity, and provide a haven for the laity to grow in awareness and compassion. Such a refuge enables the process towards enlightenment to take place with as few obstacles as possible and ensures that the teachings of the Buddha are passed on from one generation to the next.

Initially, the Buddha's followers were to "travel for the welfare and happiness of the people, out of compassion for the world, for the benefit, welfare and happiness of gods and men" (*Vinaya Pitaka*, I. 21). Soon such peripatetic wandering ceased, as places of refuge were established during the monsoon season so that communities could dedicate themselves to living strict lives of poverty, self-discipline, and compassion, based on the *dhamma*. Buddhist *sanghas* became arenas for institutionalizing the Middle Way where monks, *bhikkhus*, and nuns, *bhikkunis*, could observe lives of mindful awareness. The *vinaya* (one part of the Buddhist Scriptures) contains a code of 227 rules for monks, 311 for nuns, and a list of ordinances for the orderly running of the *sangha*; each must be obeyed as rigorously as possible. This code, *patimokkha*, is chanted at observance days at the full and new moons, and was originally a public ritual recital of personal transgressions. Like most religious codes, it emerged to encourage a strong flourishing of the community. The simple, disciplined lifestyle Buddhist monks and nuns follow (they possess only robes, begging bowl, razor, needle, belt, and water strainer) is a constant reminder to themselves and others that being content with little is an important step on the way to enlightenment.

But *sanghas* are only able to survive by maintaining a reciprocal relationship between themselves and the laity. Spiritual and material sustenance are interchanged accordingly between the two communities, as they come to rely on each other's gifts and generosity. The daily alms-round of the monks is one example of this mutual relationship, a meditative exercise through which the mindful humility of the "begging" monk acts as a spiritual catalyst to any willing lay followers who place their material offerings of food in the begging bowls of their teachers. The Buddhist laity receive the spiritual nourishment they need to encourage them on their journey, often acknowledged as a form of merit and progressive step towards a better rebirth, rather than any hope of enlightenment itself.

The teacher–pupil relationship is crucial in the *sangha* and, in this regard, Buddhism is similar to other Indian traditions which emphasize the importance of a *guru* for spiritual advancement. One of the most influential Theravada teachers of the twentieth century is the Venerable Ajahn Chah of Wat Pah Pong monastery in Thailand. His words are helpful in appreciating the primary purpose of a *sangha*:

> Don't allow yourself to speak or talk very much. Don't read books! Read your own heart (mind) instead. . . . Listening to your own heart (mind) is really very interesting. This untrained heart races around following its own untrained habits. It jumps excitedly, randomly, because it has never been trained. Therefore train your heart (mind). Buddhist meditation is about the heart; to develop the heart or mind, to develop your own heart. This is very, very important. The training of the heart is the main emphasis. Buddhism is the religion of the heart. (Ajahn Chah, 1982: 59)

I hope it is now becoming apparent why Buddhists regard *mindfulness* as an important concept and practice. Let us pursue this notion further. The Buddha taught his early followers that progression along the spiritual path consisted in mastering four essential elements – mindfulness of body, feelings, mind, and mental states. The aim of the first is to become sensitively aware of the body as it engages in the doing of physical activities, like walking, sitting, or standing. The second involves the comprehension and awareness of the experiencing of pleasant or painful feelings. The task here is to recognize them for what they are and realize that they are only passing phenomena which arise and then fall way. The third refers to the states of the mind which are conditioned by our emotions and thoughts, and the moods such factors produce. Finally, the fourth, mindfulness, focuses attention on positive factors such as joy, vigor, and tranquility as well as negative factors like sensual desire, ill-will, or torpor.

Skillful awareness is achieved by the practice of meditation and the perfection of "letting go." This entails a deliberate emptying out of the mind so that practitioners can see and experience something of the original purity of the mind. In other words, meditation requires a process of "mental cleaning out" so that positive and whole-some elements may enter. This does not demand a stubborn effort to push aside the mental defilements of greed, hatred, and delusion, but rather the ability to "let go" of them when attachment has occurred. Qualities like concentration, joy, tranquility, confidence, and wisdom can then begin to replace the harmful presence of ill-will, indolence, worry, restlessness, and doubt.

A helpful distinction is made in Buddhist meditation between the vehicle of calm, *samatha-yana*, and the vehicle of insight, *vipassana-yana*; these two forms develop the mental attributes of concentration and wisdom respectively. Both are necessary, as calm meditation by itself cannot lead to *Nirvana*. The purpose of calm meditation is to allow the mind to become as pure and radiant as it is in its original state. Insight meditation involves the investigation of the content of consciousness, which leads to flashes of awareness, knowledge, and insight, and is not unlike the Zen Buddhist experience of "direct understanding." The most common method is to start with calm meditation and then progress to insight.

Meditation is a highly delineated practice and involves a systematic series of advanced mental states with specific pointers of success along the route. One first step is to stop the mind from wandering and being restless. According to the Buddha, the mind is like a monkey jumping from one branch of a tree to another, in rapid succession, never still, constantly moving from one thing to the next. Once such restlessness is worked on and controlled, there arises a mental image or sign known as a *nimitta* which can be used as a means of stabilizing the mind. From there a process of suspending the "five hindrances" (sensual desire, ill-will, torpor, worry, fear of commitment) occurs and when these have been worked on, the meditator enters what is known as a state of "access concentration." This in turn leads to a state of "absorption concentration," the gate which leads to the building up of the four *jhana* states. During these advanced *jhana* states, a person is unaffected by any sense stimuli and mindful awareness is extremely acute.

Specific techniques for developing mindfulness have been well tested during the history of the Buddhist religion. The most common is known as *anapanasati*, a practice entailing the mindfulness of breathing, where the meditator is encouraged to concentrate on the intake and outtake of the breath. This encourages an ability to live in the present moment and prevents one from dwelling unnecessarily on the past or the future. It also enables the person to still a wavering and restless mind. Other commonly used devices include concentration on *kasina* circles, brightly colored discs to enable the mind to settle, meditations on skeletons to develop awareness of the transitoriness of existence, walking meditations to gain equilibrium of mind and body, and the practice of *metta* meditation, which consists in developing an attitude of loving-kindness – first toward oneself, then one's friends, followed by acquaintances and, finally, toward one's enemies.

Zen Buddhism and Tibetan Buddhism have developed their own distinctive forms of meditation. The Ch'an or Zen School emphasizes that enlightenment comes through direct flashes of intuitive insight, and is a strong advocate of letting go of rational thinking in order for the mind to become unmuddied and pure. Conceptual thinking and words can be obstacles to the process of liberation. Therefore, the aim is to live mindfully in the present moment, with no mediated thoughts of what one is doing. For example, when you drive a car you drive a car, you *do not think about* driving a car. When you dig the garden you dig the garden, you *do not think about* digging the garden. Such absolute unselfconscious attention to the present moment is only possible after long periods of meditation. Not geared toward the future attainment of anything (including enlightenment itself), the process encourages being content with the present. Moments of spontaneous insight emerge from such states of mind and eventually one comes to realize that there is no real difference between practice and enlightenment itself. Tibetan Buddhism is distinctive for its emphasis on the practice of *tantric* visualizations. Based on a body of texts known as *tantras*, it has developed distinct meditational methods based on ritual magic and symbolism.

Loving-kindness, *metta* (the wish for the happiness of all beings), and compassion, *karuna* (the desire that all beings become free from suffering), are important virtues to be attained in Buddhism. The notion of the *bodhisattva* in the Mahayana tradition embodies this emphasis. *Bodhisattvas* are beings who enter *Nirvana* in order to help those who still suffer. The laity began to see such figures as semidivine beings who could assist them on their own path toward liberation. But the training to become a *bodhisattva* is a strenuous one. There are ten stages of perfection along the path: first, the arising of the thought of enlightenment; second, the aspiration to become a Buddha and save all beings; third, the perfection of patience; fourth, the perfection of vigor; fifth, the perfection of meditation; sixth, the perfection of wisdom; at the seventh stage the *bodhisattva* is no longer reborn and becomes a "Great Being," a savior figure with skillful means, who can magically transform him or herself into a different form to help those who suffer. At the eighth stage, he or she becomes certain of attaining Buddhahood, and during the ninth stage, perfects his or her power; in the final, tenth stage, he or she begins to reside in a Heavenly abode.

Such figures have become highly popular and significant within Buddhist devotional practice and, unlike the Theravadins, Mahayanists are quite happy to regard faith in the salvific powers of *bodhisattvas* and Heavenly Buddhas as being helpful and appropriate ways to attain salvation. The most popular figures are *Majushri* (a formidable figure who brandishes the sword of wisdom to cut through ignorance), *Avalokitesvara* (of whom the various Tibetan Dalai Lamas are said to be human re-incarnations), and *Amitabha*, who resides in a Pure Land and promises that whoever calls on His name in faith will be reborn in that land. Such beings, perfect in wisdom and compassion, make up an elaborate and sophisticated pantheon within the Buddhist religion.

It is not surprising that, as the belief in the concept of the *bodhisattva* became widespread, a more complex and systematic account of the figure of the Buddha emerged. Eventually, a new Buddhology (i.e., a view of the Buddha) came into existence as more Mahayanists came to believe that since the nature of Buddha was pure compassion He would never abandon those still suffering and in need of help. A doctrine of "Three Bodies," *trikaya*, was formulated in the light of these specu-lations. This consisted of understanding the Buddha as having a *transcendent body* identical with ultimate truth, a *heavenly body* situated in a paradise, and an *earthly human body* like yours and mine. Mahayanists established a much more complex understanding of salvation than the Theravadins, since they believed there were many Buddhas and *bodhisattvas* who existed and were always ready to support their efforts. In contrast, the Theravada school has never changed its view that the Buddha is dead and no longer contactable for assistance.

Ethical Expression

The establishment of moral stability, *sila*, is the bedrock of spiritual awakening. The role of the teacher in the *sangha* is to encourage in pupils an unflinching adher-ence to the *vinaya*, and the honest pursuit of a rigorous lifestyle which will discip-line the heart and mind; the distractions of daily living can then have little effect. The Buddha taught his followers to live as "islands to themselves," to be their "own refuges" (*Digha Nikaya*, III. 58). See the exercise below for further consideration of this matter. This teaching does not imply a self-absorbed isolation, but the self-regulated attainment of mental stability and mindful awareness of body, thought, and speech. There is a famous story of Adhimutta, an *arahat* (a person "worthy" of respect since he has overcome *dukkha*), who was able to show complete calm and equipoise, even when his life was being threatened. Similarly, the Buddha's chief disciple, *Sariputta*, claimed that he did not know of anything which would disturb his equilibrium. The attainment of such mental fortitude and stability is a quality to be sought and is at the heart of the Buddhist religion.

Such mental awakening and equipoise is one consequence of living within a tightly disciplined monastic routine, regulated within a hierarchical framework. In some Buddhist countries, boys and girls at about seven years of age may join the *sangha*. Initiated by a lower ordination ceremony, *pabbajja* (which literally means "going forth"), they have their heads shaved as a sign of renunciation and are given robes – orange colored in Theravada tradition, russet-red in the Mahayana, black in Japan and usually gray in China and Korea. Chinese monks and nuns also make a mark by burning incense cones on their scalps. At the age of twenty, an individual may take higher or full ordination. To ordain a monk, a quorum of five ordained monks is required, representing a lineage flowing back to the time of the Buddha himself.

Temporary monkhood is acceptable and is often seen as being advantageous in moral and educational terms. This is especially true in Thailand.

The law of *karma* is central to an understanding of Buddhist ethics. As we have seen, the goal of the spiritual quest is to achieve liberation from the constant round of rebirths, *samsara*. This law refers to the fact that every action and thought has consequences, good or bad, which lead to the kind of rebirth sentient beings experience. A natural part of the way things are, this law operates by cause and effect: all actions and thoughts have results which condition the type of being we become. A person's compassionate actions and thoughts result in a better rebirth, whereas selfish actions and thoughts result in the reverse. A strict logic of cause and effect operates here, since individuals always reap what they sow.

However, such a law should not be regarded as the working out of an implacable determinism. Although karmic results affect the types of action and thinking one tends to adopt, these are never determined fatalistically. All beings are free to alter the states of consciousness and rebirth in which they find themselves and this is precisely what Buddhists attempt to do. Fate and *karma* are two very different concepts, since the former implies that one is trapped helplessly in a condition from which there is no release. Contrary to this, the *dhamma* offers a path of liberation which ensures that previous wrongdoings never affect permanently the way one will be or how one will lead one's life. Buddhism is not a religion of chance or fate, but a faith about choosing to live humbly according to the knowledge that even the smallest acts of compassion will have beneficial results. As one section of the Scriptures, the *Dhammapada*, puts it, "Hold not a deed of little worth, thinking 'this is little to me.' The falling of drops of water will in time fill a water-jar. Even so the wise man becomes full of good, although he gather it little by little" (*Dhammapada*, 1984: 52).

One of the distinctive contributions the Buddha made to an understanding of ethical action is his teaching concerning the law of *karma* in relation to the caste system. The Buddha claimed that what was of significance was the *moral intention* behind any action. This was not to be understood in relation to a hierarchy of social classes or ritual sacrificial practices. Brahminical ethics had been rooted in the caste system and was overturned by the Buddha's insistence on the relationship between inner motivation and moral integrity. What really mattered was the purity of the motive, not duty done according to caste. Behavior which is pure and good springs from a mind which has been cleansed from hindrances and obstructions. An intrinsic relationship, therefore, always exists in Buddhist ethics between moral action and mindfulness, since the former flows from and is dependent upon the condition of the mind for its auspiciousness. Such a way of understanding the process of liberation does not imply that everything which happens to a person is karmically conditioned; some occurrences are mere accidents determined by factors outside the law of *karma*.

The Buddha emphasized in his teachings that it was through skillful means, *upaya*, that a person would be released from any harmful conditioning. A skillful or auspicious action is a reflection of a state of the mind and leads to its purification, whereas an inauspicious action reflects and leads to a clouding of the mind. Even when acts are performed with the intention of gaining merit towards a better rebirth, they are still regarded as being auspicious, but inevitably, selfless acts done from the purest of motives have better karmic results.

All Buddhist practitioners undertake to lead their lives according to precepts – five for the laity and ten for the ordained. They are viewed better as promises rather than as commandments and are frequently used within devotional practice as anti-dotes to the defilements of greed, hatred, and delusion. The precepts are:

> I undertake to observe the precept to abstain from:
>
>> harming living beings,
>> taking things not freely given,
>> sexual misconduct,
>> false speech,
>> intoxicating drinks and drugs.

The additional five undertakings for those ordained are:

> I undertake to observe the precept to abstain from:
>
>> taking meals before midday,
>> dancing, music, singing and watching grotesque mime,
>> the use of garlands, perfumes and personal adornment,
>> the use of high seats or beds,
>> accepting gold or silver.

The precepts, when combined with the following of the eight-fold path (see *A World Religions Reader*, pp. 147–9), attempt to keep the Buddhist practitioner spiritually focused. One Theravada Buddhist monk described this ethical frame-work as being like the markers on a motorway which divide the lanes. They are a useful means of safeguarding the moral safety of ourselves and of others. The goal and skill is to keep within the parameters as best we can in accordance with the Buddha's teaching.

Role of Women

Although the representation of women in Buddhism has suffered from its asso-ciation with sensual desire, temptation, and suffering, the story of the Buddha's disciple Ananda requesting the admittance of women for ordination is an import-ant one and counterbalances any quick dismissal of the Buddhist religion as being irreversibly misogynist. The episode relates how the Buddha was reluctant at first to include women within an ordained framework, but finally agreed that they were competent enough to reach high levels of spiritual attainment provided eight con-ditions were laid down and followed. This is a remarkable shift of attitude toward women given the patriarchal culture of the time. Women in Indian culture were believed to possess an excess of energy or sexuality which emanated from the god Indra. It is not difficult to appreciate how a religion which had emphasized the cause of suffering as being primarily a result of desire, could slip quite easily into identifying women as temptresses and obstacles toward the pursuit of the ascetic ideal. The story of Mara's temptation of the Buddha in the form of his three daughters, Raga, Arati, and Tsna – representing lust, aversion, and craving – indicates the courageousness of the request of Ananda and the bold nature of the Buddha's eventual agreement to allow women to move from the lifestyle of the domestic "householder" to that of the religious "houseless." The sensual feminine world had been identified with *samsara* and it was not easy to overturn such deeply embedded cultural assumptions.

The Order of nuns, *bhikkhunis*, became established first of all in Kapilavattu, five years after the Buddha's Enlightenment, and was a major step in giving recognition to Buddhist women's spirituality. But it must be admitted that their status with regard to ordained monks was always secondary. Nuns had to behave deferentially to monks at all times and to make confession to the male *sanghas*. They were never to criticize monks and remained inferior to male monastics, even those very recently ordained. They were also not permitted to withdraw to the forest in order to lead a solitary life, as many male monastics chose to do. However, the following of a stringent code of discipline existed for both men and women.

Despite such hierarchical regulations, Buddhist texts show the positive goals reached by many women with some attaining the status of *arahatship*. Some women became famous for their dedication to the spiritual life, their attainment of wisdom, and for their skills in teaching the *dhamma*. The following poem taken from the *Therigatha* (Songs of the Sisters), attributed to Buddhist nuns thought to have lived during the time of the Buddha, demonstrates this clearly:

> Four or five times I went out from my cell, not having obtained peace of mind, being without self-mastery over the mind.
> That same I went up to a bhikkhuni who was fit to be trusted by me. She taught me the doctrine, the elements of existence, the sense-bases, and the elements.
> Having heard her doctrine as she instructed me, for seven days I sat in one and the same cross-legged position, consigned to joy and happiness. On the eighth day I stretched forth my feet, having torn asunder the mass of darkness (of ignorance).
>   (Extract taken from the *Therigatha*, quoted in Young, 1993: 316)

Within Tibetan Buddhism, it is regarded as being meritorious for a family to have a daughter become a nun. Girls may join an Order when they are between six and eight years of age. Three distinct categories have tended to exist: those who stayed in nunneries, those who concentrated on advanced meditation techniques and went on pilgrimage, often looking for *gurus* who would teach and advise them, and those who had taken ordination in later life and engaged in saying prayers, turning prayer-wheels, doing walking meditations and going on pilgrimages. However,

Tibetan nuns have only ever received ordination as novices and have never been allowed to receive full ordination. The thorny question of the ordination of nuns still persists today in all Buddhist schools. The Theravada tradition of the *sangha* revealed in the *vinaya* states that a nun must undergo a double ordination, one by validly ordained monks and one by validly ordained nuns. Since it is claimed there exist no such nuns, the ordination line cannot be continued. However, there are moves, particularly among western Theravadins, to challenge this viewpoint and allow nuns to be ordained. Within the Mahayana school, nuns still exist and in Tibet, as I have indicated, although nuns are only entitled to novice ordination, many western and Tibetan nuns have been encouraged to go to Hong Kong or Taiwan to obtain full ordination.

Within the Mahayana literature generally, female lay disciples are mentioned more often than nuns, but the *bodhisattva* path is open to both males and females and has gained such a prominent status in the tradition that advanced spiritual attainment by women is openly recognized. A "good daughter," who is on the *bodhisattva* path, is able to worship, teach the *dhamma*, take vows, awaken the Thought of Enlightenment, and to receive the prediction of Enlightenment. However, the literature is somewhat ambivalent in regard to the status of women as *bodhisattva* figures and the majority of the Mahayana *sutras* tend to fall into the category of acknowledging women as lower-stage *bodhisattvas*; only a few point out that women did reach the highest stage of perfection and were on the brink of attaining Enlightenment. Tantric texts, however, are mostly positive toward the equality of the sexes and emphasize the union of male and female as constituent aspects of existence; both men and women are regarded as having equal opportunities for Enlightenment through ritual practices. The rather ambivalent attitude toward women in the Mahayana tradition is also endorsed with regard to the issue of changing sex. The Pure Land school makes the point that only women who have been transformed into men may enter Paradise. However, for those who take more seriously the Buddhist teaching on emptiness, *sunyata*, all talk about such differentiations in gender is largely irrelevant; those of advanced spiritual awareness acknowledge the conditioned world of gender as being illusory and of no permanent importance.

By the end of the fourth century, female deities entered the Buddhist pantheon in a telling way. One of the most famous is the figure of *Avalokitesvara* who is said to epitomize complete compassion. This originally male figure became represented in female form in China as *Kuan-yin*. Usually she is seen as a slender white-clad figure, famous for being a protectress of women who want children, and of sailors in danger at sea. The following extract taken from the Chinese version of the *Lotus Sutra* extols her many powers and attributes:

> Kuan-yin's magnificent spiritual powers are like this. If living beings are intensely passionate and yet they always revere the Bodhisattva Kuan-yin, they will be able to give up their desire. If they are intensely hateful yet they always revere the Bodhisattva Kuan-yin, they will give up their hatred. If they are greatly disillusioned yet they always revere the Bodhisattva Kuan-yin, they will give up their disillusion-

ment. If a woman wishes to have a son and worships and pays homage to the Bodhisattva Kuan-yin, she will have a virtuous and wise son. If she wishes to have a daughter, again she will have an exceptionally refined daughter . . .

(Extract taken from *The Lotus Sutra* quoted in Young, 1993: 322)

Another well-known female figure within Tantric Buddhism is White Tara, who became identified as the consort of *Avalokitesvara* and continues to be one of the most widely venerated deities in Tibetan Buddhism.

Generally speaking, in the Mahayana literature, the feminine ideal became associated with the perfection of wisdom, the joyful, the compassionate, and the friend and instructor pointing to the truth. However, motherhood is not given any religious or sacred significance in Buddhism and falls largely within the secular realm. It is usually associated with pain, suffering, and attachment to the world of *samsara*. Bearing children is not seen as having any explicitly religious significance, and those texts which describe women as religious beings rarely refer to motherhood. Nevertheless, a mother is often portrayed as fulfilling a role of selfless love toward her children, which is much greater than a father's sacrifice. Such love places the Mother in an important position within society. However, early Buddhist texts tended to stress the importance of the ascetic over the married lifestyle or motherhood, despite the sacrifices involved.

Modern Expression

In this section the focus will be primarily on the turn to Buddhism by the West (with particular reference to Britain) during the twentieth century. By the end of the section, you should be able to glimpse something of the attraction and diversity of Buddhism which has occurred in the twentieth century.

The story of western Buddhism goes back to the eighteenth century with the work of the philosopher Arthur Schopenhauer, arguably the first western philosopher to take a serious interest in Buddhism. But, as early as 1845, Buddhist Scriptures were being translated, the most famous being the Mahayana text *The Lotus Sutra* by the French scholar Eugène Burnouf in 1852. Popular accounts of the life of the Buddha also began to be written at this time, most notably by the German scholar Hermann Oldenberg (1881) and the British scholar T. Rhys Davids (1878). In England, the poem "The Light of Asia" by Sir Edward Arnold had a popular appeal on both sides of the Atlantic. In America, Henry Clarke Warren was responsible for an anthology of translations from the Pali Canon produced in 1896. The Theosophical Society, founded in New York in 1875, also became an influential group as it promoted and encouraged discussion of Indian beliefs and practices in the West; two names are particularly associated with its success – Madame Blavatsky and Colonel Henry Olcott.

The arts also had a considerable effect on introducing Buddhism to the West. For example, the novels of the German author Herman Hesse, especially *Siddhartha*

(1922), and the writings of Jack Kerouac (with their Zen Buddhist themes which seeped into the 1950s American beat culture), did much to widen its appeal. Alan Watts' books on Zen Buddhism and the best-selling *Zen and the Art of Motorcycle Maintenance* by Robert M. Pirsig have also had their influences. More recently, films like *Little Buddha*, *Seven Years in Tibet*, *Red Corner* and *Kundun* have been responsible for introducing large western audiences to some distinctive features of the Buddhist religion.

Inevitably, immigration played an important role in opening up the West to Buddhism. Thousands of Chinese immigrants in the 1860s and 1870s descended on the west coast of America and Canada, followed by the Japanese who set up home on the sugar plantations in Hawaii. However, the majority of Buddhists in Europe are Caucasians who were converted to Buddhism. Britain now has approximately 175,000 practicing Buddhists consisting of around 130,000 "ethnic" Buddhists, mainly of Chinese, Thai, and Sri Lankan descent, and about 45,000 western practitioners.

The emergence of British Buddhism has revealed some remarkable adherents. One of the first ordained monks from Britain was Allan Bennett, who in 1901 entered a *sangha* in Burma and then returned to England in 1907 to form the Buddhist Society, which is still flourishing today. The pioneering work of one of its leaders, the lawyer Christmas Humphries, did much to establish its importance on Britain's religious agenda. At first small communities became established, the earliest being a Sinhalese *vihara* (small monastic community) in 1954, followed by a Thai community in 1966.

But it is the *range* of Buddhist traditions now established in Britain which is remarkable; the last twenty years have seen a rapid increase in the numbers finding Buddhism spiritually attractive. Zen Buddhism (originally popular in America after World War II) continues to draw loyal followers. Tibetan Buddhist Centres in Britain (particularly in the wake of the "Tibetan Cause" after the Chinese invasion of 1950) are often renowned for having distinguished *lamas* as resident teachers and continue to gain momentum. For example, Samye Ling, situated in Eskdalemuir on the Scottish borders, now boasts of being Europe's largest Tibetan community. The New Kadampa Tradition (which developed during the 1960s from the encounters between westerners and certain Tibetan lamas) now has 14 centers and 88 groups involving over 4,000 people, and it continues to draw followers.

The Soka Gakkai (currently claiming 6,000 members) is similarly attracting attention. A variant of Japanese Mahayana Buddhism based on the teachings of the thirteenth-century monk Nichiren, this tradition is characterized by the practice of chanting before a *gohonzon* (a scroll or plaque on which is written the *Lotus Sutra of the True Dharma*), which encourages faith in the power of the text. One line is repeatedly chanted: "*Namu Namu – Myo-ho Ren-ge Kyo*" which means "Honor to the *Lotus Sutra of the True Dharma*." As Richard Causton, a member of the group, claims, "Any person who believes in this object of worship and chants . . . can expiate all negative *karma* and attain Buddhahood."

Two other Buddhist groups, the English Sangha and the Friends of the Western Buddhist Order, also offer rewarding insights into British Buddhism and, in particular, show how Buddhism has been culturally translated into the West in contrasting ways. The English Sangha is a branch of the Theravada tradition. Many of the monks who established *sanghas* in England during the 1960s and 1970s had been trained under the austere forest, monastic traditions in Thailand, having responded generously to invitations from the West to set up a monastic presence in Britain. From the earliest days, the formation of such communities rested on the assurance that they were an organic and natural development of Thai forest monasticism. Based on a positive evaluation of "tradition," the English Sangha has never consciously adapted any of its features to a modern western context, although Ajahn Sumedho, the American Abbot of the Amaravati Centre in Hertfordshire, does admit that the tradition will naturally take its form in accordance with its new setting.

Such reliance on tradition is a deliberate strategy of the English Sangha. It is opposed to modernism, since this is associated with degeneration rather than progress. The monastic/lay relationship is the same as it would be in any southern Buddhist country. Guests are expected to observe the monastic precepts and conventions and encouraged to participate in the communities' activities. The monastic routine, based on the *vinaya*, is a demanding one, with a rising bell sounding at 4.00 a.m. followed by chanting and meditation between 5.00–6.30 a.m., domestic chores during the morning, a meal at 10.30 a.m. and further meditation, and then afternoon work. Evening is devoted to more meditation and a talk by the abbot or a senior member.

Proselytization is unknown in the English Sangha. Its relationship to Christianity is positive and tends to echo the Dalai Lama's recent endorsement to discover (if you are able to) the riches of your own religion rather than convert to another. There is an emphasis on the development of community rather than individual values and little concession is made to western lifestyles. Despite its lack of missionary zeal, it has been enormously successful. Lay organizations and educational establishments call on the services of the various communities which have been established, so much so that their members are unable to respond to the myriad invitations they receive each week. Traditional Theravada monastic Buddhism, it seems, is drawing many westerners into its fold.

The Friends of the Western Buddhist Order – FWBO – takes a different approach, as is illustrated in this extract from one of its publications:

> The Buddha never drove a car. He never drank Coca-Cola. He never worried about nuclear proliferation. And yet, 2,500 years after his death, his teaching is being found relevant by millions of people in the modern world. In fact, Buddhism is one of the fastest growing spiritual traditions in the West.

> The FWBO has a number of distinctive features, which make it stand out from other attempts to establish Buddhism in the West. We recognise that new social and cultural conditions may mean doing things in a new way. Before the arrival of the FWBO,

most Buddhist teaching was carried out in line with traditional forms developed in the East. Teachers came from Sri Lanka, Thailand, Burma, or Japan (and more recently from Tibet), and largely tried to transplant their own particular forms of Buddhism wholesale into the Western context.

The FWBO, however, is committed to presenting Buddhism in a way that is relevant to the modern West. It will require some new and different agents to dissolve the psychological and spiritual barriers which keep Westerners from the path to Enlightenment. We have therefore recognised that some of the forms through which the central experiences of Buddhism are expressed may need to be adapted to our new circumstances.

The view of the FWBO is that Western Buddhits should feel free to draw on the whole Buddhist tradition for inspiration. We are therefore not devoted just to Theravada, to Zen, to Tibetan Buddhism. Within the FWBO we study and practice whatever we find useful for our development, regardless of which Buddhist tradition it comes from.

The members of our Order are people who have fully committed themselves to following the Buddhist path to Enlightenment. In particular, they have committed themselves to Sangharakshita as their spiritual teacher, and to the Western Buddhist order as the context in which they are trying to gain Enlightenment.

The kind of monasticism found in the Buddhist East is not necessarily relevant or helpful to people living in modern society . . . There are no rules. Rules have a tendency to hinder rather than help, since they often have the effect of preventing people from thinking for themselves.

(Extracts taken from Dharmachari Vessantara,
The Friends of the Western Buddhist Order, 1996)

We see here an immediate contrast to the English Sangha. The FWBO makes a deliberate effort to adapt Buddhism to western norms and sees little point in perpetuating the demands of a form of eastern monasticism which has no relevance to the majority of westerners. Tradition for tradition's sake is unhelpful, they argue. Members believe that Buddhism is ideally suited to fill the spiritual vacuum left in the wake of Christianity's decline. Buddhist practice should be regulated not by rules, but by the discernment and practice of skillful means brought about by meditation. Drawing from the rich diversity found within Buddhism, the FWBO is an eclectic Buddhist group which does not align itself with any one tradition. Many westerners have been attracted to this hybrid form of Buddhism over the past thirty years. The contrast between the two groups discussed raises important questions about what might be regarded as "authentic" Buddhism today and highlights the issue of the cultural translation of any eastern tradition into western settings (see questions below).

The reasons *why* many westerners are turning toward the Buddhist religion are complex and manifold, but a few indicators might encourage you to research the possible explanations yourself. The emphasis on religious practice rather than belief in a metaphysical system is attractive to some converts who find, for example, Christianity too creedal or intellectually bewildering. Jane Compson argues that there is a simplicity to Buddhism which makes it attractive (see *A World Religions Reader*, pp. 153–5). The lack of a transcendent authority who commands allegiance through law might be appealing to those who welcome modernity's emphasis on individualism and self-autonomy – certainly, the stress in Buddhism on discovering the truth for oneself seems to reflect some of the dominant epistemological assumptions of the modern West. The centrality of the practice of meditation in Buddhism might also appeal to those seeking a spiritual path which offers peace and tranquility in a fragmented and frenzied culture. Individual charismatic spiritual leaders like the Dalai Lama (who received the Nobel Peace Prize in 1989 for his non-violent efforts to preserve Tibetan culture) are also responsible for the growth of interest in Buddhism. Many other reasons can be postulated and investigated (see the questions below).

In whatever form it may take, Buddhism is characterized by the following of the Buddha's teaching, which guides and encourages the pursuit of a spiritual path rooted in the perfection of mindfulness, moral virtue, and wisdom. But such a definition must not be viewed as a humanist philosophy. The Buddhist religion's central concern is the attainment of a state of immortal bliss after the fetters of spiritual ignorance have been broken and are unable to exercise any harmful conditioning effects. The advocacy of such a profound and challenging spiritual teaching and practice situates Buddhism among the great religions of the world.

1 Read the following extract from the Buddhist Scriptures (the *Digha Nikaya*, the Long Discourses of the Buddha) and discuss the questions which follow, in teams.

Exercises

> Herein monks, a monk fares along contemplating the body in the body, ardent, clearly conscious, mindful, so as to control covetousness and dejection with respect to the world; ... Thus monks, a monk lives with himself as an island, with himself as a refuge, with no other person as a refuge, he lives with *Dhamma* as an island, *Dhamma* as a refuge, with no other *Dhamma* as refuge. Keep to your own pastures, monks, range in your own native beat. Ranging there Mara will not get a chance, he will not get an opportunity for attack. It is thus by reason of undertaking wholesome states, monks, that this goodness-power grows. (Taken from the *Digha Nikaya*, III. 58, quoted in Harvey, 1995: 54)

(a) Why should a monk, if he is to advance along the spiritual path, "keep to" his "own pastures"? Do you consider this to be "selfish"?

(b) The Buddhist Scriptures teach that spiritual ignorance is the barrier that needs to be lifted between ourselves and others if any spiritual development is to take place. Once a monk or nun has learnt to live as an island, he or she is able to break down such barriers between her or himself and others and live without boundaries. He or she has then "lifted up the barrier," "filled in the moat" and "become a pure one with flag laid low, burden dropped, without fetters." What is your response to these ideas?

2 Consider why Buddhism has become an important religion for many people living in the West today.

3 Find out more about the English Sangha and the Friends of the Western Buddhist Order and then discuss points of comparison and contrast.

Chapter 10

Sikhism

JOHN PARRY

Historical Survey

The Sikh Belief System

The Human Condition

Rituals and Institutions

Ethics

Engagement with the Modern World

Sikhism originated in the Panjab, commonly known as Punjab, in the northwest of India. The area takes its name from the five rivers which have created a remarkably fertile environment. The area borders the Khyber Pass, one of the historical portals through which Islam entered the subcontinent.

The Panjab was a religiously diverse area. Resident traditional Hindus worshiped both Shiva and Vishnu (see chapter 8), and Guru Nanak, the founder of Sikhism, would have heard Hindu worship regularly as a young boy, born as he was into a Hindu family. Such worship was essentially devotional, centering on a personal relationship with the deity and expressed through hymns sung in the vernacular language. Amongst the Muslims in that part of India in the fifteenth century (CE) were Sufis who were known for their humility and their depth of faith, as well as the more orthodox Sunnis, who held power in the Moghul courts. Other groups were also practicing their faith in the Panjab. The **Naths** believed that release from the round of birth and rebirth, *samsara*, could be found through yoga and asceticism. Individuals such as Lalla, Kabir, and Namdev expressed their faith through poetry, speaking of the possibility of release through the "nameless One who is within." The **Sant** tradition had been established in the area. It affirmed an all-pervading reality, the God who is one, who is essentially ineffable and without form, with whom union was possible for the faithful devotee. Sant devotions were expressed through the language of the people, not Sanskrit.

The author is particularly grateful to Charanjit Ajit Singh for help and advice in the writing of this chapter. Of course, responsibility for what appears is the author's alone.

The Golden Temple at Amritsar, India. Photo: Corbis/Bennett Dean/Eye Ubiquitous.

Into this environment **Guru** Nanak was born. It was clearly a dynamic environment with some groups debating conflicting claims, while others preached simple devotion, eschewing theological controversy. No doubt the young Nanak was involved in discussions with people of a variety of religious faiths, and in later life this may have fueled his feeling that he was called by God to challenge what he felt was the misplaced piety and valueless religiosity of much that passed for religion at that time. His was a challenge that grew out of his context and spoke to the needs of many people, but it was also, Sikhs firmly believe, an independent revelation of a distinct divine message: to search the depths of one's own being for that One through whose grace alone liberation is possible.

At present there is a tension between western-trained scholars and the guardians of Sikh orthodoxy. Essentially, this revolves around the nature of possible background influences on the Sikh faith and the effects of rigorous historical–critical method on the text of the Guru Granth Sahib. This brief introduction to Sikhism aims to reflect the Sikhism of the popular belief of the ordinary Gurdwara congregational member.

Historical Survey

The ten gurus

Guru Nanak (1469–1539)
Guru Nanak was born in 1469 in Talwandi Rai, 65 km northwest of Lahore. He was of a middle-class Hindu family. His father was Kalyan Das who maintained the

accounts for the local Muslim landowner, Rai Bular. As a boy he had a good education and became a storekeeper for Nawab Daulat Khan Lodi in Sultanpur. Even
as a young man he was very interested in religious matters and talked to the religious leaders of both Hindu and Muslim communities, who traditionally had little
time for one another. Having had first-hand knowledge of both faiths, he reacted to
what he saw was the "false" religiosity of both groups, and felt called to encourage
the worship of the one God, eschewing over-concern with the outward religious
rites of either faith.

Breaking away from convention, he encouraged women to join in worship and,
furthermore, encouraged all to worship in their own Panjabi language rather than
the brahminical Sanskrit or the courtly Urdu. Worship, however, was considered
insufficient. The deepening of religious faith was also to be accompanied by selfless
service (**seva**) and honest living.

Later in life he made a number of missionary journeys and established communities – *sangats*. He eventually settled in Kartarpur on the River Ravi where he led
the community in the singing of hymns which he and other like-minded people
had composed. There he also received visitors, all of whom were invited to share
in a common meal, thus breaking down caste barriers.

Amongst those who regularly came was Lehna, originally a worshiper of the Hindu
goddess Durga, who became a disciple and thanks to his self-effacing ways was
nominated by Guru Nanak as his successor.

Guru Angad (1504–52, G 1539 ["G" symbolizes the date of recognition as the Guru])

The erstwhile Lehna was born in 1504, the son of Pheru of the Khatri caste (a
high-caste, Hindu mercantile class) in the village of Matte di Sarai in Ferozepur
District. He was converted through Guru Nanak's preaching and is said to have
invented and developed the Gurmukhi script. In this script the scriptures were eventually to be written, hence the name meaning "from the mouth of the Guru."

He had two sons, both of whom were said to be delinquents, and a daughter
who is said to have been the model of piety and obedience. Having founded a
school in Khadur, he encouraged all to learn Gurmukhi in an attempt to wean
people away from Hinduism. He wrote hymns under the name of "Nanak,"
thereby indicating spiritual continuity with Guru Nanak. He taught his followers
to meditate on the divine name, thus reducing the necessity for either temple or
priest.

Guru Amar Das (1479–1574, G 1552)

Amar Das was born in the village of Basarke near Amritsar and, like his predecessors (and indeed like the rest of the gurus to follow), was of Khatri stock. Having
heard his nephew's wife, Guru Angad's daughter, singing Sikh hymns, he was attracted
to Sikhism. He was of Hindu background and had often made pilgrimages to holy
rivers to wash away his sins, but learnt from Guru Nanak that only through God's
grace would liberation be possible. He settled in Goindwal on the River Beas where

he created a bathing place which his followers were to visit, especially at **Baisakhi** and **Diwali**.

Missionaries were appointed by him to spread the new faith, both men and women. Indeed, his concern for women was demonstrated by his rejection of *sati* (in which a widow throws herself on her late husband's funeral pyre) and consequent encouragement of widow remarriage. A practical man who was determined to consolidate a distinguishable Sikh community, he drew up a pattern for funerals. Also, as a married man, he demonstrated that there is no need to become ascetic or celibate to gain liberation.

By Guru Amar Das's time more people were being born into the faith than were converts to it. It was a period of consolidation and organization when new *sangats* (congregations) were being founded. Perhaps his most significant new development was the establishment of the *langar*, the free kitchen to which all people, irrespective of faith, caste, or status, were invited to eat together.

Guru Ram Das (1534–81, G 1574)

Guru Ram Das was Guru Amar Das's son-in-law and had been involved in missionary work. His memory stands the test of time in that he composed the *lavan* – the hymn used to this day in the Sikh wedding ceremony. The creation of new Sikh liturgies and rituals was a deliberate policy, with the intention of further distancing Sikhism from Hinduism. Through this new ceremony Sikhs would not need the aid and presence of a Brahmin priest.

Ram Das laid the foundations of the city of Amritsar in 1577. It was on the main road across north India, thus the message of Sikhism could be easily spread. Further consolidation of the community was through his appointment of *masands* – leaders – who acted on his behalf as spiritual guides and tithe collectors. He contributed to Sikh worship through his skillful hymn-writing.

Guru Arjan (1563–1606, G 1581)

Guru Arjan was Guru Ram Das's youngest son and the first Guru to be born a Sikh and the son of a Guru. In appointing Arjan, a hereditary tradition was begun, and the rest of the Gurus were all from the same Sodhi family.

Arjan excavated the pool at Amritsar and constructed the *Harmandir* (House of God). He was a prolific hymn writer and also edited a volume of poems and hymns of Sikh and other writers, which later became the Guru Granth Sahib, or the **Adi** Granth, the Sikh holy scriptures.

During his time as Guru a number of towns were founded, all of which were dominated by the Sikh presence, for example, Tarn Taran, Kartapur and Chherta Sahib. Sikhism thus became a significant socio-political factor during the political struggle after the death of the Emperor Akbar. Arjan was caught up in the struggle between the successors to Akbar's throne and eventually died in Mughal custody in 1606. Sikhs saw his death as a martydom and a call to arms, and consequently the next Guru, Hargobind, was to sit fully armed on his throne.

Guru Hargobind (1595–1644, G 1606)

Guru Arjan's son, Guru Hargobind, recognized that Sikhs would probably have to defend their faith by force if necessary. He took to wearing two swords representing temporal authority (*miri*) and spiritual authority (*piri*), emblems later incorporated into the Sikh symbol. He was detained in Gwalior fort by the Emperor Shah Jehan, who had stationed imperial troops in the Panjab. This led to skirmishes between the Mughal Emperor's forces and the Sikhs. Hargobind deliberately moved his headquarters to Kiratpur near the Shivalik Hill, outside Mughal jurisdiction.

Guru Har Rai (1630–61, G 1644)

The Sikhs continued to be out of favor with the Mughal Emperor, forcing Har Rai to move from Kiratpur further into the Shivalik Hills. The Guru is said to have been of a gentle persuasion, giving much of his time to missionary work in the Malwa region. Under his rule, as well as the eighth Guru's, political and military skirmishes abated.

Guru Har Krishan (1656–64, G 1661)

Har Krishan was Guru Har Rai's second son. He became Guru at the age of six. He lived in Delhi and died at an early age having contracted smallpox.

Guru Tegh Bahadur (1621–1675, G 1664)

During Emperor Aurangzeb's reign, Hindus found themselves denied religious liberty. Schools and temples were closed and some Hindus were forcibly converted to Islam. Sikhs fared little better. Guru Tegh Bahadur traveled the country trying to encourage his followers. Whilst doing so he was approached by Kashmiri Brahmins for help and consequently traveled to Delhi to try to persuade the Emperor to change his policies toward religious tolerance. The result was that not only were his companions beheaded when they refused to become Muslims but he too suffered the same fate when in 1675 he was arrested and executed on a charge of sedition. His head was rescued by a sweeper, Jaita, and cremated at Anandpur whilst his body was taken to a village near Delhi where it was cremated. Tegh Bahadur acquired the status of a Sikh martyr.

Guru Gobind Singh (1666–1708, G 1675)

Born in Patna and the son of Guru Tegh Bahadur, Guru Gobind Singh has always been considered the model of Sikh manhood. He was courageous in battle and sensitive and generous in nature. During his reign the relationships between Sikhs and Muslims deteriorated further and reached such a low ebb that, at Baisakhi 1699, he called his followers to assemble and warned them of dangerous times ahead when they would have to be ready to fight for their faith. This demanded courage and strength. Having drawn his sword, he asked for a volunteer who would give his head for the cause. No one responded for some time, but eventually a Sikh came forward. He was led to the Guru's tent. With his sword dripping with blood the Guru emerged again only to make the same request. A second volunteer came forward and was led away to the tent. In all, this happened five times, during which time those of a less courageous disposition quietly took their leave from the gathering. To the surprise of the remaining crowd, the "beloved five" (*panj piare*) reappeared alive and safe with the Guru. Some say they had been raised to life, others that the Guru had slaughtered five goats. Whatever was the case they had demonstrated fearless loyalty and were upheld as role models for those Sikhs who remained. The five were given *amrit* – nectar – made from sugar crystals, placed in an iron bowl by the Guru's wife, and water stirred with a two-edged sword by the Guru. In turn the Guru and his wife were similarly initiated by the five. To this day all who are initiated as Sikhs of whatever caste, or none, follow the same process.

A new code of conduct was instituted for the "Pure Ones" – the *khalsa* – which forbade the use of tobacco, the eating of meat slaughtered in the Muslim *halal* fashion, and sexual intercourse with Muslim women. Male membership in the *khalsa* was symbolized by the *panj kakke* or "five Ks": uncut hair, a comb, a steel bangle, a sword, and undershorts. We will consider the five Ks below. It was also at this time that the men took the name *Singh*, lion, and the women *Kaur*, princess. All, irrespective of previous caste or gender, were regarded as equal members of the *khalsa* once initiated.

A final step was to end the Sikh custom of appointing a human successor as Guru. Supposedly, just before his execution, Guru Gobind Singh proclaimed that the word of the Guru was now to be found within the scripture, in whose presence all major decisions with regard to the Sikh **panth** were to be made. So the Tenth Guru is in fact the Adi Granth, or Guru Granth Sahib, which we will discuss in more detail later.

Struggles with the Mughal Empire continued after Guru Gobind Singh's death, though by this time the empire was in decline. Nevertheless the Sikhs were contained, but not without the continued skirmishes by the *jathas* – small cavalry groups – against the governors of Lahore. Repression continued with the slaughter of the Sikh forces in 1746 and the defilement of the *Harmandir*. From the northwest in the following year, an Afghan force was next to attack the Sikhs through a series of invasions led by Ahmad Shah Abdali. The sixth invasion, in 1762, saw the massacre of very many Sikhs and was dubbed "the Greater Holocaust."

In Sikh history and legend this was a period when the Sikhs seemed to be the only ones willing to stand against the Afghan invaders. Since the Afghans were unable to firmly establish their grip over the Panjab, it was one of the Sikh chieftains, Ranjit Singh, who was able to gain control over much of the Panjab. He eventually ruled as Maharajah of Lahore until his death in 1839. Ranjit Singh was able to remain independent from the British in India and maintained a stable administration, during which time the "Golden Temple" complex was developed.

With Ranjit Singh's death, however, no single Sikh leader came to prominence, leaving the British able to gain the advantage in the hard-fought Anglo-Sikh wars of 1845–6 and 1848–9. Sikh troops were then recruited by the British, to whom they remained loyal during the 1857 War of Independence.

Under British administration, the Panjab became a center for Christian missionary activity, to the extent that when four young men announced their intention to convert to Christianity, Sikh concern for the decline in faith resulted in the formation of the Singh Sabha movement. Its express intention was to reawaken Sikh doctrinal purity and faithful practice in the light of threats from both Christians and especially the Hindu *Arya Samaj*.

Control of the Sikh Gurdwaras and the lands associated with them was also an area of concern. Many were in the hands of Hindu custodians – *mahants* – who thought nothing of installing Hindu images, even within the precincts of the *Harmandir* itself. Mass campaigns were launched to gain Sikh control with the *Akali Dal* – the "army of immortals" – demanding that the Central Gurdwara Management Committee (SGPC), established in 1920, be given necessary powers. These they received in 1925 when the Sikh Gurdwaras Act gave the SGPC full control over Gurdwaras, their lands, and their revenues.

Sikhs played a prominent role in the Independence movement and had hoped for an independent Panjab in 1947, only to find themselves as part of India. The influence and increased powers of the central Indian government over the Panjab led to further dissatisfaction on the part of many Sikhs. Calls for a Sikh homeland were made, and echoed in the Sikh diaspora. By the 1980s Sant Jarnail Singh Bhindranwale emerged as a leader in the Sikh call for an independent homeland, *Khalistan*. It had been hoped by Mrs. Gandhi's government that he would embarrass Sikh leaders, but, rather than tow a central government line, Bhindranwale took it upon himself to occupy and defend the Golden Temple in Amritsar. An Indian "anti-terrorist" operation to clear him out of the complex resulted in considerable structural damage, a loss of trust between Sikhs and the central government, and eventually to Mrs. Gandhi's being assassinated in 1984 by her Sikh bodyguard.

The tensions are still not resolved. The Hindu-based Bharatiya Janita Party is not trusted by Sikhs and tensions between India and Pakistan, now again at the forefront of political life in the subcontinent, leave the Sikhs of the Panjab in a particularly vulnerable position.

The Sikh Belief System

God

The opening words of the Sikh scriptures deal with the Sikh understanding of God, who is usually referred to as *Akal Purakh*, or the "timeless person." The language of the Guru Granth Sahib is not gender specific and the poetic and economic nature of the text means that any English translation can only be a paraphrase. Nevertheless, it will be useful to look at the first verses in order to come to some understanding of the Sikh doctrine of God.

> There is one God,
> Eternal Truth is His Name;

Maker of all things,
Fearing nothing and at enmity with nothing,
Timeless is His image;
Not begotten, being of His own Being;
By the grace of the Guru, made known to men.
(*A World Religions Reader*, second edition, edited by
Ian S. Markham (Oxford: Blackwell Publishers, 2000),
p. 334. See also Adi Granth [the Sikh Scriptures], p. 1)

God is One

"My master is the One. He is the One, brother, and He alone exists" is among many of the sayings of Guru Nanak about God. Discussion arises as to whether the Sikh understanding is one of monism or monotheism, that is, do they believe, respectively, that all is one, impersonal Reality or that a single personal ultimate deity exists. The monistic view seems to be indicated if one reads the words of Guru Gobind Singh: "all embodied beings are absorbed in you," while the monotheistic view is demonstrated by the experience of the Gurus, and their followers, of a God of grace to whom they respond with love and devotion.

God as Supreme Reality

The universe reflects God's divine power. God is both omnipotent and omniscient – "the sovereign Lord created this visible world. He sees all, comprehends all, and knows all, permeating (all creation) both within and without," says the Adi Granth. It is this God who is the Lord who has absolute authority over all life: "you are able to do whatever pleases you and no one can question it." God is often referred to as "Wonderful Lord" – **Waheguru**.

Immanent yet Transcendent

Sikhs affirm the seemingly paradoxical truth that God is both known or manifest in and through the world, yet is immeasurably beyond it: God is both immanent and transcendent. So God is in all humans and the whole created universe, "the whole phenomenal world which is before you is the visible image of God, in it I see the face of God" (Adi Granth p. 622, henceforth AG). Yet God is ineffable and transcendent: "beyond human grasp or understanding, boundless, infinite, the all-powerful supreme God . . . beyond understanding, infinite, unreachable, beyond perception . . ." (AG, p. 597).

God as Creator and Sustainer

"When it pleased you, you created the world" (AG, p. 1036), sings the Guru, affirming further "the fearless One, the formless One, the True Name – the whole world is his creation" (AG, p. 465). However, this is praise of no absentee God but rather one who sustains that which has been created: "He who created the world watches over it, appointing all to their various tasks" (AG, p. 765). Sikhs place their faith in one who is seen to participate in the life of the universe and, therefore, one with whom a personal relationship is possible.

Yet this creator and sustainer is also one who destroys, though not without re-creating: "God breaks down and rebuilds and by divine order all is sustained" (AG, p. 579).

God is without fear and without enmity

That which is feared is usually something that holds one in its power. Thus the Sikh affirms, by this understanding of the nature of God, that there is nothing that is beyond God's power.

God is not subject to time, rather God is eternal

In speaking of the divine, Sikhs will tend to use the term *Akal Purakh*, meaning "the Being which is beyond the limitations of time." While the world may be imper-manent, God is not: "The one who is the True Lord is eternally true. God is and will be, for unlike creation God will not pass away" (AG, p. 6). Thus union with God, which is the essence of liberation and the goal of one's spiritual quest, takes one out of the confines of this world and its temporal limitations and beyond to that which is true and not *maya* – the contingent or "relatively real." God is absolute, unconditioned, and beyond human perception: "From God's absolute con-dition the divine, the pure one, became manifest; from *nirguna* (without form) the divinity became *saguna* (with form)" (AG, p. 940).

God is self-manifesting and gracious

This last quotation from the Adi Granth does not imply that God manifests Godself in terms of an *avatar*. Rather, because God is creator, humanity is able to under-stand something of the nature of God, God's purposes and praiseworthy qualities. These are understood through God's *saguna* aspect, and reflected in the deeds and lifestyle of his faithful people. Notice that personal divine qualities, such as loving concern for others, steadfastness and justice, are qualities which are usually ascribed to either males or females. Sikhs believe that with God, however, no such gender distinctions can be made. Indeed, God is beyond gender epithets and referred to, by Sikhs, as both "father" and "mother." The fact that the language of the Sikh scriptures is inclusive is, theologically, exceedingly helpful. Translations into English usually leave much to be desired since they do not reflect the inclusive nature of the original language.

God is ultimately ineffable, beyond human comprehension. Yet this same God can be comprehended through God's grace since "only the one upon whom God's grace rests understands" (AG, p. 1256).

God is the True Guru, the one who speaks through the Word

Those to whom we refer as "Gurus," both human and the scripture, ultimately find their authority in God who is the Guru, whose Word – **shabad** – the gurus must proclaim: "The true creator is known by means of the Word" (AG, p. 688). This being so, "whoever meditates on your true word is united with you" (AG, p. 1290).

1   Guru Nanak said that the more you speak about God the more you need
        to speak about God. In speaking of God, the Guru used many paradoxes
        and metaphors. Does this use of poetic and figurative language leave the
        believer more confused or rather even more determined to continue the search
        for greater understanding? Give reasons for your answers.

The Human Condition

As with the Hindu understanding of time, Sikhs understand time and the progression of the human soul to be cyclical. The state of humans in time is one of attachment and ensnarement. Pride, self-centeredness, and sin are of the nature of unregenerate humanity and are to be avoided, otherwise they lead to rebirth. They must be overcome if release is to be found.

The Sikh understanding of humanity starts with the **man**. There is no single satisfactory translation of this word, but it represents that within the individual which takes decisions. One may begin to scratch the surface of understanding through the terms "innermost sense," "mind," "soul," or "heart." So "the *man* acts as the *man* determines, sometimes expressing virtue, sometimes vice." Notice that mankind is not inherently evil, for "in one's *man* is truth and so truth is spoken also" (AG, p. 839). The *man* is erratic, unsteady and does not know the true way. Thus one should not place one's trust in one's *man*, rather in the name of God (see AG, pp. 1187–8).

As a result humanity is essentially self-centered. This is the result of one's "*haumai*" which is sometimes translated "ego" and means literally "me-I." "Sin" may also be a translation, but this is more a reflection on the outcome rather than the meaning of the word itself. "Self-centeredness" may be the best translation. As a result of this self-centeredness life and its aftermath is dictated:

> In *haumai* one comes, in *haumai* one goes;
> In *haumai* one is born and in *haumai* one dies;
> In *haumai* one gives and in *haumai* one takes;
> In *haumai* one acquires and in *haumai* one throws away;
> In *haumai* one is truthful and in *haumai* one tells lies;
> In *haumai* one sometimes espouses virtue and sometimes evil . . .
> (AG, p. 466)

Anyone who is influenced by *haumai* will become **manmukh**, that is, "self-willed" and by their very nature unable to follow God's will to become **gurmukh**. Such a person will be caught up in *maya* – the mistaken belief that this material world may be the ultimate reality (this does not mean to imply that this physical world is unreal):

> She who is caught up in greed, avarice and pride is sunk in *maya*.
> Foolish woman! God is not found by such means.
> (AG, p. 722)

Rather the opposite is likely to happen as is graphically described by Guru Nanak:

> Day and night are the two seasons when people crop their land; lust and anger are their two fields. They water them with greed, sow in them the seed of untruth and worldly impulse, the plough-man cultivates them. Their evil thoughts are the plough and evil is the crop they reap, for in accordance with the divine will, they harvest and eat. (AG, p. 955)

There are five evil passions, all of which lead to violence, evil deeds, falsehood and consequently the continuation of transmigration. Self-willed people are shown by their inability to control *kam* (lust); *krodh* (anger); *lobh* (avarice); *moh* (worldly attachment); and *hankar* (pride). These constantly attack human nature:

> I have five adversaries and I am alone. How shall I defend my house
> O *man*? Daily they attack and plunder me.
>
> (AG, p. 155)

Further:

> No one can say when their turn will come. The way is difficult, frightening, over seas and impassable mountains. I waste away because of the evil within. Without the necessary merit how can I enter (God's) house? (AG, p. 936)

For Discussion. How true to life is Guru Nanak's understanding of the human condition? Explain the reasons for your answers.   **Exercise**

How does one find liberation?

"By meditating on God, in my heart I shall become like him. (My heart) is filled with evil, but in it there are redeeming qualities" (AG, p. 936). Without the true Guru these qualities are not perceived and, until they are perceived, one does not meditate on the Word of God. Thus liberation is possible only through the grace of God unlocking the individual's effort to cleanse him or herself from evil. Note the order in which this occurs and the fact that it is through God's grace alone.

Guru Nanak and his followers rejected rituals, asceticism, notions of cleansing oneself from impurity and the like, arguing, rather, that if the inner *man* is not clean, then it cannot be made so by worshiping stones, visiting places of pilgrimage or living in the jungle as an ascetic (all of which are Hindu practices). Only unity with the True One will convey honor.

The individual believer needs, therefore, to comprehend the will and purpose of God who communicates through *Shabad* (the Word); *Nam* (the Name); the *Guru* and his *Hukum* (God's will); and *Nadar* (grace). God reveals Godself and God's will through his *hukum* – the order of creation. "Truth is there for those who perceive it," as the scriptures say. Such perception, however, is brought about only through God's grace:

> If thou dost impart thy grace then by that grace the true Guru is revealed. (AG, p. 465)

The Sikh understanding is not one of God giving liberation, but a prior act of grace which enables the individual to hear and understand God's Word and to respond to it. So, a person understands the need for liberation and also understands the means to be followed in order to respond/attain it. Human beings have to respond and themselves make an effort.

The nature of the response

An outward show of religion is not true religion. God is not found through maintenance of caste, status, idolatry, bathing in pilgrimage centers, ascetic practices, or forms of yoga, but in the inward disciplines of love, faith, mercy, and humility expressed in righteous and compassionate acts and upholding the truth.

Guru Nanak illustrated this by turning on their head the so-called religious practices of those who claimed to be fulfilling the requirements of their faith:

> Make mercy your mosque, faith your prayer-mat, and righteousness your Qur'an.
> Make humility your circumcision, uprightness your fasting, and so
> You will be a (true) Muslim.
> Make good works your *Ka'bah*, truth your *pir*, and compassion your
> Creed and your prayer.
> Make the performance of what pleases (God) your rosary and, Nanak,
> God will uphold your honour.
>
> (AG, pp. 140–1)

Loving devotion of God is vital, requiring absolute surrender to God's will and purpose: "Accept whatever God does as good, put no trust in your own cleverness and abandon the exercise of your own will. Fix your mind . . . (on God) . . . through whose love the priceless treasure is obtained" (AG, p. 722).

A further requirement of the devotee is *nam simran*, which connotes more than its literal meaning of "repetition of the name." It is about keeping God in mind at all times so that the whole of one's life is a reflection of God's nature: "Let your actions be those of love. (The seed) will then sprout and you will see your home prosper" (AG, p. 595). The results are two-fold: there will be the potential for liberation from the round of transmigration as the ultimate result. Secondly, there is the possibility of becoming a *jivan mukat*, one who attains liberation whilst in this present body which is "sanctified and God dwells in that person's heart as the only love" (AG, p. 931).

At this level of devotion the faithful may go through five spiritual stages. First comes *dharam khand* in which one realizes the moral consequences of all actions. Second is *gian khand* at which point one's understanding of the nature of the purposes of God weakens one's inclination to self-centeredness. The interpretation of the third stage is debatable but might represent either the element of humility and surrender needed to follow God's will, or the effort the devotee needs to make. Fourthly, there is *karam khand* which may either represent the stage at which God's grace comes further into play, or may be the realm of action. Finally comes *sach khand*, the realm of Truth, the dwelling of the Formless One. At this point the devotee would in effect be in union with the divine. It is the ultimate end and purpose of human existence:

> The body is the palace of God, God's temple and dwelling place in which shines the infinitely radiant light. By the Guru's Word one is summoned within the palace; there one meets God. (AG, p. 1256)

Rituals and Institutions

Five Ks

The *panj kakke* – Ks – are symbols of the faith that initiated male members of the *khalsa* must wear.

1   The hair should never be cut and is known as *Keshas* – uncut hair. Holy men in India customarily have been distinguished by their long, uncut hair. To trim the hair, even body hair, is regarded as an act of apostasy.
2   The comb – *Kanga* – is used to keep the hair neat and tidy. As one should comb the hair twice a day, so too should one's prayer life be similarly maintained. Hair must always be kept clean and is washed regularly.
3   A sword – *Kirpan* – is worn to remind Sikhs of their need to maintain dignity and self-respect and their willingness to fight for truth and justice. The actual length of the sword varies from a formal one about three feet long carried at important ceremonies to one of only a few inches in length which would be carried in a belt. It should be used only in a just cause: "when all other means have failed," said Guru Gobind Singh, "it is right to draw the sword."
4   Recalling the days when Sikhs sometimes had to fight for their very lives, Sikhs are required to wear the *Kara*, a steel bracelet which once would have been used for protection for the sword arm and had already become a symbol of devotion to the Guru. It is also a reminder of the unity of God, for there is no beginning and no end to the circle.
5   Knee-length shorts – *Kaccha* – are the final symbol. They are practical in purpose, especially in battle, and are also a reminder to the wearer that he must remain faithful to his marriage partner.

Langar

When he settled in Kartarpur, Guru Nanak encouraged his followers to eat together, but by the time of Guru Amar Das all those who wished to visit the Guru were obliged to take food. This obligation was even placed upon the Emperor Akbar when he visited the Guru. Vegetarian food must always be served so as not to place any restrictions on those who eat. The term "*langar*" actually refers to both the place in which the food is served and the food itself. It is a symbol of the Guru's generosity and also of the egalitarian nature of Sikhism, for all, irrespective of caste or religious affiliation, are invited. Similarly all may be involved in serving, both women and men.

The ingredients are often supplied by members of the congregation, usually in thanksgiving for God's grace active in their families. However, Gurdwara trustees will always ensure that stocks are well maintained. The food is usually simple, nourishing, and generously served. Traditionally, those who eat would sit on the floor in rows and be served from stainless steel vessels. In the Sikh diaspora there has been a tendency to serve from the kitchen hatches in fast-food style, a development not entirely favored by some of the older members of the *sangats*.

Rahit Marayada

The *Rahit Marayada* is the Sikh code of conduct agreed in 1945, when the Shiromani Gurdwara Parbandhak Committee (set up in 1925 to oversee the management of Sikh places of worship) was obliged to define the nature of Sikhism and who is a Sikh. Their definition shows that a Sikh is a person who has faith in the one God, the ten Gurus and their teaching, and in the Adi Granth. Such a person must also believe in the necessity of the *amrit* initiation and must not espouse any other religion.

The *Rahit* goes on to indicate how Gurdwaras must be open during the day for worship, the nature and function of such worship, the way the scriptures should be handled, stored, and read and who is permitted to do so, the sharing of *kara prasad* (a mixture of wheatmeal, sugar, and clarified butter used in ritual worship); the way a Sikh should live out her or his life, eschewing anything which may smack of caste, pollution, horoscopes, and meaningless religiosity. The details of rites of passage are also outlined as are matters concerning community discipline.

Marriage

Since the path to liberation – *mukti* – is possible in the householder state, according to Sikh understanding, marriage and family are of great importance. In normal circumstances there would be little delay after the completion of a young person's education in finding a suitable partner from a compatible family. This is particularly important since the bride will leave her own family to live with that of her husband.

Sikhs usually hold a betrothal ceremony when the parents of the bride, together with family members, visit the groom's parents to exchange presents for the bride and groom in the presence of the Guru Granth Sahib. Promises are then publicly made. A suitable date for the wedding is found, but astrological calculations should not be involved since this reflects mere superstition.

Whilst some Sikhs dress their daughter in very costly clothes for her wedding, others, especially Namdharis, do not put on such a lavish display. On the morning of the wedding in India the groom and his party would make their way to the bride's parents for the wedding ceremony. In the West, if the Gurdwara is not registered for weddings, a civil wedding would take place. This would take place in a Registry Office or before a Justice of the Peace, followed by the religious ceremony – the *Anand Karaj* – which would take place usually in the Gurdwara and certainly in the presence of the Guru Granth Sahib. The men of both families would meet together with the bride's family, giving turban lengths and token gifts of money to show that the wedding represents the joining not simply of bride and groom but of their families as well. The guests then gather together in the presence of the scriptures for the religious part of the ceremony.

Both bride and groom sit together before the Guru Granth Sahib, the bride to the groom's left and dressed, traditionally, in a *Shalwar Chamise*. The *granthi*, the reciter of the Adi Granth, explains the responsibilities of married life to the couple, asking God's blessing on them, and reminding them that Sikh marriage is not simply a social contract but the bringing together of two souls in unity with and before God – "They are not man and wife who have physical contact alone, but only those who have one spirit in two bodies are truly married" (AG, p. 788).

At that point the *granthi* opens the Guru Granth Sahib, and the *Lavan*, a hymn composed especially for weddings by Guru Ram Das, is read and sung verse by verse, during which the couple walk clockwise around the scriptures, once for each of the four verses. Thereafter further excerpts from the scriptures are sung, the advice of the Guru is sought by opening the scriptures at random and finally *kara prasad* is distributed, first to the couple and then to all other guests. All leave to make their way to a wedding feast, sometimes in the *langar*, otherwise in the home of the groom or a suitable meeting hall.

Death

The impermanence of human life is well recognized by Sikhs – "nothing is everlasting" (AG, p. 1429) so when someone is about to die they are encouraged to die with God's name on their lips – **Waheguru** – Wonderful Lord. The body is washed and clothed by the family members, making sure the five Ks are in place.

The body would be taken to the cremation ground outside the village or town if the family were in India. In the West it is taken to a crematorium. Sometimes a service of remembrance would take place in the Gurdwara, but the coffin would not usually be taken inside. At cremation the evening hymn would be sung and prayers, including the *Ardas* offered.

Mourners would then make their way to the family home where they would wash their hands and faces, or, in India, take a bath and then eat together signifying that though a death may have occurred life must go on and what is there to mourn? "If God dwells in you undisturbed you will not be reborn" (AG, p. 13).

Festivals

While there are a number of ceremonies celebrated in India, usually at the scene of the event they commemorate, the number of universally held Sikh festivals is but few. Essentially these are the birthdays of Gurus Nanak and Gobind Singh, the anniversaries of the martyrdoms of Gurus Arjan and Tegh Bahadur, and the anniversary of the founding of institutional Sikhism at Baisakhi.

The former two *gurpurbs* – holy days held in honor of the Gurus – are celebrated by a continuous reading of the Guru Granth Sahib lasting 48 hours, when a team of readers would complete an "uncut" reading – *akhand path* – from beginning to end of the scriptures. Whilst this is being done *kara prasad* would be available to any who come to the Gurdwara as, indeed, would food cooked and served by family or congregation members. As the reading comes to an end, usually early in the morning, it would lead into a service of worship when there would also be sermons explaining the significance and teachings of the Guru whose birthday was being celebrated. In the West there is a tendency to hold the *gurpurb* on the nearest weekend to the actual day.

Often a procession is organized. It would be led, sometimes on horseback and with swords drawn, by five Sikhs of good standing who would represent the five "beloved ones." The Guru Granth Sahib would be taken on a specially decorated vehicle, leading the faithful who would chant passages of the scriptures.

Two further festivals are important: **Baisakhi** and **Diwali**. These are the *jore melas* – seasons for meeting, when Sikhs recognize the importance of celebrating their unanimity and concord. Baisakhi, held on 13/14 April, was originally a Hindu festival, but Guru Gobind Singh chose that day to gather together his followers and challenge them to the recognition that they must be prepared to fight for their faith. It was the time that the *khalsa* was formed and nowadays would be the time when young Sikhs are initiated into the faith. In the West the festival would be celebrated on the nearest weekend and would start with an *akhand path* followed on the Sunday by lectures, hymn-singing, and worship. Each year at this time the flag (*nishan sahib*) flying above the Gurdwara would be taken down and renewed and the flag-pole cleaned with yoghurt or milk and water. Sikhs may also recall other events which occurred at Baisakhi, such as the 1919 massacre of those involved in the quit-India campaign by the British General Dyer in Jallianwala Bagh in Amritsar.

Like Baisakhi, Diwali, too, is a Hindu festival in origin. For many Sikhs it serves as a reminder of their persecution often at the hands of the Mughals. An example is the freeing of Guru Hargobind who had been imprisoned by the Emperor Jehangir.

Worship and the Gurdwara

Anyone entering a Sikh Gurdwara will be struck by the fact that much of the service of worship is set to music. Hymns – *shabads* – are sung to tunes selected long ago and to sing them is considered a means of liberation. Congregational worship is pivotal, for it is in the company of good people that one finds the presence of God – "Just as a castor oil plant takes on the scent of sandalwood nearby, so the fallen are emancipated by the company of the true ones" (AG, p. 869). Guru Nanak started the practice of hymn-singing during his missionary travels and also when he settled in Kartarpur. It was, and often still is, accompanied by a meal after the service since the Gurdwara building will always have a kitchen – *langar* – attached.

Gurdwaras change little in basic design. A large hall would have at its far end a dais with a canopy, under which the scriptures would be placed during the early morning. Nearby would be a lower dais for three musicians to lead the singing and expound the scriptures. The walls would be bare with little if any religious iconography to be found. The congregation would sit on cotton sheets on the carpeted floor, men on one side, women on the other, and the younger children crawling or running in between until encouraged to settle down and sit quietly.

There are no priests within Sikhism, but someone who is well respected and who has good knowledge of the scriptures may be appointed as leader of worship. In some Gurdwaras in the West a full-time official may be appointed whose task would be to lead formal worship and look after the buildings. Overall responsibility, however, would be taken by a Gurdwara management committee, normally appointed through elections held each year at Baisakhi, and also by the trustees whose appointment is more permanent.

Whilst the Gurdwara is essentially a place of worship, a visitor may often find older members of the congregation gathering there during the day sometimes to say their prayers or, more often than not, simply to sit and talk or read the newspapers. In addition, the India tradition of providing a room for travelers to sleep in is also found in many western Gurdwaras.

In the West many congregations gather on Sunday. It is not a Sikh holy day but quite simply a day when many people do not work and are, therefore, free to worship. Typically, services in the Gurdwara start at daybreak when the scriptures are brought into the sanctuary and a lesson is read. It is regarded as guidance for the day and is written up on a prominent notice-board. Hymn-singing begins, starting with *Asa-di-Var*. Many Sikhs will also make their way to the Gurdwara on their way to work during the week.

In the formal service in the Gurdwara there may also be an explanation of a particular hymn or passage of scripture. There might be time as well for making known important information for the congregation. *Ardas*, a set of prayers recalling lives of Sikh leaders, and prayers of intercession are followed by a number of hymns. *Kara Prasad* is then served and people make their way to the *langar*.

> 2   Gurdwaras in India are open every day from dawn to dusk. In North America
>   and Europe they are often open only at weekends and in the evening. What
>   effects do you think will this have on the Sikh community? Is
>   "Westernization" something to be worried about for the believing Sikh?

Ethics

The nature of authority

In that there is no sacred–secular divide within Sikhism, the whole of life is to be
lived to God's glory. Hence all authority with regard to ethical matters is essentially
God's. Human beings, therefore, must seek the will and guidance of God in all
they do. To this end the Guru Granth Sahib becomes that in which authority rests,
as it guides any decisions made by the consensus of the *khalsa*. The ultimate authority in human terms is the *khalsa*, who meet within the presence of the scriptures
in the *Akal Takht*. Religious authority may be mediated through the *jathedar*, the key
Sikh leader who would pronounce a *hukum nama* such as one recently delivered
which forbids the use of chairs in the *langar*.

However, from time to time Sikh leaders have produced guidelines, such as the
Rahit Marayada, which indicate behavior with regard to specific issues. Social pressure will also influence many Sikhs who would be most disturbed if they as individuals or a family member were to undermine the honor – *izzat* – of the family.

Personal life

Hospitality to strangers, respect for the elderly, and the imperative to maintain justice would be primary concerns in one's individual life. Honesty in dealings with
people, sexual restraint, and showing no hatred are central characteristics of an upright
Sikh since they reflect his or her concern for the maintenance of God's justice within
the world. The individual has a duty to worship regularly. This is not merely a
matter of the outward show of praise, but in the practice of *nam simran*, the repetition of God's name, one keeps the will of God at the forefront of one's mind.
The Adi Granth advises, "do not do deeds which make you regretful in the end"
(AG, p. 918).

Family Matters

Sikhs have a high regard for marriage and the maintenance of its sanctity. For the
Sikh there is no need to abandon the family home to seek spiritual liberation. As
the wedding hymn avows, the spiritual unity of man and wife leads to unity with
the divine – "they are not husband and wife who simply dwell together" (AG,
p. 788).

For Sikhs, the marriage is not simply a matter of two people joining in matrimony. It is a union of two families and to this end everything is done to make sure they are compatible through similar background and religious persuasion. Family relationships are of great importance, reflected in the practice of the bride leaving her own family and joining that of her husband. Girls tend to be brought up to recognize that one day this will happen. There is a tendency among families in the subcontinent to indulge young boys, but as both boys and girls grow, things become a little more strict – certainly for many teenage girls. In the West both girls and boys tend to resent the authoritarianism of the traditional ways, which seem more concerned with the maintenance of the family *izzat* than with the welfare and happiness of the younger generation. While this is often the case in many religious communities, Sikh emphasis on the importance of family can make matters particularly problematic.

Older people are always treated with great respect. A young bride would usually do her utmost to please her in-laws. The treatment rendered by westerners to the elderly when they are banished into residential homes leaves many Sikhs horrified and ashamed. Many retired people are able to maintain their dignity by the service they give to their local Gurdwaras, either in terms of rebuilding, refurbishment, or simply being of service to the congregation through cooking or cleaning.

The status of women

Guru Nanak's teaching condemned the attitudes toward women held amongst both Hindus and Muslims of the time. Hindu belief had it that during menstruation or childbirth women were ritually unclean. Further, girls were regarded as a liability because of the financial outlay necessary for dowries. Widows were not allowed to remarry, rather the loyal wife would be considered to have done an extremely honorable deed if she immolated herself on her husband's funeral pyre – a practice which was perhaps less frequent in reality than in folklore and gossip. In Muslim circles women would have been encouraged to veil themselves in public. All these practices were condemned by Guru Nanak and in various codes of practice (*rahitnamas*).

It is one thing for these practices to be condemned; alleviating the force of custom and cultural ethos is another matter. Until the twentieth century in some places baby girls continued to be smothered at birth. Amongst **Bhatra Sikhs** (small traders) women tend to cover their heads in the presence of male in-laws, and the practice of dowry-giving is maintained in some communities.

From a theological perspective women do not have to wait until they are reborn as men in order to attain release from the cycle of rebirth, nor are they necessarily considered to be temptresses, since liberation is possible in the householder state for both men and women. Sexual fidelity is, therefore, equally important for both partners, though male promiscuity is not unknown.

Women may be highly regarded, though in affirming this their high esteem is more a matter of the dependence of men upon women than a matter of women having significant position in their own right. This is illustrated by Guru Nanak's dictum:

> It is through woman, the one who is despised, that we are conceived and from her we are born. We are engaged to a woman and later marry her. She is our life-long friend and on her depends the survival of the race. On her death a man seeks another wife. Through women we establish social ties. Why denounce her, through whom kings are born? (AG, p. 473)

This history of Sikhism shows the courageous acts of many women, starting with the support given Guru Nanak by his sister Nanake. Likewise the Gurus' wives played a significant role. There were women preachers and those who fought in battle such as Mai Bhago, and both men and women work together in the running of Gurdwaras, though there is a tendency for men to dominate management committees.

The increasing present-day consciousness of the role and place of women has caused many Sikh women to re-evaluate their heritage and thus play a greater role in the life of their communities in terms of the professions, scholarship, and daily life.

Lifestyles

Three concepts dominate a good Sikh's lifestyle – worship, work, and charity. Hard work is a *sine qua non* of Sikh life, begging is seen as a disgrace. "All work is worship" may sometimes be found written on buses in Panjab. Generosity in terms of time and money is an often-seen characteristic.

In whatever continent they find themselves, Sikhs will unhesitatingly buckle down to hard work in order to maintain their families. But that does not mean they do not play hard as well. Sikhs are traditionally excellent at sports and Sikh communities may take pride in this tradition. Smoking is strictly forbidden, as is gambling, and the consumption of alcohol, but this last vice is not unknown amongst some.

Education

The very name "Sikh" implies someone who is a learner, so young people are very much encouraged to apply themselves to education. Medicine and engineering are the favored occupations, but the teaching profession is still highly regarded. Gurdwaras have traditionally been places where people have learned to read and write since, without that skill, reading the scriptures, the Word of God, would be impossible. Competence in literacy is not simply a blessing, it is a spiritual obligation.

Equality

There have been a number of examples of prominent Sikh women active as much on the battlefield as in the professions, diplomacy, and education. Guru Nanak is said to have established a more egalitarian environment for women but many Sikh women will tell you that it is as much honored in the breach as in reality.

Business ethics

Honest work

"He alone has found the right way who eats what he earns and shares his earnings with the needy" (AG, p. 1245) is the advice of the Guru. This means that there is an obligation upon the Sikh to be honest in all his or her dealings. Money should be honestly earned with one-tenth given away in charity. The exploitation of the poor is forbidden. In recognition that human beings are but sojourners in this world, the Gurus reminded their followers that material wealth is impermanent and it must not distract people of faith from their spiritual obligations.

This will have implications for one's work and how it is done. Advertising, for instance, will necessitate honesty; accountancy will demand integrity; and for shop-keepers profit is a necessity but excess profit anathema.

Ethics

The general ethical principles of Sikhism might best be understood through the concept of virtue. The virtuous person, he or she who follows the teachings of the Guru, will best be able to choose rightly in any given morally charged circumstance. This should be seen, however, in the context of the larger Indian ethos in which Sikhism developed. The Hindu concept of **karma** stresses that it is what one does, that is the moral character of actions, which determines one's ethical status. While rejecting the theory of karma in its specific form, the stress on action, specifically caring service to others, was stressed by Nanak and his followers. Ethical, socially relevant activity is a duty of all Sikhs.

Abortion

There is no direct guidance with regard to abortion but the Sikh reverence for life will indicate that it is normally to be avoided. In some circumstances, such as rape, there may be grounds for a termination, as may well be the case for medical reasons, but on religious grounds this might not be defensible since it is interfering with God's creativity. The increasing use of amniocentesis, however, has resulted in an escalation of the number of abortions of female fetuses, particularly in cultures where male children are more greatly prized. Contraception, however, is not frowned upon and decisions on its use are left to the couples involved.

Euthanasia

As with abortion there is no direct guidance. Care for the elderly is a very real part of Sikh life but any thought of terminating the life, even of those who are terminally ill or senile, is considered by many to be unacceptable. Life is a gift of God and is God's to give and to take away.

Engagement with the Modern World

Since early in their history Sikhs have traveled widely, at least from Baghdad in the west to Dhaka in the east. Many were traders whose later descendants made their way to other parts of the world to the extent that today Sikhs are to be found well established in South Asia, the Pacific, North America, and throughout Europe. What took them to these places?

In 1849 the Panjab was annexed by the British. Sikhs were not in favor of Mughal rule and accepted their new rulers as a better, though of course not ideal, situation. Having what was considered by the British to be a fine military bearing, Sikh soldiers soon found themselves in other parts of the British Empire either as soldiers or policemen or, when they retired, guards and security personnel. Thus Sikhs were to be found in Malaya, Singapore, Thailand, Burma, and Hong Kong. The early migration practice was essentially chain migration with younger members of the family following older relatives. Although many would have indicated that poverty had driven them to find employment elsewhere it must be borne in mind that it takes relative wealth to be able to travel to seek new opportunity. Some were driven to this because family land was being divided among sons with the result that some farm-holdings were becoming too small to maintain family life with any degree of dignity. Hence, those who sought employment abroad were often in a position to send money to their families in the Panjab and in so doing settle debts, possibly buy more land, build substantial houses, and marry their daughters or sisters honorably. Later, many sent for their families, staying on in their new homes having found that local customs did not undermine their own values and the practice of faith.

The USA and Canada

Presently, there are in the region of 150,000 Sikhs to be found in each of Canada and the United States. The Sikh presence dates from the turn of the twentieth century when, at the Coronation of Edward VII, some Sikh soldiers were taken to Vancouver, Canada, to which they later returned. Others made their way to the interior of British Columbia and were involved in logging or railway building. From 1907 onwards, migration to Canada was closed except to dependants. This continued until the 1950s. The USA denied even the right to bring in one's wife. Thus those Sikhs who made their way South, down the west coast, were obliged to find wives among Mexican migrant women. Many such families are to be found in California, for example near Stockton, where the riparian nature of the countryside enables the practice of the farming skills dear to the hearts of *Jat* Sikhs.

In the USA a number of white people have found their spiritual home within Sikhism. Many are the followers of an Indian spiritual teacher, Harbhajan Singh Puri, sometimes known as Yogi Bhajan. His is a strict regime of daily spiritual discipline, monogamy, the prohibition of alcohol, tobacco, and drugs, and service to the community, all of which are attractive to those who seek an honorable lifestyle.

The United Kingdom

By far the largest number of Sikhs in the diaspora, some 400,000 plus, are those living in the United Kingdom. Although the first Gurdwara in the UK was opened in Putney in 1911, it was not until the mid-war period that Bhatra Sikhs were to be found in more significant numbers trading in the various port cities. After the Second World War many arrived to work in the factories of Britain, then desperately seeking employees who were often willing to work anti-social hours. The first groups of Sikhs to come were men. Racist bigotry on the part of landlords meant that many lived in cramped conditions in overcrowded houses. Virtually all had the intention of making sufficient money to give them a reasonable lifestyle back in the Panjab to which they had every intention of returning. However, legislation in the 1960s presented them with the dilemma of the expense of bringing their families to the UK or returning to India with little or no chance of repeated access to the UK. Many chose to bring their families, and for them a new predicament arose.

Remaining faithful in an alien environment

Whereas in the Panjab one experiences and absorbs Sikhism and its ethos, it is much more difficult to enter its ethos in a western environment, sometimes very hostile to new immigrants. This created difficulties for Sikh children brought up and born in the UK.

Such young people found that they had to learn their faith in a non-traditional way. In the Panjab one learns the stories of faith on the grandmother's knee. Who is there to teach the faith in London, Leeds, or Bristol? Gurdwaras rapidly had to recognize educational responsibilities and rose to the occasion.

Yet education was not all. Many young Sikhs understood Panjabi, but had little, and often no, ability to read and write twentieth-century Panjabi let alone the scriptures written almost four hundred years previously. Thus many young people in the 1970s and 80s had little or no understanding of their parents' faith. Sikh leaders were understandably perturbed about this situation. Sikhism is a religion of a book, the Guru Granth Sahib. If young people cannot read the sacred language, how can the faith be communicated to the coming generation? Admittedly there are some translations into English, but certainly not the colloquial English of the present day. Should these be installed in the Gurdwara? Purists certainly resist this option.

Many of those who came as children in the 1960s are now themselves parents. Some have learnt Panjabi, though often only when their children arrived. Denied the facilities for Panjabi learning when young, often because it was not a language thought conducive to preferment in employment, they now encourage their own children to learn Panjabi for fear of losing their root culture. Though relatively successful for the youngest children, much still has to be done. Sermons in the Gurdwara services, usually on Sundays (a capitulation to the western work week), are often in Panjabi and given by a *granthi* of an older generation from the Panjab who does not understand the cultural milieu of his younger listeners.

In other respects the maintenance of faith is difficult. The demand made by Sikh initiation for the wearing of the *kirpan* can bring with it potential conflict with the police on the grounds that the *kirpan* could be assumed to be a dangerous weapon. The orthodox use of the turban has been the center of disputes with regard to safety regulations and dress code, even to the extent of various police and armed forces rejecting Sikh candidates, notwithstanding a history of courageous Sikh military service.

Note has already been made with regard to matters of Sikh ethical requirements and their effect on present-day life. In the UK, Sikh doctors usually follow the British Medical Association's codes of practice. Likewise the lifestyle of many younger Sikhs is more likely to be influenced as much by the cultural milieu of the major ethnic group as by ancestral norms. Assisted marriages are more likely to be the case than arranged, but the assistance given will not be inconsiderable.

These are early days yet for any detailed study of the contextualization of the Sikh faith. Over the coming decades this will take place. In what manner it will do so few can foresee with accuracy, but it would be hoped that the common-sense approach taken by the Gurus to faith and its manifestation in everyday life will continue to prevail. Theirs was a concern for humanity which has much to say about present-day hedonism and, by implication, issues of ecology, economics, and the creation of a just world.

Exercise   3   The Guru Granth Sahib installed in any Gurdwara is written in the language of sixteenth-century Northwest India. What are the broader issues this raises for young Sikhs born in the West? Should they attempt to remain pure to the old traditions and languages, or should some form of accommodation be found? If the latter, how far should this accommodation go?

In conclusion, I have tried to present Sikhism as believed and practiced by the orthodox, modern faithful. As one of the newest of the "great" religious traditions, Sikhism has had to face change and development to a greater extent than other, older traditions. This was due in part to the geographical locale of its genesis, in part to the religiously diverse context in which it developed, but perhaps mostly due to its leadership in its earliest days. Sikhism continues to develop and change today, and the dynamism, deep values, and praxis orientation that have served it so well through its history will surely continue to do so.

GLOSSARY

Adi   First.

Baisakhi   Originally a Hindu spring harvest festival, now for Sikhs the commemoration of the founding of the khalsa.

Bhakti   Belief in, and devotion to, a personal god.

Bhatra Sikh   A Sikh of the trader/peddler profession.

Diwali   A festival of lights.

Gurmukh   One who follows the will of God.

Guru   A spiritual teacher, usually a human-being, but sometimes considered to be the divine inner voice.

Haumai   Self, self-centeredness.

Janam-sakhi   Biography usually of Guru Nanak.

Jats   Hindus and Sikhs who are traditionally farmers.

Karma   A person's destiny thought to be dictated by one's deeds in a previous incarnation.

Langar   Kitchen or refectory.

Man   Heart, soul, mind, psyche.

Manmukh   One who follows his/her own impulses rather than the will of God.

Nath   A yogic sect amongst Hindus who rejected the external ceremonies of religion.

Panth   Path, sect, community.

Shabad   Word, divine self-communication.

Sant   (1) A religious devotee; (2) a tradition which considers the supreme being to be non-incarnated.

Samsara   The cycle of birth and rebirth.

Satsang   Fellowship of true believers.

Seva   Devotionally inspired social service.

Takht   Throne/seat of one who is of spiritual authority.

Waheguru   "Wonderful Lord," God.

Chapter 11

Chinese Religion

Mythological Rulers

Historical Survey

Worldviews

Ethical Expression

Role of Women

Rituals and Institutions

Calendar

Engagement with Modernity

In this short introduction to Chinese religion we will seek to discern the indigenous strands of thought which have permeated and fashioned the Chinese way of
life since antiquity. For the most part we will look at Confucianism and Daoism,
not as separate self-contained religious traditions, but focusing on how some of
the teachings associated with them have grafted onto, and developed, pre-existing
animistic beliefs. We will explore also the problematic question of Confucianism;
scholars both in China and abroad are divided as to whether it is a religion or merely
a social doctrine, and the issue is unlikely to be resolved soon. So this chapter is
not so much intended to present a definitive view, as to point out some of the
complexities in the study and perception of Chinese religion. This should not dis-
appoint or dishearten us, because this is only a starting point for the exploration
of an alternative way of interpreting the world around us; it can engage us also in
a stimulating reflection about how we categorize knowledge.

The Pinyin system of romanization, the standard adopted by the United Nations, has been used throughout
the chapter. To aid the pronunciation of unfamiliar terms, where it differs, the traditional Wade–Giles equivalent is given in square parentheses.

Unless indicated to the contrary, quotations from the Chinese Classics are taken from the following translations: A. Waley, *The Analects* (Ware: Wordsworth Editions, 1996); A. Waley, *Book of Songs (The Classic
of Poetry)* (London: George Allen Unwin, 1954); R. Wilhelm, *I Ching (The Classic of Changes)*, English
trans. Cary F. Baynes (Harmondsworth: Arkana, 1989); D. C. Lau, *Mencius* (Harmondsworth: Penguin, 1970);
D. C. Lau, *Tao Te Ching (Daodejing)* (Harmondsworth: Penguin, 1963).

Elderly man burning "paper hell money" in front of grave, Kaili, Guizhou, China.
Photo: Corbis/Keren Su.

China is essentially an agricultural country, as it always has been, where three-quarters of its 1.2 billion inhabitants live in rural areas. As the ancient Chinese toiled on the land they learnt to revere the natural environment. The spirit of Chinese religion reveals a deep affinity between humankind and the rest of nature, and it is this characteristic which makes it strikingly relevant to contemporary religious debate.

In pre-modern China the spiritual and the secular spheres were indistinct. Religion was an integral part of the experience of life. The State was then the principal religious institution, at the head of which was the emperor, a universal monarch whose rule was divinely sanctioned. There was never a contest between Church and State as witnessed in medieval Europe. In China there are no soaring cathedrals to testify to the power of the Church or the ingenuity and pride of humankind. With the exception of the suburban altars at Beijing, such as the Temple of Heaven, which were particular to the imperial–state cult, temples differed from domestic buildings only in size and embellishment. The absence of an ecclesiastical style of architecture astonished English visitors to China in the eighteenth century. Only recently has a distinct style begun to evolve as Chinese have ordinarily ceased to build in the traditional manner, so increasingly people have come to associate religious buildings with traditional stylistic features, such as colored glazed-tile roofs.

Today, the family can be regarded as the principal Chinese religious institution. The inhabitants of a village often belong to the same clan and they share a communal ancestral hall. Distinct from this is the local *miao*, or temple, dedicated to a certain deity. In the practice of Chinese religion there is no obligation to visit the temple, as daily worship is performed at domestic shrines. Unlike a synagogue, church, or mosque, it is not a place for communal worship. It is the audience hall of a deity. It is not uncommon to find Daoist and Buddhist deities in the same temple. When asked to which religion their temple belongs, often local villagers do not know. Even the caretaker might not know. It is not a question Chinese would ordinarily think of asking. In the introduction to Chinese religion in *The World Religions Reader*,[1] Ian Markham comments on the eclectic nature of Chinese beliefs. This in itself suggests that here exists a different understanding of the nature of religion from that of the Judaeo-Christian tradition.

This question of religious affiliation is just one of many problematic areas, both practical and theoretical, in the study of Chinese religion. A practical issue which colored the interpretation of Chinese philosophy and religion was the complicated script. The principal religious texts are composed in Classical Chinese. A certain mystique was attached to it because for millennia it was the preserve of the educated ruling class. To put it into context, in the early part of the twentieth century only 10 percent of the population were literate; and this encompassed the erudite scholar and the peasant with only rudimentary knowledge of writing. The written word was a revered medium of communication, to the extent that some people attached potent occult power to it, and to this day, Chinese writing is often a constitutive part of a Daoist magical charm.

Classical Chinese is heavily dependent on context since there is no built-in indication of whether a word is functioning as a noun, verb, or any other part of speech. When a word is used as a noun there is no indication of conjugation, except in the negative. The terse style of grammar and syntax contributed to the illusion that Classical Chinese is a pictographic or ideographic language, that is to say it conveys meaning through characters which appeal directly to the mind and bypassing speech.

One of the earliest western commentators on China was a sixteenth-century Portuguese friar, Gaspar da Cruz. He said that the Chinese wrote characters, which represented concepts rather than words. This was repeated by Juan Gonzáles de Mendoza, in his book, *Historia de las cosas más notables, ritos y costumbres, del gran reino de la China*; published in Rome in 1585, it was the first major European work on China which enjoyed a wide circulation.

Subsequently, the ideographic concept was widely accepted among scholars. This misunderstanding probably arose because many of the key concepts in Chinese philosophy and religion descend from picture writing. In studying religious texts which were composed over two thousand years ago, western scholars were confined to working with a restricted vocabulary of about three thousand or so characters. This led to the impression that the Classical Chinese language was ideographic. In reality, in the *Kangxi Dictionary*, which was promulgated in 1716, out of over forty-eight thousand characters only about 3 percent are ideographs.

Examples of key terms in Chinese religion which descend from picture writing

1   mound + now + cloud = **yin** – shadow, darkness
2   mound + light = **yang** – light
3   human + need, weak = **ru** – scholar, literati
4   head + walk = **dao** – way
5   human + two = **ren** – humaneness
6   elder + child = **xiao** – filial piety
7   sheep + I = **yi** – rightness
8   divine + sacrificial vessel = **li** – ritual, propriety
9   like + heart = **shu** – reciprocity
10 court + shelter = **miao** – temple

Before China engaged in intellectual discourse with the West in the nineteenth century, there was no equivalent word in Chinese for "religion." A new phrase was coined, *zongjiao*, which means *orthodox teaching*. This term, however, encapsulates an essentially Judaeo-Christian concept of religion which is alien to the Chinese experience. When western scholars approached Chinese religion they could only articulate it within the conceptual framework that was available to them; and to complicate matters, Chinese scholars who wanted to engage in dialogue with the West accepted this framework because there was no alternative.

Consequently, Chinese religion was articulated by scholars in terms of the "three religions": Confucianism, Daoism, and Buddhism. These were sometimes categorized under the heading of "greater traditions," which have the characteristics of organized religion: with a founder, leaders, institutional structures, written scriptures and liturgical orders. They were presented, if not as mutually exclusive creeds, then at least as though they exist in pure forms, and practiced by an educated elite. They were complemented by a "lesser tradition," the popular or folk religion of the common people, which was often perceived to be a superstitious melange of ancient Chinese beliefs. Designated as the lowly "lesser tradition," it often failed to attract the attention of scholars, although in practice the religious observances associated with it, such as the domestic rituals, permeated through all levels of Chinese society.

One of the pioneers of revisionism was C. K. Yang who recognized the importance of the fourth tradition, which he called "diffused religion." In a sociological study, *Religion in Chinese Society*,[1] he inverted the conventional model for studying Chinese religion; diffused religion was of primary importance, its beliefs, practices and organization were intimately merged with the social order and its institutions. It was the social glue which bound traditional Chinese society together. It is significant to note the adjective "traditional" and that the past tense is used, for the revolutionary upheavals of the twentieth century overturned the social–religious order that existed in pre-modern China. Today, religion is officially discouraged by the

Chinese government, though across the country there is a renaissance; religion in China is reinventing itself.

Meanwhile, the arduous task of reappraising Chinese religion is earnestly in progress. Not only is the problematic relationship between the "greater" and "lesser" traditions being examined, but scholars are also questioning the normative conceptual frameworks and language used in religious discourse. For the present, however, to make sense of Chinese religion we are still very much constrained to follow conventional terminology, but we should recognize that these are culturally conditioned.

Mythological Rulers

The mythological rulers are important Chinese cultural heroes. In the course of history they have been variously designated. The Box on p. 245 follows the arrangement of the Confucian *Three Character Classic*.

Historical Survey

According to one of the earliest Chinese historians, the Grand Scribe Sima Dan [Ssu-ma T'an] (d. 110 BCE), there were six main schools of philosophy in ancient China. In *The Records of History* he says that the six schools had good government as their common goal, although each followed and taught different ways to reach that goal. These six schools developed during the Warring States period (403–221 BCE). During this time the kings of the Zhou [Chou] dynasty (1122–256 BCE) had lost their paramount authority over the confederate states which constituted the "Middle Kingdom," which we know as China. The states contended for supremacy, a process which shook Zhou society to its very foundations. The sense of dislocation and yearning for peace is captured in the following extract from the *Book of Mencius*:

> Now in the empire among the shepherds of men there is not one who is not fond of killing. If there is one who is not, then the people in the empire will crane their necks to watch for his coming. This being truly the case, the people will turn to him like water flowing downwards with a tremendous force. Who can stop it?[2]

Zhou China was a feudal society. This meant your position in life was fixed by birth. At the bottom were the common people. Above them were feudal lords who led the confederated states. The Zhou King was at the top of the pyramid. The philosophers addressed their teachings to the feudal lords, each offering a solution to the socio-political crisis. The philosophers never intended to set up their own religions. Of the six schools enumerated by Sima Dan, Confucianism and Daoism were to shape and influence Chinese civilization to the present day.

Three Sovereigns
Fu Xi [Fu Hsi], the Conqueror of Animals
Shen Nong [Shen Nung], the Divine Farmer   Third millennium BCE
Huang Di [Huang Ti], the Yellow Emperor

Two Emperors
Yao   2357–2258 BCE
Shun   2255–2208 BCE

Three Kings
Yu, founder of the Xia dynasty   2205–2198 BCE
Tang, founder of the Shang dynasty   1765–1760 BCE
Wen and Wu, co-founders of the Zhou dynasty   1122–1116 BCE

Table of Dynasties
Dates prior to the eighth century BCE are approximate.

Xia [Hsia]	2205–1766 BCE
Shang	1766–1122 BCE
Zhou [Chou]	1122–256 BCE
Spring and Autumn Period	722–481 BCE
Warring States Period	403–221 BCE
Qin [Ch'in]	221–206 BCE
Han	206 BCE–220 CE
Western Han	206 BCE–8 CE
Xin [Hsin]	9–23 CE
Eastern Han	25–220 CE
Three Kingdoms	221–264 CE
Jin [Chin]	265–316 CE
Northern and Southern Dynasties	317–588 CE
Sui	589–618 CE
Tang	618–907 CE
Five Dynasties	907–960 CE
Song [Sung]	960–1279 CE
Yuan (Mongol)	1279–1368 CE
Ming	1368–1644 CE
Qing [Ch'ing] (Manchu)	1644–1912 CE
Republic	1912–1949 CE
People's Republic of China	1949–

The school of philosophy associated with Confucius is known as **Rujia** [Ju-chia], the *School of the Scholars*. **Ru** [*Ju*] is an ancient word which is translated today as *scholar* or *literati*. Some etymologists think it originally meant *weakling* because the Ru were said to have descended from the Shang (Yin) dynasty which the Zhou had defeated. When the teaching of the Scholars was introduced to Europe by the Jesuits in the seventeenth century CE it was associated with the name of Confucius; "Confucius" being a latinization of Kong Fuzi [K'ung Fu-tzu] (551–479 BCE), which means *Master Kong*. In China, however, the school is identified not by the man but

the social group to which he belonged. This was how Sima Dan summarized the
School of the Scholars:

> The Confucianists are very broad in their interests but do not deal with much that
> is essential. They labour much and achieve but slight success. Therefore their discip-
> line is difficult to carry out to the fullest. But in the way they order the rules of
> decorum between lord and subject and father and son, and the proper distinctions
> between husband and wife and elder and younger, they have something that cannot
> be altered.[3]

Confucius was a minor official in the confederate state of Lu. He was a teacher
belonging to the Ru, or Scholar class. Their task was to educate the sons of the
feudal lords in the six arts, archery, charioteering, rites, music, writing and mathematics, to prepare them for leadership. Following the Zhou religious tradition, he
understood the supreme deity, which he called **Tian** [*T'ien*], or Heaven, to be a
just and righteous being who expected and demanded the same from humankind.
The answer to all of society's problems, he thought, was contained in the **Five Classics**.
These Classics record a time when rulers governed not by fear or force, but by
moral charisma. Confucius believed that if the feudal lords could reinstate the customs and manners which prevailed during the reigns of the "Three Kings," peace
and harmony would exist on earth. For many years Confucius went from place to
place, searching for a feudal lord who would implement his teachings. He found
no success.

The Analects, a collection of his sayings, was compiled after his death by his followers. Retrospectively his most distinguished follower was Mencius (ca. 379–289
BCE). He lived at a time when Legalism was in the ascent. Legalism was a political
doctrine which advocated a strong centralized state, governed by an absolute
monarch according to a strict legal code. Draconian laws were justified, they claimed,
because humans are inherently evil and are geared solely toward selfish gain. In
contrast, Mencius stressed that humans were naturally predisposed toward goodness. It was also legitimate for a tyrant to be deposed, although this duty, it must
be stressed, rested with the feudal lords. Mencius retained his faith in divine
justice, but by no means was this the consensus, even within his own tradition.
The Legalists' negative view of human nature derived from another follower of
Confucius, Xunzi [Hsün Tzu] (ca. 298–238 BCE). For him Heaven was no longer
a just and righteous being, but a dispassionate cosmic force. This loss of confidence
in the supreme deity was echoed by Laozi [Lao Tzu], the traditional founder of
Daoism.

Daoism, which the Chinese call **Daojia** [Tao-chia], the School of **Dao**, takes its
name from the philosophical concept Dao [Tao]. They claim as its principal scripture the **Daodejing** [Tao Te Ching], *The Classic of the Way and Its Power*. This classic is attributed to Laozi, the "Old Master", a mysterious figure about whom little is
known. Some sources say he lived in the third century BCE, others identify him as
an elder contemporary of Confucius. Laozi never intended to found a school of

philosophy, less still a seemingly polytheistic religion which was to worship him as a manifestation of the Dao. By the end of the second century BCE there was a thriving Daoist school of philosophy. As the Grand Scribe Sima Dan records:

> The Daoists teach men to live a life of spiritual concentration and to act in harmony with the unseen. Their teaching is all sufficient and embraces all things. Its method consists in following the seasonal order of the yin-yang school, of selecting what is good from the Confucian and Mohist teachings, and adopting the important points of the Logical and Legalist schools. It modifies its position with the times and responds to the changes which come about in the world. In establishing customs and practices and administering affairs it does nothing that is not appropriate to the time and place. Its principles are simple and easy to practice; it undertakes few things but achieves much success.[4]

The "unseen" is the Dao, the impersonal law of nature which took the place of the just and righteous supreme deity. Disorder arises when the law of nature is flouted. To live and act in accordance with the Dao was to refrain from artificial activity. Laozi saw that the only way to survive the turbulent upheavals of the day was to withdraw from conventional society. Which was what he did. The *Daodejing* is supposed to be his last testament to civilization, written just before he rode off into the mountains on the back of a black ox.

The ambiguity of the *Daodejing* allows for many interpretations of the text, which appears to be a compilation from several different sources. It was adopted by many different groups to endorse their teachings and to add a gloss of respectability. The term Daoism, therefore, encompasses many different things. The description by Sima Dan indicates the eclecticism of the Daoist School. Theoretically Laozi advocated a return to a primitive agrarian lifestyle, but this was impracticable as a basis of government. However, the original radical message remained attractive among rebel political movements. The Tianshi Dao and the Taiping Dao were two such movements. Zhang Daoling [Chang Tao-ling] (34–156 CE) founded the Tianshi Dao, *The Way of the Celestial Master*. This movement is sometimes known as religious Daoism. Drawing from the shamanistic tradition of ancient Chinese religion, with a pantheon of anthropomorphic deities, elaborate religious rituals, and magical charms aimed at manipulating the forces of nature, it seems far from the spirit of the *Daodejing*. The other famous movement, the Taiping Dao, *The Way of Great Peace*, inspired the millenarian rebellion of Yellow Turbans in the second century CE.

Daoism reached the height of political prestige when the emperors of the Tang dynasty (618–907 CE) claimed Laozi, with whom they shared a common surname, as the grand ancestor of the ruling house. During the Tang period the *Daodejing* was added to the state examination syllabus. Although in practice its political application was minimal, Daoism strongly influenced other aspects of Chinese culture, especially art and medicine. It is most apparent in landscape painting. Nature dominates in these compositions. Mountains, rivers, and vegetation take precedence over humankind. The Daoist emphasis upon self-preservation and avoidance of physical death spurred an interest in alchemy and the elixirs of immortality. These arcane arts influenced the development of Chinese science and medicine. This association with the magical strand of Daoism meant that after the triumph of Confucianism in the thirteenth century, advances in Chinese science and medicine virtually ceased.

Qin Shi Huangdi [Ch'in Shih Huang-ti], the first Qin emperor, whose tomb at Xi'an is guarded by the mighty terracotta army, unified the warring states in 221 BCE and began the imperial period in Chinese history. "China" is widely thought to be an Anglicism of the dynastic name Qin [Ch'in]. The Qin emperor was an advocate of Legalism. In 213 BCE he instigated the **Burning of Books**. All books that contradicted the new Qin regime, especially books on history, were consigned to the flames. The Confucian *Classic of History* and *The Classic of Poetry* were singled out for particular criticism, and it became a capital offence to quote from either of these books. His harsh and amoral methods of government alienated people and, soon after his death, a popular uprising overthrew the Qin regime.

Qin unification brought an end to the feudal system of government. The emperors of the Han dynasty (206 BCE–220 CE) had no intention of reverting to the pre-Qin order. Legalism was officially discredited, but in practice its structures were retained, and they searched around for an alternative theory of government which would enhance their prestige, albeit superficially. Eventually they were swayed in favor of the Confucianists, not by the wisdom of Ru teaching, but by the splendor of the rituals with which they enveloped the monarchy. Although privately they were adherents of Daoism, the Han emperors found in Confucianism an instrument for controlling a vast united empire. The scholar official Dong Zhongshu [Tung Chung-shu] (ca. 179–104 BCE) reinvented Confucianism to accommodate this new world order. He fused together Confucian ethics, Legalist political theory, and traditional religious beliefs into a systematic theory, which has become known as Han Confucianism. Henceforth Confucianism became the state doctrine, a position it was to hold for two thousand years. During the early Han period the Five Classics were reconstructed from fragments which survived the Burning of Books and were inscribed on tablets of stone. Since the feudal lords had been displaced by a centralized bureaucracy at unification, knowledge of these Classics, rather than the accident of birth, became one of the routes to political preferment.

Han China was an outward looking society. It was engaged in trans-continental trade through the so-called "Silk Route." This period saw the arrival of Mahayana Buddhism from India in 65 CE. It was to take root and acculturate on Chinese soil. It became the dominant religious tradition in China between the end of the Han (220 CE) and the Song [Sung] dynasty (960–1279 CE). In this period of Buddhist ascendancy its most distinguished critic was the Confucian scholar Han Yu (768–824 CE). During the reign of the emperor Wuzong [Wu Tsung] (841–6 CE) all foreign religious teachings were suppressed in China, and like Buddhism, Nestorian Christianity was numbered among the casualties. Yet in spite of these sporadic periods of persecution, Buddhism enjoyed an unrivaled hold over Chinese culture. The reign of Wu Zetian [Wu Tse-t'ien] (624–705 CE), the only woman emperor in Chinese history, was partly legitimized by the Buddhists. Prior to her usurpation they circulated the *Great Cloud Sutra* which identified her as the Maitreya, the Buddha of the Future. Throughout this period the imperial–state doctrine officially remained Confucian and its teachings were preserved in the state examination syllabus. An aspiring minister of state was still obliged to master the Confucian classics.

The growth of Buddhism in China coincided with a prolonged period of social and political disorder between the collapse of the Han dynasty in the third century CE and the rise of the Sui and Tang dynasties in the sixth to seventh centuries. Unlike Confucianism, which emphasized the social dimension of human existence, whereby one was defined by a network of social relationships, Buddhism specifically addressed the individual psyche. It was a welcome source of solace to a long-suffering people. What helped its progress was the borrowing of Daoist philosophical terminology in the translation of the Buddhist *sutras* into Chinese. Chan, or Zen as it is known in Japan, is the most enduring fruit of this cultural interaction. Prominent schools of Buddhism, founded on the interpretation of various *sutras*, flourished in China. However, as Tang China started to slip back into political turmoil, Buddhist prestige declined. The An Lu Shan rebellion (755−63 CE) was a pivotal moment, after which the Chinese became introspective and suspicious of all things foreign.

The legacy and influence of Buddhism in Chinese culture is more pervasive than is at first apparent. Printing is thought to have been invented by Buddhists wishing to accrue religious merit by distributing *sutras*. The earliest printed book is thought to be an edition of the *Diamond Sutra* dating from the ninth century. Another example is incense, which is probably the item most readily associated with Chinese rituals. Confucianists of the Tang dynasty wanted to ban its use in the imperial–state rituals because it was a Buddhist innovation which had no precedence in the Five Classics. In the visual arts, Buddhism inspired the creation of spectacular rock sculptures and frescoes, notably at Dunhuang. The popular Xieyi, *writing an idea*, style of painting is inspired by Chan Buddhism; the technique involves lengthy concentration on the subject, which is then translated onto paper as swiftly as possible and with the minimum number of brush strokes. In architecture, the Indian stupa inspired the development of the pagoda, which was originally intended to house *sutras* and relics. It soon became an aesthetic object, shorn of its religious connotations, and has become readily associated with the Chinese landscape.

Despite its status as the imperial–state doctrine, Confucianism was regarded much of the time as a system of social ethics. Its success hung on its usefulness as a political doctrine. Compared with Buddhism it had little to offer to suffering humanity. During the Song dynasty, Confucianists sought to change the situation. They created a new system, known in the West as Neo-Confucianism. Unconsciously it assimilated many Buddhist ideas which had become part of the Chinese intellectual culture, and where it differed fundamentally from the Buddhists was over the question of the reality of material phenomena. Neo-Confucianism is principally associated with the name of Zhu Xi [Chu Hsi] (1130−1200 CE). Under his influence the **Four Books** were added to the civil service examination syllabus, and within the Confucian canon itself they now took precedence over the Five Classics. The inclusion of the *Book of Mencius* confirmed Mencius' status as the orthodox successor of Confucius as Han Yu had first advocated three centuries earlier. Zhu Xi's own commentaries on the Confucian books were to acquire definitive status, which remained unchallenged, in theory, until the end of the Qing [Ch'ing] dynasty (1644–1912). For the next seven hundred years the words "Confucian" and "Chinese" became synonymous.

Worldviews

An English visitor to China in the eighteenth century observed that the Chinese *"are seldom said to carry the objects, to be obtained by their devotion, beyond the benefits of this life."*[5] A western observer may assume that the Chinese have a materialistic attitude to religion, but the Chinese do not see the spiritual as something entirely separate from the natural world in which we live.

To understand the Chinese worldview it is necessary to begin in the second millennium BCE. The limited knowledge that we have about ancient Chinese religion concerns only the ruling class. Little is known about the beliefs of ordinary people. The oldest written records are the oracle-bone inscriptions. These are divination records from the Shang dynasty (ca. 1766–1122 BCE). The inscriptions reveal a belief in a supreme deity called **Shang Di**, which translates as *God-on-high*. Under him were lesser spirits, including nature deities such as the genies of rivers and mountains; the royal ancestors dwelled also with Shang Di.

According to the oracle-bone inscriptions, the Shang kings consulted the spirits on a range of practical matters relating to the maintenance of the State and government. Naturally for an agrarian society, there were frequent petitions for rain and good harvests. Therefore, from the beginning of Chinese civilization, politics was linked to religion. It was a shamanistic religion, whereby the king's power was derived from his association with the spirits, who could be manipulated through magic and ritual sacrifice. At first this included human sacrifice, though animals were more commonly offered. The kings enjoyed a reciprocal relationship with the spirits; in exchange for sacrificial offerings they were granted material blessings, as this song from *The Classic of Poetry* expresses:

> Ah, the glorious ancestors –
> Endless their blessings,
> Boundless their gifts are extended;
> To you too, they needs must reach.
> We have brought them clear wine;
> They will give victory.
> Here, too, is a soup well seasoned,
> Well prepared, well mixed.
> Because we come in silence,
> Setting all quarrels aside,

> They make safe for us a ripe old age,
> We shall reach the wither cheek, we shall go on and on.
> With our leather-bound naves, our bronze-clad yokes,
> With eight bells a-jangle
> We come to make offering.
> The charge put upon us is vast and mighty,
> From heaven dropped our prosperity,
> Good harvests, great abundance.
> They come, they accept,
> They send down blessings numberless.
> They regard the paddy-offerings, the offerings of first fruits
> That T'ang's descendant brings.[6]

Ancient Chinese religion affirmed that the physical world is good. This is confirmed by the belief in an afterlife, which is a shadow of the present. The survival and well-being of the individual after death depended not on ethical behavior in life, but on the continued offering of ritual sacrifice. This remains a basic tenet today. Ancestor worship is perpetuated through the patrilineal family. As a colloquial saying has it, sons are produced "to continue the incense smoke."

Morality did not seem to concern Shang religion. This was to change during the succeeding Zhou dynasty The Shang had ruled by **de** [te], or magical power. Under the Zhou this was transformed into a moral quality when an ethical dimension was introduced into government. The new rulers introduced the concept of a divine commission, which they called the Mandate of Heaven, to support their claim to power. **Tian**, or *Heaven*, was synonymous and used interchangeably with Shang Di. As *The Classic of Poetry* says:

> May you never shame your ancestors,
> But rather tend their inward power [de],
> That forever you may be linked to Heaven's charge
> And bring yourselves many blessings.
> Before Yin lost its army
> It was well linked to God above.
> In Yin you should see as in a mirror
> That Heaven's high charge is hard to keep.[7]

This mandate was conditional. According to the Zhou, the last Shang king had forfeited his kingdom because he was a tyrant and had neglected the ancestral temple. So, like the Shang (also known as Yin) before them, the Zhou were equally liable to lose the heavenly commission if they failed to govern well. The concept of the Mandate of Heaven became the guarantor of dynastic legitimacy up until the beginning of the twentieth century. During the Zhou there was also a gradual shift in the understanding of Heaven. In the West it is usually perceived as a place outside time and space. In China, the word referred to the supreme deity, but it also became identified as the law of the universe.

What we know of early Chinese civilization, apart from archeology, comes primarily from books which circulated at the Zhou court. These include: *The Classic of Poetry, The Classic of History, The Classic of Changes, The Record of Ritual*, and *The Chronicles of the Spring and Autumn Period*. At one stage there was also a *Classic of Music*, but it is now lost. Confucianists later dubbed these books the *Five Classics* and they were to shape the development of Chinese culture.

The most influential of these books is *The Classic of Changes*. Its authorship is attributed to King Wen and the Duke of Zhou, the co-founders of the Zhou dynasty. It originated as a manual of divination to replace the tortoise-shell oracle (oracle bones). In the oracle-bone method the divine messages were elucidated from the random patterns which formed after the application of a hot pointer to the surface of the shell. This meant there was an unlimited number of possible answers. The Zhou kings restricted the number of patterns to sixty-four. A cycle of hexagrams (diagrams made up of six lines) were modeled after the tortoise-shell patterns and arranged in a sequence. Subsequently the Confucianists added the *Ten Wings*, or commentaries.

This book became the basis of philosophy and science in China. The commentaries wrought a consistent philosophical system out of *The Classic of Changes*, in which the sequence of hexagrams is interpreted as a microcosm of the universe. As *The Great Commentary* says:

> The Book of Changes contains the measure of heaven and earth; therefore it enables us to comprehend the dao of heaven and earth and its order.[8]

This knowledge was deduced by an intuitive human, such as the ancient sage Fu Xi [Fu Hsi], through the observation of nature. *The Great Commentary* continues:

> They put themselves in accord with dao and its power, and in conformity with this laid down the order of what is right. By thinking through the order of the outer world to the end, and by exploring the law of their nature to the deepest core, they arrived at an understanding of fate.[9]

The first and second hexagrams in *The Classic of Changes* are call Qian [Ch'ien] and Kun [K'un]. Qian is made up of six whole lines, and Kun, of six broken lines (see *A World Religions Reader*, pp. 160–1). These represent polar but complementary opposites which later became known as **yang** and **yin**. The remaining hexagrams are made up of a combination of whole and broken lines. All things that exist, seen and unseen, are seen as a mixture of yin and yang. Yin and yang literally mean *shadow* and *light*, but they are sometimes described as female and male forces respectively. This should not be interpreted literally. They are neither forces nor material entities. Yin and yang are simply metaphorical tags to describe how things relate to each other. According to this doctrine, the whole of the universe is interconnected.

Behind yin and yang is the **Taiji** [T'ai Chi], or *Great Ultimate*. This is the state of undifferentiated being out of which all things evolve. It consists of a basic substance called **qi** [ch'i], which can be translated as *psycho-physical stuff*. Everything that exists in the universe, visible and invisible, including mental thoughts, is simply differentiated *qi*. The universe is characterized by the law of change. No state of being is permanent. As commentary on the fifty-fifth hexagram says: "*When the sun stands at midday, it begins to set; when the moon is full it begins to wane.*"[10] When an entity reaches its supreme expression it will revert to its opposite, so whenever yang reaches its zenith, it reverts itself into yin and vice-versa. This is illustrated by what many people outside China know as the yin–yang symbol, the Taiji Tu [T'ai Chi T'u] or *Diagram of the Great Ultimate*, a device invented by the Neo-Confucianist scholar Zhou Dunyi [Chou Tun-yi] (1017–73 CE).

During the Zhou period, government was considered the highest sphere of human activity. It was the issue that concentrated the minds of the major philosophers

CONFUCIUS
Le plus celebre Philosophe de la Chine

Confucius, engraving ca. 1650. Photo: Corbis/Historical Picture Archive during the Warring States Period. Confucius and Laozi each had a solution to the political turmoil. It is important to remember that the *Daodejing* of Laozi also contains advice on government, something which is sometimes forgotten because of the emphasis on its mystical aspects. In identifying the cause of the political disorder the two philosophers came to a consensus; humankind had fallen away from Dao, which means *the Way*.

For the Daoists, Dao was the underlying principle of the universe. It is identified with the law of nature. To achieve peace and harmony it is necessary to live in accordance with the flow of nature. This concept is known as *wu-wei*, which means *non-action*. Human society, with its institutions and conventions, including language, is artificial and unnatural, separating humans from their true nature. The solution is to retreat to a primitive agrarian existence. As a plan for government, it could not, of course, be implemented. The attraction of Daoist utopian vision is captured in the famous tale, *The Peach Blossom Fountain* by Tao Yuanming (365–427 CE). This story inspired the famous phrase, "Shi wai taoyuan," literally meaning *the peach orchard beyond this world*, a traditional literary device which expresses the yearning to escape from the trouble and strife of conventional society.

The Confucianists saw the Dao as the moral law, the way of humaneness and goodness. Peace and harmony comes through humane behavior and the observation of the *li*, or rituals. It is very difficult to encapsulate the concept of *li* with a single English word. When it is used as a noun it encompasses religious rituals, social manners, and etiquette. In this case it is best translated as *ritual*. These rituals are ceremonial expressions of humaneness. As an adjective, *li* means *propriety* and it is manifested in the correct observance of the rituals. In *The Analects* Confucius laments the abuse and decline of these rituals. Peace and harmony lay in their restoration.

Confucianists also use the concept of **wu-wei**. Here it refers to government by moral charisma. In *The Analects* the sage-emperor Shun was the model of government by non-action. To govern a state efficiently, all it requires is for the ruler to behave morally and the people will follow his example. *The Analects* says:

> He who rules by moral force is like the pole star, which remains in its place while the lesser stars do homage to it.[11] Among those who "ruled by inactivity" surely Shun may be counted. For what action did he take? He merely placed himself gravely with his face due south; that was all.[12]

For Confucius the imperative for individuals to behave morally was decreed by Heaven. He failed to convince the feudal lords to accept this. There was no obligation for anyone to accept this heavenly decree. Mencius sought to provide a solution. He maintained that the imperative to do good is programmed into the very atoms of the human body. Human nature is essentially good and is inherently orientated toward goodness. He calls this "original heart"; and this heart distinguishes humans from other animals. It is more than a cognitive sense of conscience as he links it with the actual physical organ. Consequently, moral action does not require the intervention of an external source of power or grace, but is achieved by actualizing human nature. Mencius cites *The Classic of Poetry* to endorse his theory.

> Heaven produces the teeming masses,
> And where there is a thing there is a norm.
> If the people held onto their constant nature,
> They would be drawn to superior virtue.[13]

As the poem says, people will be drawn to virtue if only they hold onto their original nature. Human beings, says Mencius, begin to lose the original heart from the moment of birth. Life's duty is to retrieve this lost heart, and in so doing, the individual becomes fully human. In this light, the scholar D. C. Lau suggests that Mencius rather than Laozi is the true mystic, for behind the mystical speculation in the *Daodejing* is a very pessimistic view of human nature. Mencius, by contrast, has absolute faith in the moral purpose of the universe, and that man can become one with it by perfecting his moral nature.[14] The opening chapter of *The Doctrine of the Mean* puts this succinctly: "*What heaven has conferred is what we call human nature. To fulfill the law of human nature is what we call the Way.*"

So far we have established that human nature is good and that this present life is to be enjoyed. As to the lost heart, this can be regained though ethical action. To this end, education has a fundamental part to play, which is why the Chinese have traditionally put great emphasis on education. Although it can improve one's employment prospects, that is only of secondary importance; its true purpose is to enable human beings to regain the lost heart. The awesome role assigned to education stems perhaps from the fact that the Confucianists belonged to the scholar class who were originally entrusted with the education of the sons of the feudal lords. In *The Analects* and the *Book of Mencius* the ideal person, the model of humane behavior, is the **Junzi** [Chün-tzu], which often translates as *gentleman*. Literally it means *son of a lord*. The concept of the gentleman was originally a code of ethics for the ruling elite, but through the passage of the centuries, it assumed universal application.

Ethical Expression

The status of Confucianism as the imperial–state doctrine meant that its system of ethics was once observed throughout Chinese society. In order to survive, Buddhism and Daoism had in practice to acknowledge this in their respective ethical systems. In theory, the classic Daoist approach to ethics is the very antithesis of the Confucian position. As the *Daodejing* says:

> when the way was lost there was virtue; when virtue was lost there was benevolence; when benevolence was lost there was rectitude; when rectitude was lost there were the rites.

The rites are the wearing thin of loyalty and good faith
And the beginning of disorder;
Foreknowledge is the flowery embellishment of the way
And the beginning of folly.[15]

For the Daoists, the idea of virtue arises only after the fragmentation of the undifferentiated Dao, symbolized in the *Daodejing* by the "uncarved block." The prescribed forms of social behavior advocated by the Confucianists only serve to separate
humans from the ineffable Dao. In practical terms, the Daoist idea of "going with
the flow [of nature]" cannot be reconciled with human society as it exists. The
Confucian ethic, on the other hand, centers on the well ordering of human relationships within society.

> There is a common expression, "The Empire, the state, the family". The Empire has
> its basis in the state, the state in the family, and the family in one's own self.[16]

According to Mencius, each person belongs to three basic communities: the
empire, the state, and the family. In ancient China, the empire and the civilized
world were perceived to be one and the same. Just as the state is a microcosm of
the empire, the family is the state in miniature. As the basic unit in society, the
family is where humans first learn to relate to one another. It is through the community, beginning with the family, that the individual is defined through a web of
social relationships.

Human relationships fall into five categories. These "five relationships" are
between: ruler and subject, parent and child, husband and wife, elder and younger
sibling, and finally, between friends. These categories determine and regulate all
human relationships. The well-being of society depends on the observance of the
correct forms of behavior pertaining to each.

Correct or ethical behavior is motivated by the principle of **ren** [jen]. It is the
root of **yi** [i] rightness, *xin* [hsin] sincerity, *zhi* [chih] wisdom, and *li* [li] propriety.
Together they constitute the five cardinal Confucian virtues.

Confucian ethics is summed up in the principle of *ren*, or *humaneness*. This term
can be translated also as *benevolence* or *goodness*. Underlying it is the belief that there
is a moral purpose to the universe; for the Confucianists, the moral law is identified
with the law of nature. Humans, as social creatures, can perfect their own nature
by fulfilling the moral law. The Chinese character "*ren*" consists of the components for "human" and the number "two." Only when humans are in the company
of others can they demonstrate humaneness, as Mencius says:

> "Benevolence" means "man." When these two are conjoined, the result is "the Way"
> benevolence is the distinguishing characteristic of man. As embodied in man's con-
> duct, it is called the path of duty.[17]

To accomplish the path of duty one achieves **yi**, or *rightness*. Sometimes this is translated as *righteousness* or *rectitude*, which can be misleading, as in a western religious

context these terms tend to imply something which is imputed from outside the human person. *Yi* refers not to the moral status of the one who acts, but to the ethical quality of a particular act.

Ren is exemplified in **xiao** [hsiao] or *filial piety*, which simply means proper behavior toward one's parents. Individuals owe their parents a debt of gratitude for bringing them into the world. This is repaid through deference and respect while the parents are living and it continues after their deaths through the observance of mourning and the ancestor rituals. It does not entail blind obedience. For example, the sage–emperor Shun, an exemplar of filial piety who heads the list of the *Twenty Four Examples of Filial Piety*, married without parental consent. In Shun's case, his motives meant that his parents were as good as told. He had to marry to produce a son. Failure to do so would in itself have been a breach of filial piety. In general terms, this was how Confucius described filial piety:

> Behave in such a way that your father and mother have no anxiety about you, except concerning your health.[18] (See Markham, *A World Religions Reader*, p. 178)

Filial piety operates within the family environment. Beyond this immediate confine, the golden rule of **shu** [shu], or *reciprocity*, may be taken as a guide. When asked by a follower if there is a single saying that one can act upon all day and every day, Confucius replied:

> Never do to others what you would not like them to do to you.[19]

This was a sentiment repeated by Mencius who saw *shu* as the quickest way to achieve humaneness:

> Try your best to treat others as you would wish to be treated yourself, and you will find that this is the shortest way to benevolence.[20]

Reciprocity should not be interpreted as in any sense utilitarian. That would compromise the dignity of each individual human being. The Confucian tradition is vehemently opposed to utilitarianism, which in ancient China was represented by the doctrines of Mozi [Mo Tzu]. Mencius was one of its most celebrated adversaries, in whose lifetime the Mohist School enjoyed greater popularity than that of the Confucianists.

Humans achieve perfection by realizing their inherent inborn nature. In Confucian temples there are no images of heaven, hell, purgatory, or divine saviors. The journey along the path to perfection is aided by the experience of chi [ch'ih], which translates as *shame*. Confucius describes it as one of the qualities of the gentleman. It is not a negative trait, for it is recognized as a sign of genuine self-consciousness. Shame is instinctively experienced when one fails to act in accordance with humaneness and propriety. In the end, it is an incentive for self-improvement, as Mencius says:

> Great is the use of shame to man. He who indulges in craftiness has no use for shame. If a man is not ashamed of being inferior to other men, how will he ever become their equal?[21]

What is termed Confucian ethics today has its roots in the chivalric code of the feudal ruling class in ancient China. Confucius began the move from its particular to universal application. Although he maintained that there was nothing new in his teaching – I have *"transmitted what was taught to me without making up anything of my own"*[22] – the manner in which he went about teaching was innovative. As no feudal lord would implement his teaching, he retired to his home town and established a school. The radical innovation was that students did not have to belong to the ruling class. Students from humble backgrounds were accepted, the entrance criteria being that they had a genuine desire and ability to learn. The gentlemanly goal was no longer an elite preserve. In this way, Confucius fulfilled his obligation to hand down to posterity what he himself had received. Mencius took Confucian ethics another step forward toward its universal application with his concept of original heart. All humans can retrieve their original nature, so everyone could, in practice, aspire to become gentlemen. Finally, the old class distinctions disappeared when feudalism was abolished at the unification of China in 221 BCE.

The shift from the particular to the universal application of Confucian doctrine is illustrated by the fate of *The Great Learning*. This book is the most widely read of the Confucian Four Books. A systematic presentation of Confucian doctrine, it is a blueprint for Confucian civilization. It consists of two sections, the opening text attributed to Confucius, and a commentary by a follower of the Confucian School. From the thirteenth century CE to the beginning of the twentieth, *The Great Learning* constituted one of the three elementary school textbooks, the other two being *The Three Character Classic* and *The Thousand Character Essay*, both of which date from the Song dynasty. Every child who went to school learnt to read through these three texts, which they also had to commit to memory. The two Song texts are didactic summaries of cosmology, history, and ethics, the "Confucian worldview for children."

Unlike the two Song texts, *The Great Learning* was not originally intended for general circulation. Compiled as a textbook in the fourth century BCE, it was meant for the education of the sons of the feudal lords, the future leaders of society. The book concentrates on the means of achieving good government and, ultimately, world peace. This was to be accomplished through moral charisma. To achieve this end Confucius identifies eight steps in a chain of being. In linear progression, it begins with the investigation of things, the extension of knowledge, sincerity of thought, the rectification of the heart, the cultivation of the person, the regulation of the family, the ordering well of the state, and finally, the pacification of the world.[23]

The commentary embellishes on the opening text. To illustrate how the ruler should set a moral example before the people, the commentator draws extensively from *The Classic of History* and *The Classic of Poetry*. For example, with the theme of self-cultivation, he cites a song from *The Classic of Poetry*:

> Look at that little bay of the Ch'i,
> Its kitesfoot so fresh.
> Delicately fashioned is my lord,
> As thing cut, as thing filed,
> As thing chiselled, as thing polished.
> Oh, the grace, the elegance!
> Oh, the lustre, oh, the light!
> Delicately fashioned is my lord;
> Never for a moment can I forget him.[24]

This is evidently a love song. The lines "*As thing cut, as thing filed, as thing chiselled, as thing polished*" originally referred to the lord's physical appearance. In the context of *The Great Learning* the commentator interprets these lines allegorically. The reference to physical grooming is taken to mean moral self-cultivation. This is explained in the elementary text, *The Three Character Classic*, which says:

> If jade is not polished, it cannot become a thing of use. If a man does not learn, he cannot know his duty toward his neighbor.

In Confucian vocabulary "cutting" and "polishing" are customary phrases for the cultivation of character. It was common practice in the Confucian tradition to give existing terms and vocabulary new meanings. As previously noted in this chapter, **de**, which meant magical power, was reinterpreted to represent moral virtue. Further on in the commentary, a marriage song from *The Classic of Poetry* is used, rather tenuously, to illustrate good government. Like the new bride at her home, the ruler must rightly order his household, for in so doing, the state would be properly governed.

> In the Classic of Poetry is the saying:
>
> > How charming the peach tree
> > Its leaves thickly massed!
> > The bride is coming to her home:
> > The bride will rightly order her household.
>
> True! Order your household and then you can teach good principles to influence the nation.[25]

Role of Women

It was noted earlier in this chapter that some Chinese characters, or words, descend from picture writing. "Woman" is one such word; it is made up of two components, "girl" and "broom." When a girl married, she had to attend to domestic chores, and cleaning the house was one of her jobs. The origin of this character is sometimes cited as evidence of the subservient role of women in Chinese society. Women bound their feet in the pursuit of beauty, according to norms dictated by men. Women were traditionally defined as either wives or concubines, subject first to their fathers, then their husbands, and finally, their sons. The memoirs of Jung Chang, *Wild Swans*, and films such as Zhang Yimou's *Raise the Red Lantern*, vividly reveal how little control women had over their own lives as recently as the first half of the twentieth century. In her discussion on women in Islam (chapter 15), Victoria La'Porte draws attention to the influence of Orientalism in western representations of the East. Likewise in China, it should be borne in mind that the commonly perceived negative images of the role of women do not represent the totality of their experience.

A further consideration to bear in mind is that in contemporary Chinese society, women officially have full equality with men. Often discussions about the role of women in Chinese religion ignore this contemporary fact. The impact of this change on traditional religious beliefs and practices has yet to be fully worked out. What is apparent, however, is that despite the significance attached to the male role in Chinese religion, it is primarily through the efforts of women that many traditional religious practices have survived through the twentieth century.

The ideal Confucian society described in *The Record of Rites* ran along strict gender divisions, where each occupied distinct social and physical spheres. From a very young age these boundaries were delineated and instilled in children. The woman's place is at home; the man's in public life. Only in exceptional circumstances were women able to participate in public affairs, although Confucianists traditionally regarded this as a perversion of the law of nature. The most notable example was the Empress Wu Zetian [Wu Tse-t'ien], who in 690 CE usurped the throne and proclaimed herself emperor of a new dynasty. This clear distinction of roles should be understood in the light of the concept of yin and yang. An object is defined in relationship to something else. Conventionally, as an accident of history, the female takes the lower yin position in relation to the male yang. It does not mean that women are intrinsically inferior to men, only that they have different but complementary roles to play. Both sexes are equally necessary as one cannot exist without the other.

In addition, the ideal Confucian society was only prescription rather than a description of real life. *The Record of Ritual* may prescribe marriage for men at the age of thirty, but Confucius married at twenty. Take another example, archery and charioteering were two of the six arts which a gentleman, the chivalric knight of feudal China, was supposed to acquire, yet in imperial China, especially from the Song dynasty onwards, the gentleman was characterized by the languid scholar–aesthete.

Without lessening the gravity of the maltreatment which Chinese women have experienced, the portrayal of the pampered but enslaved life of concubinage in the film *Raise the Red Lantern* is unbalanced. In the West today, marriage and childbirth are sometimes regarded as a constraint on women, but in Confucian China, only as a wife or concubine could a woman achieve her full potential. It was a religious imperative for her to bear children, who would secure her well-being and status during her lifetime, but more crucially, also after her death. It is by producing sons that the familial ancestor cult is perpetuated.

Domestic life is the setting for *The Dream of the Red Chamber*, the famous eighteenth-century semi-autobiographical novel by Cao Xueqin [T'sao Hsüeh-ch'in]. This book is widely recognized today as a reliable social document, which vividly describes the life of the educated ruling elite in eighteenth-century China. An indispensable text in the study of Chinese religious belief and practice, it demonstrates how Confucianism, Daoism, and Buddhism can interact with each other in practice. The most powerful and revered character in the novel is not a man, but the dowager matriarch of the family. Contrary to the popular idea that widowed mothers were subject to the whims of their sons, the obligations of filial piety mean in fact that her sons are constantly obliged to accede to her wishes.

Women are generally portrayed sympathetically throughout *The Dream of the Red Chamber*, as talented administrators or cultured scholars. It reveals how the daughters of scholars and the well-to-do enjoyed an education alongside their male siblings. These accomplished fictional characters had historical antecedents. In the elementary textbook *The Three Character Classic*, Cai Wenji [Ts'ai Wen-chi] and Xie Daoyun [Hsieh Tao-yun], two "quick and clever" young women from the third and fourth centuries CE respectively, are included among the prodigies whom young boys should seek to emulate.

Rituals and Institutions

The word "revolution" has characterized China in the twentieth century. The unfavorable treatment in the Treaty of Versailles in 1919, which transferred German rights in China to Japan, sparked off a student protest at Tiananmen in Beijing. This became known as the May 4th Movement. It was to inspire the New Culture Movement which proclaimed "Mr Science" and "Mr Democracy" as China's salvation. Prefiguring the Great Proletarian Cultural Revolution, which lasted from 1966 to 1977, all vestiges of the past, its old customs, old habits, old culture, and old thinking, which included traditional religious beliefs, were to be erased from Chinese consciousness. This destructive period in Chinese history is vividly recorded in the book entitled *Wild Swans* by Jung Chang. For many decades people were coerced to abandon long-held beliefs and customs, but since the end of the Cultural Revolution there has been a revival of traditional Chinese religious practices.

Daily worship of Heaven, Earth, and the ancestors is an integral part of the traditional Chinese way of life. If the family is the principal religious institution, then the family home is its temple. It is as much a dwelling for the spirits as for humans. Daily worship is performed at the household shrines by family members, without the aid of clergy or religious specialists. In terms of religious affiliation these household rituals are neither strictly Confucian nor Daoist. There is much speculation about how the spirits of the ancestors are involved in them but there is no definitive view.

Xunzi [Hsün Tzu], who lived in the third century BCE, noted that there were different levels of apprehension of the unseen world. Regarding ritual sacrifice he says:

> among gentlemen it is considered the way of man; among the common people it is considered as having to do with the spirits.[26]

The worship of Heaven was once the exclusive prerogative of the emperor. Anybody who attempted the worship of the supreme deity was committing treason. In southern China people circumvented this ban by worshiping Heaven by proxy, through a Daoist deity called the Official of Heaven. For many people the distinction between Heaven and its representative is vague, if it exists at all. The local God of the Earth is also a Daoist deity, and often this anthropomorphic spirit, who is responsible for overseeing a particular geographical area, is conflated with the God of the Soil who properly belongs to the imperial–state cult. Although the Earth is conventionally perceived to be yin and is sometimes referred to as "mother," it is important to stress that the Earth and Soil deities have always been understood to be male. Ancestor worship pre-dates both Confucianism and Daoism. It is based on the idea that life continues after death in a parallel world similar to the present one. There the spirits of the ancestors require sustenance and nourishment in the form of ritual offerings from their living descendants, which they reciprocate with material rewards. Overall, the exact status of these deities and spirits is inconsequential for Chinese. What matters is that Heaven, Earth, and the ancestors are accorded due reverence and worship.

The customs for performing the household rituals differ considerably from village to village throughout China, but they usually involve the offering of food, drink, incense, and paper goods. Underlying the rituals are two key points: the bond between Heaven, Earth, and humankind; and the maintenance of family solidarity, both among the living and with the dead. A visit to the home of a wealthy peasant in the southern province of Guangzhou [Canton], who made his fortune on the plantations in California in the late nineteenth century, reveals how religious rituals are incorporated into the fabric of everyday life.[27]

The traditional Chinese house is built around an internal courtyard. It is a self-contained universe, surrounded by high walls and often without external windows. It is as much a home for the spirits as for humans. The main entrance leads into a courtyard, where to one side, halfway up the wall, is a stone tablet bearing the words "Official of Heaven." Beneath it is a container for incense sticks. Directly opposite this shrine is the main hall, which is open to the courtyard. Inside, the entire upper section of the rear wall is dominated by a structure of carved and gilded wood, at either end of which are inscriptions commending Confucian virtues and family honor. It is called the Spirit Platform. The platform is divided into tiers supporting the wooden boards inscribed with the names of ancestors. These boards, the spirit tablets, are arranged in generational order, the most senior occupying the uppermost shelf. Before the tablets stands a censer between a pair of candlesticks, next to which are vases containing stalks of bamboo, which are a symbol of wealth and distinction. Finally, to one side is a wooden box containing the robes of a scholar. An ancestor had obtained the *Xiucai* (licentiate) degree toward the end of the Qing dynasty (1644–1912). It is displayed in this prominent position in acknowledgment of the blessings granted by the ancestors and to encourage the living to succeed in the world. Directly beneath the Spirit Platform is a small stone tablet at ground level and set against the wall, with the inscription "Lord of the Earth," the shrine of the local Earth god. Before it stand vessels for incense and candles. In the middle of the hall is the household altar, a simple square table, and four seats, all made of wood.

Each day, at morning and evening, offerings are made to Heaven, Earth, and the ancestors. This involves nothing more than bowing solemnly and placing a few sticks of incense at each of the three shrines. On the first and fifteenth of each month, and during the major festivals in the Chinese calendar, the offerings are supplemented with food, rice-wine, and imitation paper money in accordance with the Record of Rites, which prescribes the offering of animal flesh, agricultural produce, and drink in religious rituals. This ritual takes the form of a meal, and like a Christian Eucharist, only "family" members participate. Three pairs of chopsticks and three small cups of rice-wine are laid in a row on one side of the square table next to the food offerings, which usually consists of meat, poultry, fruit, and confectionery. These offerings, as well as incense, are presented first to the deities and then to the ancestors. Standing at the table and facing each shrine in turn, the worshiper performs the usual bows. The cups of rice-wine are then poured onto the ground between the table and the seat, recalling an ancient belief that the spirits are present at the table to partake of the gifts. When this has been done, paper ingots of gold and silver are burnt before each of the shrines. Finally, firecrackers suspended over the main entrance are ignited. The piercing noise adds to the festive air and is intended to frighten away malicious spirits who are believed to linger wherever ritual offerings are being made. Afterwards, the remaining food offerings are eaten by those present.

Household shrines can be seen today in the principal room of many Chinese homes, in China and in the Chinese diaspora, but rarely do they take on the grand proportions of the old shrines as described earlier. Because of the restrictions of space, they often resemble a narrow bookcase with two or three shelves. Each of these is illuminated by a red lamp and furnished with a censer, flowers, and offerings of fruit. The bottom shelf is dedicated to the local Earth god who is represented by either an inscribed tablet, a stone, or an image. On the top shelf usually stands a single collective spirit tablet dedicated to all the family ancestors, and sometimes the photographs of recently deceased relatives are placed here as well. Few modern Chinese houses have an internal courtyard and for that reason an incense holder is attached to a wall near the front door or even on the doorpost itself for the representative of Heaven. In this contemporary setting the traditional household rituals continue, but a fundamental difference is that while at the beginning of the twentieth century they were unquestioningly observed in all Chinese homes, today they are optional.

Calendar

There are four principal methods of keeping time in the current Chinese calendar. First is the Jiazi cycle, which reflects a cyclic understanding of time. Two sets of Chinese characters, one made up of a sequence of twelve, known as "earthly branches," the other of ten, called "heavenly stems," are paired in sequence to create sixty different combinations which constitute one Jiazi cycle. On the Shang dynasty oracle bones this cycle was used to record days, but subsequently it was extended to number other divisions of time. The bazi or *eight characters* used in Chinese astrology are the stem and branch character combinations for a person's year, month, day, and hour of birth. Other than for astrology and designating the years, the Jiazi cycle is too cumbersome and impractical for everyday use.

A lunar calendar is ordinarily used to number the days and months. There is also a solar calendar, which was once essential for regulating the times of sowing and reaping in an agrarian society. The solar year is split into twenty-four divisions, called "joints" and "breaths," which occur approximately at two-week intervals, two of which make one solar month. The names of these "joints" and "breaths" refer to the seasons (four of which are the equinoxes and solstices), the weather, and agriculture. To keep the lunar and solar years in synchronism, an intercalary month is inserted into the lunar calendar every two or three years, thus ensuring that the equinoxes and solstices always fall in the same lunar months. Lastly, at the founding of the Republic in 1912, the Chinese government officially adopted the Gregorian calendar.

The twelve creatures in the Chinese zodiac, unlike its western counterpart, do not denote constellations or any other astronomical phenomena. They are figurative substitutes for the sequence of earthly branches. The creatures were probably adopted as general year titles because they were easier to remember than the earthly branches. Precisely when this began is not known, but it was possibly invented by Buddhist monks during the Tang dynasty (618–907 CE) to simplify the calendar.

Each year the calendar is updated and published in the almanac. It is the most widely consulted religious book among Chinese. The Confucian and Daoist Canons do not enjoy a popular readership. In addition to the calendar, between its covers are charts designating lucky and unlucky days for performing various human activities, ranging from the mundane, like washing hair, to marriage and funerals, which are the major rites of passage. It also offers advice on how to deal with malevolent spirits, complete with the requisite magical charms. Moreover, the book itself is an exorcising charm. In parts of South China it was traditional for sick children to use an old copy as a pillow, the belief being that illness was caused by malevolent spirits. The almanac is also the basic handbook of the astrologer, containing information for casting horoscopes and other methods for predicting the future, such as palmistry and physiognomy. Despite its importance in religious belief and practice, the almanac rarely features in studies of Chinese religion, mainly because it is extremely difficult to render comprehensibly into English without heavy annotation. Many of its esoteric passages are an inscrutable mystery even among Chinese.

Daoism and Buddhism have each introduced festivals into the Chinese calendar, but none except a handful of major festivals are universally observed. The major Chinese festivals mark the passage of the seasons. The calendar echoes the ceaseless process of cyclic change visualized in the Book of Changes. Festive customs vary from place to place but a common chord is that they usually involve a celebratory meal preceded by the ritual worship of Heaven, Earth, and the ancestors. They are family occasions, when ties are renewed between the living and the dead.

The cycle of major festivals begins at the Lunar New Year, which is also known as the Spring Festival. It falls on the second new moon after the winter solstice, which appears sometime between January 21st and February 20th in the Gregorian calendar. The solar year begins at Lichun, the Inauguration of Spring, which coincides with February 4th. After the Spring Festival comes Qingming, the day of Pure Brightness, one of the twenty-four solar joints and breaths, which usually corresponds to April 5th. Of the major feasts, it is exclusively dedicated to the commemoration of the dead and the main activity takes place outside the family home. Family graves are renovated, and incense, food, drink, and paper objects are offered and then shared among the living.

As summer approaches, on the Double Fifth (the fifth day of the fifth month), dragon boats take to the waters to commemorate the death, by suicide, of Qu Yuan [Chü Yuan], a distinguished official of the Warring States period, though the festival itself is thought to pre-date Qu Yuan. In Chinese culture, dragons are auspicious creatures who bring rain. Some scholars have suggested that the dragon boats originated as a waterborne rain dance. The noisy beat of the drums was supposed to incite the dragons to bring rain, which was crucial at this point in the year for the success of the rice crop.

The Mid-Autumn Festival falls on the fifteenth day of the eighth month. The full moon, a symbol of yin, is believed to be at its fullest and most brilliant. Yin, the feminine force, is at its zenith. By this time the crops have been harvested and people celebrate after their labors.

Celebration and thanksgiving are also the keynotes during the winter solstice. During imperial times, at dawn on the Winter Festival, the emperor performed the most solemn worship of Heaven, which he alone, as Son of Heaven, was entitled to do. Yang, the masculine force symbolized by the sun, has reached its lowest point and hereafter the days get longer. With the advent of spring the cycle begins anew.

Engagement with Modernity

In contemporary China an avowedly atheistic state claims and exercises many of the religious prerogatives enjoyed by the last Qing emperor at the beginning of the twentieth century, including the authority to determine the incarnation of the Dalai Lama. Although religion is officially discouraged, the Chinese government recognizes the existence of five major religions within China, which it supervises through the Religious Affairs Bureau of the People's National Congress. These include: Buddhism, Daoism, Islam, Catholicism, and Protestantism (the last two being regarded as distinct and separate religions). Daoism and Buddhism are at present enjoying a revival. Confucianism is notably absent from the list of authorized religions, yet as the focus of the "Asian Values" debate, it has caught the limelight in recent cultural discourse between East and West.

Late imperial China was lauded throughout western Europe during the seventeenth and eighteenth centuries as a model of civilization, worthy of emulation, particularly the idea of the enlightened despot. The sixty-year reign of the great Qianlong emperor [Ch'ien-lung] (1736–96) could be described "like the sun at midday," Confucian civilization in all its blazing glory, but it also saw the beginning of its decline. China was undoubtedly the wealthiest and most powerful country in the world at the beginning of the reign. As it drew to a close, the industrial revolution in Britain had transformed the world stage. China, an insular self-sufficient civilization which disdained profit, was confronted by a seemingly insignificant, yet ambitious, trading nation which demanded to be treated as an equal. The British Embassy to China led by Lord Macartney (1792–4) finally shattered the romantic illusion of Confucian China. Even the famous Voltaire, who had once sung the praises of its venerable antiquity, turned against it. Henceforth, relations between China and the western nations rapidly deteriorated and in the process undermined the Confucian worldview. The Chinese ruling elite nevertheless continued to maintain their faith in the Confucian order. As late as 1894, the Guangxu emperor [Kuang Hsü] issued an edict proscribing criticism of Zhu Xi [Chu Hsi], the Song dynasty Neo-Confucianist whose teachings formed the basis of the imperial–state doctrine.

In heated debate, orthodox Confucian scholars firmly continued to place the reform of life before that of institutions, while others, such as Kang Youwei [K'ang Yu-wei] (1858–1927), advocated modernization. At the heart of the matter was to what extent a universal Confucian civilization could adapt to the modern world in which China had lately become just one of many independent states. A radical Confucianist and a leading figure in the "Hundred Days' Reforms" of 1898, Kang believed that political and economic changes could take place within a Confucian framework. He was confronted by a barrage of opposition, typified by scholars such as Zhu Yixin [Chu I-hsin] (1846–94) and Ye Dehui [Yeh Te-hui] (1864–1927) (see Markham, *A World Religions Reader*, p. 191). For these orthodox Confucianists, good government lay in moral charisma, in men of virtue rather than new laws and institutions. Self-cultivation alone could solve all political problems and usher in a perfect society. Above all, government should not be based, as they saw in the West, on the principle of utilitarianism. Citing Mencius, Zhu reiterated:

> A gentleman goes back to the norm. That is all. When the norm is properly set then the common people will be roused; when the common people are roused then heresy and aberration will disappear.[28]

The abandonment of Confucian norms, such as the "five relationships," was seen as a perversion of fundamental principles. Ye Dehui was equally convinced of the superiority of Confucianism, although he was more conciliatory toward the West. Ultimately they sought to reaffirm the universality of Confucian doctrine, and even ventured to speculate on its eventual adoption in the West.

The valiant efforts of the defenders of the Neo-Confucian tradition served only to seal its fate. As the imperial state doctrine, Confucianism was repudiated by the revolutionaries in the early part of the twentieth century. Never for over two millennia had there been such a wholesale rejection of Confucian ideals. It was now held responsible for China's ills. Confucius, or rather the system which bore his name, was indicted as the perpetrator of great suffering and misery. Joseph Levenson, a renowned American sinologist, once remarked that May 4, 1919 was the day Confucius died. This date, on which began a student protest in Beijing, is traditionally taken to represent the start of the New Culture Movement. Its luminaries, such as Lu Xun [Lu Hsün] (1881–1936), author of *The True Story of Ah Q*, and the early communist Qu Qiubai [Chü Ch'iu-pai] (1899–1935), reviled their own culture as one of extreme barbarism.

Although nominally Confucius enjoyed moments of patronage by various republican governments in China, notably those led by Yuan Shikai, the renegade prime minister of the last imperial dynasty, and later by Chiang Kai-shek, Neo-Confucianism effectively ceased to be a living tradition. The attempts by Chiang, a professed Christian, to rehabilitate Confucius from the late 1920s onwards was ridiculed by many Chinese intellectuals. In any case, it was a very selective and peculiar interpretation which would hardly qualify as genuine revival. After Liberation, the Chinese term for the Communist victory in 1949, Confucianism was even less likely to find favor with the new masters. With its elaborate system of social distinctions, it sat incongruously with the culture of equality in the new China.

According to Chinese-Marxist historiography the imperial period is confusingly designated as the feudal period, although historically speaking, feudalism was abolished in the second century BCE. During the Cultural Revolution Confucius was singled out as the archetypal feudal reactionary. Anything that was deemed to be "rightist," or allegedly tainted by traditional culture, was to be destroyed. A vilification campaign was orchestrated to purge the government of so-called reactionaries, including the head of state, President Liu Shaoqi; the author of *How to Be a Good Communist*, he was hounded from office and died in captivity in 1969.

The prospects for Confucianism took an about turn after the Cultural Revolution. Following the death of Mao Zedong in 1976, the pragmatic open-door policy pursued under Deng Xiaoping brought much foreign investment into China, which resulted in dramatic economic growth in the 1980s and early 1990s. Astonished by the growth and success of the budding "tiger economies" in China and Southeast Asia, people around the world sought an explanation. Thrift, frugality, hard work, and family values were identified as the characteristics which contributed to the change of fortune. Though not dissimilar to the Protestant work ethic, these characteristics were quickly claimed by some people in the tiger economies as quintessential "Asian values" which derive from time-honored

Confucian culture. The concept of Confucianism was revived as one of the principles underlying Asia's new-found prosperity, though ironically, the idea of profit
is inimical to the Neo-Confucian tradition. This is expressed in *The Great Learning*,
and also in the opening chapter of the book of *Mencius*, where the position is clearly
stated: *What is the point of mentioning the word "profit"? All that matters is that there
should be benevolence and rightness.*[29]

Confucius is part of an eclectic amalgam of cultural images that makes up the
iconography of contemporary China. In 1979 the Confucius Mansion and its adjoin-
ing temple at Qufu [Ch'u-fu] was opened to the public. It now joined the Great
Wall and the Terracotta Army, monuments associated with the first Qin emperor,
on the tourist trail. Confucius is a strange bedfellow alongside the tyrannical
emperor, who in his lifetime was an implacable opponent of the Confucian tradition, but few seem to notice.

Neo-Confucianism, as it stood at the beginning of the twentieth century, was
a doctrine which claimed universal application. It was not meant as an ethnic
peculiarity belonging only to the Chinese, or to East Asians in general, as contemporary Confucianism seems to be. Almost a century on, during which he has
fluctuated in and out of favor, Confucius has been reinvented as a national hero,
as someone who is quintessentially Chinese. Like the twelfth-century general Yue
Fei [Yüeh Fei], he has been recruited from the extensive cultural archive to
promote modern Chinese patriotism and nationalism. Within living memory, these
cultural heroes were representatives of a dark and backward "feudal" society.
Today, they are the torchbearers of a great, glorious, and correct living culture with
a history stretching back five thousand years.

At Hangzhou the temple and tomb of Yue Fei, an impetuous general and martyr for Chinese nationalism, has been restored and opened to the public. During
the Song dynasty, the Jurchen, ancestors of the Manchus who later ruled China as
the Qing dynasty, attacked and conquered parts of northern China. The Song Court
was split on the issue. Yue Fei belonged to the war faction which advocated recon-
quering land regardless of the cost in human lives. The peace faction led by the
prudent prime minister, Qin Kui [Ch'in Kuei], sued for peace and successfully con-
trived to have the general executed. Peace endured for almost twenty years and,
for a brief period, Qin was posthumously honored in the Confucian temple; when
the war faction regained their influence at Court, Qin's spirit tablet was cast from
the temple, and to this day, his name is a byword for treachery.

The Confucian school primer, *The Three Character Classic*, emanated from the
circle of the war faction at the Song Court. This text is a summation of Confucian
doctrine, encapsulating the basic tenets and principles which inspired traditional
Chinese society. The publication of a new, officially approved edition of *The Three
Character Classic* in 1995 sheds light on the nature of contemporary Confucianism. In
the original text, the famous opening lines runs as follows:

> At man's beginning, human nature is basically good; all are close in nature, but become
> different through experience.

The new edition reads:

> At man's beginning, his nature is uncarved jade; both nature and feelings are capable of being molded.[30]

The original text opens with the affirmation of the orthodox, Neo-Confucian position, namely the essential goodness of human nature. The new text does not acknowledge this, and in its place it substitutes another Confucian image, that of carving and polishing jade. As previously noted, this is a metaphor for self-cultivation, one of the basic tenets in Confucian practice. It has to be remembered, however, that self-cultivation has a very different meaning in contemporary China. Instead of looking inwards to regain our Heaven-bestowed essential humanity, one should look, theoretically, toward the ruling Communist Party for guidance. At a stroke, the spiritual dimension of Neo-Confucian doctrine has been erased. Contemporary Confucianism as advocated by vociferous exponents of "Asian values" is a secular doctrine concerned purely with social ethics. It has been evacuated of its religious elements. The language and ideals of Confucianism are utilized where and when it can be accommodated with contemporary thinking; but where it conflicts, it is discarded.

GLOSSARY

Burning of Books Literary inquisition ordered by Qin Shi Huangdi [Ch'in Shih Huang-ti], the first Qin emperor, in 213 BCE to destroy all books, except those on divination, medicine and agriculture. Particular criticism was directed toward *The Classic of History* and *The Classic of Poetry*, books which articulated views on history conflicting with those of the first Qin emperor.

De [Te] *Inner power and moral virtue.* Originally perceived to be the power which characterized a thing, the Confucianists later transformed it to mean moral virtue.

Dao [Tao] *The Way.* A philosophical concept common to both Daoism and Confucianism. In Daoism it refers to the law of nature, or the universe, which is beyond words or thought. In Confucianism it refers to the path of moral perfection.

Daodejing [Tao Te Ching] *The Classic of the Way and Its Power,* the central scripture of the Daoist tradition.

Daojia [Tao-chia] *The School of Dao,* the name of the philosophical Daoist School. Religious Daoism is sometimes called Daojiao [Dao-chiao], but the distinction between the two is not so clear cut in practice.

Five Classics The principal books of the Zhou Court. Adopted by the Confucianists as the foundation of their scriptural canon. They include:

Classic of History (Shujing) [Shu Ching]
Classic of Poetry (Shijing) [Shi Ching]

Classic of Changes (Yijing) [I Ching]
Record of Rites (Liji) [Li Chi]
*Chronicles of the Spring and Autumn
Period* (Chunqiu) [Ch'un Ch'iu]

Four Books The principal books emanating from the Confucian School. Together with the Five Classics they constitute the basic Confucian canon. The Four Books are:

Analects of Confucius (Lunyu) [Lun Yu]
Book of Mencius (Mengzi) [Meng-tzu]
Great Learning (Daxue) [Ta-hsüeh]
Doctrine of the Mean (Zhongyong)
[Chung-yung]

Junzi [Chün-tzu] The *Gentleman*, or literally, *son of a lord*. A person who is the embodiment of Confucian ethics in practice and a role model for others.

Li *Ritual and propriety*. It is a central ethical tenet in Confucianism. It is meant to be an outward expression of humane sentiment.

Qi [Ch'i] *Psycho-physical stuff* or primordial energy-matter from which all things are made.

Ren [Jen] *Humaneness*, the guiding moral principle in Confucianism. It is the perfection of human nature. Some scholars equate it with the Christian concept of *agape*.

Ru [Ju] The *Scholars* or *Literati*. The Chinese term for Confucian, Confucianist. Confucius belonged to the scholar class in ancient China.

Rujia [Ju-Chia] The *School of the Scholars*, the Chinese term for the Confucian tradition.

Shang Di [Shang Ti] The *Lord on High*, name of the anthropomorphic supreme deity in ancient China. Used by some Christian missionaries to translate the term *God*.

Shu *Reciprocity*, the golden rule of Confucian ethics, "Treat others as you would wish to be treated yourself."

Taiji [T'ai Chi] The *Great ultimate* or *primal origin* of all things. It is illustrated by the Taijitu [T'ai Chi T'u], the Diagram of the Great Ultimate. This is sometimes known in the West as the yin–yang symbol.

Tian [T'ien] *Heaven*, an alternative name for the supreme deity. Also used to mean the impersonal natural law of the universe.

Wu-wei *Non-action*, the state of harmony with the law of nature, or the universe. For the Confucianists, this means acting ethically; for the Daoists it means abstinence from artificial or unnatural activity.

Xiao [Hsiao] *Filial piety*, a central ethical tenet in Confucianism. Dutiful, or proper behavior toward one's parents.

Yang *Light*, the creative principle. Polar opposite of yin. By extension it came to signify, for example, Heaven, male, and firm.

Yi [I] *Rightness*, or ren in action. A central ethical tenet in Confucianism, it describes the quality of an act rather than the moral status of the one who acts.

Yin *Shadow or darkness*, the receptive principle. Polar opposite of yang. By extension it came to signify, for example, Earth, female, and yielding.

Notes and References

1   Ian Markham, *A World Religions Reader*, second edition (Oxford: Blackwell Publishers, 2000).
2   *Mencius* 1A: 6.
3   Ssu-Ma T'an, *Discussion on the Essentials of the Six Schools*, in De Barry, *Sources of Chinese Tradition*, vol. 1 (New York: Columbia University Press, 1971), p. 189.
4   Ibid., p. 189.
5   A. Peyrefitte (English trans. Jon Rothschild), *The Immobile Empire* (New York: Alfred A. Knopf, 1992), p. 110.
6   Song 204.
7   Song 241.
8   Ta Chuan Commentary 4: 1. R. Wilhelm (English trans. Cary F. Baynes), *I Ching* (Harmondsworth: Arkana, 1989), p. 293.
9   Shuo Kua Commentary 1:1; ibid., p. 262.
10 Tuan Chuan Commentary, ibid., p. 670.
11 *Analects* 2: 1.
12 *Analects* 15: 5.
13 *Mencius* 6A: 6.
14 D. C. Lau, *Mencius* (Harmondsworth: Penguin, 1970), p. 46.
15 *Daodejing* [Tao Te Ching] 38: 83–4.
16 *Mencius* 4A: 5.
17 *Mencius* 7B: 16.
18 *Analects* 2: 6.
19 *Analects* 15: 23.
20 *Mencius* 7A: 4.
21 *Mencius* 7A: 6.
22 *Analects* 7: 1.
23 See Markham, *A World Religions Reader*, pp. 182–3.
24 *Great Learning* 3: 4.
25 *Great Learning* 9: 6, trans. E. R. Hughes, p. 157. E. R. Hughes, *The Great Learning & The Mean-in-Action* (London: J. M. Dent & Sons, 1942).
26 Hsün Tzu, chapter 19, in De Barry, *Sources of Chinese Tradition*, p. 110.
27 The following description is based on recollections of the author's grandfather about domestic life in China during the days of the Republic (1912–49). The ornate woodwork of the Spirit Platform and the spirit tablets at the author's ancestral home no longer exist. They were destroyed during the Cultural Revolution.
28 *Mencius* 7B: 37.
29 *Mencius* 1A: 1.
30 Quoted in Peter R. Moody Jr., *"Asian Values,"* *Journal of International Affairs*, Summer 1996, vol. 50, no. 1, Colombia University, New York, p. 179, n. 38.

Chapter 12

....

Judaism

ELIZABETH RAMSEY

Historical Survey

Worldviews

God

Election

Torah

The Land

Institutions and Rituals

The Main Festivals

Ethical Expression

Modern Outlook

Secularism

The Holocaust

Israel

Jewish Humor and Story

From Moses to Einstein, Judaism has produced some of the greatest thinkers the world has ever known. Even today, in spite of the near destruction of Europe's Jewish communities, the influence of Jews is out of any proportion to their numbers, whether in the professions such as law, medicine, and scientific research, or in the worlds of politics, entertainment, and the media. In religion, Judaism introduced **monotheism** to the world and was the inspiration behind the rise of both Christianity and Islam. Yet many Jews experience a deep-seated sense of unease about the defining of Judaism as a "religion" and, indeed, about the whole use of the term "Judaism."

Interestingly, there is no equivalent word for "religion" in Hebrew and no word for "religion" or for "spiritual" in the major early Jewish sources. Jews will often describe Judaism as being "not so much a religion, more a way of life." This reflects

A boy and rabbi reading the Torah. Photo: Corbis/Hanan Isachar.

the fact that Judaism, understood as a "religion," is essentially more concerned with actions and the refinement of ways of behaving, than with abstract statements of belief. Another complicating factor these days is that many Jews are not "Jewish" in any religious sense of the word. You are Jewish regardless of "Judaism," as long as you are born a Jew. Religious belief is just one ingredient in the makeup of a Jew. Only converts to Judaism have to be religious and, even then, they may not be acknowledged as Jewish by all Jews unless they go through the full orthodox process of conversion. This leads in turn to the complex question not only of "What *is* Judaism?" but "Who is a Jew?"

Judaism is difficult to define. There are so many possible approaches that can be taken and, ideally, all of them need to be taken together for a complete knowledge and understanding of Jews and Judaism. To be a Jew for many Jews, religious and otherwise, means, first and foremost, to belong to a group of people. Having said that, the groupings within Judaism are numerous, and spread throughout the world. The majority of Jews live in the USA but Jews also live in countries and cultures as different as India, Ethiopia, Russia, England and, of course, Israel. In Israel itself, over one hundred different cultures are represented.

The story of Judaism is, simultaneously, the history of a religion and the history of a people – and much more besides. For Jews, there is an inseparable link between religion, history, and cultural and social circumstances. No other people have struggled to exist in so many different parts of the world for so long. If we seriously want to understand Jews and Judaism, we must, at one and the same time, take account of the centuries of history which have helped to form them, and seek to understand their religion, or, indeed, lack of it.

One way of understanding "what it is to be a Jew" is to stress the significance of memory. Memory forms a basis for the most important rituals which most Jews, religious or secular, perform, from Passover to the celebration of the anniversary of the State of Israel. Unfortunately, intrinsic to that memory is the experience of persecutions. These can be traced from the time of Nebuchadnezzar, through the Roman period, the Crusades and the Inquisition, the ghetto and the Jew-badge and the pogroms, to Hitler's "Final Solution." The very fact that Jews continue to exist has been seen by many people, both inside and outside Jewry, as evidence in itself for the existence of God.

Historical Survey

Jewish history has shaped Jewish religion. From the time of the fall of Jerusalem to Nebuchadnezzar in 586 BCE, until the State of Israel was set up in 1948, wherever Jews lived they were continually under foreign rule, except for a very short period of independence under the Maccabean kings (140–163 BCE). We shall briefly outline the main components of Jewish religion and locate them in their historical setting. We will start with the Torah (1200 BCE), then examine Pharisaic Judaism (1 CE), which led to the emergence of the Synagogue, the Rabbi, and the production of the Talmud. Then we will examine the growing popularity of Mysticism (especially 1280 CE), followed by more recent assimilation and Zionist movements.

The written and the oral Torah

We start with the Torah: the written Torah is the first five books of the Hebrew Bible, which according to tradition were written by Moses; the oral Torah is the interpretation and teaching built on the written Torah. According to Orthodox Jewish belief, God was revealed to the whole of humankind through the experience of the presence of God by Moses on Mount Sinai. Moses probably lived in the thirteenth century BCE. The experience was recorded in the book of Exodus to bear lasting testimony to this revelation. Viewed as God's will, Torah is the source of all wisdom, offering guidance on the nature of ultimate reality and on ways of living in accordance with that nature. Traditionally, the Sinai experience is regarded to have included the revelation of both the written and the oral Torah. The oral Torah is a body of teachings intended to enable correct understanding of the written text. It was framed by the early Rabbis in the first few centuries of the Common Era.

Pharisaic Judaism

Most of the great Rabbis and followers of the Oral Law were Pharisees, like the famous Hillel. Unfortunately, the Pharisees get a "bad press" in Christian sources, particularly in the Gospels and these negative perceptions have been reinforced in recent times by films and musicals depicting the life of Jesus. The Pharisees believed that the religious needs of the people could not be altogether satisfied by the Temple priesthood because of what they considered to be an excessive emphasis on rites and ceremony. Rabbi Hillel tried to make the moral and social truths of the Torah meaningful in terms of people's experience of daily living. Jesus' moral beliefs were similar to the Pharisaic school of Hillel, which emphasized the love of God and neighbor: "What is hateful to you, do not do to your neighbor." This could be considered the "whole Torah," said the school of Hillel, "the rest is commentary." Hillel died about 10 CE. It was Pharisaic Judaism which survived when the Romans finally destroyed Jewish sovereignty in 73 CE, three years after the destruction of the Second Temple. The destruction of the Temple was very traumatic for the Jewish people. However, Pharisaic Judaism found ways of adapting the traditions of Judaism to this. After 70 CE, the synagogue and Rabbi became much more important.

The center of community life became the Synagogue; and the Rabbi was the leader of the community. First and foremost the Rabbi is an expert in the Torah and is its teacher and commentator. One of the most ancient parts of the **Synagogue** service is the public readings from the scrolls of the Torah. Traditionally, Moses is credited with instituting readings from the Torah on the Sabbath and at festivals. Ezra is credited with being the person who instigated the attempt to make the Torah accessible to the people. In the four centuries between Ezra and Jesus, every effort was made to see that Jewish boys learned and followed Torah.

The other accomplishment of Pharisaic Judaism was the continuing work on the formulation of the Oral Law, which is found in the Mishnah (ca. 200 CE). Its clarification and detailed application are given by the Gemara (virtually completed by 500 CE). The two together form the Talmud. Anyone wishing to understand the methods of Rabbinic exegesis needs to be familiar also with the Midrashim, the commentaries on the Hebrew Scriptures which date from about the same time as the Talmud. Torah has been likened to an inverted pyramid. The tip of the pyramid is the Written Teaching and this gradually widens out to include further commentary based on changing experiences.

The Rabbis deduced from the first five books principles and codes of behavior which would cover the whole of life. These principles and codes form the Oral Teaching. The Written Teaching and the Oral Teaching are traditionally regarded as having equal authority and together they form the second "layer" of Torah for the Rabbinic Jew. The twenty-five closely printed folio volumes which form the

Talmud basically consist of records of the discussions that took place in the Rabbinic academies.

Undoubtedly there were Jews who enjoyed the sheer mental entertainment of casuistic hair-splitting for its own sake. Others would simply keep the laws in the hope that they would receive some reward in the future. However, neither of these approaches is typical of Rabbinic Judaism at its best. The emphasis given by the Rabbis is that laws should be kept primarily out of devotion to God, not for reasons of personal accomplishment or gain. Because God is believed to be right-eous, it is true to say that reward was expected but only because God's will had been performed, for God's sake. The Rabbis stressed that the main purpose of God's revelation was to give *life* and in order to save life, any commandment might be broken, except those against murder, unchastity, and idolatry.

Mysticism

Mysticism has played an important role in Rabbinic Judaism from at least the second century CE. The influence of mysticism provided a constant balance to any tendency toward an overly-legalistic approach. It is only possible to mention Kabbalism and its famous work, *The Zohar* (ca. 1280), and Hasidism. Kabbalah is currently undergoing an increasing popularity as part of the modern search for spiritual experiences. *The Zohar* is the fundamental Rabbinic work of Jewish mysticism and the primary reference text for Kabbalistic studies. Arranged in the form of a commentary on the Bible, *The Zohar* brings to the surface the deeper meanings behind the commandments and biblical narrative.

Hasidism has been described as one of the most colorful movements within Orthodox Judaism. Founded by Rabbi Israel Eliezer (1698–1760) it provided a wel-come alternative for the people who, for good practical reasons, were unable to devote the major proportion of their lives to study. Also known by the title Baal Shem Tov, or "Master of the Good Name," Eliezer was concerned to bring the experience of enjoyment in serving God more to the forefront. He popularized mysticism among the Jewish people of eastern Europe and Russia thereby revitalizing the Judaism of his day, at least for ordinary people, and his influence continues.

Although today Hasidism can be associated with the strictest, most uncom-promising forms of Orthodoxy, the early Hasidim were accused of "corrupting" the people. Introducing joy and song into the lives of ordinary people coping with life in a hard and often very unpleasant world, sometimes meant jettisoning the formalistic conventions of the day for the sake of the warmth and mysticism of deeply emotional prayer and song. Gradually, Hasidism began to follow a more level path which combined emotion and mysticism with the way of life of the Talmud.

Assimilation

In the Biblical period, the name Jew had both a religious and a national meaning. During the long centuries of the dispersion of Jews (known as Jews living in **Diaspora**), the existence of Jewish people was increasingly explained in purely religious terms. With the rise of modern liberalism, many Jews wished to repudiate any national or racial connotation in the name. Indeed, there was a period in the eighteenth century (and again more recently) when it was the ambition of the average west European Jew to assimilate to those among whom they lived in everything except religion. In the last twenty years of the eighteenth century, it became increasingly and tragically clear that a policy of assimilation was not in any way contributing to a check on the rapid increase in anti-Semitism.

The Holocaust

Anti-Semitism is centuries old; persecution and movement have characterized the Jewish people since the Exodus out of Egypt. However, when the Nazis came to power in Germany in the 1930s, technology and bureaucracy gave anti-Semitism a wicked opportunity. The murder of six million Jews devastated European Jewry. As a result the survival and security of the Jewish people remains the major issue for contemporary Judaism.

Exercise

1 To understand Judaism, it is essential to attempt some sort of understanding of the nature of the Holocaust. Take any one of the suggestions outlined below and do some background research into the Holocaust.

Establish contact with the Holocaust Memorial Centers in Washington or Yad Vashem in Jerusalem or the Anne Frank Centre in Amsterdam.
Use the Internet and locate the register of survivors' testimonies.
Martin Gilbert, one of the greatest historians of the twentieth century, is a foremost historian of the Holocaust. His books *An Atlas of the Holocaust* and *Holocaust Journey* are very accessible.
Watch Spielberg's film *Schindler's List*, and Claude Lanzmann's film *Shoah*.
Roberto Benigni's film, *La vita è bella/Life is Beautiful*, is unique to the extent that the "victim" is the hero. The humor highlights the horror while diminishing the perpetrators.
Read the novels of Elie Wiesel and Primo Levi, both survivors of the death camps. Of particular interest is Binjamin Wilkomirski's memoirs as a child survivor of the liquidation of the Riga ghetto and two death camps. His slim book, *Fragments*, has been translated into sixteen languages since its publication in Switzerland in 1995.

Zionism

Partly as a result of the anti-Semitism developing in the 1880s, the nineteenth century saw the beginnings of a movement for the Jewish resettlement of Palestine.

This movement, which became known as **Zionism**, was given an increased impetus by the pogroms taking place in Russia. The outbreak of **anti-Semitism** in Germany in 1879 reinforced thoughts of a homeland for Jews. As anti-Semitism gained supporters throughout Europe, many Jews questioned whether they had any future in European society at all.

The Zionist movement held its first congress in 1897, in Basle. Theodore Herzl's book *Der Judenstaat* (1896) gave expression to this new trend. The 204 delegates were representative of worldwide Jewry, and they opened the eyes of the western leaders of the new movement to the mass support they might expect from the younger Jews of eastern Europe. Further encouragement was given to resettlement when the British Government issued the Balfour Declaration in 1917 viewing "with favour the establishment of a Jewish national home in Palestine."

Groups of young Jews expressed a determination to settle on the land. It should be remembered that the land was inhospitable. Not only had it been deserted and neglected but it was scattered with an amazing number of rocks and boulders. There were few natural resources. Mrs. Golda Meir is often quoted as saying: "Let me tell you something that we Israelis have against Moses. He took us 40 years through the desert to bring us to the one spot in the Middle East that had no oil."

However, the cooperative settlements known as the **Kibbutzim** and described as the greatest experiment in communal living of the twentieth century were founded by the pioneers. A revival of national feeling began to replace the old Orthodoxy. This revival was powerfully supported by young Jews in Russia who had abandoned religion in despair on account of their experiences of persecution. Increasingly, the establishment of a homeland was seen as a way of maintaining Jewish existence. The Liberal might be opposed to Zionism on principle but nevertheless could not resist a growing feeling of pride in the achievements of the pioneers of the Kibbutzim. The Orthodox gradually decreased their opposition and apart from small extreme groups (such as the Naturei Kartei) they have been willing to accept the fruits of its success.

So we have seen how Judaism is grounded in the revelation of God to Moses, yet it has developed a means of modifying and adapting the tradition over time. In the next section we shall look at the ways in which Judaism understands the world.

Worldviews

"On three things does the world stand – on Torah, on divine service, and on acts of kindness (charity)." (Teaching of "Shimon the Righteous, ca. 200 BCE Mishnah" Avot 1: 2)

These words encapsulate the essential features of Judaism in terms of religious belief and practice. The belief that humanity is in partnership with God in sustaining the world is intrinsic to Judaism. This is to be interpreted not only in the popular ecological sense of stewardship, but in a more mystical sense. Religious action, it is believed, can put us in contact with a hidden source, the source, in fact, of *all* being. This includes the world itself. Although it makes sense to study beliefs and then institutions and rituals for the sake of a certain clarity and comparison between different religious traditions, belief and action are irrevocably bound together in Judaism. A similar case of course can be made out for other religions. It is specifically the Christian West that places emphasis on religion as a set of beliefs.

Consider the following:

> Beware of looking upon religion as an ideal to be yearned for: it should be an ideal to be applied. (S. Dubnow, cited in *Forms of Prayer for Jewish Worship*)

> The chief thing is not to study but to do. (*Pirke Avoth* 1: 17)

> If one studies in order to teach, one is granted the opportunity to study and to teach; but if one studies in order to practice, one is granted the opportunity to study and to teach, to observe and to practice. (*Pirke Avoth*)

Judaism is an intensely practical religion and it can be quite a challenge to realize that religion can infuse every dimension of life from the moment of waking each morning. For Jews, their whole day, their weeks, months and years, their food and their dress, their ethical standards and family life are defined by their religious commitment. For Jews, practice is more important than belief. Having said that, belief about God is implicit in the practice of Judaism. And the "thirteen principles of faith" written by Maimonides (Rabbi Moshe Ben Maimon, great thinker, Talmudist and codifier, 1135–1204) are signficant because they have been in the Jewish prayer book since the early-sixteenth century.

However, it is essential for gaining insight into the nature of Jewish belief and practice to realize that Maimonides did not sit down to state simply and categorically what every Jew is expected to believe. Judaism is not a religion which is centered on creedal statements. Maimonides was actually making a deliberate attempt to respond to particular circumstances and his main purpose was to defend the Torah. His "thirteen principles of faith" were appended to his Commentary on the Mishnah which states that "One who says the Torah is not from heaven has no share in the World to Come" (Sanhedrin 10: 1). Increasingly it was being claimed that the Torah of Moses had been superseded by Christianity and Islam while other people (in particular the Karaites) were insisting that the oral Torah is an invention of the Rabbis. Attempts to systematize and categorize Jewish beliefs have been rare and usually ignored. Until recently, with the development of post-Holocaust theology, it has even been difficult to speak of Jewish theology. Theology is somewhat alien to traditional Jewish thought and in fact arouses suspicion among Jews. To be a Jew is to be part of a family, a culture, a history, a spiritual system, and much more beside.

Jews will almost always claim personal responsibility for their views and they hesitate to appear to put forward what might be regarded as any kind of platform of Jewish belief, particularly when communicating with non-Jews. Unless we are able to break out of the mindset which needs to define Judaism in those restrictive terms, then we shall never understand the significance of Zionism to Jews, the effect of the Holocaust on the Jewish people, or the way in which a Jew may be extremely proud of his or her Jewishness without being "religious" in any way. Nevertheless, an attempt will now be made to explore Jewish perspectives on the following: God, Election, Torah, and the Land.

God

The prayer known as the Shema (Hebrew for "Hear") is central to Judaism. The poignant words, "Hear O Israel: The Lord our God, the Lord is One" (Deuteronomy 6: 4–9, together with Deuteronomy 11: 13–21) reveal the heart of Judaism and point to the soul of Jews everywhere, religious or "secular." The Shema is the most frequently used reminder of God's presence in a Jewish household. The words from the Torah, best translated as "Teaching" (of which the basic layer of meaning is the first five books of the Bible), written on a tiny piece of parchment scroll protected by a special container called a mezuzah, are to be found on each doorpost of a house. The religious Jew will kiss the mezuzah (Hebrew for "doorpost") as a way of praying. These same words are used at the end of the Synagogue service on the Day of Atonement, the holiest day in the Jewish year. Traditionally, they are the final words uttered when a person is dying.

Through this central statement that God is One, Jews understand, at least implicitly, that everything, everywhere and forever is part of one wholeness. This explains why early Jewish sources had no word for "religion" or for "spiritual." Judaism, as Brian Lancaster explains, "makes no such division between religious and non-religious spheres; it has no concept of non-spiritual, or material, things existing devoid of any ongoing reference to the divine."[1] Monotheism, in Jewish terms, implies that the whole of reality is brought together in a single unity through its ultimate dependence on God.

Because God is infinite and has no form or likeness, God is far beyond the grasp of human, finite minds. This is the reason there are no pictures or statues of any kind in Jewish (or Muslim) places of worship. Judaism recognizes, in other words, that God encompasses male and female and transcends gender. To attribute gender to God is close to idolatry. Unfortunately, this complex male/female God has not been incorporated into everyday Judaism. Traditionally, the limitations of language have inevitably led to various human attributes being applied to God and this is where male symbolism has become predominant. These attributes include, for example, those of Lord, Father, King, Creator, and Saviour. Today the case is increasingly being made, particularly by women scholars and human rights activists, for the retrieval of the feminine which is considered to be built right into Judaism's God. "He" is purely a product of human convention but the power of the patriarchal system that developed as a result should not be underestimated. The title of Judith Plaskow's book, *Standing Again at Sinai*, represents the determined efforts of many Jewish women to ensure that the female experience which is undoubtedly within the tradition is uncovered and reclaimed.

Election

The covenantal relationship to God lies at the very heart of Jewish consciousness. God has chosen (elected) the Jewish people. Basically, this relationship consists of an agreement between God and the people which promises, "I will be your God if you will be my people." Culturally, the relationship binds Jewish people into the confines of literal history. In religious terms, the covenantal relationship binds them into the perspective of sacred history. The whole spiritual center of Judaism stems from the historical encounter between the people and God. The power of the beauty, the mystery, and the dynamism of Judaism to enchant is to be encountered at the points where the literal and the sacred forms of history intersect. It is for this reason that the yearly cycle of festivals is crucial to the Jewish experience.

The idea of Jews being a chosen people has often been a source of misunderstanding. The great medieval Jewish commentator Rashi tells a story which puts the idea of being "chosen" into a proper perspective. God, so the story goes, was searching for a people who would be prepared to live their lives according to God's will and thereby set an example in living to the rest of the world. One by one the different groups of people whom God approached turned down the invitation. People very often wish to get quietly on with their own lives without too much feeling of pressure and obligation. After all, how many of us, given the choice, would opt to live a good life, in the full spiritual and ethical sense, *all the time and forever*? Eventually, and with some reluctance, the Israelites agreed to take up the challenge and Rashi concludes, "We haven't made a very good job of it ever since!"

2   In the light of this story and the following quotations, what do you under-   **Exercise**
    stand by the idea of being "chosen"?

    You have chosen us out of all the peoples, loved us and cherished us. You
    have raised us up out of all the nations, set us apart through your com-
    mandments, and drawn us close to you, our king, so as to serve you, pro-
    nouncing over us your great and holy Name. (From *The Service for Festivals*)

    God, I know we are your chosen people, but couldn't you choose somebody
    else for a change? (Shalom Aleichem)

Jewish people in fact *chose* to accept the responsibility to witness to the one God and for implementing God's teachings throughout the generations. They have paid an enormously high price for their efforts. The ultimate goal of life for Orthodox Jews is not political power or wealth but the keeping of God's teaching. This is the most basic characteristic of Rabbinic Judaism. A life of study is regarded as a noble pursuit, study, that is to say, of Torah and thus God's will. The Talmud in fact grants a higher position to the scholar than to a monarch. It is this traditional love of learning and propensity for study that ensures that, whenever possible, Jews take education extremely seriously. This in turn is an important reason for the disproportionately high number of Jews in positions of prominence in the world, particularly in the fields of science and the arts. One of the tensions within Israel today is the resentment shown by some secular Jews toward those Orthodox Jews who are paid to spend their lives studying.

Many Jews consider it a special privilege that they have been given what they interpret to be a full and perfect revelation of God's will in the Law of Moses. But the consequence of election has not been the experience of power for Jews, but rather the acquisition of the fortitude and the motivation to enable them to survive powerlessness and yet retain their identity. Suffering and oppression have regularly been interpreted as evidence for the wrongdoing of God's people.

Being "called out" or "chosen" then is to be regarded as a burden of responsibility. There is nothing intrinsic to Jewish teaching which sets Jews apart in terms of superior status. In fact, Leviticus 19: 34 clearly specifies the Jewish approach to equality among nations: "The stranger that lives with you shall be as the home-born and you shall love him as yourself for you were strangers in the land of Egypt."

Torah

The study of Torah is largely concerned with the clarification of the written text by means of the insights of the oral tradition. Such study has traditionally been regarded as the highest of all possible human endeavors. Non-Orthodox Jews generally share the view that Torah embodies some form of higher truth, even though many may question not only the literal notions of the nature of Biblical revelation but also the whole authority of the oral tradition. The source of true spiritual nourishment is to be found in Torah and the rational mind is often harnessed to the service of sacred history, which does not inevitably mean that the rational mind is compromised. Through the study of Torah, Jews actually enter into the process of creation and revelation. Torah is much more than a collection of stories and commandments. The more closely we engage with Torah, the clearer the meaning of sacred history becomes. Torah is the essential focus of meaning for the religious Jew and therefore essential to any attempt to understand Judaism.

From a non-Jewish perspective however, Torah, commonly translated unfortunately as Law (through the influence of the second-century BCE Greek translation – the Septuagint) has very often been seen as a stumbling block to attempts to gain insight into Jewish religious experience. Judaism is often assumed to be an overly legalistic religion. Traditionally, Christians have taken the view that the "old" way of the "Law" was superseded by the "new" way of love. The Torah, the "Old" Testament, has been polarized against the "New" Testament. The Torah does not exist as an end in itself, but rather so that through the *keeping* of Torah, men and women may come to know God better. Leviticus 19 in fact makes it clear that loving God and neighbor is pure Judaism.

Exercise

3   What do the following examples of the nature of Torah tell us about Torah?

> Torah has been compared to the love-letters that a man sends to his betrothed when he is away. Her friends mock her for waiting for a man who will never return, but she reads the letters daily. When at last he comes back as he promised, he asks her how she had managed to be so faithful. And she shows him his letters to her ... (Cited in J. H. Hertz, *A Book of Jewish Thoughts*)
>
> The letters must be read because ... while in the womb, it is said, a child learns the entire Torah but at the moment of birth an angel strikes it on the mouth, making it forget all that it learnt. The rest of our lives are spent remembering what we once knew.... (Niddah 30b)
>
> The whole world, not only the individual human soul, is the object of religious activity.

The Land

"By the rivers of Babylon, there we sat down, yea we wept, when we remembered Zion" cries the Psalmist. (Psalm 137: 1)

Jewish prayers have focused on Zion for two thousand years. Jewish history is ultimately defined in relation to Israel and most religious Jews view the return to Israel as part of the purpose of history and as a prelude to the days of the Messiah. To extract Jerusalem from Judaism could be compared with extracting a heart from a body. Many of the commandments are only operable in relation to the Land of Israel. The meaning of Israel is fundamentally religious before it is political.

Zionism is not to be equated with what is usually understood by nationalism. This kind of thinking has paved the way for a modern form of anti-Semitism. The Zionist ideal is not simply a political target. The biblical word "Zion" refers to Jerusalem, and Jerusalem and Israel itself are fundamental to Jewish teaching and tradition. A key element of Jewish experience and identity is the religious meaning of Israel as an inner spiritual ideal. The conquest of the kingdom of Judah by the Babylonians in 586 BCE created the first Jewish exile. Expression was given to a sentiment which has remained in the Jewish heart ever since: "If I forget thee, O Jerusalem, may my right hand wither." Then, in 70 CE, came the second drastic disruption of Jewish national life – Jerusalem was sacked by the Romans. Many Jews stayed in Palestine, but thousands were taken into captivity in various parts of the Roman Empire. The love of Zion (Palestine) continued to occupy an important place in Jewish prayers and hopes. Jews still turn their faces towards Jerusalem when praying. In the twelfth century, Europe became a persecuting society. The historian R. I. Moore illustrates this by including the example of Jews alongside those of witches and lepers. His argument is that Europe has remained a persecuting society ever since. In the Middle Ages, many Jews therefore left Europe and returned to cities such as Jerusalem, Hebron, Tiberias, and Safed with the aim of re-establishing those ancient communities.

The fact that the State of Israel exists is a very strong unifying influence within contemporary Jewry, while also being a source of dissension. Israel provides a vision and a hope for the future, as well as a sense of security, even for Jews who do not see themselves as ever living there. It unites the majority of Jews in a common cause which includes making joint efforts not only for Israel, but for Soviet and Arab Jewry. The first political conference of the Zionist movement did not take place until 1897 (in Switzerland). The belief in the restoration of the Land of Israel to the Jewish people, evidenced by the frequent recital of the words "Next year in Jerusalem," began on the day the Romans destroyed the Temple in Jerusalem.

To move from the Diaspora to live in Israel is seen as a religious obligation to be fulfilled if circumstances allow. The reality of the State has injected a spirit of creative renewal into Judaism throughout the Diaspora. The revival of Hebrew as an everyday language and the State's astonishing cultural activity in a short period have provided a source of strength to Jewish people everywhere. As a Sovereign State, Israel elects its own government and has developed its own legal and administrative structures. Jews throughout the world feel a special responsibility to integrate Jews from different backgrounds into Israeli society and the challenge this presents has a bonding effect. Jews from all parts of the world jostle together and add to the special character of the streets of Jerusalem and Tel Aviv. A melting pot such as this must surely contain ingredients for creative renewal. If these creative impulses can be harnessed to the causes of peace and increasing democracy, then Israel may well be judged to have been a miracle of the twentieth century in the Common Era.

Institutions and Rituals

Given the importance of practice in Judaism, it is inevitable that ritual will be central. In this section we shall examine the following important rituals: Pidyon Ha-ben (birth of a son), *Bar-Mitzvah* and *Bat-Mitzvah*, the Sabbath, the main festivals, and the role of the Synagogue.

The birth of a child needs to be celebrated. A Jewish mother from Liverpool, UK, explains: "When my first child was born, there was delight as it was a boy and we were able to celebrate with a 'redemption of the first-born male.' This involved family and friends gathering for a simple ceremony which involved my son being brought into the room on a cushion by a Kohen, a descendant of the priestly tribe of the Levites, and being redeemed by paying money for him. The book of Numbers tells us: 'And I, behold, have taken the Levites instead of every first-born; and the Levites shall be mine.'"

The best remembered event in the life of the young Jew is the *Bar-Mitzvah*, which literally means "son of the commandment," or, more recently, the *Bat-Mitzvah* meaning "daughter of the commandment." In Jewish law boys attain legal majority at thirteen and girls at twelve. The ceremony as it takes place today evolved in the late-Middle Ages. On the Sabbath nearest to a boy's thirteenth birthday he has the privilege of being called up to the *Torah* and generally reads the weekly portion from it. In traditional communities it is also the time when he first puts on the *tefillin*, leather phylacteries strapped to the forehead and the left arm. In the sealed boxes of the *tefillin* are parchments with the texts of Deuteronomy 6: 4–9 and 11: 13–21 hand-written on them. This is in fulfillment of the commandment that "these words, to love God with all of one's heart, mind and might, shall be bound upon the hand and serve as reminders between the eyes."

In Reform and Liberal communities girls as well as boys are given the privilege of *aliyah*. The *Bat-Mitzvah* ceremony for girls is gaining popularity in an increasing number of Orthodox congregations. The *Bar-Mitzvah* is celebrated both in the Synagogue and in the home. The rituals to mark a child's birth and entry to adulthood are the beginning of a whole lifetime of rituals that shape every day, every week, and every year.

The weekly observance of the Sabbath (Shabbat in Hebrew) from sundown on Friday until sundown on Saturday contributes greatly to Jewish identity and supplies people everywhere with a reminder of the vision of "rest" and its creative potential. In the Ten Commandments, the emphasis is on the Sabbath as a day of abstention from work. It needs to be emphasized, to counteract a long history of misunderstanding, that according to Rabbinic law, everything possible must be done to save a human life, if in danger, on the Sabbath. The whole purpose of the Sabbath is to ensure that every week, as "an everlasting sign between Me and the Children of Israel" (Exodus 31: 17), the creation of the world is celebrated by remembering that God rested on the seventh day. Space is therefore created on Shabbat for people to rest from the chores and pressures of the week and to enjoy the company of family and friends.

Families are important in Judaism, and under the guidance of the mother the home is intended to be a constructive educational environment. The home complements the Synagogue as a focus for worship and participation in observances. Every effort is made to involve the children in as many active and enjoyable ways as possible so that pleasant memories may be implanted from an early age. So on the Sabbath, children are blessed by the father as they sit round the family table. Moving on to the main annual festivals, it is intended that a child should recite the ritual Four Questions at the Passover–Seder celebration. Children lead the noise-making whenever Haman's name is mentioned during the reading of the Book of Esther at the festival of Purim. The children have the places of honor in front of the lights of the *menorah* at the festival of *Chanukah*.

The Main Festivals

The major Jewish festivals are memorials of God's acts in the past. Orthodox traditional Judaism expects strict observance of the Sabbath and festivals, dietary

September–October	Rosh Hashana (New Year is marked with solemnity because it is the day on which the whole world is judged), 2 days, 1–2 Tishrei
	Yom Kippur (Day of Atonement, whole day spent fasting and praying for forgiveness), 1 day, 10 Tishrei
	Sukkot (Festival of Tabernacles, a holiday of happiness and a reminder of God's protection), 8 days, 15–21 Tishrei
November–December	Chanukah (Festival of Lights, marks victory of Jews over Greeks and re-dedication of the Temple by the Maccabees), 8 days, 25 Kislev–2 Tevet
February–March	Purim (celebration of rescue from near destruction of Jews owing to Haman's scheming with the King of Persia, 14 Adar, 1 day
March–April	Pesach (Passover, celebrates the story of the Exodus from slavery in Egypt), 8 days, 15–21 Nisan
May–June	Shavuot (Pentecost), 2 days, 6 Sivan

laws and other ceremonies. Most Jews will come together for occasions such as Yom Kippur and Pesach.

The festival chart is intended to illustrate the variety of Jewish festivals and does not attempt to list them all. Basically, there are "Biblical" Festivals, Traditional Festivals, and Israeli Holidays such as Yom HaShoah (Holocaust Day, 27 Nisan). In almost every month of the year, there is either a major or a minor festival, which highlights another dimension of Jewish self-awareness, history, or sense of relationship with God. There is the 3,500-year-old festival of Pesach (Passover), with its specifically national and agricultural dimensions. Passover, together with the two other "pilgrim festivals" of Weeks and Tabernacles is an annual re-enactment of the special events through which Israel was forged into a people dedicated to the service of God. These festivals marked the three occasions each year when the people went to Jerusalem to offer thanks to God during the time when the Temple played a central part in the life of the people.

Most Jewish festivals are in some way based on a story, but in Purim and Pesach the stories themselves constitute the festival celebrations: they cannot be "told" without the telling. The Exodus story is retold every year at a special meal. The Passover supper follows a set program (Seder). The dominant theme, perennially relevant, is liberation, the constant struggle in all our lives to aspire to freedom, that is to say, liberation from oppression and bondage. The festival of Passover serves as a regular reminder that the Exodus marked the beginning of the process by which Israel became a people. This process was sealed at Sinai and culminated in the entry into the promised land after the death of Moses.

The holiest day in the year is Yom Kippur. There are other fasts during the year but this day has the most significance. Yom Kippur or Day of Atonement, with its universalistic implications, reminds Jews that however carefully the Law is kept, human beings are ultimately dependent on the forgiving grace of God. Fasting means not drinking as well as not eating for the twenty-five hours of Yom Kippur.

Even so-called non-religious Jews may still identify with aspects of Judaism's ritual life, particularly on Yom Kippur and at Passover. Judaism is in many ways a culture as well as a religion. Ritual life, especially as it revolves around the family, is the primary root of its cultural identity. It is the active involvement in the ritual life of Judaism that cements identity as a Jew for the average Jew today. In today's world, with the assimilation of Jews into non-religious society, the legal status through birth is less pressing than the more psycho-social one of involvement in Judaism's ritual life. It is particularly in relation to historical experience of Jews as "outsiders" that these issues of cultural and sociological identity have come about.

Progressive Jews only enact those ceremonies which they consider to have contemporary meaning and relevance as they do not believe that either the Hebrew Bible or the Oral Teaching (Talmud etc.) carries permanent authority in all respects. Men and women therefore worship together in Progressive Synagogues. Instrumental music, usually the organ, is allowed as an accompaniment to singing. A shorter service is employed and some use is made of the vernacular as well as Hebrew. Initiative is encouraged and new prayers are used.

Finally, this section will conclude with a brief description of the place of the Synagogue in Judaism. We have already described its historical significance, now we need to examine its contemporary role. The Synagogue is a house of study as well as prayer on account of Jews' love of knowledge and study. Power is not invested in persons, or in their office, to the extent that there is a hierarchy in Judaism and an "us and them" division between rabbis and laity. So, worship cannot proceed in a Synagogue without a minyan, or a quorum of ten males over the age of thirteen. Any male over thirteen can lead a service. The real point behind this is that worship is centered within the Jewish home.

In the Orthodox tradition, men and women sit separately, women usually seated in a gallery so as not to give cause for distraction. There is no instrumental music in orthodox Synagogues on the Sabbath and festivals and, apart from the sermon, only Hebrew is used for conducting worship. The restriction on the use of musical instruments has been maintained as a reminder of the destruction of the Second Temple in Jerusalem in 70 CE. To stand at the Western Wall, the only surviving wall built by King Herod (37–34 BCE), is still a highly emotional experience for many Jews. As one Jewish woman describes it: "My visit to Jerusalem enabled me to write a note and push it into a crack in the Kottell (Wailing Wall), a custom which is carried out by almost every person who visits the Wall. I was very proud as my husband donned his Tefillin and prayed at the Wall. The custom of Tefillin, or Phylacteries arises from the commandment: 'And thou shalt bind them for a sign upon thy arm, for frontlets (or headgarments) between thine eyes.'"

The Western Wall was part of Herod's expansion of the Temple Mount area. The Shield of David (Magen David) is the Hebrew title for the symbol (two superimposed equilateral triangles) which is usually referred to as the "star of David." It is found in many Synagogues, it adorns many ritual objects and is a central feature of the Israeli flag. The term did not appear in Jewish literature until the twelfth century. During the Middle Ages, the Kabbalists (Jewish mystics) interpreted the six points as representing the four directions of the compass and the two directions of above and below – thereby encompassing the entire universe. As time went on, the Shield of David began to mean simply "hope" – for Jews today and in the future. The name of "David" is always linked with prayers for Jewish freedom and happiness.

Ethical Expression

To the extent to which Judaism is a way of life, it is an ethical way of life. The whole purpose of a religious Jew's existence is to live a way of life which is pleasing to God. This is achieved by being Torah, true, that is, by keeping God's mitzvoth contained in the Torah. In this way, human behavior may be brought in line with the Will of God. Such are ways of holiness. The whole of the Torah is concerned with behavior. It is important to appreciate that all aspects of life are covered by this teaching, not merely those which tend to be classed as "religious" by today's outlook. As far as Judaism in daily life is concerned, belief in God is scarcely an issue. The way one acts is much more important than the kinds of beliefs one holds.

As Harold Kushner says (see Ian Markham, *A World Religions Reader*, pp. 247–9): "There is nothing intrinsically wicked about eating pork or lobster, and there is nothing intrinsically moral about eating cheese or chicken instead. But what the Jewish way of life does by imposing rules on our eating, sleeping, and working habits is to take the most common and mundane activities and invest them with deeper meaning, turning every one of them into an occasion for obeying (or disobeying) God. If a Gentile walks into a fast-food establishment and orders a cheeseburger, he is just having lunch. But if a Jew does the same thing, he is making a theological statement."

Orthodox Judaism regards eating kosher food as right solely because God requires this discipline. Kosher is therefore primarily a spiritual concept not a matter of hygiene. Because kosher is often translated as "clean" there is the unfortunate assumption that non-kosher food is "unclean." It is possible to identify rational historical reasons for eating kosher food but these are not going to demonstrate how, by not eating a ham sandwich, a person may feel closer to God. As Kushner points out, "People have tried to find ecological and hygienic reasons, but with limited success" (in *A World Religions Reader*, pp. 247–9).

In addition to these particular obligations of the Jew, there are many other commandments that have become central to western European morality. Judaism teaches love of neighbor. The actual term "ethics" is not to be found in the Jewish sources, yet there is the strong ideal of the *tzaddik*, a "good Jew," a person who has reached the height of Jewish perfection and who additionally can work miracles. In every form of Judaism the practice of justice is encouraged without compromise. For Jews justice would rank before forgiveness. But no treatise is to be found in Jewish thought which would compare with a Socratic analysis of the nature of justice. As Louis Jacobs points out, classical Jewish thinking is organic not systematic.[2] The implication in this is that no one, whether Jew or Gentile, male or female, has to be a practiced philosopher to recognize that justice and righteousness are categorical imperatives.

The Halakhah, says traditional Judaism, gives the guidance needed to put these ideals into practice. "Even if the Halakhic system is seen as a process, as a quest rather than as a given, the human quest involves a search for the will of God in often new and complex situations." "It would seem to follow," says Jacobs, "that one can as little speak of a specific Jewish ethic as one can speak of kosher mathematics."[3]

The teachings of Judaism have to be examined in depth in order for their relevance to contemporary challenges to be fully comprehended and appreciated. Many features of Judaism, including attitudes towards women, can be seriously misunderstood mostly on cultural grounds. It is difficult for many people to explore Judaism without seeing it through glasses tinted by Christianity and the whole outlook shaped by the western Enlightenment. Many Orthodox Jews today would contend that Judaism conveys an outlook which is entirely consistent with contemporary knowledge, including issues in psychology, modern physics, and ecology, for example. A position adopted by many Jewish thinkers is that the sense of duty must have been implanted by a source beyond persons, i.e., God. The "ought" that is the basis for all ethical conduct cannot be grounded in the person who acts; it must be "outside." The ground of ethics is God, even if religious people are not always very ethical.

Judaism insists that Jews must live by the Commandments, not die by them. The laws regarding work on the Sabbath, for example, must be set aside if a human life is in danger. Historically, Judaism has taken a more liberal attitude to marriage and divorce than Christianity. The formula "until death us do part" has no place in Judaism. Marriage is considered to be a union between man, woman, and God but the rabbis have always accepted that there will be situations in which bringing a marriage to an end is the humane and necessary course of action to be taken. Serious incompatibility has always been one of the grounds for divorce. Traditionally, it is the man who hands the wife the bill of divorce, *get* in Hebrew, whoever is the aggrieved party. In countries outside Israel, marriage is both a civil and a religious act. Civil divorce has to be given in addition to a *get*.

It is true that orthodox Judaism does stress the importance of the woman's role in the home. This may strike a discordant note in the minds of the many women who see their self-worth in terms of emancipation from the kitchen and the chores which the kitchen has often come to epitomize. It is important to understand that, traditionally, Jewish women's spiritual fulfillment was achieved through the active role they played in the creation of the home as the major focus of religious life. "The Jewish woman is the foundation of the home" (Lancaster, *The Elements of Judaism*). Many Orthodox Jewish women continue to view this responsibility positively, particularly as the religious activities of the home are a vital part of children's Jewish education. However, traditional Judaism, like any other tradition in the modern world, is challenged by changing roles in society, and contemporary Judaism reflects a whole spectrum of attitudes toward female spirituality.

While recognizing the importance of women's spiritual needs and hopes, Orthodox Judaism does maintain that certain features of traditional roles regarding Jewish practice cannot be changed. Reform Judaism, on the whole, views positively the filling by women of roles traditionally performed by men. What is important for the person seeking to understand the varying facets of Judaism is to realize that the differences represent ways of approaching deep spiritual principles.

Modern Outlook

Perhaps the most important contemporary challenge facing Jews and Judaism is the reconsideration of the role of Jewry in the Diaspora, a Diaspora which is vanishing by some accounts. The traditional definition of a Jew is that to be Jewish, you need to have a mother who is Jewish. This raises the further question of what makes a mother Jewish, but against the background of continuous persecution of Jews in one part of the world or another, and the consequent implications for women, the identity of the mother has seemed to have more reliability than the identity of the father. Certainly, the defining feature of identity is established by birth rather than some declaration of faith.

The laws concerning "who is a Jew?" are more complicated than the basic definition "a Jew is someone who has a Jewish mother." The legal and Halakhic (Jewish laws and customs) views are changing. This is largely due to the existence of the State of Israel. The Law of Return of the State of Israel gave the right to every Jew to become a citizen of the State. This sharpened the problem of defining "Jew." One much discussed case was that of a Christian priest who was born a Jew, who therefore claimed the right to Israeli citizenship by the Law of Return. The Israeli court decided by a majority decision not to grant this right although according to traditional Halakha, Jewish status depends on the status of the mother (or conversion by the due processes of Halakha). The court argued that it was a question of what was in the minds of those who framed the Law of Return rather than being a matter of what Halakha says. Those who framed the Law presumably did not intend it to apply to anyone who converted out of Judaism.

But what about those who convert in to Judaism in the Reform tradition where Halakhic procedures are not considered to have been carried out in a proper manner? It could be argued that although Halakha does not consider the person to be a Jew, the people who framed the Law of Return presumably did consider such a person to qualify. Fortunately, the persons affected are very few in number but for those who are affected the situation is heart-breaking.

Although Judaism has various schools of thought, in the main, Jews are divided into only two sections – Orthodox and Progressive. The attitude to revelation is crucial. All religious Jews regard the Bible as God's message to humankind, which contains divine truth relevant to contemporary men and women. In the main, however, it is Progressive Judaism, also known as Reform or Liberal Judaism, which views the Hebrew Bible as an "inspired work," rather than a sudden, miraculous revelation, which gives an account of human efforts to understand and to enter into relationship with God. Progressive Jews maintain that the Bible contains divine truth while also being the product of human needs and longings. They contend that neither the Bible nor the Oral Law is permanently authoritative in every way, so Progressive Jews only keep the ceremonies which they consider to have meaning in the modern world. Many Progressive Jews do not keep the dietary laws because they believe they were framed by human beings (not God) for reasons that are no longer relevant.

However, it is not uncommon for Jews to belong both to Orthodox and to Progressive Synagogues. The words "denomination" or "sect" are not appropriate words to express the diversity within Jewish religious belief and practice. The teaching of the living God is the crucial unifying factor within Judaism and all traditions seek to express this teaching. "Schools of thought" is probably the most accurate term which we can use.

In some Orthodox circles there have been attempts, which many Jews would dismiss as absurd, to demonstrate by the use of modern methods of computer research that the Torah is true in the traditional sense of being God-given. These have attempted to show that the Torah contains a hidden code which could only have been placed there by God. This "code" has been said to refer to AIDS and Hitler as well as predicting the assassination of a President. Most Orthodox Jews would regard this as misguided: it is wrong to reduce the Torah to a book of magic.

The number of truly Orthodox Jews is relatively small and many think they can only preserve their Orthodoxy by avoiding contacts with non-Jews as far as practicable. Very many of them are strongly influenced by Hasidism, which places much emphasis on joyful devotion to God alongside the keeping of the Law. Their followers place great reliance on their rabbis or *tzaddikim*. These are respected and valued for their spiritual gifts rather than their Talmudic knowledge and are considered to be mediators between their followers and God.

Many Jews in Britain and America would call themselves Orthodox, but a fairer name would be "Conservative." Few unquestioningly accept the divine authority of the Torah, but, in practice, most keep as much of it as they consider reasonable for the conditions in which they live. Many are prepared to admit that they keep the ritual demands of the Law because they are part of what it means to be a Jew, not because they necessarily consider them divine commandments.

Even among the strictly Orthodox there have been the possibilities of stricter and laxer interpretations of the Law. It has always been recognized, at least in theory, that rigor is not necessarily a sign of spirituality.

Early in the nineteenth century the spirit of the age led to the founding of "Reform" Synagogues. The first Reform Synagogue opened in Germany in 1810. Reform Synagogues then opened in Britain, then in other European countries and, somewhat later, in America. The emphasis of the Reform movement varied from one country to another. In Britain, it was the repudiation of Rabbinic authority. The Written Law was set above the Oral Law. What was retained of the Oral Law was that which was considered to have spiritual value. Arguably, the Reform Jew is doing deliberately and systematically what many Conservative Jews do anyway.

Occupying in the above sense a sort of halfway house, the Reform Synagogue never became very influential, particularly as many of the laxer Conservative Synagogues came to occupy almost the same position. The same spirit, however, which queried the inspiration and authority of the Oral Law passed on to query those of the Written Law. The resultant faith is known as Reform Judaism in America, but in Britain, perhaps more appropriately, as Liberal Judaism. The largest number of Reform congregations are today in the United States and in spite of a Conservative and even Orthodox revival, Reform Judaism is probably dominant.

Secularism

There is some evidence that a "secular" attitude has touched some Jewish lives. Although it is true that historically the Jewish religion has kept the Jew a Jew and that most Jews try to keep some sort of connection, secular outlooks are discernible in several areas.

For some Jews, there is a growing "secular" trust in military might. Centuries of life in the Diaspora created an image of a meek and downtrodden people, although there has always been a strong tradition of fighting the oppressor when there was no apparent alternative. However, today, the image of the "fighting Jew" has taken on new meaning since World War II. The men and women who fought against the might of the Nazi armies in the Warsaw Ghetto in 1943 followed in the tradition of the men and women of Masada, the last stronghold to fall to the Romans after the destruction of Jerusalem in 70 CE. The State of Israel has attracted many secular Jews, who want to make sure that the state is militarily strong. However, the "fighting Jew" has led to a new form of anti-Semitism.

In education, one can see a secular tendency. The Rabbinic dictum that "The ignorant person cannot be a pious one" may be an exaggerated statement but it was an important motivation for education. Teachers in Jewish society are honored and learning is a lifelong enterprise. Today, learning continues to be valued as a lifelong enterprise and, as a result, the setting up of schools has taken precedence over the building of synagogues. The respect for learning has been secularized, so parents tend to be more keen on Mathematics than on Jewish studies. The encounter with the modern western world, secular society, and the profound effects of the last war – evacuation and extermination – have made huge inroads into the effectiveness of the Jewish home as an educational and reinforcing agency. The Jewish learning destroyed by the Holocaust can perhaps never be compensated for. The social pressures which once existed to conform to Jewish norms have been severely diminished. The Jewish community today is a small minority group, tossed by the waves of an open society, extensively assimilated, troubled by intermarriage and apathy.

On doctrine, we also find secular pressure. The Messiah traditionally has been viewed as a human figure, endowed with special qualities of wisdom, courage, and leadership, who will be sent by God. The Messiah will herald the coming of a better world, when all human beings will worship the One God and live together in justice and peace. The Messiah will appear either when human behavior merits it or towards the end of the world's allotted span of time. The Messiah will be the key figure in the restoration of full national and religious autonomy to the Jewish people. The Days of the Messiah will be a time when earthly life will be infused with a clear vision of the Oneness of God and God's purpose. There is a tendency, particularly in the writings of the Reform movement, to abandon the personalistic aspect of the Messiah and to emphasize instead the notion of a Messianic Age as a kind of final golden age to world history. Today, only the very Orthodox believe that the Messiah is still to come.

So to conclude this section, although there are not very many atheistic Jews, the secular pressures are considerable. These pressures are being expressed in the form of significant adjustments to traditional priorities. Undoubtedly, it is secularism that has made the Progressive strands of Judaism more popular.

The Holocaust

No understanding of contemporary Judaism is possible without an informed awareness of the impact of the Holocaust on Jewish communities everywhere. A total of something like 80 percent of all European Jews and 90 percent of all the world's greatest Jewish teachers were exterminated between the years 1939 and 1945. The world maintained almost total silence as the million Jews of Germany, Austria, and Czechoslovakia were humiliated and tortured. Jews were forced, for example, to stand in public with notices hung round their necks saying, "Jews for sale. Who wants them?" Between World War I and World War II, Jews were increasingly made the scapegoats for all the troubles of the world, including Communism, in spite of the fact that Jewish leaders in the USSR were being steadily liquidated.

By the time of the actual outbreak of World War II, the Nazis had no reason to have any qualms whatsoever concerning their treatment of Jews. It was already obvious that no one with any real power to prevent it was going to object to the treatment Jews were receiving. So it was that centuries of hatred, persecution, and massacre culminated in the deliberate attempt to annihilate Jews from the heart of so-called civilized, and Christian, twentieth-century Europe. The most advanced technology, devised by some of the leading scientists and engineers in the world, ensured that the greatest possible number of Jews were gassed and burned in the shortest possible time.

Exercises

4 The question, "Where was God in Auschwitz?" has obviously been a crucial question for Jews, with their belief in a God who is revealed in human history. However, all religious people will want to reflect on this question.

5 Arguably, a universal question is: Where was "man" (and woman) in Auschwitz?

6 Where do you consider men and women to have been in the experience that is epitomized in the name Auschwitz?

7 Why should this be considered to be a universal question?

Since the Holocaust, an increasing number of scholars, particularly in the United States, are acknowledging the implications for Christianity, as well as for Judaism, of a renewed perception of the Hebrew Scriptures. Fortunately, Jewish and Christian scholars have begun to work together to explore the origins of Christianity as a sect within Judaism and prejudices implicit in traditional Christian theology are being broken down. Since the Holocaust, all the Christian Churches have made progress in this area. However, much work remains to be done and it is still unclear how Christianity might look if the anti-Judaism within it were to be completely removed.

Israel

Even when the war was over, survivors were murdered when they tried to return to their homes. Many survivors were retained behind barbed wire under military discipline in "Displaced Persons" Camps. Initially, the survivors were retained alongside possible perpetrators of the Holocaust. Not surprisingly, Jews were unwilling to live in countries that had become a nightmare to them. In fact, when asked what their second choice would be if it proved impossible to settle in Palestine, the majority replied "the crematoria." For the first time since the start of the Zionist movement, every major Jewish organization supported the idea of a homeland, a land where Jews would be "safe" from slaughter. This was the reality that led the United Nations to agree in principle to the partition of Palestine, which in turn led to the setting up of the State of Israel in 1948.

In spite of the many problems that have beset Israel and the ongoing tragedy of the situation for Jews (and for Arabs), Israel continues to symbolize hope and survival for Jews all over the world as expressed by the Ha-tikva, the National Anthem. The Kibbutz movement, possibly the greatest experiment in communal living in the twentieth century, expressed the Jewish will to live and to build for a future. Schools were established in order to teach what have been described as the two sustaining faiths of the survivors – "Judaism" and "Israel." A vital part of Jewish consciousness is the passionate belief that, "We owe it to the dead to live."

Jewish Humor and Story

It would not be true to the spirit of Jews and Judaism to conclude this section without referring to Jewish humor and the capacity for story. "A Jew is someone who tells Jewish jokes . . . ," tautologous but true. For Jews, life is full of humor. But Jewish humor, born of accumulated anguish, actually takes life very seriously. Its purpose has been to root out the meaning of experiences, to penetrate the heart of suffering so as to rise above it, to save some sanity, and to find just a little compensation. It bespeaks the paradox and poignancy of Jewish life. Perhaps the deepest and most authentic approach to the study of Judaism will be formed as we develop a taste for Jewish stories:

> "Learn in the place where you are, within the circumstances, complexities, joys and sorrows in which you find yourself; learn *through* these involvements, to understand – with heart, not head – the meanings that emanate from them. No one can take this task from you. No one else can do this work for you. (S. H. Bergman cited in *Forms of Prayer for Jewish Worship*)

> From my teachers, I have learned a lot; from my colleagues, even more; but from my students, most of all. (Ta'anit 7b)

Probably the most typical Jewish form of story is the *midrash*. From the root "investigate" or "search," midrash is in effect a story behind, within, and beyond another story. It is said that a midrash is like a king who loses a precious pearl and finds it with the aid of a candle that costs only a penny. One midrash often told to Jewish children concerns Abraham and the idols and illustrates monotheism:

> While Abraham is minding his father Terah's idol business for him, God reveals to Abraham God's one nature. Recognizing the folly of idol worship, Abraham smashes all the idols in his father's shop, except for the largest one. Abraham places his hammer beside this remaining statue. When Terah returns, he is naturally shocked and angry at the devastation which has befallen the family's income and asks Abraham what on earth has happened. Abraham points to the large statue with the hammer beside it and says, "It was *him!*" "Don't be so ridiculous!" his father retorts. "It's only made of stone. It has no power to do anything!" "Oh?" says Abraham, "then why do you worship it?"

In conclusion, in the spirit of Judaism this chapter closes with a story. As Elie Wiesel, the Holocaust survivor and novelist, explains, "My father, an enlightened soul, believed in man. My grandfather, a fervent Hasid, believed in God. One taught me to speak; the other to sing. Both loved stories. . . ." (Elie Wiesel, *Souls on Fire*).

> When the great Rabbi Israel Baal Shem Tov saw misfortune threatening the Jews it was his custom to go into a certain part of the forest to meditate. There he would light a fire, say a special prayer, and the miracle would be accomplished and the

misfortune averted. Later, when his disciple, the celebrated Maggid of Mezritch, had occasion, for the same reason, to intercede with heaven, he would go to the same place in the forest and say: "Master of the Universe, listen! I do not know how to light the fire, but I am still able to say the prayer," and again the miracle would be accomplished. Still later, Rabbi Moshe-Leib of Sasov, in order to save his people once more, would go into the forest and say: "I do not know how to light the fire, I do not know how to say the prayer, but I know the place and this must be sufficient." It was sufficient and the miracle was accomplished. Then it fell to Rabbi Israel of Rizhyn to overcome misfortune. Sitting in his armchair, his head in his hands, he spoke to God: "I am unable to light the fire and I do not know the prayer; I cannot even find the place in the forest. All I can do is to tell the story and this must be sufficient." And it was sufficient. (Elie Wiesel, cited in *Forms of Prayer for Jewish Worship*)

GLOSSARY

Anti-Semitism Prejudice and hostility toward the Jewish People.

Diaspora A Greek term meaning scattered abroad which is applied to Jews living outside of Palestine.

Kibbutzim Democratically run, voluntary agricultural communities set up in Israel.

Kosher Term given within Jewish dietary law for food that is ritually clean and fit to eat.

Monotheism The belief in only one God.

Mysticism Aspect of religion associated with the achievement of direct experiences of God, through the use of various mystical systems and processes.

Synagogue Place of worship and meeting for Jews.

Zionism Movement to return Jews to Israel, and to return Israel to the Jews — using political and ideological means.

Notes and References

1 Brian Lancaster, *The Elements of Judaism*, p. 7.
2 Louis Jacobs, *Ethics*, p. 151.
3 Ibid., p. 151.

Chapter 13

Shintoism

Ian Markham

Shintoism in the Past

Shintoism Today

Winston Davies, a leading authority on Shintoism, walked into a tea shop in Tokyo just before it officially opened:

> As I sat waiting, the employees joined hands and chanted the following credo:
> We are grateful to the people of the world.
> We will not forget that our shop has been set
> up for the sake of the customer.
> Sharing both happiness and sorrow, we will cooperate
> and not forget to encourage each other.
> Setting aside the past and anxiety of the 'morrow
> we will not forget to give our all
> to the work set before us today![1]

The credo begins with a sense of gratitude. This sense of gratitude is, perhaps, the key to understanding Shintoism. One is grateful to one's parents – for life, food, clothing – and grateful to village gods and one's ancestors – for land, possessions, and employment. It is this sense of "givenness" that generates the famous sense of Japanese obligation.

As with most religions, generalizations are difficult. It is often said that Shintoism represents the values and dispositions of Japanese culture. Although this is true to an extent, it is important to remember that most nations are made up of many cultures. As with all the traditions examined in this book, Shintoism embraces considerable diversity. In particular it is not at all clear where Shintoism ends and Buddhism starts. This is partly due to the lack of organization. As we shall see, one had to wait until 1900 for a comprehensive, national organization. Yet it is right to describe Shintoism as the indigenous religion of Japan, which for centuries did not need a name. The name "Shinto" (taken from *shen do (dao, tao)*) arose in the sixth century CE precisely to distinguish itself from Buddhism. As Buddhism was the "Way of the Buddha" so Shintoism described itself as the old way, "The Way of the Gods" or a better translation "The Way of the Kami." **Kami** is a difficult term to describe.

Torii gates at the Fushimi-Inari Shinto shrine, Kyoto, Japan.
Photo: Corbis/David Samuel Robbin

In brief, kami are the forces and powers that pervade everything; they are seen best in "extraordinary" things of life – the sun, thunder, great people (such as Emperors) and animals. As this idea is very important, more shall be said about the kami later on.

Shintoism distinguishes itself from the other faith traditions in a number of ways. Although it has books that are revered, it does not really have a scripture. Although it does make ethical demands, it does not really have a strong code of ethical behavior. It is also extremely significant historically. After World War II, the postwar surrender treaty built in a requirement that the Shinto religion must be disestablished. This chapter will explore all these elements. However, to begin with we shall start with a brief historical survey, which will be followed by a systematic account of Shintoism.

Shintoism in the Past

The early period

The first Japanese histories were written down in the eighth century BCE. Prior to this, we have a small number of clues. There are Chinese documents from the third century, which describe visits of people to Japan, and a significant archeological record. Everything seems to suggest that the Japanese had a strong appreciation of the beauty of the natural world. They loved their island home. The power of nature and the miracle of fertility preoccupied them greatly. They wanted to merge with nature rather than fight or resist it. Anything provoking awe, either in nature, amongst people, or beyond, provoked worship. This is where the idea of kami comes from. In early Japanese history, considerable prominence is given to the story of the descent of the Imperial family from the supreme Sun Goddess.

It also seems that from the "start" (whenever that was) government and religion were closely linked together. Sacred leaders, who in early times were female shamans, were responsible both for organizing the worship of the kami and for the organization of human affairs. There was no clear philosophy or ethics. Instead the focus was a sense of gratitude and joy for life and a real intimacy with nature. This intimacy partly depended on "ritual purity." One had to be clean to be close to the kami. The theme of purity has continued to be a major part of Shintoism right up to the present day.

A link between the political and religious realms can be found in the very earliest Japanese clans. The government of eighth-century Japan saw it as their responsibility to organize the major religious festivals and to maintain the shrines. The Emperor's function combined administrative duties with his religious ones. The stability of the cosmic order depended on this combination. It is not surprising that it was during this period that the two major texts of Shintoism were written. *Kojiki* was written in 712 and *Nihongi* in 720. These two texts outline two central themes of Shintoism: the existence of kami throughout Japan and the "semi-divine" descent of Japan and her people.

Period 2: Heian period

Shintoism has shown itself remarkable in its capacity to assimilate different influences. Two centuries before the Heian period (794–1185), the sophisticated Chinese had arrived. The Japanese welcomed the highly developed and complex system of Confucian political life. They worked hard to impose order on their informal tribal systems. Although the Chinese political system dissipated over time, the Confucian ethic (see chapter 11, Chinese Religion) became a significant part of Japanese life that continues to this very day. However, in the Heian period, Buddhism emerged as a major influence. Although Buddhism had already arrived and taken root with Nara Buddhism, the Heian period saw the emergence of two further Buddhist sects. As in many other countries in Asia, Buddhists were good at accommodating local religions. A popular Buddhist strategy was to suggest that the local deities were simply the local expression of Buddhist experience. So, for example, the Buddhist monks of the Shingon sect described the local kami as expressions of **bodhisattvas** (enlightened beings). Kobo Daishi was the founder of Shingon: he introduced a highly esoteric Buddhism that had its roots in the Tantric traditions of India. The second sect emerging in this period was the Tendai, founded by Dengyo Daishi. The famous Chinese text the *Lotus Sutra* was its central scripture and its Japanese headquarters was the Hieizan mountain. It was also during this period that Taoism became important. Japanese religion was a hybrid of Shintoism, Buddhism, and religious Taoism, which took distinctive Japanese expression. Shugendo, for example, was a highly organized pilgrimage movement of this period: it stressed the need to make pilgrimage to sacred mountains and acknowledge the power of the local Kami on these mountains, which were linked to the local bodhisattvas of Buddhism. Shintoism was now inescapably linked with other religious traditions. Scholars disagree as to the extent of this linkage. Helen Hardacre insists that the practice of Shinto was for centuries a "mere appendage to Buddhist institutions."[2] Brian Bocking insists that "For most of its history what we call in retrospect Shinto was mainly Buddhism, with generous helpings of Taoism, Yin–Yang philosophy, Confucianism, folk religion and more recently European-style nationalism."[3] Edwin O. Reischauer is more nuanced and more accurate when he writes, "[T]he two religions became institutionally very much intertwined. . . . And yet, throughout, Shinto retained its distinctiveness and strength."[4] Although it is true that we have to wait until 1900 for the basics of a national Shinto organization, it is wrong to deny the existence of distinctive Shinto beliefs and dispositions before this. It is true, however, that Buddhism and Shintoism were both operating together in Japanese culture up until 1868.

Period 3: Kamakura period

The Heian period was marked by political and social stability. The Kamakura period (1185–1333) was much more troubled. Political power shifted from the Court to the shoguns (the feudal powers). Struggles between these feudal powers, which had their roots in the Heian period, now dominated the political scene. Religiously, many of the syncretistic tendencies of the Heian period continued. However, as is common in troubled times, a widespread belief arose that the people were living in the third and final age of the world. (The first age was a period when people practiced the Buddha's teaching and obtained enlightenment; the second was a period of practice but few expected to obtain enlightenment; and the third was a period of indifference to the teaching and virtually no observation.) Given that this was the final age, an expectation developed that the world would end soon, probably through a great catastrophe. The forms of Buddhism that emerged in this period reflected these expectations. It is not surprising that the Pure Land Sects and the Zen Sects emerged during this period.

Period 4: Tokugawa period

Perhaps partly in reaction to the unsettled nature of the preceding period, the Tokugawa period was marked by strong central government, peace, and order. Its attitude to religion was strongly conservative. Helen Hardacre suggests that Shintoism in the period operated differently within the three different layers of Japanese society. The first layer was the "ritual practice of the imperial court, which maintained a formal schedule of elaborate ritual for both Buddhas and kami."[5] It was during this period that the widespread Japanese practice of Shinto ritual to mark birth and Buddhist ritual to mark death became a commonplace. The second layer consisted of the large shrines that had sufficient resources to support an hereditary priesthood. Many were branch shrines (i.e., linked with an original shrine through a ceremony); often these shrines were a result of the migration of members from the original shrine and as they settled so they created a new shrine dedicated to the clan deity. Many of the most prestigious shrines, such as Usa Hachiman, Inari, Kasuga, Tenjin, Konpira, Munakata, Suwa, and Izumo, developed branch shrines throughout Japan. The third layer involved the many thousands of local shrines dedicated to a local tutelary deity. Often these shrines did not have a professional priest, but simply survived through the support of the local community.

Toward the end of the Tokugawa period, two distinct developments emerged. The Ise pilgrimage was the means by which many Japanese people found themselves involved in the worship of kami. Villages would support certain carefully chosen pilgrims as they traveled to the shrine to offer prayers for a bounteous harvest. The second development was the Shinto school of thought known as National Learning. This school has its roots in the work of Kada no Azumamaro (1669–1739), but in the nineteenth century was heavily shaped by Hirata Atsutane (1776–1843). The key issues for this school were the separation of Shinto from Buddhism, the need for Shinto funerals taken by a Shinto priest, and the re-establishment of a department of religion within the government.

Period 5: The Meiji Restoration

Tokugawa feudalism came to an end with the Meiji Restoration (1868). Earhart sees this date as the movement of Japan into the modern world. Although ostensibly the restoration is so called because the Emperor was restored to his position as head of state, in fact it was the period when a modern nation state was formed. Earhart outlines the extent of the change, when he writes: "The whole system of government was reorganized along the lines of a nation-state. The office of the military ruler was abolished and the emperor formally ruled a centralized government with a constitution and elected legislators. The feudal clans were replaced with prefectures which administered local government as a branch of the central authority. The new capital was established at Tokyo. To finance the government a tax system was adopted."[6]

On the religious front, it was the period when the state started to support Shinto as the state religion. A campaign was waged against Buddhism. In the same way that the Emperor had been "restored" so, the argument went, the original religion of Japan had to be "restored." This meant the removal of Buddhist statues and Buddhist priests from Shinto shrines.

During the 1870s, the government found it difficult to insist on Shintoism as the main and most important religion in Japan. Japanese Buddhism was not going to be so easily dismissed. Between 1872 and 1875 the government had a Department of Religion which included both Shintoism and Buddhism. Matters were finally resolved in 1882, when the government formally recognized State Shintoism. Legally State Shintoism was not religious; it was simply the values and institutions that supported the State. Sect Shintoism was a religion (i.e., the 13 groups which were linked with Shintoism) and this was distinct from State Shintoism. The government argued that religion was separate from the State, thereby protecting religious liberty.

Although religious diversity was permitted in Japan, Shinto dominated the scene right up until 1945. After the 1890s, every child in Japan was given a complete introduction to Shinto and a strongly nationalistic ethic (see Markham, *A World Religions Reader*, pp. 203–5). It is a widespread perception that Shinto is responsible for Japan's military aggression. Actually most religious traditions in Japan supported Japan's war activities. Although it is true that the State used Shinto to encourage a patriotic and nationalistic outlook, it would be wrong to simply link the Japanese war machine to the Shinto religion.

Period 6: After World War II

The surrender and occupation of Japan in 1945 brought State Shintoism to an end. William K. Brunce headed up the Religions Division of the Civil Information and Education Section and produced the Shinto Directive on December 15, 1945. This directive prohibited the funding of Shinto doctrines and the supporting of any ideology that encouraged militarism and ultranationalism. It also prohibited any creed asserting the superiority of the Emperor or the Japanese people. The Emperor duly announced that he was only human and not a god (see *A World Religions Reader*, pp. 212–17). The occupying powers were insisting that Shintoism should be treated just like Buddhism and Christianity. Shinto priests no longer worked for the State; Shinto shrines did not receive a state subsidy; and religious nationalistic sentiments were removed from the school textbooks.

The result was a crisis within Shintoism. Its popularity waned rapidly; it was a religion directly associated with the defeat. Once isolated from government it found itself lacking sufficient organization, which hampered the tradition's capacity to recover. For many years it looked as if Shintoism was in serious trouble. However, in recent years it has recovered, or perhaps, to be more accurate, it has demonstrated how it has remained part of the Japanese psyche.

This perhaps can be best illustrated by the controversy surrounding the death of Emperor Hirohito who died on January 7, 1989. The Crown Prince Akihito succeeded him on January 8, 1989, but the enthronement ceremony was not held until November 1990. During the intervening period, the whole issue of state funding for the enthronement had to be confronted.

Article 89 of the Constitution of Japan (1946) states explicitly: "no public money or other property shall be expended . . . for the use, benefit or maintenance of any religious institution or association . . ." This article would appear to prohibit funding for either the funeral or the enthronement. However, the strength of the "traditionalists" (i.e., those who insisted that Japanese traditions must be maintained) was sufficient for the government to be persuaded to pay for these rituals. For the funeral, the government divided the occasion into a "religious private ceremony" and a "secular public part," both of which were paid for out of the public purse. For the enthronement, the government made a similar distinction. The actual enthronement ceremony (Sokui-no-Rei) was considered a state affair and paid for out of state funds. The Daijosai ceremony, which is the occasion when the Emperor assumes spiritual power by spending part of a night in a special Shinto shrine, was to be funded out of the Imperial court budget. The court budget comes from the government, so it is a moot point whether this careful distinction made any difference.

There are some movements that would like the government to extend further funding to certain other shrines. Such movements are vigorously opposed, especially by Christians, who fear a repeat of the 1930s. The result is that Shintoism continues to gain widespread recognition, although the government tries to keep its distance.

1   The most contentious aspect to Shintoism is the perceived relationship between religion, nationalism and the Japanese war machine. The purpose of this exercise is to encourage you to reflect on this complex relationship. There are two central issues: the first is the dangers of a religion being used for military purposes; the second is the appropriateness of the conquering powers to require the Emperor to insist that he is only human and to insist the State does not continue to support Shintoism.

Exercise

(a) Debate: be it resolved that the Allies were right to insist that the Japanese government's relationship with Shintoism must change.

(b) Divide into two groups: those who maintain that the Allies were right to insist that the Japanese must change the relationship between government and Shinto, and those arguing that the Allies were wrong in this demand. In your groups analyse the issues and devise as many arguments as possible for your case. You might reflect on the following issues: the limits of metaphysical beliefs as political tools; freedom of belief; the problem of persuading people to change their views; the link between nationalism and religion, especially in the Japanese context; the nature of State Shintoism; confronting the causes, not just the symptoms, of militarism.

(c) Reconvene to debate the issues in the light of your group work. Take a final vote to discover those who have changed their view during the exercise.

Shintoism Today

Worldviews

Kami

The concept of kami probably has its roots in the Japanese love of nature. According to tradition there are many thousands (*yaoyorozu no kami* – vast myriads of kami) of these life powers. Although the Sun Kami Amaterasu-o-Mikami is considered the head of the kami, she is not considered the source or the overall creator. Indeed she pays respect to the other kami. This means that unlike many other traditions there is a fundamental plurality of forces in control of the world.

The central texts that describe the main kami are the **Kojiki** and **Nihongi** (see *A World Religions Reader*, p. 200). It is here that the marvelous Japanese story of the creator is recorded; the emergence of the Japanese islands from the love of two creator kami – Izanagi and Izanami. Kami are found throughout nature: mountains, trees, rocks, sea, rivers, and animals. Even people can be described as kami, not least the Emperor. Naturally there are those kami which are destructive and cause suffering, for example Magatsuhi-no-kami (the kami of misfortune). Traditionally such destructive kami are located in the nether-world (the land of Yomi). Evil, in Shintoism, is not inherent in humanity but comes from outside.

The primary human duty toward the kami is to worship them. All deserve respect, even the destructive kami. There are thousands of shrines in Japan. All insist on approaching the kami having observed the fundamental rituals of purfication. Then it is possible to offer food, offer dances and music, and chant prayers. Some homes have a kami shelf (*kamidana*). This is a miniature shrine, which is often decorated with pine sprigs or the sacred *sasaki* tree. The family will deposit various offerings on the shelf (e.g., rice cakes or seaweed) and demonstrate their acknowledgment of the kami by clapping, bowing, and praying in front of the shrine.

The concept of kami is a distinctive Japanese contribution to the understanding of the spiritual in the world. Only certain forms of Hinduism and animism are similiar. It is the acknowledgment of the many varied powers that maintain the balance of the cosmos. The worship of the kami is essential to maintain the harmony of the human with nature.

Kojiki (Records of Ancient Matters) and Nihongi (Chronicle of Japan)

These are the earliest texts of Shintoism. Emperor Temmu (672–86) felt that existing histories were unreliable and offered to provide a corrected text. The Kojiki was compiled first in 712 CE, closely followed by the Nihongi, which according to tradition was compiled in 720 CE. The major theme of the Kojiki is the origin of kingship. Book 1 explains the origins of the world through the marriage of two kami, Izanagi and Izanami. Together they create the Japanese islands and many other kami. Izanami is then killed by the kami of fire, so Izangi descends to the underworld to try and find her. When Izangi returns to the earth, the act of purification brings about the existence of the Kami of the Sun, Amaterasu. She is the historic ancestor of the Imperial family. She is the administrator of the heavenly domain. It is her grandson Ninigi who descends from heaven to Mount Takachiho to rule the Japanese islands.

Book 2 starts with the great-grandson of Ninigi, Jimmu, who becomes Japan's first Emperor. Jimmu goes to war against the forces of evil and finds the center of the land, which is where he builds the Imperial Palace. We are then provided with a careful record of 13 other Emperors before arriving at Emperor Ojin, who historians have evidence lived in the fifth century CE. Book 3 continues to document the achievements of the great Emperors. It describes their exploits, from Emperor Nintoku to Empress Suiko.

Nihongi covers similiar ground. There are thirty volumes, of which the first two deal with the age of the kami and the remaining twenty-eight tell the story from Emperor Jimmu to Empress Jito. It seems that the two books are intended for different audiences. The Nihongi has made use of more sources; it seems to be intended as an official chronicle, comparable to the historical records of the Chinese.

Institutions and rituals

The Shrine Association (Jinja Honcho)

On February 3, 1946 the Shrine Association was formed. This is the body responsible for coordinating and governing "shrine Shinto." After the breakdown of "State Shintoism," this was the body that emerged to coordinate continuing Shinto activities. Although some shrines are independent of the Association, more than 80 percent of Japanese shrines are affiliated to it. Relatively recently the headquarters were moved from Tokyo to Meiji jingu. The central teaching is the "guidance of the spiritual leadership of the Ise shrines" because this embodies the spiritual homeland of Japan. The Ise Shrine is the Imperial household shrine, which is identified with the Emperor; it remains popular as a place of pilgrimage. The Association retains certain traditional convictions about the character of Shinto: for example, it assumes the Shinto is a national faith, which is separate from Buddhism. The president is responsible for the recognition of priestly rank and the appointment of priests to shrines. On certain other occasions the president stands in for the Emperor.

Festivals

The Shinto word which is closest to "festivals" is *matsuri*. According to Brian Bocking, this term may be rendered "festival," "worship," "celebration," "rite," or even "prayer," which actually captures the range of activities connected with Shinto festivals.[7] The main Shinto festivals are organized around the annual seasonal celebrations. Most are held at a shrine and will involve offering, prayers, rites, gratitude to the kami, and straightforward entertainment.

Major Festivals

Oshogatsu (New Year)	1–3 January
Ohinamatsuri (Dolls' or Girls' Festival)	3 March
Tango nu Sekku (Boys' Festival)	5 May
Hoshi matsuri/Tanabata (Star Festival)	7 July

Ethics

Shintoism is not preoccupied with "ethics." Bocking explains that Japanese do not associate the Shinto word *shushin* with morality and behavioral norms, but with "the pre-war ethics courses and textbooks used in Japanese schools to underpin the emperor system."[8] For Bocking, the ethics of Shinto are simply Japanese versions of Confucianism or Buddhism.

Insofar that Shintoism has an ethic, it is one that stresses the corporate dimensions of human life. Sokyo Ono writes, "The Shinto faith brings not only the individual, the neighbourhood and society into direct relationship with the kami and makes them more ideal; it does the same for the political world."[9] As we saw in the examination of the history of Shintoism, it is true that Shintoism has been a bond that linked the people with nature and the state. This, of course, partly created the problems that led to the Allies requiring the disestablishment of State Shinto at the end of World War II. Sokyo Ono insists that the use of Shinto for nationalistic purposes was a distortion of the tradition and writes, "[F]undamentally, Shinto is a faith which is based on the belief that many kami cooperate together. Shrine Shinto is worship to unite and harmonize the various kinds of kami. The spirit of tolerance and cooperation is a hitherto unnoticed aspect of Shinto."[10] Generally, however, there is little that is distinctive about Shinto ethics. Japanese ethical traditions do not draw heavily on the Shinto tradition.

Women

Some feminist scholars suspect that Shintoism historically was positive about women.[11] There is some evidence that prior to the sixth century CE there was a female shamanic cult and that menstruating women were viewed positively as possessed by kami and pure. Problems arose with the arrival of the more male-dominated Buddhist traditions, which marginalized Shinto shamanesses and, perhaps, women more generally. However, as Martinez has shown, the domination of the major festivals by men can easily lead scholars to ignore the way that women dominate the minor rituals and festivals.

Martinez provides a study of a Kuzaki village. She shows how the bulk of household rites are organized by women. The daily offerings to the kami and the prayers to household ancestors are almost always performed by the women. Even the monthly climb up Sengen, the sacred mountain, is an activity of the working women. This monthly pilgrimage is to ask the kami for good fortune. It was only when the village celebrated a major festival that the men became involved. All the political leaders were present, all of whom were men, and they dominated the occasion.

For Martinez, the interesting feature is the way that the regular acts of rituals are being dominated by women. She suggests that "women, . . . because of their innate power, always have the potential to mediate directly for the deities."[12] In other words there is a constructive message underpinning this, largely rural, participation in religious activities.

Modern expression

It is commonplace that western scholars of Japanese religions find themselves denying the existence of Japanese religion. The education system stresses the worlds of technology and science and is impatient with the "spiritual." Book shops are full of books on ghosts, avoiding pollution, and UFOs. Ian Reader insists that there is considerable evidence that Japanese young people are reacting against such reductionism. He writes, "The processes of modernisation, rationalisation, scientific development and increased education thus tend to stimulate rather than diminish interest in spiritual matters and the world of the irrational."[13] Religion is alive and well in Japan.

Yet traditional forms are struggling. The evidence is that it is anti-establishment traditions that attract the interest. Shintoism continues to be identified with the "establishment." However, Ian Reader writes, "the rising numbers participating in festivals, . . . the various occasions which memorialize the ancestors, the current interest in pilgrimages, the large numbers who acquire amulets and talismans and visit religious centers to pray for benefits, the small but growing interest in meditation . . . , the contemporay focus on ascetic and charismatic figures of power, and the seemingly endless emergence and growth of new religions, are indicative of the energies inherent in the religious world of Japan today."[14]

Shintoism remains significant because underpinning many festivals and customs are Shinto traditions. In the 1980s, growing Japanese prosperity enabled the Japanese to revisit their traditions with pride. In the 1990s, the economic miracle was less strong and interest in religious traditions waned. It seems to remain true that interest in Shintoism runs in parallel with Japanese self-perception; when the Japanese nation is doing well, Shintoism is viewed positively; when it is doing less well, Shintoism attracts less interest.

---

2   Does Shintoism exist? Evaluate the main arguments for and against the **Exercises**
    distinctiveness of Shintoism.
3   What is the traditional Shinto view of the Japanese Emperor? What does
    this say about the nature of the kami?
4   Analyze the relationship of Shintoism with Nationalism. Are there any
    other parallels in the world?
5   Who or what are the kami?

GLOSSARY

Bodhisattvas A term from Buddhism for an enlightened being.

Kami The forces and powers that pervade everything; they are seen best in "extraordinary" things of life – the sun, thunder, great people (such as Emperors), and animals.

Kojiki Along with *Nihongi*, this is the central source for Shinto doctrine and history, which was written in 712.

Nihongi Along with *Kojiki*, this is the central source for Shinto doctrine and history, which was written in 720.

Notes and References

1   Winston Davis, *Japanese Religion and Society: Paradigms of Structure and Change* (New York: State University of New York, 1992), pp. 18–19.
2   Helen Hardacre, *Shinto and the State 1868–1988* (Princeton: Princeton University Press, 1989), p. 5. Hardacre makes much of the lack of official organization and follows Kuroda Toshio's argument at this point.
3   Brian Bocking, *A Popular Dictionary of Shinto* (Richmond: Curzon, 1995), p. viii.
4   Edwin O. Reischauer, in Roger Eastman (ed.), *The Ways of Religion* (Oxford: Oxford University Press, 1993), p. 243.
5   Helen Hardacre, *Shinto and the State* (Princeton: Princeton University Press, 1989), p. 10.
6   H. Byron Earhart, *Japanese Religion: Unity and Diversity* (Belmont, California: Dickenson Publishing Co., 1969), p. 76.
7   Brian Bocking, *A Popular Dictionary of Shinto* (Richmond: Curzon, 1995), p. 117.
8   Ibid., p. 186.
9   Sokyo Ono, *Shinto: The Kami Way* (Rutland, Vermont, and Tokyo: Charles E. Tuttle Co., 1962), p. 75.
10 Ibid., p. 79.
11 Much of the material in this section is taken from D. P. Martinez, "Women and ritual," in Jan van Bremen and D. P. Martinez (eds.), *Ceremony and Ritual in Japan* (London and New York: Routledge, 1995), pp. 186ff.
12 Ibid., p. 194.
13 Ian Reader, *Religion in Contemporary Japan* (Basingstoke: Macmillan Press, 1991), p. 236.
14 Ibid., pp. 236–7.

Chapter 14

Christianity

ALEX SMITH

Historical Survey

Second and Third Centuries

Third and Fourth Centuries

The Middle Ages

The Reformation and Counter-Reformation

The Modern Period

Worldviews

Institutions and Rituals

Ethical Expressions

Modern and Future Expression

The impact of Jesus of Nazareth, the center of the Christian faith, is already recognized in the western calendar. The numbering of the years in western calendars is calculated from the supposed date of his birth. In Christian circles everything before his birth is still referred to as "before Christ" (BC), and everything after is "anno domini" or "in the year of the Lord" (AD). As the western world enters into the third millennium, it is the third 1,000-year period following his birth. It is surprising that a carpenter from a small village in a not very significant country, dominated by Roman power, should be seen as such an epoch-making person.

Jesus of Nazareth was born a Jew and for the last years of his life conducted himself as an itinerant prophet and teacher before his execution by crucifixion, about 30 CE, under the Roman governor of Judea. Not a very auspicious start. However, during his itinerant ministry he had gathered together a band of followers, who

All quoted references from the Christian Bible are taken from the Revised Standard Version: the book is given first, then the chapter, then the verse(s). References to Ian Markham, *A World Religions Reader*, second edition (Oxford: Blackwell Publishers, 2000), are from the section on Christianity.

Mosaic of Christ as Pantocrator, Kariye Mosque, Istanbul, Turkey.
Photo: Corbis/Chris Hellier

listened to his preaching and propagated the message of Jesus after his crucifixion. It was these same followers that made a stupendous claim: Jesus, who had been crucified, dead and buried, was alive. They understood the manner of this experience in the only terms available, borrowed from the language of the apocalyptic literature concerning the hope, held by many Jews, of what would happen when God finally established his Kingdom where his purposes would find full expression. Into this Kingdom would be drawn all the righteous, both living and dead, thus the dead would be raised to share in the life of God. If Jesus was alive, they believed that it could only be because God had raised him from the dead, had resurrected him. There was no other way for them to image the experience. Further, if he had been raised then God's kingdom had arrived.

Jesus, for these early followers, could only be the **Messiah**, which is a Hebrew participle meaning "the anointed one." In the literature which concerned itself with what the Kingdom of God might be, this term had become a title denoting a figure specially commissioned by anointing, who would be the sign and occasion of its arrival. The conviction that Jesus was alive, which triggered the belief that God's Kingdom had erupted, meant that he was identified with that figure. This term, now attached to Jesus and none other, ceased to be just a title and became in time an alternative name, becoming, at the present time, almost a surname. The surname however is not Messiah, but Christ. When the new faith went out into the Greek world Messiah was turned into its Greek equivalent, Christ, and it is from this that the faith and its adherents take their name. It should be recognized, however, that Jesus was never considered to be the Messiah by Jews. He did not fulfill the Jewish criteria; he did not fit the job specification.

Christianity, then, is the faith that holds that in Jesus (the) Christ God's purposes find their fulfillment. Christians are those who believe that this is the case, are called by that name, and further believe that they find life in it.

Historical Survey

Christianity began as a sect within Judaism. In the New Testament, Christians are call "the sect of the Nazarenes" (Acts 24: 5). Christianity today is a worldwide faith with over 1.5 billion adherents. This survey will attempt to trace the path from the former to the latter position, highlighting those events, trends and dominant beliefs which have determined the direction of the path, and help to explain the texture of the faith.

The New Testament tells the first part of the journey, and takes us up to the early second century. In it we can note three important steps. The first had to do with the earliest expectations of the first Christians, which accompanied their conviction that their master was alive and their understanding of this as resurrection. Christ's resurrection sparked the expectation that he would return in the very near future to bring the historical sequence to an end and fully establish God's kingdom. This expectation is mirrored in several writings of the New Testament (e.g., 1 Thessalonians 4: 13–18). As time went by this "coming again," which is often referred to as the **Parousia**, was pushed further and further into the future and lost its immediacy with the effect that, increasingly, Christians saw their place not apart from a world soon to come to an end, but immersed in that world and its business. The end would come but it was no longer of immediate concern.

The second step is closely connected to the first and has to do with ways of life and ethics. Jesus seems to have taught his disciples some very challenging precepts (e.g., Luke 14: 26). Opinion differs about whether this ethic arises because of the needs of an itinerant ministry or a belief in the imminent end of the world. But certainly, in the early days, when such an imminent end was in the forefront of Christian minds it was not surprising that it was accompanied by a radical

"interim" ethic. Such an ethic however was too drastic and radical for people set-
tling down for long-term community life, and other communally edifying codes
were adopted, borrowed from the prevailing moral systems.

The third step was taken largely because of Paul, whose influence on
Christianity has been, and continues to be, immense. Paul was a converted Jew and
one of the stories of his conversion is recorded in Acts 9, which can be found in
the *World Religions Reader* (pp. 276–7). His writings, and those of his disciples, occupy
the lion's share of the New Testament. It was Paul who brought the nascent Christian
church from being a sect within Judaism and set it on its way to being a universal
faith. The earliest Christians were Jews and they "bolted on" Christian additions
to their already existing Jewish beliefs and practices. As Paul took the Christian
message out into the non-Jewish (Gentile) world, the question became one of deciding to what extent these Jewish practices were necessary for Christian living. Chief
among the practices that affected everybody were the dietary laws, and the one that
affected males in particular was circumcision. Paul gave a very clear answer to the
question about whether Gentile male Christians need be circumcised, and that answer
was an unqualified "No!"

This position, after some argument and dissension, won the day and had two
main effects. As Christianity was seen to be more and more different from Judaism,
so it was seen as a radical break with that out of which it had come, and it developed its own distinctive identity. As this identity bore less and less the traces of
Jewishness, so Judaism became more hostile. The break came in the eighties of the
first century of this era, when the Jewish authorities ejected Christians – until that
time considered a sect – from the synagogue. That was the first effect. The second
was the appropriation by the new religion of the status, promises, and privileges
under God associated with Judaism. Christianity was not content to be an alternative to Judaism; she was her replacement. Christianity was the new Israel of God.

The pages of the New Testament bear witness to the process of these three steps
and explain the tensions which are endemic in Christianity, especially for those for
whom the Scriptures are the chief guide and inspiration. Catastrophic, unsettling,
and threatening occurrences revive an imminent expectation of the end of the world,
of which parts of the New Testament speak: the apparent ineffectiveness of comfortable Christianity drives some to seek renewal in the radical itinerant lifestyle or
interim ethic, of which too the New Testament speaks. Unfortunately, the New
Testament also records the growing disagreement and conflict between Christian
and Jew and does so, in places, through some very acrimonious anti-Jewish
rhetoric. It is not hard to envisage how these words can be, and have been, used
in support of anti-Semitism, both in attitude and in practice.

Exercise   1   Before we move on to the second century you might like to reflect upon what
living under the radical "interim" ethic might be like. We start with the text
given above, the Gospel of Luke 14: 26:

"If anyone comes to me and does not hate his own father and mother and wife and children and brothers and sisters, yes, and even his own life, he cannot be my disciple."

And when "the twelve" were sent out by Jesus they were charged to

"take no gold, nor silver, nor copper in your belts, no bag for your journey, nor two tunics, nor sandals, nor a staff..." (Gospel of Matthew 10: 9–10)

Would you judge Christians by their obedience to these sayings?

Second and Third Centuries

By the end of the first century, Christians had settled down in the Empire and were trying to be model citizens. The latest books of the New Testament testify to this. Prayers are to be offered for "all men, for kings and all who are in high positions, that we may lead a quiet and peaceable life, godly and respectful in every way. This is good . . ." (1st Letter to Timothy 2: 2–3). Christians are to be "subject for the Lord's sake to every human institution, whether it be to the emperor as supreme, or to governors as sent by him to punish those who do wrong and to praise those who do right. For it is God's will that by doing right you should put to silence the ignorance of foolish men" (1st Letter of Peter 2: 13–15).

They proved to by highly successful. It was true that they were sometimes regarded as a danger to the stability of the Roman state because of their refusal to acknowledge the divine status of the Emperor, and to accompany this with the titular pinch of incense to his deity. They were actually accused of being atheistic; they refused to acknowledge the Roman national gods, thought to be responsible for the security and success of the Empire. They were also regarded as unpatriotic for refusing to serve in the army. This led to periodic bouts of persecution and frequent misrepresentations of the Christian position. The last and severest persecution occurred under Diocletian, who died in 305 CE; in this many churches were destroyed or confiscated, many books burnt, and not a few lives lost. However, slowly but surely, in the words of Peter quoted above, the high ethical seriousness and the exemplary citizenship put to silence the ignorance of the foolish and misguided.

If nascent Christianity was attractive on the ethical front, it also proved to the world-weary civilization of the early centuries of this era a real alternative to the mystery religions. It offered in the sacraments (see later) the possibility of union with the Saviour and the protection of the divine power; moreover, there was the promise that death was not the end. To carry the Christian message to the imagination pagan ideas and images were pressed into service: the late second-century Clement of Alexandria spoke of Jesus in terms of Orpheus storming Hell to gain the release of his loved ones.

On an intellectual level, Christianity quickly came to terms with ancient and contemporary Greek philosophical thought and through its earliest thinkers used this medium to propagate the new faith. They were called the **Apologists**, not because they were expressing regret for being Christians, but, as the original meaning of that term suggested, they presented persuasive reasons for the reasonableness of Christianity. It was not long before distinguished seats of learning appeared, the most famous being the catechetical school in Alexandria.

The Church continued to grow and flourish. The records show that by the middle of the third century synods at Rome and Carthage (in what is now North Africa) were attended by 60 and 87 bishops respectively. And then came Constantine.

Third and Fourth Centuries

Diocletian (Emperor 284–305) reorganized the sprawling Roman Empire, dividing it into two, the East and the West, each part having its Emperor and each Emperor having his Caesar. The Caesars were not averse to calling themselves, and being called, Emperor, which meant that there were in effect four emperors. But, after the death of Diocletian, his reorganization began to fall apart and at one time there were as many as seven emperors, all waging war against each other. By 312 Constantine had made himself supreme in the West, and by 324 he was the sole Emperor. In 313, by the so-called Edict of Milan, freedom of worship was granted to all religions in the Empire. However, because Constantine had espoused the Christian cause, Christianity increased in power and dignity. When, in 380, Theodosius declared Christianity to be the sole state religion a new age began, marked by a close association between church and state. This association was to determine the shape Christianity was to become.

The association started with Constantine. It must not be thought that he treated the new ascendant religion as an individual's private affair. He expected Christianity to function and perform in a way neither the old polytheism of Rome nor the newer syncretistic system, which had formed around the cult of Jupiter, had done. The word religion comes from a Latin word which suggests the sense of "binding." This vast multinational and multicultural structure, which was Constantine's Empire, needed holding together and Constantine looked to his newly adopted faith to provide the basic religious and moral values which would act as the cement to do just that. Moreover, he regarded his relationship to the church as in every way similar to the emporial relationship to the state religion it had replaced. He retained the title "pontifex maximus" (chief pontiff) and he expected the church to deliver what he expected religion to do. After such a long period of hostility and persecution the church rejoiced, perhaps with too much enthusiasm, to have this powerful protector. Its leaders received gratefully the many favors bestowed, but they were now under his bidding. It was the Emperor that summoned the ecumenical (worldwide) councils, the first of which met at Nicea in 325.

When he became sole Emperor, Constantine decided to found a new capital in the East, and chose the small town of Byzantium on the Bosphorus. In 330 it was consecrated and named Constantinople (Istanbul in modern Turkey). This change of capitals was another factor to have momentous consequences for the Christian church. The imperial center of gravity moved East and less interest was given to affairs in the West. The "New Rome" soon rivaled the Old Rome and with this rivalry came the germ of future division which was to gravely infect the church.

By the time Theodosius died in 395, the influence and power of the Emperor had declined to such an extent that the real political figure in the West had become the pope in Rome. (The term pope was used in the West for all bishops until the fifth century, when it became reserved for the bishop of Rome and the first letter became upper case.) There was a titular western emperor, but he carried little weight, and the West was increasingly vulnerable to attack and plunder from Germanic tribes.

Alaric the Visigoth captured and sacked Rome in 410 before proceeding with his followers to settle in what is now southern France and Spain; Attila the Hun invaded the West in 451 and was only persuaded to withdraw by Pope Leo the Great; the same Pope managed to persuade the Vandal Genseric not to torch Rome in 355, though he failed to stop its plunder. The last western emperor was dethroned by yet another barbarian in 476 and the ancient Roman world in the West had ceased to be; it had become a plethora of independent barbarian kingdoms. In Rome, however, the papacy remained, and with it the political power that came through its being the only guarantor of the culture and tradition that still exercised and excited the memory and imagination. This political clout was eventually to re-emerge in the form of the Holy Roman Empire. So, from the ruined empire of the fifth-century West emerged a politically powerful papacy that increasingly viewed itself as exercising not only spiritual power but also the secular power associated with the Emperor still flourishing in the East.

In the East things were completely different. There the Roman Empire still existed with its new capital of Constantinople. The East too was still the center of ecumenical/worldwide Christianity; all the ecumenical councils of the church in the first millennium of the Christian era were held in the East, most of them convened by the eastern Emperor. This dominant position of the Emperor, established by Constantine, continued to be a most important factor, for eastern Christianity became, to all intents and purposes, a state religion where the sacred and the secular were so intertwined that religious enactments were approved by the state and state laws were given religious sanction. The Emperor, helped by the associations which his office had enjoyed in the pagan imperial cult, became God's regent and, as such, was given a prominent role in church deliberations. It is interesting that this "caesaropapism," as it is sometimes called, continued after the capture of Byzantium in 1453 by the Turks. The Russian Czar took the title of Emperor but also assumed the position of head of the Orthodox Church. When this dynasty ceased to be, in 1917, the function of the Russian church continued to be that of a state church even though the state had declared itself atheist.

Two things coming from this period may be worthy of note before we pass on to the medieval church. In church art, seen especially in the decorations of the many churches which were built following Constantine's conversion to Christianity, an interesting change comes over the portrayal of Christ. Before the fourth century, to judge from the pictures in the catacombs, he is portrayed as the Good Shepherd and as the one to deliver from oppression and persecution. After 324 Christ is increasingly represented, especially in the apses of the new churches, as the King and Lord holding universal sway, but no longer being near and comforting; he is the austere ruler of the world. Another figure takes on the loving, tender side of the divine and she is Mary, the **theotokos**, the Mother of God.

The other trend can also be noted in the drawings and paintings of the fourth and fifth centuries, and in the plastic arts associated with the ornamentation of sarcophagi, the stone coffins in which the dead were interred. The crowing of the cock, marking the denial of Jesus by Peter, becomes increasingly common. New dangers and temptations have made themselves felt in this period of imperial patronage, when the secular and the spiritual became so conjoined that they became confused; the more austere demands of the spiritual life could easily be forgotten. It is at this time too that we find the beginnings of asceticism and a movement to shun the world. This took two forms. There were the solitaries (anchorites or hermits) who took themselves off to the wilderness, and there were those who formed and lived in communities (coenobites). Antony is generally regarded as the founder of the former, and Pachomius the father of the latter. Both forms of what is now called monasticism were to grow in strength and popularity.

Exercises

2 *Pause and consider*: What significant temptations do you see creeping into religion in general, and Christianity in particular, when a religion occupies a central place in social and political structures?

3 How are today's secular societies still religious? You may wish to consider the religious themes running through popular and civic culture.

The Middle Ages

The term used for this time span is a rather demeaning one; it was coined by historians to describe the period between what was considered the high culture of the Graeco-Roman world and its **Renaissance** (or Rebirth) in the fifteenth century. Culturally it may have been a time of small things, but in the history of Christianity (and, as we saw in chapters 13 and 15, for Judaism and Islam as well) it was otherwise. During this time the concept of Christendom arose, the Church split into eastern and western churches, the Crusades occurred, the Inquisition was founded, Universities emerged, and Christianity became layered into its various strata of the good and the not so good.

During the eighth century the various kingdoms of western Europe, formed by successive waves of barbarian invaders since the fifth century, and gradually evangelized, and partially civilized, by a succession of missionaries, were faced with two threats. The first was the weakening that occurred through incessant warring, and the second was that posed by the Arab (Muslim) advance up through Spain. These perceived threats were met by a family of warriors; Charles Martel, his son Pepin the Small, and his grandson Charlemagne (Charles the Great). They strengthened the unity of western Europe and pushed the Arabs back into northern Spain. The new state of affairs was legitimated and sacralized by the Pope, who had been helped by the family to retain and strengthen his position in Italy, then under threat, when his traditional ally, the Emperor in Constantinople, was no longer able to help him owing to the new Muslim pressure from the East. When, on Christmas Day 800, Pope Leo III crowned Charlemagne Emperor, a new empire had arrived to succeed the Roman Empire, inspired by the old ideals of peace and stability founded on unity. Papacy and Empire had entered upon a mutually acceptable symbiosis and the idea of Christendom was born. Time would reveal a tussle for supremacy and the claim that the Pope had authority not only in matters spiritual but also in matters temporal, an authority that extended as far as the deposition of emperors.

Needless to say, the court at Constantinople regarded Charlemagne as an interloper: there was no Christian emperor save he who lived in Byzantium. This was but one of the causes of the split or schism that overtook the church in the eleventh century. The other was the growing power of the papacy and its claims of universal sovereignty. To this the patriarch of Constantinople did not take kindly. The matter came to a head in the eleventh century, when, following a Roman delegation to the East for negotiations, each part of the church, with great acrimony, accused the other of every conceivable heresy and proceeded with excommunication. The Great Schism occurred in 1054 and it had mostly to do with authority and supremacy. Hereafter, the eastern church claimed to be the Orthodox (that is, correct belief) Church, and the western church appropriated the title of the Catholic (that is, universal) Church.

What came over Christianity that it entered upon its holy wars, called the Crusades? After all, in its earlier days it had renounced all shedding of blood and had forbidden its adherents to serve in the Roman army. All that, of course, was before the rise of Christendom and the increasing threat from a militant Islam. The Muslim advance into what is now France had been halted by the Martel family, but the places associated with the earthly life of Christ in Palestine, the most holy places for pilgrimage, were under Muslim control and were increasingly being denied to the earnest and pious. This was an affront to a Europe discovering unity and purpose under the concept of Christendom. Things came to a head in the eleventh century when a new Muslim power, the Turks, threatened the position of Byzantium itself; the Emperor appealed for help. The pilgrimage to Palestine had long been considered a ritual of purification, and to die in battle against infidels, as the Muslims were called, had recently been decreed as meriting salvation. Interestingly, this might well be called a Christian Jihad! A crusade to the Holy

Land to rid the sacred places of the infidel could only be doubly rewarding. Any account of the Crusades will reflect no credit on Christianity; the control of the holy places was only temporary, and the experience coarsened the Christian spirit and indelibly blackened its history. The great Bernard of Clairvaux, the promoter of a stricter form of the Benedictine monastic rule practiced by the Cistercians, urged battle not only against the enemy without but also against the enemy within. The armies of Christendom, before proceeding to the East, destroyed many of the Jewish communities in a Europe that was being persuaded that its unity and peace was being threatened by an alien belief in its midst. Systematic persecution of the Jews had begun.

Any deviation from orthodoxy, the perceived correct form of belief, had similarly to be stamped out. Heresy was sought out and destroyed, and the organ for this task was the Inquisition. The systematic eradication of any dissent was in place, under the direction of the Dominicans. This was a new preaching order, founded in 1216 by Dominic, to bring the Gospel to the enlarging cities of medieval Europe. It was proud to number among its members great theologians like Thomas Aquinas (1225–74) and great mystics and exponents of personal piety like Meister Eckhart (1260–1327), but it acquired a dark reputation by the way torture and burning were used in the service of the Inquisition. The reputation was stained darker still by the way the Spanish Inquisition operated in a Spain recently reconquered from the Moors; Jews and Muslims were expelled and exterminated unless they converted. But far from making Christian Europe more secure and united, this attempt to eradicate all questioning and dissent only made Christendom more unsure of itself and less confident about its identity.

The twelfth and thirteenth centuries were times of intellectual ferment. The growth of cities led to a new social class which demanded access to learning. Up to this time, all learning was under the close control of the Church in monasteries and episcopal schools, and tended, given the climate encouraged by the Inquisition, to be concerned with traditional studies in Scripture and orthodox texts. Control over the curriculum was closely guarded. However, the students gathering in increasing numbers in the cities wanted more and there was much to whet their appetite. New texts were becoming available, such as those offering translations of the ancient Greek philosopher Aristotle and the explorations in mathematics and science coming in from the Arab world. The result, after a period of conflict, was the institutions we know as universities. These began as associations of teachers and pupils, and gained a degree of autonomy by removing themselves from the direct control of the local bishop, who zealously claimed the right to decide upon the curriculum and to licence the teachers, and placing themselves under the papacy. In 1231 the University of Paris was recognized by Pope Gregory IX and granted the right to decide their own courses and order their own administration.

In medieval Europe, to be a citizen meant also to belong to the Church; there was no escape, except in the case of the Jews and their position was precarious. This meant that all activity, whether religious, social, or political, occurred within a Christian ambit. That, however, did not mean that every activity was equally good or meritorious, for some were perceived to belong to a higher order then others. This resulted in a layered society, each layer having its own status, duties, and obligations. Two obvious layers were the clergy and the laity; the former responsible for worship, prayer, and the things of the Spirit, while the latter tended to the things of the world, like business and commerce, politics and war, and of course procreation. The divide became all the greater when, in the twelfth century, clerical celibacy became obligatory. Clergy and laity had become different not just in degree but also in kind. And then there were the religious orders of monks or nuns. These formed another layer and were witness to an early ideal of simplicity, peace and order, and the sharing of possessions. This represented the best way. The common practice of burying laymen in a monk's habit clearly indicates how the monastic life was appraised, and its superior status in the layering of life.

The Reformation and Counter-Reformation

Christendom at the end of the medieval period was showing signs of strain. The vision of the Holy Roman Empire had faded and was replaced by the desire for local autonomy and development, free from the interference of outsiders amongst whom was numbered the Pope, who by this time claimed jurisdiction over not only spiritual matters but also affairs temporal. The power of the lesser nobility had declined while that of the local ruler had increased: nationalism had broken out in Europe, bringing with it monarchies concerned above all with what promoted narrow national interests.

An educated middle class had emerged, for the most part hungry for education. It was not, however, the narrow Christian education of church and cloister that they craved, but rather an education in the values of the old pre-Christian culture of Greece and Rome. These were now increasingly available following the capture of Constantinople by the Turks in 1453, after which Christian refugees brought to the West the glories of Graeco-Roman culture. The **Renaissance** (or Rebirth) had broken in.

The Church, in the main, was slumbering. The Church was dominated by very rich prelates and a largely uneducated clergy. But worse, the Church's grip on the majority of people was through its promise to provide the way to heaven, and avoidance of the torments of Hell. They were only too aware that their occupation in the "wicked" world put them at a disadvantage, for they were unlikely to be pleasing to God. The clergy and the monastics were better placed. Perhaps they could go to Heaven on the backs of these meritorious people, and also through the merits of the saints whose lives they most certainly could not possibly emulate. The pious among the people were increasingly turning their minds to avoiding the pains of Hell, from which it was becoming ever more difficult to escape. The ordinary people just sank into superstition.

There were attempts at reform, but they came to very little. Any reform would mean a change in the institutional church, but the institutional church resisted any change that would threaten its privileges and authority. Things were brought to a head through the growing use of **indulgences** as a means of raising money. Good deeds and pilgrimages, the intercession of the saints, and the endowment of worthy causes, were all commonly considered as counting toward a shortening of the time of punishment for sin that would follow death. A further step was taken when it was suggested that such remission would take place on the straight payment of money to the Church authorities. And then the Church actively promoted this payment. The occasion was the building of St. Peter's in Rome; in order to finance the project Pope Leo X issued an indulgence in 1517. In Germany half of the proceeds were to go to him and half to the Archbishop of Mainz. Later the same year, Martin Luther produced his now famous Ninety-Five Theses against the indulgence, and the Reformation was on its way.

There followed the charge of heresy and the threat of excommunication, as a response to which Luther produced the first of his many theological and reforming works. When he refused to withdraw what he had written he was placed under the imperial ban, but he had acquired a protector in the Elector of Saxony, one of the local rulers who were seeking ways of expanding their power and influence against the centralist authority of Pope and Emperor. This was a political backing that the earlier attempts at reform lacked, but for the eventual success of the movement more was necessary. That more was the new theological vision and religious experience, based on Luther's own personal experience of release and peace when he replaced his most strenuous efforts to be accepted by God with the conviction that it was God's grace alone that would bring the salvation he so dearly sought. He had read in Paul's letter to the Romans that the just and righteous shall live by faith (Romans 1: 17) and this convinced him that the only response to God's gift was trust or faith. Good works then were not the condition for acceptance by God, but what flowed from the gratitude of being so accepted. This was heady stuff and it came as a great balm to those who were uncertain about their escape from the unworthiness they believed to dwell within them.

The dam had burst and the old containment within a uniform Christian Europe was shattered. Unfortunately, the containment dispersed into many religious rivers; it was not limited to a stream of Lutheranism. Once the old certainties had gone there were many contenders to show how a reformed church should be ordered and governed, and indeed these contenders continue to the present day. This was inevitable, because the authoritative position of the **magisterium** (the teaching organ of the Church), which claimed to decide matters of belief and practice, had been replaced by a frozen authority, the Christian Scriptures.

All wanted to return "*ad fontes*" (to the fountainhead of Christianity), and all looked to Scripture to find that clear, unsullied spiritual drink. But the Christian Scriptures are open to many interpretations; their diversity invites a variety of understandings. Consequently, the sixteenth century was witness to other forms of church reform: there was the form which developed in Zurich, Switzerland, under Ulrich Zwingli; and the form which emerged from Geneva, also in Switzerland, under Jean Calvin, which is better known as Calvinism in its theology and as Presbyterianism in its church government. At the same time in England, the

Church of England was developing yet another pattern, which it described as Catholic yet Reformed. Two centuries later, Methodism was to separate itself from this church.

The movement called the Reformation resulted in the division of western Christendom into Protestant and Catholic. The Roman Catholic Church retrenched. What is commonly called the Counter-Reformation was indeed a reformation of abuses, but the word "counter" suggests that it took its orientation from the new Protestantism and set itself against it; the Counter-Reformation's position of certainty and authority was not surrendered, nor indeed demonized. This Catholic Reformation, to use the term preferred by Catholics, was shaped by the deliberations of the Council of Trent, which extended over the long period from 1545 to 1563.

The Modern Period

The Reformation in the sixteenth century resulted in a religiously divided Europe, which in turn led to persecution of those of a different religious persuasion within countries, and even to wars of religion which soaked the soil of Europe with blood. Toward the end of the seventeenth century, a general weariness resulted in mutual toleration, if not of the other's beliefs and practices, at least of the other's presence. The damage to Christianity, however, had been done. The religious conflicts seemed incapable of being resolved, and the reason for this was seen to be the intractable nature of competing ideologies. Something other than unverifiable ideology was needed to establish peace and to promote the smooth running of the body politic. Reason was seen to be the answer. The so-called Age of Reason had arrived, and with it the modern mind. The "moderns" refused to accept "truths" merely on traditional authority; all was to be held up and judged by the light of reason.

Another name for the shift of personal, social, and political life from ecclesiastical tutelage is the **Enlightenment**. As the name suggests, moving to a reason-directed life was considered to be analogous to moving from darkness into light. The Christian faith was seen by many to be founded on myths and fables; certainly it had inhibited free thinking. Galileo was a case in point. The Church seemed to prefer error to accepting the new finding of science; it preferred its own myth, of the Earth being the center of the universe, to the plain evidence supplied by Galileo's telescope. Christianity, once the patron of the arts and sciences, was seen to be their gaoler.

Two significant offspring of the Enlightenment were toleration and liberalism. The toleration of Christian minorities was followed by the toleration of other faiths, in particular the Jews of Europe. With toleration came a great variety of thought and action. Curiously, this aspect found free expression in religion. Christianity itself, in its Protestant representation, continued to fragment and assume forms that would have been unthinkable, and indeed unrecognizable, in an earlier age. Outside Christianity, a wide variety of religious practice was generally tolerated. Pious superstition, for so long controlled by the churches, was given free rein and found expression in many new cults and movements.

The eighteenth century saw, too, an increase in colonialization. Colonialism did not, of course, start then, for it could be said to have begun with the discovery of the "New World," and the opening up of Africa and India, and points further East. The colonists took their religion with them, but they also used it as an excuse and a legitimization. To colonialize was seen to be bringing "savages" out of "pagan darkness" into the enlightenment provided by the Christian message; it was to do "God's work". Such claims hardly hid the fact that colonialization would not have been pursued so vigorously by most of the European powers had it not produced great wealth in precious metals and stones, in commercial commodities, and in cheap labour. By the end of the eighteenth century, however, the possession of territories abroad laid upon the Christian churches a newly-discovered obligation to go out into the world and make disciples of all nations (Matthew 28: 19). Active missionary endeavor, dormant for a millennium, had begun once again. If the political powers were competing for overseas territories, the various Christian denominations began to compete for the souls of their inhabitants. To be fair, the concern was for more than souls; minds were educated in Christian schools, and bodies tended in Christian hospitals.

Interestingly, it was the denominational competition in the fields of mission that produced what is now generally called the **Ecumenical Movement**, the movement to heal the divisions within Christianity, one of the significant and hopeful stirrings of this age. Europe had grown used to the divisions, and what the divisions stood for was considered important. The scandal of these divisions, however, was felt particularly sharply overseas, when the effectiveness of the missionary endeavor was vitiated by rivalry and competition. Christianity should speak in a single voice; the bitterness caused by European squabbles should not be exported.

Worldviews

In *A World Religions Reader*, Ian Markham begins the section on worldviews in Christianity with the heading "Monotheism and the Incarnation." Near the beginning are these words: "Monotheism is the belief that there is only one God, but if Jesus is God as well, then doesn't that mean that there are two Gods, or at least two bits of God?" The answer given to this question determines the unique Christian worldview or mindset.

The experience of Jesus of Nazareth was such that his followers wanted to say he was more than a man, and they ended up by claiming that he was nothing short of God. And yet they wanted to affirm that they were still monotheists. They did so by developing the doctrine of the Trinity. The acknowledgment that Jesus was divine did indeed explode the idea of monotheism but, Christians claim, not in the sense of making the idea untenable; it exploded the idea to accommodate the divinity of Jesus, and also that of the Holy Spirit. How could this be possible? The attempt was made at the first two general councils of the Christian Church at Nicea (325 CE) and Constantinople (381 CE). It is summarized in the Nicene Creed, which was started at Nicea and finished at Constantinople, and can be found on pages 275–6 of *A World Religions Reader*. The claim, which had to resist all attacks, was that he who became Jesus was not a semi-god but God in every sense of the word. This explains the emphasis contained in the words "very God of very God . . . being of one substance with the Father . . ." This creedal statement was accompanied by much theological explanation, which sought to explain the Trinity by stating that there was one "substance" which eternally existed in three "persons." The words are used in a special way and are therefore placed in warning marks to alert readers to the difficulty of translating Latin or Greek words while still retaining the meaning and nuance of the original. The idea of "person" today certainly carries the idea of separateness from other persons; this is not what the Latin word "persona" meant. The three "persons" were one God because of the principle of co-inherence, an essential togetherness.

If there were difficulties in producing and defending ways of thinking of differentiation within God while retaining the oneness of God, these were as nothing compared with the difficulties in producing and defending ways of thinking of Jesus as being both God and human while still being a single being. There were many attempts to express what was believed to be the "specialness" of Jesus, but this was new ground and no one had traveled it before. It was not surprising that some mistakes were made; at least they were seen as mistakes, and labeled **heresy** (the Church labeled heresy any interpretation which was later seen as incorrect, and therefore corrupting), when viewed from the position of the explanation that was finally accepted as **orthodox** (and the Church labeled orthodox the interpretation which was viewed as correct, and therefore proper). This position was arrived at during the second two general councils of the Christian Church held at Ephesus (431 CE) and Chalcedon (451 CE). At the latter there appeared what became known as the Chalcedonian Definition concerning the person of Christ, though it was more a statement of the orthodox position than an explanation of it. The Definition states that Jesus Christ is fully human and at the same time fully divine, and goes on to say that the two natures are "unconfused and unalterable, indivisible and inseparable." These negative terms indicate why what was said at Chalcedon is a statement of what Christ is not, rather than an explanation of what Christ is.

The Christological settlement was not without its casualties. The two councils produced division in the Church. The decisions of 431 created the Nestorian divide. Nestorius and his followers were those who were at pains to stress the humanness of Jesus and objected to the title "**theotokos**" (god-bearer) being given to the mother of Jesus; he who was born of Mary was not God but a human being. Nestorius' opponents accused him of positing two persons, a human being and a divine one. Nestorius, they claimed, had divided the person of Christ and had produced two persons. The decision at Ephesus not only created a separate Nestorian group of Christians, which stretched as far as India, but gave encouragement to see in the mother of Jesus, as "theotokos," a person removed from the ordinary. This was to have very important implications in the future.

The second division occurred at Chalcedon. If the Nestorians felt that the ortho-dox position threatened the humanness of Christ and as a result opened themselves to the charge that they had produced two Christs, one human and the other divine, there were others who were so keen to promote an undivided Christ that they went so far as to say that in the incarnate Christ there were not two natures but one, and that one was the divine which had added to itself humanity. These folk were called monophysites (one-nature people: the humanity in Christ did not bring about any change in the divine). Following Chalcedon, the eastern churches includ-ing those of Egypt and Armenia, who favored the monophysite understanding of the nature of Christ, split from the rest of the Church. These divisions eventually made it all the easier for Islam to expand and establish itself in those areas where there existed a weakened Christianity, cut off from the main body of Christians.

You will note that all that has been covered so far under worldviews has had to do with how Jesus of Nazareth, who was called Christ, was to be evaluated with respect to the divine on the one hand, and to the human on the other. Christian theology calls this evaluation **Christology**. Simply put, it is the question of un-derstanding the person of Christ. It can be simply put, but it is far from being a simple task, which you are perhaps beginning to appreciate. It becomes more com-plicated when the term is expanded to include an understanding of the difference this person is believed to have brought about by his life, and particularly by his death. At one time it was conventional to keep these two separate; thinking about the person of Christ was called Christology and thinking about his accomplishment was termed **Soteriology** (salvation theory). Today these two are increasingly brought together, for it is impossible to separate what this person is deemed to be from what he is thought to have accomplished.

| Exercises | 4 | Before proceeding, pause and reflect on those four negative terms used at Chalcedon. Decide which might be designed to exclude the Nestorians and which the Monophysites. |
| | 5 | *Something more to ponder*: Is Jesus who Christians claim him to be because he has to be that in order to accomplish what it is claimed he has done, or is he who he is claimed to be irrespective of what he is thought to have accomplished? Do you judge someone by what he does or what he is? Are we human beings or human doings? |

You may by now be thinking, and perhaps hoping, that there is more to Christian worldviews than considerations about Jesus Christ. But Christianity is just that. It has to do with Christ and everything is understood in relation to what is believed about him. What makes Christian thinking what it is is its Christo-centricity. Theology in a Christian context is not just any "talk about God," but talk about God as a consequence of what is believed about Christ. It is not too wide of the mark to state that all distinctive Christian theology is Christology.

Consider the assertions made by Christians in respect of four very common religious questions. One recurring question is, not unnaturally, about God. The Christian reply is that God is like Christ. A lot of sophisticated answers can be given but, basically, the bottom line to them all is that the person who would know God will know him through Christ, and, perhaps more surprisingly, as being Christ-like.

Another question, often asked, concerns the human condition, its ambiguity and messiness. In this, Christianity's questions are no different from the questions posed in other religious faiths. The answer, however, is very different. The solution is in Jesus Christ, or, as Christians are more likely to express it, salvation is only possible through this person. Pushing this matter further Christianity provides, as it has to, both an explanation for the human condition, which needs redemption, and the way in which this redemption is received and appropriated. To these two explanations we must turn, but not before considering the Christian answer to another two common religious questions.

What is the shape of the religious life? The answer is strange. It is one thing to say that this Christ displays what God is like; it is perhaps on the same level to claim that only in him can there be deliverance from the fallen or broken human condition; but Christians go on to say that the Christian life should be defined by the way in which it exhibits Christ-like qualities. The paradox is obvious: God is Christ-like and the Christian life is Christ-like. Is there a connection? The importance of the Chalcedonian statement, with regard to the humanness of Jesus, moves into prominence at this point.

The last question concerns the sphere of religious living. Christianity, as you will probably be aware by now, is full of ambiguities and tensions. There are those who are convinced that the trials, but more the temptations, of this corrupt world nudge the Christian to have as little to do with it as possible. We noted in the historical section the beginning of the ascetic trend within Christianity, which sought escape from the trials, tribulations, and temptations of a world experienced as corrupt. The world cannot be the true resting place for the Christian. As this trend developed, there was a danger that the Christian life might be seen primarily as a period for developing the soul and preparing it for heaven. But this has been increasingly balanced by the recognition that the world and its affairs matter. As Christ took flesh and immersed himself in the world for its benefit, so the church, his body commissioned to do those things that he would have done, cannot be separated from the world. Like its master all Christians are called to show a worldly interest, but in holiness, and conduct the Christian life not just for the benefit of themselves but for the world. Perhaps it is now clearer why Christian theology is at heart Christology.

There remains the two explanations, which will of necessity form part of the Christian worldview, of why the human condition needs redemption and how this redemption is made one's own. The Christian view is that something has gone wrong with the good and perfect creation which God intended and to which imperfect state the human condition only too well witnesses. Humans are not what they are capable of being, what they were meant to be in the purposes of God. It is here that the story in the first book in the Christian Bible has dominated the explanation: humans have fallen from an original "un-fallen" state and are henceforth in a condition of **original sin**, from which there is no natural escape. Humans were created above all else to enjoy a relationship with God, but disobedience has fractured this. What is needed is a healing of the fracture, and it is here that Christ is considered to work his work as the great mender of what has been broken.

But how is this received and how is it related to the Christian life, which we have already observed should be Christ-shaped? The answer is odd. Most would expect that the healing would occur when the Christian adherent followed the Christ-shaped life. The answer, however, takes a different track and it owes its direction to Paul, and it is well charted in his writings in the Christian New Testament. The healing is offered gratuitously by God, and it cannot be obtained through any reward-earning activity. To put it in the words of what has become in some circles a slogan, "Christians are saved by (God's) grace through faith (in what God has done for humans in Christ)." The importance of this cannot be overlooked for it helps to explain why Christians emphasize correct belief in God, and what he is conceived to have done, above correct action, which might be construed as meriting some reward from him. Right belief, or **orthodoxy** (for a fuller explanation, see the glossary), and not right behavior, is that which determines a believer's final relationship with God. This goes a long way to explain, though of course not to excuse, such past Christian evils as the Inquisition and the burning of witches.

Institutions and Rituals

The institution without which Christianity would be but an idea, however beautiful, is the Church. You will note the upper case C in Church; it is used to distinguish the theological or abstract, universal entity from its human fragmentation into many churches. It would be difficult to envisage what this faith would be without this corporate manifestation. It is the Church which gives Christianity its corporate identification; above all else it is a people. All the great images witness to this fact. Those drawn from Christian scripture speak of "the people of God," "the body of Christ" in which all are as parts or limbs, "the Temple of God's praise" for which all are as building blocks, or "the household of God" the occupation of which is never conceived as single. Perhaps the most evocative image is that of the body of Christ for it carries with it the obligation for those incorporated in that body to continue the effects of Christ in this world and, in the words of a well used prayer, "to continue to do those things that he would have done." It is here that the division in the Christian Church, which has produced such a choice of different churches, makes this task an impossibility and leads, for many Christians, to a desire to work for the reunification of the Church. To put it in theological terms, the Church should reflect the completeness and harmony of the Trinity, in the light of which, to borrow a slogan from another place, "united we stand and divided we fall." But, divided the Church undoubtedly is. The reasons for this we traced earlier in the historical survey.

All other institutions within Christianity bear witness to the Church as the primary institution. The totality of Christ's presence, with all its manifold aspects and operations, is often divided up into societies and associations which seek to promote a particular aspect or operation that is perceived to be of special importance. These, however, can never claim to be the total continuance, or the essence, of the Christian business in the here and now. There are many claims that this or that is "real Christianity", but they are easily shown to be but a slice of the whole operation. A major element in Christian thinking is concerned with the nature and function of the Church and is called **ecclesiology**, a term which emerges from the Greek word for Church.

And so to rituals. All these become more understandable when they are viewed within the context of the Church as primary institution. *A World Religions Reader* begins with prayer and rightly so, for the common and "up front" feature of most religious activity is words addressed to the deity. As an example there is the prayer that Christians refer to as the Lord's Prayer, because the records suggest that Jesus taught his followers to use it in their prayer to God (see *A World Religions Reader*, pp. 279–80). Interestingly, if there is any weight in the first clause, the hallowing of God's name could be seen to be the primary obligation of Christian discipleship. Certainly, in the Christian vision of Heaven, hinted at in the last book of the Christian Bible, called the Revelation (what will be hereafter), the blessed seem to do little else than fall down on their knees and offer praise to God. Prayer and praise would seem, for the Christian, to be not a means to an end but the end itself!

There are of course more rituals in Christianity than prayer, and as suggested above they all have to do with the institution of the Church. More correctly, they have to do with the meaning that has been attached to the totality of the Christ happening, just as the meaning attached to the Church takes as its point of departure its relationship to that event. This is yet another indication of the centrality of Christology in all Christian thinking.

The other rituals which Christian practice demonstrates to be central are the **sacraments**. By a sacrament is meant a special kind of symbol or effective sign, which makes real what it signifies and by so doing becomes a particular means of grace. In many Christian circles they are described as outward and visible signs of an inward and spiritual grace. There is some disagreement among Christians about the number and precise meaning of the sacraments. The Protestant churches tend to limit them to two, Baptism and Eucharist, sometimes called Communion. They do so because they claim that these were the only two instituted by Christ himself, and all others are human creations. Other Christians have as many as five more, and justify them by seeing in them a continuation of some aspect of the ministry of Christ. For example, as Christ forgave sins and made people whole, so this activity is continued in the Church through the rites (or sacraments) of reconciliation and anointing. But all Christians agree about the centrality of Baptism and Eucharist.

Baptism is Christian initiation. Through Baptism one becomes a member of the Church and is incorporated into Christ, and for this reason the rite is sometimes referred to as Christening, being "Christed." The use of water is suggestive: where adult baptism is practiced as immersion, the waters of baptism become the grave wherein lies the old corrupt nature and through which the believer rises to new life; and where baptism is administered as sprinkling, the water is seen as a cleansing for renewal. Water determines the primary significance but other aspects are often found within the rite, such as enlightenment signified by the giving and receiving of a candle.

One cause of Christian division is the age at which Baptism should be administered. Baptists, once called Anabaptists for their opposition to infant baptism, will only baptize adults who will make a public confession of Christian faith. Others will baptize infants, believing that God's grace is prior to any human response to it, though increasingly the active faith of the parents and friends has become a determining reason for admitting a baby into the Church.

There is general agreement among Christians about the meaning and function of Baptism, but there is no such agreement over the common meal of Christians. Just compare the names given to this sacrament: the Holy Communion, the Holy Mysteries, the Lord's Supper, the Breaking of Bread, the Eucharist, and the Sacrifice of the Mass. All these names are witness to the many meanings generated by this central act of Christian worship. That it is a meal is clear from the elements of bread and wine and the record of the institution of the sacrament in the New Testament, where it is in the context of the meal called by all Christians the Last Supper. That it is more can be seen in the name given by some Christians to what others simply call a table: the altar. The suggestion offered by this word is that what is happening at this service is the offering of a sacrifice. This is one of the features which deeply divide Christians and the point of division is the question whether this service is a memorial of Jesus' death on the cross interpreted as a once-for-all, never to be repeated sacrifice for the sins of the world, or a representation of that sacrifice afresh.

Another feature of this sacrament which tends to divide Christians is the manner of the sacramental presence of Christ. Catholic Christians tend to see it in terms of the medieval doctrine of transubstantiation, where the bread and wine become the body and blood of Christ while retaining all the features of bread and wine offered to the senses. Other Christians prefer not to define too precisely just how Christ is present, but insist that present he most assuredly is. These refer to "the real presence," a quaint phrase bearing witness to the religious polemic of yesteryear when these Christians were accused of practicing a mere memorial of a past event. After all, no Christian now believes in the real absence!

It is a cause of much sorrow among Christians that this sacrament, in which all are thought to be enveloped in the healing peace or wholeness of Christ, should prove to be so divisive. As a result, over the last few decades many Christian churches have adopted a policy of the "open altar or table"; these churches believe that there is already a great deal that is held in common, and further believe that the desired unity of all Christians might be helped and hastened by the sharing of this sacrament of unity. Others believe that the sharing of this sacrament should be the fruit of unity, and intercommunion should not be a feature of the churches until this has been achieved.

It should be recognized that some Christian groups do not have any sacraments, believing that the presence of Christ is always with them and nothing can alter or increase this. These groups include the Religious Society of Friends and the Salvation Army.

Under this heading would normally come an explanation of the use and function of the Christian Scriptures within that faith. This however can be found in chapter 4, where the Christian use of Scripture is described and compared to the function of holy books in other faiths.

6   Task: Attend a baptism or Eucharist and try to attach meaning to five   **Exercise**
    separate things you hear or observe happening.

Ethical Expressions

A World Religions Reader begins this section by drawing attention to the priority of love, and presents a portion of Paul's great hymn to love in 1 Corinthians 13. What is interesting here is the way, in some Christian devotions, the suggestion is made to replace the word love in the passage given with the word of Christ. This may seem strange, but is in accord with the point made above, when we were considering worldviews, about the way the figure of Christ defines many things in Christianity, one of which is the expected shape of Christian living. To love, for the Christian, is to follow Christ, for, as the 1st Letter of John says, "we love because he first loved us." (1 John 4: 19)

A World Religions Reader then passes on to the important observation that love entails justice, and illustrates this through the words of a Christmas sermon preached by the celebrated civil rights leader Martin Luther King. Justice, as has been observed, is love distributed.

All religions exhibit an ethical dimension, as all religions exhibit their belief systems and worship patterns, but what is surprising in Christianity is the amount of time and energy given to produce moral maps. It is surprising because, as stated above (the final paragraph of the section headed Worldviews), what is regarded as Christian healing is appropriated not by a succession of approved actions but by grace through faith. But even Paul, who was at pains to stress that what Christians call salvation is received in this way, was also at pains to stress the importance of those actions which conform to the new situation in which Christians find themselves. Paul could at times lay down the law, and his letters contain many ethical bits spelling out in no uncertain terms the actions that are appropriate to the new life begun at Baptism and those that are not. In many of his lists of approved and condemned actions we can trace the influence of contemporary moral systems which he has made his own. This is to be expected as the early Christian community turned from the "interim" ethic of an immanent return of Christ to a settled life lived among others in the Roman Empire. You might like to have a look at one of these lists in his Letter to the Galatians, 5: 19–24.

The concern for the right and proper thing has continued in Christian thinking down the centuries and finds expression in moral theology (discourse in the light of belief on the matter of behavior) and, because the practice of borrowing the ethical ideas of others was continued, in moral philosophy. In the search for the correct action, Christian thinking has been concerned with three areas of moral thinking. They are:

- the moral status of the act in itself;
- the effect of the act; and
- the motive for the act.

The second has rather fallen into the background of late due to a reaction to **utilitarianism**, which tends to judge any action by whether it promotes well-being or lessens discomfort and pain. Although the results or effects of actions continue to be a factor in Christian ethics, there is a long tradition in its thinking which is suspicious of the dictum that the end justifies the means and all that really matters is a promising end. The poet T. S. Eliot expresses this suspicion eloquently:

> This is the last and greatest treason
> To do the right for the wrong reason.
> (*Murder in the Cathedral*)

The other two areas continue to dominate Christian ethical thinking. Those from a Catholic position home in on the first, while those from a Protestant position focus more on the matter of motive. The latter are anxious lest right actions proceed from a desire to earn merit. For them, Christian action should proceed from gratitude for what God has done and continues to do, with no thought of reward. Because the emphasis here is on the right motive perhaps insufficient attention is paid to the nature of the act done or the program proposed. It is here that the Catholic emphasis acts as a corrective; for them it is the correctness of the act or program that is up front, though for many outside that camp the judgments of past generations on the nature of certain acts were based on incorrect or incomplete information, and decisions based on such judgments seem at times to be unnecessarily prohibiting and restrictive.

7   *Reflection:* Think of a great issue at present under public debate in the media   **Exercises**
    of communications and consider what might be the proper response to
    it in the light of the three guiding principles which have determined moral
    thinking.
8   How does Christianity define the Good? Is it determined by God or is God
    determined by it?

A World Religions Reader ends the section on ethical expression with a consideration of the status and role of women within Christianity. Ian Markham makes the
point clearly that the Church, instead of opposing the oppression of women, participated in it. But it was not so from the beginning as Luke 10: 38–42 and Galatians
3: 28 (see *A World Religions Reader*, p. 288) suggest.

The picture seems to be that during the ministry of Jesus, and in the first few
decades that followed his crucifixion, women had been close followers of his, had
held ministerial office in the Church, and had been accredited and successful emis-
saries for the faith. They had played their part in leading worship, speaking, and
praying in public. That had been in the early, heady days. Things changed when
Christians settled down to be good model citizens, for on no account should offence
be caused. Christian women had to behave like all other respectable women in the
Empire; they had to be modest and submissive. Although restrictive views find expression in the latest books in the New Testament they are borrowed from contemporary moral norms. When the writer of the 1st Letter to Timothy says "Let a
woman learn in silence with all submissiveness. I permit no woman to teach or to
have authority over men; she is to keep silent" (verses 11 and 12), this is forward-
ing the new program of assimilation with a vengeance. Christians must not be seen
to be too different; their women must be as subservient as all others. The rest, as
they say, is history, a history of patriarchal domination which, judged by the pattern of the earliest days, was not the earliest picture. If it was contemporary patterns of status, behavior, and expectation in the first two centuries of this era that
began the process whereby women were disempowered, it could be that the present patterns might reverse the process. There is, of course, the possibility that the
traditionalists in all Christian churches will regard this as dangerous novelty, forgetting that novelty has been part of the Christian scene from the beginning. Perhaps
like all reformations and renewals the return "*ad fontes*" (see above) will allow women
to play a full part in the Christian Church, which has been impoverished by being
denied their full ministry, to build up the "Body of Christ." The Church can take
courage; it did stop, in the end, burning witches! Hard as it may seem at the turn
into the third millennium, people did at one time think that by burning women
considered to be witches they were doing God's will. More than that, to stop burning witches would be a betrayal of a tradition sanctioned by the Bible and encouraged by the Church. But they did stop in the end burning witches, as indeed Christians
stopped owning slaves.

Exercises

9   Read the Acts of the Apostles 2: 17–19. Then consider why this prophecy of Joel has yet to be realized in the Christian Church.

10   Why do there still exist gender divisions, generation divisions, and social divisions? Should they be resolved? Would that be the wonders and signs referred to?

11   Are the genders equal under God? What are those who say that they are equal but different asserting? How is this difference to find expression?

Modern and Future Expression

In this concluding section of this chapter, we will attempt to describe and even predict some of the trends within Christianity that will prove significant in the coming century.

1   We start where we left off in the last section. Women are already in some parts of the Christian family not only increasingly playing an important part in the councils, and indeed the inner councils, but also beginning to occupy positions of authority and power. Already, some ecclesial communities have willingly undertaken this momentous step, momentous that is for the traditional mind which thinks that it is attempting something new. In this they will only be allowing women to reclaim their ancient birthright. There will be resistance in other groups, but it will be difficult to withstand the high tides of change that are sweeping over the contemporary world. Reluctantly perhaps, most bastions of male power will give way and allow at least half of the Christian faithful to occupy the position referred to in Paul's epistle to the Galations (see *A World Religions Reader*, p. 288).

2   Of course a modern expression of a faith will have to take notice of just that, modernity, and indeed postmodernity. Doubtless in their intellectual activity Christian thinkers will continue the noble task of **apologetics** (see **Apologists** above) which their second-century predecessors did with such success, but many doubt that they will enjoy a similar success, at least in the West. There has been an observed shrinking in the numbers committed to the mainstream churches in this area of the globe, and the perceived answer is to attempt to make the faith acceptable in terms of its intellectual content. This is the legacy of orthodoxy; intellectual acceptance is everything. Elsewhere on this planet, unencumbered by the need for intellectual respectability as understood in the West, the Christian Church appears to fare rather better. There it is not detached, even semi-detached, from the main business of living in this world; it is offered as a way of life which addresses the trials and tribulations of human existence, and a satisfying spirituality which speaks to the hopes and aspirations of people where they are. For many, the churches in the West are still answering questions no one is asking and not listening sufficiently to the questions that are in people's minds, if not always on their lips. The slogan of the

1960s still carries persuasion: "Let the world write the agenda." But the agenda is not solely intellectual, for it is as much moral, and spiritual, and aesthetic.

3   It is often remarked that there are as many Catholic Christians in Latin America and as many Protestant Christians in Africa as there are in Europe. While many of these continue to practice the faith in its exported form, increasingly local ways of expressing and living it out are finding expression. Christianity is becoming more pluriform. Uniformity as a lodestar probably never operated globally and certainly has fewer and fewer adherents today. Pluriformity exists in the worldwide expression of Christianity, which has become (or rather come to realize itself as always having been) the rainbow faith. In so doing, a remarkable shift has occurred in the way Christianity understands itself. If right belief was all that mattered in the time of the Inquisition it seems to be no longer the case today. Though still hotly debated, lifestyle and observable action seem to have become the criteria for judging the genuineness of this faith. Paul must be spinning in his grave!

4   The West, it is said, must now be considered to be post-Christian. Judged by its past there is some truth in this observation. What cannot be denied is that this post-Christian West is seen by those Christians who live in it as an area of evangelization and mission. No longer can it be assumed that those who live there have any residual understanding of Christianity and what it represents. Christendom has long departed. The result is that churches become more "gathered" and separate from the communities in which they are set, and the community has become a mission area. But more, already those whose forebears in the past were evangelized by Europeans are now seeing it as a Christian duty to repay their debt by sending missionaries to a no longer Christian Europe.

5   Christianity, because of its history which held together the good and the not-so-good, has tended to see the good as being more of the Church than the not-so-good. At the very center of the good has been the ordained clergy. Becoming a member of the clergy has, in some circles, been referred to as "going into the Church." This, of course, was not how it was in the beginning but was something that developed over the years, especially in medieval Europe. At the present there has been in the Christian Church an "*ad fontes*" renewal, in which every member is encouraged to find a proper vocation and ministry. There are to be no "idle" Christians, for all have a part to play. This renewal of the Church through the activation of everybody goes by the ungainly term **laicization**, which merely means that the non-clerical part of the Church, commonly called the laity, is beginning to exercise a ministry which was theirs from the beginning. This process of laicization is likely to gather pace. But whether this will be extended to sharing real power with the ordained clergy, and making real decisions for the ongoing welfare of the Church, remains to be seen.

6   A movement within Christianity which has been a particular feature in the twentieth century is likely to become an all absorbing issue in the twenty-first

century. It concerns the principal institution in Christianity, viz. the Church, and its unity, or **ecumenism**. As pointed out in the historical section, it began because of a concern for credibility in what was then considered the mission lands. It has gathered a pace and an urgency. Unkind critics will say that it has only done so as the churches of the West have declined in numbers and influence. There is probably more than a grain of truth in this observation, because those Christian groups that are flourishing often show very little interest in the ecumenical thrust. Great strides have been made toward greater understanding, and the unkind and wounding words of yesteryear are being increasingly seen in the context of competing polemic, now for the most part a thing of the past. All sorts of common statements have emerged and concordats been agreed upon. This momentum is unlikely to slacken for the movement is commonly seen as bringing together the broken body of Christ, and so fulfilling the words of Jesus found in Chapter 17 of John's Gospel, where he prayed "that they may be one even as we are one . . . so that the world may know that thou hast sent me . . ." That is the Christian hope; that is the Christian vision.

7   So far in this section we have looked only at the internal housekeeping of what some Christians call the Household of God. But in an ever-shrinking world the other households of Faith which can be found along the religious street in our "global village" can no longer be ignored, and good neighborliness is the order of the day. The third millennium will bring increasingly to the fore Christianity's relationship with other faiths. There will continue to be fear and suspicion, from which will emerge conflict and rivalry, but increasingly there will be learning and discussion, from which will emerge a degree of understanding and convergence.

Two questions in particular arise in the Christian mind when it considers other world faiths; they concern revelation and salvation. How is the inner core of belief and practice in other faiths related to the inner core of Christian belief and practice which Christians will say is the outcome of the special revelation to which the Christian Bible is witness? This is the easier question. Christians can easily envisage God making himself known in other times and in other places. Further, they can appreciate that this must be appropriated and shared through the medium of the dominant culture with its particular questions and interests, all of which can account, at least in part, for the differences, or most of them, in these inner cores. But the second question, concerning salvation, is the more intractable. Christians are likely to hold to the uniqueness of their experience of liberation and renewal, so that they will find it difficult to envisage anything similar elsewhere. A fruitful avenue, along which faiths have begun to travel, is that of the spirituality and sanctity of life, for it is well nigh impossible to undervalue peace and goodness, and their source.

The major, and some would say the only, difficulty in this area is that which lies at the center of all Christian thinking, namely Christ. It tends to skew from the very start all interfaith conversations. Christians seem to start from a position that proclaims that their faith is by definition superior to all others, because God himself in the incarnate Christ delivered the revelation and secured the salvation. Of course other faiths make similar claims and so the religious and non-religious alike are left to try to decide which claims to believe, if in fact they can be compared, and in the absence of clear direction to this question, there remains only the imperative to love others and remain open to growth and humble in the face of truth wherever they find it.

12 As a final task you might like to reflect on what form Christian mission   **Exercises**
    might take in the third millennium, in the age of Interfaith.
13 What might Christianity have to learn from other faiths? What can it share
    with them?

GLOSSARY

Ad fontes A Latin phrase, referring to the act of going back to the beginning or the fountainhead.

Apologetics The work that an apologist does.

Apologist One who seeks to show the reasonableness of Christianity.

Christology The understanding of the person and work of Christ.

Ecclesiology Views about the nature and function of the Church, from a Greek word meaning "church."

Ecumenism The process of bringing together the various churches of Christianity, often called the **Ecumenical Movement**.

Enlightenment The name applied to the period, beginning in the eighteenth century, in which reason became the principal way of solving the questions of human living.

Heresy A belief which is viewed as wrong and dangerous from an orthodox position.

Indulgences The promise, by ecclesiastical authority, that the punishments for sin would be lessened through good works and, increasingly, the giving of money to the church.

Laicization The process whereby the laity, a word which now refers to the non-clerical bit of Christianity, is increasingly being brought into the official thinking and action of the churches.

Magisterium The teaching office of the Church, which in the Roman Catholic Church is the supreme arbiter on matters of faith and morals.

Messiah A Hebrew word meaning the "anointed one" (of God), which became, in Greek, Christos, from which comes the English Christ.

Original sin The belief that all human life has a basic defect which inevitably results in corruption and sin. Some Christians see this as the result of the Fall (Genesis 3).

Orthodox The correct way of believing and practicing Christianity. The incorrect is labeled heretical, or a heresy.

Parousia A Greek word which has become the technical word for the return, or "coming again," of Christ.

Renaissance The term, meaning "rebirth," applied to the cultural revival in the fifteenth century which was triggered by the rediscovery of Graeco-Roman civilization.

Sacraments A visible sign or action accompanying the reception of a spiritual grace to which the sign points.

Soteriology From a Greek word meaning "salvation." It stands for the understanding of how what Christians call salvation is related to Jesus Christ.

Theotokos A Greek term meaning "bearer of God" which is applied to Mary, the mother of Jesus.

Utilitarianism The ethical position that judges an action by the amount of pleasure and well-being it produces, or pain and discomfort it diminishes.

Chapter 15

Islam

VICTORIA LA'PORTE

The Life of the Prophet Muhammad

The Sunni\Shia Split

Sufism

Worldviews

The Philosophical Tradition

The Prophets and the Message of Jesus

The Significance of the Prophet Muhammad

Life after Death

Institutions and Rituals

The Role of Women

Modern Expressions

The purpose of this chapter is to offer an introduction to the main beliefs and practices of the Islamic faith. The account is fairly selective but does examine the basics
of the faith as well as focus on more controversial issues such as the status of women
in Islam and *The Satanic Verses* controversy.

Many Muslims believe that the Islamic faith distinguishes itself in its appealing
straightforwardness. Its belief system is, for the most part, rational and intelligible.
Islam offers its believers certainty and this could be one of the reasons why it is
one of the fastest growing religions in the world. However, this is not to suggest
that certain aspects of belief are not open to interpretation. It is quite wrong to
treat the Muslim community as a totally homogeneous entity. Although there is
general agreement among Muslims concerning, for example, the oneness of God,
the authority of the Qur'an, and the prophethood of Muhammad, we shall see that

All quotations from the Qur'an are taken from A. J. Arberry's translation published by World's Classics,
Oxford, 1982.

A Muslim man prays inside the Zamboanga Mosque in the Philippines.
Photo: Corbis/Dave Bartruff

as regards more ambiguous issues such as the role of women within Islam there are a variety of different interpretations.

Islam has been given a fairly bad press by the western media. Events in Iran, Iraq, and Afghanistan, for example, color western perceptions of Islam but it is vital to remember that the real Islam is comprised of its sources. Beliefs and practices that do not derive from these sources (Qur'an and *Sunnah*) cannot be given any real credence within the religion itself; however, Islam, like all religions, is subject to misuse.

This chapter will begin with an historical overview of the life of Muhammad and the beginnings of the Islamic religion. Muhammad is the highly revered Prophet of Islam whose revelations from Allah comprise the Muslim Holy Book, the Qur'an.

The Life of the Prophet Muhammad

Recent historians have challenged the idea that Islam began violently. The belief that Muhammad spread his message by aggressive means is far from universally accepted. Increasingly, historians have become more sensitive to the fact that Muhammad was the initial victim rather than perpetrator of persecution.

Muslims are able to appeal to the Qur'an for some details concerning the life of the Prophet. However, although the Qur'an is clear on the status and authority of the Prophet it is less informative concerning the events of the life of Muhammad. The main source for the life of Muhammad is contained in the second most important source for Muslims (as its authority never precedes that of the Qur'an), the **hadith** material. The hadith material consists of the sayings and traditions of the Prophet collected by Islamic historians such as Ibn Ishaq (704–67 CE), al-Bukhari (810–70 CE), Muslim b. al-Hajjaj (817–75 CE), al-Tabari (839–923 CE) among many others.

The hadith material basically records the sayings and actions of the Prophet Muhammad, transmitted by Muslims throughout the ages. Not all hadith are accepted as historical, and Muslims have devised an historical tool for deciphering which hadiths are genuine and which are not. This tool revolves around whether or not a chain of authority (Ar. (Arabic) **Isnad**)[1] can be traced back to Muhammad himself or one of his close followers and whether the transmitters involved are reliable. An example of hadith material is as follows (note the list of sources at the beginning of the hadith):

> Al-Harith b. Muhammad – Muhammad b. Sa'd – Muhammad b. 'Umar – 'Ali b. Muhammad b. 'Ubaydallah b. 'Abdallah b. 'Umar b. al-Khattab – Mansur b. 'Abd al-Rahman – his mother Barrah bt. Abi Tajrah: When God willed that Muhammad should be ennobled and should enter upon prophethood, it came about that whenever he went out to attend his business he would go a great distance, out of sight of houses, and into the ravines and wadi-beds, and then every stone and tree he passed would say, "Peace be upon you, Messenger of God." He would turn to the right and the left and turn around but could not see anyone.[2]

This particular hadith can be found in al-Tabari's account of Muhammad's life at Mecca. However, al-Tabari is not considered by Muslims as one of the most reliable sources for Muhammad's life as Tabari is known to have just collected material regarding Muhammad without critical judgment as regards its authenticity. There are, however, six main collectors of genuine hadith reports, and these are as follows; al-Bukhari (d. 870) (who separated the reliable from the unreliable), his pupil Muslim ibn al-Hajjaj (d. 875), Ibn Maja (d. 887), Abu Da'ud (d. 889), al-Tirmidhi (d. 892) and al-Nasa'i (d. 915).

As well as hadith material, biographies are also an important source for the life of the Prophet. These range from the earlier biographies such as Essad Bey's *Muhammad*, to much more recent biographies such as Abdula Pasha's *Sixth Century and Beyond*.

Again, these biographies vary greatly in content, scope, and reliability, though there
are common elements such as the status and authority of the Prophet Muhammad.
For example, if we look at the two aforementioned biographies we find that both
talk with much reverence of the characteristics of Muhammad (who, although not
a divine figure, was as near perfect as any man could be). Essad Bey writes:

> His was the straight and narrow path and none could find the slightest fault with
> him.[3]

Pasha writes:

> Although rich, he was never extravagant. Equally however, he was not mean. He
> lived a simple life showing generosity to the poor and orphans in the community and
> distributed his wealth amongst the poor. In times of famine, he was the first to offer
> organised help. He had a great sense of humour and would smile, and occasionally
> laugh.[4]

It is very difficult to reconstruct the life of Muhammad without running into
questions of historicity. However, the following brief overview attempts to offer a
simplified picture of the main events in the life of the Prophet.[5]

Muhammad was born around 570 CE into the clan of Hashim who were members of the tribe of **Qur'aysh**. He was born in Mecca, which was at that time
pagan as was the tribe of Qur'aysh. Muhammad's father died fairly early on in his
life and when his mother died when he was still a child, his grandfather cared
for him. Afterwards, he went to live with his uncle Abu Talib and his family.
Muhammad's mission started when he was forty years old (610 CE) when he began
to receive revelations from the angel Gabriel. The angel would visit the Prophet
on a mountain known as Mount Hira. The revelations from Allah through the angel
Gabriel, according to Muslims, make up the contents of the Qur'an.

According to certain traditions, Muhammad found these experiences deeply disturbing and had to be reassured by his first wife Khadijja that the revelations he
received were genuinely from Allah. Muhammad spent another fifteen years in Mecca
where his revelations continued. The **Isra'** (or night journey) of the Prophet
Muhammad is believed to have taken place in the tenth year of the Prophet's
mission. It is believed that during this time the Prophet ascended into the seven
heavens after being transported to Jerusalem from Mecca by the winged horse **al-
Buraq**. It was as a consequence of this journey that Muhammad instituted the five
daily prayers required by all Muslims to enact.

According to sources, Muhammad made a number of followers among the Meccans.
Muhammad's main message, the central message of Islam, was one of **monotheism**. The polytheistic tribes in Mecca became increasingly more hostile to
Muhammad and his followers, owing to the direct challenge his message made to
their gods and goddesses. According to Michael Cook, in his book *Muhammad*,[6] it
is worth remembering that at that time Mecca was a stateless society. In other words
there existed no central authority, and tribal strife inevitably led to the possibility

of civil war. As a consequence, Muhammad and his followers were especially vul-nerable to persecution as there was no central body to protect them.

It was north of Mecca that Muhammad found some relief from the hostility there, and this was among the Jewish clans in Yathrib, now called Medina. After negoti-ating with members of the tribe of Khazraj in Yathrib, Muhammad and his fol-lowers were invited to settle there peacefully. According to Cook, Yathrib also lacked a central authority and was torn by civil strife, so the unifying of the people of Yathrib in pursuit of Muhammad's cause was seen as beneficial. Muhammad then sent his followers from Mecca to Medina and later emigrated himself. This emigration took place in 622 CE and marks the beginning of the Islamic calendar.

However, Muhammad still wanted to convert the inhabitants of his homeland, which resulted in a series of confrontations with the Meccans until 624 CE when Muhammad and his followers won a decisive victory over the Meccans at **Badr** (southwest of Medina). In 625 Muhammad suffered a horrendous defeat at the hands of the Meccans at the Battle of Uhud (a hill to the west of Medina). However, circumstances altered in favor of Muhammad, and Mecca peacefully surrendered to Muhammad in 630.

After Muhammad's death in 632 there occurred the problem as to who would take over leadership of the Muslim community, which was now a significant group covering practically all of central and western Arabia. Leadership was taken over by a number of Caliphs, the first being Abu Bakr (573–634 CE), followed by 'Umar (d. 644), 'Uthman (d. 656) and 'Ali (d. 661). Under the Caliphate, Muslim control continued to expand. Muslims took over a large area of the Middle East including Egypt, Palestine, Syria, Mesopotamia, Iran, Damascus, Jerusalem, Cairo, Alexandria, and Isfahan. After the death of 'Ali, the fourth Caliph, the Muslim community split into **Shias** and **Sunnis**. From the Sunni community, who make up the majority of Muslims, there emerged the two glorious dynasties of the Ummayads (661–750) and the 'Abbasids (750–1258).

The Sunni/Shia Split

The Muslim community split over successorship. Shias (or Shi'ites)[7] believe that 'Ali should have been the first Caliph and thus they reject the first three Caliphs – Abu Bakr, 'Umar and 'Uthman. This is because 'Ali is related to the prophet as his cousin (and son-in-law). Shias point out numerous *hadiths* where Muhammad actually named 'Ali as his successor. A decisive moment in Shi'ite history occurred at the Battle at Karbala in 680 CE where the son of 'Ali, Husayn, was killed by Caliph Yazid.

Before we look at the deeper significance of the split it may be useful to briefly list some of the main differences between the two communities regarding sources and practices:

1   Differences emerge between the sunni and shia communities concerning the tombs of the saints. Sunnis reject the practice of revering saints; regarding these

practices as un-Islamic. According to Ahmed these differences reflect deeper theological differences:

> For Sunnis, God and human beings have a direct relationship; saints and scholars cannot be intermediaries to God but are only formal interpreters of religion. Belief in shrines and saints was often viewed by the Sunni orthodox as heretical and even dangerous deviation form the true and singular worship of God (*bida*).[8]

However, according to Shi'ite beliefs intermediaries between man and God are vital for salvation.

2   As regards sources the Sunnis take the **Qur'an** literally; whereas Shias believe that there is a hidden meaning within the text given by the Prophet Muhammad to 'Ali.

3   Sunnis use four sources from which to derive matters of law or a code of conduct (Ar. **Shariah**). These are the Qur'an, *Sunnah* (specific actions and sayings of the Prophet), *qiyas* (analogical reasoning), and finally **ijma** (consensus of the community). Four major schools of interpretation (Ar. *fiqh*) emerged in Sunni Islam, named after its founders. These are as follows:

> Hanafite – named after Imam Abu Hanifa (d. 767)
> Hanbalite – Imam Ahmad ibn Hanbal (d. 855)
> Malikite – Imam Malik (d. 795)
> Shafi'ite – Imam Shaf'i (d. 820)

Shias, on the other hand, have their own system of law and differ legally over inheritance and marriage. The Ithna 'Ashari (the main branch of Shi'ism – see below) allows temporary marriage (*mut'a*), prohibited in Sunni Islam. As far as hadith material is concerned, Shi'ites give special emphasis to hadith material affirming the authority and status of 'Ali.

One of the most significant differences between the two communities, which carries with it far-reaching political consequences for the Shi'ite community, revolves around the concept of the Imamate. It may be helpful here to illustrate this concept in reference to the events that occurred in Iran in 1978–9.

As mentioned above, Shi'ite Muslims believe that 'Ali should have been the first Caliph as he was related to the Prophet Muhammad. According to Shi'ites, God would not have left the Muslim community without a spiritual or religious leader after the death of Muhammad. The Sunni community elects Caliphs, who are political rather than religious figures within the Muslim community. The Shias call the leaders of their community Imams (for the Sunni community the term Imam only denotes the leader of the Mosque) and they are invested with religious as well as political authority. They are allowed to perform **itjihad**, which basically means that they are allowed to make independent legal decisions according to their interpretation of sources. The main branch of Shi'ite Islam is known as the Ithna 'Ashari

and this is the state religion of Iran (the majority of Shi'ites populate Iran and southern Iraq). The **Ithna 'Ashari** became the state religion in Iran in 1501 and was
imposed by the Safavid Dynasty (1501–1732). By the eighteenth century, roughly
85 percent of the population in Iran was Ithna 'Ashari. The Ithna 'Ashari belief
system centers on the existence of twelve principal Imams, the descendants of 'Ali,
all of whom have supreme religious authority. These are as follows;

'Ali abi Talib, d. 661
Hasan, 'Ali's son, d. 669
Husayn, 'Ali's second son, d. 680
Zayn al-'Abidin, Husayn's son, d. 712 or 713
Muhammad al-Baqir, Zayn's son, d. 735
Ja'far al-Sadiq, Muhammad's son, d. 765
Musa al-Kazim, Ja'far's son, d. 799
'Ali al-Hadi, Musa's son, d. 818
Muhammad al-Taqi al-Jawad, 'Ali's son, d. 835
Hasan al-'Askari, 'Ali's son, d. 868
Hasan al-'Askari, 'Ali's son, d. 873 or 874
Muhammad al Mahdi, Hasan's son, born 868[9]

The Ithna 'Ashari believe that the twelfth Imam did not die but instead remained
hidden (he is the hidden infallible **Mahdi**) and when he reveals himself it will be
to create a more just society. In this sense the Ithna 'Ashari is a millenarian movement. In the absence of the *Mahdi*, religious authority is given to learned scholars
(called **Mujtahids**) such as Imam Khomeini (given the title "Ayatollah" as a sign of
respect).

The factors that led to the revolution in Iran are both numerous and complex.
They revolve around not only religious ideals but also socio-economic factors.
The revolution was influenced greatly by the Imam Ruhollah al-Musavi Khomeini
(1902–89) who was very critical of the current leadership of the country at the
time. Basically, at that time Iran was ruled by a series of dynasties – the Safavids,
the Qajars (1721–1924), and the Pahlavis (1924–79).

During the rule of the Pahlavis, particularly Shah Mohammed Pahlavi, a large
proportion of Iranians grew discontented. Shah Pahlavi wanted to rule a progressive
state in Iran and as a result introduced anti-Islamic measures while infiltrating Iran
with western ideas. He was backed first by Britain and then by the United States.
Imam Khomeini rejected what he believed to be the "Westoxification" apparent
during Pahlavi's rule and subsequently fought the Shah and his regime. The
Ayatollah was immensely popular and revered by the Iranians. He was regarded as
a martyr who was willing to die for the cause of Islam, much in the same way as
Husayn died at the Battle at Karbala in 680. This is where Shi'ite history played
a significant role. Khomeini was identified with Imam Husayn and the Shah
identified with Caliph Yazid who defeated and killed Husayn at Karbala. Martyrdom has always been of central importance to the whole Shi'ite framework of

beliefs and during the revolution this was no exception. 'Ali Shari'ati (d. 1977), a leading pro-revolutionary thinker, gave two famous speeches in Tehran between 1972 and 1975 in which he refers to Karbala and martyrdom. According to Shari'ati, martyrdom

> is not the sad death of a hero on the battlefield; it means that you are there, an observer, a witness, an informed informer and lastly, a model. Naturally, it means also death, but not the death an enemy inflicts on a warrior. It is a strong-willed death, consciously sought so as to bear witness in the absence of being able to conquer . . .[10]

The revolution was so successful that the Shah was forced to abdicate in January 1979 and leave the country.

Sufism

Sufism is another important strand in Islam. It is incorrect, however, to regard Sufism as a distinct strand from within Islam, as Sufism is incorporated within the beliefs of many Sunni Muslims. Sufis also traditionally do not regard themselves as a *sect* within Islam. Sufism basically emphasizes the inner elements of the faith, rather than the outward practices.

The main aims of Sufism involve, first, a commitment to search for a spiritual life and in so doing become closer to God (thus Sufism has sometimes been interpreted as mysticism), and secondly, the abandoning of worldly materialism and wealth. Sufis reacted against what they perceived to be a legalistic interpretation of the faith by Muslims, and much conflict existed between orthodox Muslims and Sufis. Orthodox Muslims objected to what they believed were the blasphemous elements (Ar. *Shirk*) within Sufism such as Sufic claims that their souls had merged with God. Furthermore, their form of worship was frowned upon as they used traditionally un-Islamic practices such as music and dancing in order to bring about their transcendental experiences.

The most successful period for Sufism is usually regarded as the thirteenth century when Jala ud-din Rumi of Qonya (1207–73) founded the order of the whirling dervishes, where Sufis danced in spiral circles in order to induce ecstasy and closeness to God, as the movement, they believed, replicated the movement of the heavenly spheres.

Worldviews

The Qur'an

Islam is a relatively straightforward religion in regards to its Holy Scriptures. The Qur'an was revealed to Muhammad over a period of 23 years. Thus it was revealed to one man over a relatively short period of time (unlike the Bible which took centuries to complete and was composed by numerous authors). The Qur'an, it is believed by Muslims, is the literal word of God. The scriptures are not merely inspired but revealed by Allah to the Prophet Muhammad.

The Qur'an comprises 114 chapters (Ar. *Suras*) that are arranged in order of length, thus the final order is not believed to be chronological and accordingly does not originate from Muhammad himself. However, it is important to remember that the Qur'an is not an academic text and thus to apply to it the rigors of academic scholarship is inappropriate. Instead, the document is believed to be the words of Allah to humankind.[11] It is believed that the contents were written on palm leaves or flat stone, and remembered by Muslims and later compiled during the time of the third Caliph, 'Uthman, who commissioned a number of scholars to assemble together the contents of the Qur'an.

Each sura contains the heading "*Bismallah ar-Rahman ar-Rahim*," which translated from Arabic means "In the name of Allah, the Beneficent, the Merciful." The Qur'an is rich with theology. The uniqueness and sovereignty of God forms one of the central messages (see Sura 6.95–104). God has full control over the events in his creation (see Sura 3.191; 30.10). Humankind is entrusted to His providential care. God has a purpose for His creation; though it is left to human beings to exercise their free will in accordance to God's will as determined in the Qur'an (see Sura 3.86). The Qur'an is thus primarily a book of guidance, guiding humankind toward the fruits of salvation. If one looks at Sura 17, Muslims are instructed to always be respectful and kind to parents, to give to the needy, care for orphans, and never squander. Muslims are forbidden to kill their children for fear of poverty, and fornication is strictly prohibited (see also Sura 4.40f). Fundamentally, the Qur'an instructs Muslims to follow the straight path:

> Surely this Koran guides to the way that is straightest
> and gives good tidings to the believers
> who do deeds of righteousness, that theirs
> shall be a great wage,
> and that those who do not believe in the
> world to come — we have prepared for them
> a painful chastisement.
>
> (Sura 17.10)

As well as the emphasis on God's uniqueness and sovereignty there are numerous references pointing to the mercy and compassion of Allah,[12] who forgives those who truly repent. For example, Sura 11.90f:

> O my people, let not the breach with me
> move you, so that there smite you the like
> of what smote the people of Noah, or
> the people of Hood, or the people of
> Salih; and the people of Lot are not
> far away from you.
> And ask forgiveness of your Lord, then
> repent to Him; surely my Lord is
> All-Compassionate, All-Loving.

Allah is the Creator and the Qur'an affirms the Genesis account that the world was created in six days (see Sura 32.4; 41.9f). The Qur'an also talks about *Iblis* (the Qur'anic name for the archangel Lucifer). In the Qur'anic account (see Sura 7.10f) God commands the angels to bow down to his creation – Adam. The angels obey with one exception only, **Iblis:**

> We have established you in the earth
> and there appointed for you livelihood;
> little thanks you show.
> We created you, then We shaped you,
> then We said to the angels: "Bow yourselves
> to Adam"; so they bowed themselves,
> save Iblis – he was not of those
> that bowed themselves.
> Said He, "What prevented thee to
> bow thyself, when I commanded thee?"
> Said he, "I am better than he; Thou
> createdst me of fire, and him Thou
> createdst of clay."
> Said He, "Get thee down out of it;
> it is not for thee to wax proud here,
> so go thou forth; surely thou art
> among the humbled."

The Qur'an also talks about *jinn*. It seems that *jinn* have the capacity to perform both good and evil and are depicted as mischievous beings that appear on occasion alongside "men":

> Say: "If men and jinn banded together
> to produce the life of this Koran,
> they would never produce its like,
> not though they backed one another.
> (Sura 17.90)

The Philosophical Tradition

Philosophical explorations by Muslims seem to have begun fairly early (seventh century CE). John of Damascus (a Christian theologian and hymn writer of the eastern Church) debated with the "Saracens" concerning the meaning of attributes such as "word" and "spirit" given to Jesus in the Qur'an. Philosophical issues such as the origin and problem of evil were discussed along with the conflict between God's divine will and human freedom. For example, if God commands a person to murder someone else, should not the murderer be praised for obeying God's command?[13]

However, it was during the reign of Caliph Mamun in Baghdad, in the early ninth century, that scholars were instructed to translate major Greek philosophical works, such as those of Plato and Aristotle, into Arabic. William Montgomery Watt suggests that the reason behind Muslim interest in Greek philosophy lay mainly in the practical desire of the Caliphs, who were concerned with improving the health of themselves and others and believed that the "practitioner of Greek medical science"[14] could help them. Also, according to Watt, it is important to keep in mind the importance of logical method among Muslim thinkers, which began, as stated earlier, as early as the seventh century CE.

Philosophical questions directly affected Muslim theology in three specific areas: (1) the nature of God, (2) the nature of the Qur'an, and (3) man's relation to God. The school of thought that grappled with these theological issues was called the Mu'tazila. This school did not form a distinct strand within Islam; rather it encompassed a diverse number of scholars who disagreed with some issues whilst agreeing on others. Generally all agreed upon, first, the doctrine of a created Qur'an. The Mu'tazila denied that the Qur'an was eternal and uncreated as this challenged the uniqueness of God, implying that the Qur'an was another God. Secondly, the oneness of God: according to the Mu'tazila, God had no essential or eternal qualities with the exception of eternity. If God was attributed all the qualities allocated to Him in the Qur'an, this would imply division and plurality within the Godhead. They also rejected any anthropomorphic (human-like) qualities given to Allah in the Qur'an where it speaks of, for example, God's hands and eyes. According to the Mu'tazila, God is infinite and could not be restricted to one particular place and one particular time. As a consequence, they denied the belief of orthodox Muslims that the faithful would be rewarded in heaven by actually seeing Allah.

Finally, the Mu'tazila found difficulties in the belief that God willed evil to be committed by some humans and then punished them in hell as a consequence of their evil. The Qur'an is ambiguous on this point. In some places freedom of action is emphasized (see Sura 16.104), and at other places human freedom is restricted in passages which seem to imply predestination (see Sura 76.29f). According to the Mu'tazila, predestination must be rejected in favor of human freedom as the former implies a harsh and unjust God.

Orthodox responses to the philosophical conclusions of the Mu'tazila were not favorable. Orthodoxy accused the scholars of subordinating the power of God who could do as he willed even if the consequences for humans were less than beneficial. Secondly, if humans have freedom over their actions then humans become God, as God is the creator of all actions. This of course is unacceptable.

Hostility and distrust of philosophy has had a long history among Muslims. This dislike became very much explicit in the work of al-Ghazali (d. 505) who attacked philosophers in his book entitled *Tahafut al-Falasifa* (*The Incoherence of the Philosophers*). Al-Ghazali criticized many philosophical ideas such as the wide-spread belief that the world had no beginning. The response came from Averroes (Ibn Rushd, d. 1198) in Spain, who in his book *The Incoherence of the Incoherence* deals with Ghazali's points one by one and offers decisive answers to each. However, al-Ghazali remains one of the greatest theologians within the Islamic tradition, having made an enormous contribution to Islamic theology that lessened with his conversion to Sufism.[15]

The Prophets and the Message of Jesus

The prophets mentioned in the Qur'an number twenty-nine including Muhammad. A prophet is anyone who is commissioned by God to convey His messages to humankind. The majority of prophets in the Qur'an are also figures delineated in the Bible (however, there are exceptions). The main message of these prophets is that of monotheism. Many of the stories connected to these biblical prophets closely follow that in the Bible; for example, Adam is the first man created; Noah is the builder of the Ark, which saved him from the flood and God's retribution. Abraham, Moses, David, and Jesus are also mentioned among others; their main task being to convince the people of Allah's message. Because of the close correlation between the Bible and the Qur'an, Muslims were accused of deliberately contriving a document by plagiarizing the Bible and adding some unique material of their own. However, it is worth keeping in mind the opinion of one Muslim, who maintains that:

> Many committed Christian (and a few Jewish) writers assert, with a dramatic dogmatism as offensive as unfounded, that Muhammad selectively appropriated biblical ideas into the Koran and simultaneously enriched his version with a few curiously original incidents. . . . The Koran, it should be noted, explicitly claims to be the final and definitive edition of revealed scripture incorporating the truths of the Jewish and Christian dispensation.[16]

Muhammad was sent as the final prophet and is described as the "seal of the Prophets" (Sura 33.40). Muhammad's mission was to correct earlier distortions caused by the deliberate misreading and interpretations of the messages of previous prophets; particularly Moses and Jesus. The Qur'an was revealed to correct the mistakes of Jews and Christians.[17]

According to the Qur'an, Christians have elevated the status of Jesus to a patently blasphemous level. In considering Jesus to be the Son of God, the second *person* of the co-equal Trinity, Christians have committed *shirk* (blasphemy) by casting doubt on the oneness of God (*tawhid*). The Qur'an also denotes further difficulties with the belief in the divine incarnation.[18] First, the irrationality of the concept; how could one possibly believe that Allah became a human being or that Allah himself conceived a son. Secondly, the concept poses doubt concerning the omnipotence of God; for Allah could never be born, or exist as a helpless baby (Sura 15.20). Thirdly, in line with certain New Testament scholarship, Jesus' self-understanding precluded any sense of divinity in that he never claimed explicitly to be God and furthermore did not demand that people worship him. Rather, he emphasized his subordination to God. While it is true that Jesus performed miracles, it is also apparent that other prophets have performed similar miracles, such as Elisha who fed one hundred people with twenty barley loaves and a few ears of corn (II Kings 4: 44). It is also true that, in the Bible, Jesus is referred to as the Son of God. However, again this title is not exclusive to Jesus and is used in reference to other prophets, such as David in the Psalm 2: 7:

> I will declare the decree the Lord hath said unto me (David), Thou art my son; this day have I begotten thee.

Muslims therefore understand the term to be metaphorical rather than literal as it denotes anyone beloved of God.

As there is no scriptural support, according to Muslims, for the sonship of Jesus, there is likewise no support for belief in the Trinity. As previously stated, the concept of the Trinity challenges the Islamic notion of *tawhid* (oneness of God), a concept which, Muslims point out, is repeatedly emphasized in both the Old and New Testaments (for example, Deut. 4: 39; Isa. 43: 10–11; Isa. 44: 6; Exodus 8: 10; 2 Samuel 7: 22; 1 Kings 8: 23; Mark 12: 29; 1 Cor 8: 4; 1 Tim. 2: 5).[19] Furthermore, there is no biblical basis for this concept and it was never mentioned or taught by Jesus.

The virgin birth is accepted by the Qur'an. An account of the virginal conception and birth of Jesus is given in Sura 19.16–34 where it is written:

> And mention in the Book Mary
> when she withdrew from her people
> to an eastern place,
> and she took a veil apart from them;
> then we sent into her Our Spirit
> that presented himself to her
> a man without fault.
> She Said, "I take refuge in
> The All-merciful from thee."
> "If thou fearest God . . ."
> He said, "I am but a messenger
> Come from thy Lord, to give thee
> A boy most pure."
> She said, "How shall I have a son
> Whom no mortal has touched, neither
> Have I been unchaste . . ."
> So she conceived him, and withdrew with him
> to a distant place.

However, the doctrine of atonement (that is, the belief that Jesus died to save the sins of humankind) has no place within Islam, where it is firmly believed that humans must accept full responsibility for their actions. Furthermore, the crucifixion of Jesus is firmly rejected by the Qur'an; the main reason revolving around the unlikelihood that a prophet of Allah would be left to die in this way. Instead, similar to Docetic belief, it is believed that a likeness of Jesus was crucified. According to mainstream Islamic belief Jesus ascended into heaven. The Ahmadiyya community (a branch of Islam rejected by both Sunnis and Shias), however, purport that Jesus departed to India to continue preaching his message and it is in India where Jesus died of natural causes and is buried.

For Muslims, then, Jesus is a human being who demands both respect and status as a prophet of Allah. The exact position of Jesus is clearly depicted in the words he utters as a baby in his cradle:

> Lo, I am God's servant;
> God has given me the Book, and
> made me a Prophet.
> Blessed He has made me, wherever
> I may be; and he has enjoined me
> to pray, and to give the alms, so
> long as I live,
> and likewise to cherish my mother;
> He has not made me arrogant,
> unprosperous.
> Peace be upon me, the day I was born
> and the day I die, and the day I am
> raised up alive!
> That is Jesus son of Mary
> in word of truth, concerning which
> they are doubting.
>   (Surah 19.31–35)

Muhammad is the final prophet commissioned by Allah to correct the mistaken interpretations of the messages of the former prophets. Love and acceptance of the Prophet Muhammad is common to all the different schools of thought within Islam and it is to his significance within Islam that we turn next.

The Significance of the Prophet Muhammad

At the beginning of the last section we looked briefly at some of the main events in the life of the Prophet Muhammad. Now we turn to look at the role of the Prophet in Islam.

All Muslim believers share love and respect for the Prophet. The Prophet's life sets an example for Muslims to emulate. Even when writing about Muhammad, Muslims treat him with reverence adding the words *salla Allahu alayhi wasallam* (peace be upon him). Many Muslims copy the Prophet's idiosyncrasies and social behavior, this is known in Islam as **Sunnah**. The *Sunnah* (or sunna) denotes the actions and sayings of the Prophet derived from the hadith material.

To illustrate the central position that the Prophet fulfills in Muslim life, Malise Ruthven in his book entitled *A Satanic Affair* draws on the writings of the medieval Islamic theologian al-Ghazali (1058–1111) in his work *Ihya uhum al din* (*Revival of the Religious Sciences*). This extended quotation captures Islamic reverence for their Prophet,

> Know that the key to happiness is to follow the sunna (path) and to imitate the Messenger of God in all his coming and going, his movement and rest, in his way of eating, his attitude, his sleep and his talk. I do not mean this just in regard to religious observance. For there is no reason to neglect the traditions which were concerned with this aspect. I rather mean all the problems of custom and usage; for only by following them unrestricted succession is possible. God has said: Say: "If you love God, follow me, and God will love you" (Sura 3. 9), and He has said: "What the messenger has brought – accept it, and what he has prohibited, refrain from it!" (Sura 59.7). That means you have to sit while putting on trousers, and to stand when winding a turban, and to begin with the right foot when putting on shoes. . . ."[20]

Life after Death

Both the Qur'anic and hadith literature are rich with theology concerning judgment day and the destinations after death. In the Islamic scheme of things every single person will be dealt with equitably on the day of judgment. All good deeds and bad deeds will be weighed up precisely in order to determine a person's fate.

In order to build up the picture of life after death in Islam it is necessary to begin with the tradition concerning the interim period between the grave and judgment day. According to al-Ghazali,[21] everyone dies at his or her appointed time. After the deceased person has been buried in his or her grave, according to tradition, two angels by the name of **Munkar** and **Nakur** begin questioning the dead person concerning their faith. This aspect is vividly described in Imam 'Abd ar-Rahim ibn Ahmad Qadi's collection of hadith concerning the afterlife where it is written that:

> when the dead man is placed in the grave, two black angels with green eyes whose voices are like thunder and whose glances are like quick lightning and whose fangs burn the earth, come to him before his head.[22]

The angels ask him or her the question – "What do you say in respect to Muhammad, peace be upon him?" If the person responds correctly – "Muhammad is His (Allah's) Messenger" – then he will rest in peace until the day of judgment. However, if the wrong reply is given, certain hadiths suggest that the person will be punished by the angels either physically (by being beaten with sticks) or mentally (by showing him or her the torture that awaits them) until the day of judgment.[23] It is worth pointing out that the intermediate period between death and the day of judgment, that is, the period in the grave, is not described explicitly in the Qur'an; only in the hadith material.

It is not entirely clear as to the specific identity of the two questioning angels. However, the hadith material does talk about two angels that accompany a man throughout his life. A person has one angel on his right who makes note of the right actions of the person, and one angel on the left who inscribes the wrong actions. In the Imam's collection of hadiths concerning the afterlife, it is written:

> If he sits down, one is on his right and the other on his left. If he walks, one is behind him and the other in front of him. If he sleeps, one is at the head and the other at his feet.[24]

According to the Imam, the Prophet has said:

> The companion of the right is the trustee over the companion of the left. When the slave does a wrong action, and the companion of the left wishes to write it down, the companion of the right says: "Wait!" And he waits seven hours. If the slave asks pardon of Allah, he does not write it down. If he does not ask pardon of Allah, the companion of the left writes one wrong action . . .[25]

In the Qur'an it is also stated that a person has two accompanying angels:

> He has attendant angels, before him and behind him. (13.11)

The day of Judgment (sometimes just referred to as "day") in the Qur'an is colorfully described in the Qur'an and hadith. According to the Imam's collection of hadith, it is written that on the day:

> The Trumpet will be blown, and its tremor will reach the people of the heavens and earth except whomever Allah wills. The mountains will melt and the sky will sway and the earth will shake greatly like a ship in the water. Pregnant women will drop their burdens, nursing mothers will forget their suckling children, young children will become grey-haired and the *shayatin* will be confused. The stars will be scattered and the sun eclipsed and the heavens removed above them. People will be neglectful from all this, and that is His Word, may He be exalted.[26]

In the Qur'an too a trumpet will herald the beginnings of judgment day (Sura 23.104) when the earth shall shine with light (Sura 39.65–70), the heavens will split open (Sura 82.15), the stars will scatter, and the tombs will be overthrown. The dead will then emerge from their tombs. Sura 54.7 reads:

> Upon the day when the Caller shall call into a horrible thing,
> abasing their eyes, they shall come forth from the tombs as if they were scattered grasshoppers,
> running with outstretched necks to the Caller. The unbelievers
> shall say, "This is a hard day!"

Events pertaining to the last days are vividly described by al-Ghazali, who draws on both hadith material and the Qur'an. Al-Ghazali talks about a messianic figure, sometimes equated with Jesus, who defeats the one eyed anti-Christ Dajjal and Gog and Magog "the enemies of peace and justice." Waines in *An Introduction to Islam*, using hadiths from Al-Ash'ari (873–935 CE), talks about the Prophet's description of the day of judgment whereby twelve different classes of people will be gathered together according to their sin:

> Usurers, for example, will emerge from their graves as dogs; those who incited discord among people will emerge as monkeys; those who pursued passion and pleasure will be gathered bound hand and foot with their own hair. Each group is identified with those who committed an offence cited in scripture, from stealing the property of orphans to disobeying one's parents, but who did not repent of their actions. The warning to the living is evident.[27]

According to the Imam's collection of hadith (*Concerning the rising of creatures from their graves*), those who have kept to their fast will be recognized for their virtue after they have emerged from their grave:

> In another Tradition, the fasters will come out of their graves, and they will be known by the aroma of their mouths by their fasting. They will find tables and jugs. It will be said to them: "Eat! You were hungry when people were full. Drink! You were thirsty when people's thirst was quenched. Take your rest. They will eat and drink and take their rest while people are at the Reckoning.[28]

There are two destinations in Islam after death. The righteous will enter the Garden of Paradise, the wrongdoer will be ushered into Gehenna or hell. Luscious descriptions of the Garden are contained in the Qur'an. See, for example, Sura 76.10–22, where it reads that for a believer,

> God has guarded them from the evil of
> that day, and has procured them radiancy
> and gladness,
> and recompensed them for their patience
> with a Garden, and silk;
> therein they shall recline upon couches,
> therein they shall see neither sun nor
> bitter cold;
> near them shall be its shades, and its cluters hung
> meekly down,
> and there shall be passed around them vessels of silver, and goblets of crystal,
> crystal of silver that they have measured
> very exactly.
> And therein they shall be given to drink a cup whose
> mixture is ginger,
> therein a fountain whose name is called Salsabil.

Immortal youths shall go about them;
when thou seest them, thou supposest them
scattered pearls,
when thou seest them then thou seest bliss
and a great kingdom,
Upon them shall be green garments of silk
and brocade; they are adorned with
bracelets of silver, and their Lord shall
give them to drink a pure draught.
Behold, this is a recompense for you, and
your striving is thanked.

The torments of hell or **Gehenna** are also graphically described in the Qur'an. However, it is not clear whether hell involves eternal punishment or temporary punishment and there is disagreement among Muslim theologians owing to the ambiguity within the Qur'anic text. Hell is depicted as a dreadful place full of every conceivable torment;

Surely the tree of Zaqqim will be the
food of the offenders, like molten metal it
will boil in their insides, like the boiling
of scalding water. Secure him and drag
him into the midst of the blaze, then
pour over his head from the penalty of
boiling water, taste! Surely, you once
were mighty, honored. Surely, this is
what you used to call in question.

So how, then, can one attain salvation and inherit the rewards of Paradise? The Qur'an emphasizes beliefs and actions as the path to salvation. To be one of the saved one must believe in Allah and his messenger as well as follow the straight path, which is represented by the Islamic way of life (Sura 2.172f):

It is not piety, that you turn your faces
to the East and to the West.
True piety is this:
to believe in God, and the Last Day,
the angels, the Book, and the Prophets,
to give of one's substance, however cherished,
to kinsmen, and orphans,
the needy, the traveler, beggars,
and to ransom the slave,
to perform the prayer, to pay the alms.
And they who fulfill their covenant
when they have engaged in a covenant.
and endure with fortitude

misfortune, hardship and peril,
these are they who are true in their faith,
these are the truly godfearing.

There are also certain practices that are important for Muslims to follow. These
are called the Five Pillars of Faith.

Institutions and Rituals

The following five practices make up what is known as the Five Pillars of Faith.
In Shi'ite Islam these pillars comprise part of the main beliefs of Islam. In other
words, Shi'ites do not call them "pillars"; however, their content and significance
are more or less the same. This section will offer a brief outline of each pillar and
note its religious and social significance within the lives of Muslims. Both the Qu'ran
and the hadith require Muslims to follow the Five Pillars.[29]

The *Shahada*
This pillar is perhaps the most important of the five because it is the words of initiation into the Muslim community. There is no initiation ceremony. To become
a Muslim, a person has to recite the *Shahada*. The *Shahada* consists of two central
Islamic beliefs; the oneness of God and the prophethood of Muhammad. It is a
declaration of faith and reads: "There is no God but Allah and Muhammad is his
Prophet."

Salat (or prayer)
A Muslim is required to pray at least five times a day; at dawn, after mid-day, in
the late afternoon, after sunset, and in the late evening. A Muslim can pray any-
where as long as the spot they pray on is clean. Therefore, some institutions in
non-Muslim countries provide Muslims with a special place in which to carry out
their prayers. A Muslim is also required to attend the Mosque on a Friday for congregational prayers.

Each Muslim faces the *Ka'ba* when they pray. The *Ka'ba* is situated in Mecca
and is the first place dedicated to the worship of the one God, Allah. It is also
believed to have been built by the Prophet Abraham. The purpose of prayer is both
to remember God throughout the day and also to protect one from the temptation of sin. A Muslim must also be physically clean before prayer, so they perform
wudu, which involves the washing of hands, feet, and face.

Sawm (or fasting)
A Muslim is required to fast once a year during the Muslim month of *Ramadan*.
For twenty-nine (or thirty) days a Muslim must restrain from food, drink, sexual
relations, and smoking, from dawn to sunset. There are a number of reasons why
Muslims fast: First, it helps them remember the plight of the poor and needy;

secondly, the month of *Ramadan* commemorates the revelation of the Qur'an to the Prophet Muhammad; and finally, it helps one to grow stronger spiritually. At the end of the fast Muslims celebrate *Eid al-Fitr*, which involves a great feast and the exchanging of presents.

Hajj (or pilgrimage)

Muslims try to visit Mecca at least once in their lifetime. They are required to do so only if their health permits and they have the resources to finance the trip. Mecca is the Holy City where Muhammad was born and received his revelations.

Muslims perform a variety of different actions when they are on pilgrimage and many of these actions seek to commemorate events in the life of Abraham – such as running between the two hillocks where Abraham's wife Hagar searched desperately for water with her son Ismail. God showed mercy on her and rewarded her with a spring of water known as *Zamzam*. Muslims also walk in circles around the *Ka'ba* seven times in respect and remembrance of its significance to the Prophet Muhammad himself. At the end of the pilgrimage *Eid al-Adha* is celebrated. This particular feast commemorates Abraham's willingness to sacrifice his son (believed to be Ismail rather then Isaac as in the Christian tradition).

Ethical expression

Zakat (or almsgiving)

The fifth pillar is an ethical duty incumbent upon all Muslims, and involves the payment of normally 2.5 percent of one's earnings to the Muslim community or, in an Islamic country, the state. This money is then distributed among the needy. However, it is important to remember that *Zakat* does not have be a financial payment; it can involve doing a kindness to someone. The whole system reminds a Muslim that all wealth and gifts in life belong to Allah.

The Role of Women

The status of women in Islam has preoccupied western minds for centuries. The whole issue concerning women in Islam is a difficult one to examine for the main reason that so many different perspectives are involved. Therefore, it is necessary not only to address the issues preoccupying the West but, and perhaps more importantly, to look at the role of Muslim women within Islam itself by consulting the main Islamic sources; the Qur'an and hadith. It is also of considerable importance when thinking about the status of women in Islam to engage with the actual voices of Muslim women themselves.

So how has the West perceived the status of women in Islam? The Palestinian scholar Edward Said brought the damaging effects of a discipline termed Orientalism into sharp focus in his book entitled *Orientalism*.[30] Orientalism basically involves the study of the East by western scholars, academics, Islamicists, and travel writers among others. According to Said, this kind of study was for the most part distorted as the Orient was identified and manipulated by the West. Orientalists made it their business to know and write about the Orient in a disparaging way. The truth was rapidly obscured as it assumed less importance than a hidden agenda to undermine the East, and in doing so elevate the West. The Orientalist debate is an important one. When discussing questions surrounding the status of women in Islam it is worthwhile to remain vigilant when confronted with media images and stereotypes of Muslim women, and also to take care not to impose a western liberal feminist framework when analyzing the status of women in Islam. In a booklet entitled *Women in Islam*, B. Aisha Lemu has written:

> According to these assumptions (*i.e.*, Western assumptions), the Muslim woman is spiritually a non-person existing in a world of shadows, oppressed and suppressed, from which she will at death pass into a sort of limbo for soulless non-entities.[31]

And later she asserts:

> The best source of information on this must not be taken from imagination and Hollywood's choicest offerings but the source-book of Islam – that is the Qur'an, and the hadith, the recorded sayings and actions of the Prophet Muhammad.[32]

Rana Kabbani explicitly relates Orientalism to the western perception of women in Islamic countries. She argues that eastern women were depicted by Orientalists according to their own fantasies rather than how they really were.[33]

Films such as *Not Without My Daughter* and documentaries such as *Stolen Brides*, based on real events involving the maltreatment of women by Muslim men, must certainly color western perceptions of the treatment of women in Islam. However, two points must be remembered here; first, such examples cannot, in effect, be taken as typical in any way; secondly, the way some women are treated in the name of Islam does not always reflect the way women should be treated in reference to the Islamic sources, the foundations of the Islamic belief system. A thought-provoking poem, written by an Indian woman, appeared in *20\20 Visions*. The poem challenged the way in which western minds (with little touch on reality) picture Asian women:

> "What
> White woman?
> You say
> I am
> who?
>
> Your sister?
> You have
> a picture?
> Me?
> You have come to

help?
Why? When? How
Here?

The picture
White woman,
let me see it.
I remember no
picture
I gave you.
You have made a
picture of
me.
All by yourself.
Still,
let me see.

Indian woman,
Sati.
Child bride.
Dowry murder victim.
Traditional Hindu.
Untouchable.
Ostracised Widow.
Traditional Muslim.
Wife No. 1, No. 2, No. 3, No. 4.
Raped.
Uneducated.
Illiterate.
Too many children.
Backward environment.
That's all?

Is that all,
White woman?
Is that me,
my sisters, my mothers?

Now
hear me speak
in my own voice,
GET OFF MY BACK.

GET OFF MY BACK
for I am Kali
and will surely
destroy
all those who
trample on
Me.[34]

To attempt to tackle all the specific areas which have caused controversy is a very difficult task, but I do think they revolve around the following issues; polygamy, the hijab, education, divorce and inheritance laws, as well as the problematic passages within the Qur'an itself.

Polygamy

A man's right to marry up to four wives is given in the Qur'an, specifically Sura 4.3, which reads:

> . . . marry such women
> as seem good to you. Two, three, four;
> but if you fear you would not be equitable,
> then only one, or what your right hand owns;
> so it is likelier you will not be partial.

It is also testified in the hadith material that Muhammad had many wives. Therefore, because a man has been given the right to practice polygamy and Muhammad practiced it, should it then become practice for all Muslim men? There is no uniform answer to this question as responses vary from Muslim to Muslim. Twentieth-century reformers such as the Egyptian Muhammad 'Abduh argued against the practice on the basis of Sura 4.3, which stipulates that a man should only marry up to four wives if he can treat them all equally. The unlikelihood of equitable treatment renders the right to polygamy unassailable. Scholars such as Akbar Ahmed[35] point out that the political climate during Muhammad's life necessitated that he marry more than one wife as the occurrence of numerous battles meant the widowhood and consequent financial desolation of many women. Furthermore, owing to the fact that Muhammad needed to make political alliances it was expedient (in the sense of being beneficial for the Muslim community at that time) for him to marry women of different nationalities.

A totally different perspective on the issue of polygamy was expressed by writer Annie Besant, who described western society as permitting polygamy in the guise of extramarital affairs whereby the man is absolved of all responsibility and the situation for the woman is inherently bad:

> One man and one woman, that is the true marriage; all else is evil. But most men are not yet pure enough for that, and in the scales of justice the polygamy of the East which guards, shelters, feeds and clothes the wives, may weigh heavier than the prostitution of the West, which takes a woman for lust, and throws her on the streets when lust is satiated.[36]

B. Aisha Lemu in her booklet *Woman in Islam* expresses similar views:

> And it is no secret that polygamy of a sort is widely carried on in Europe and America. The difference is that while the Western man has no legal obligation towards the

second, third or fourth mistresses and their children, the Muslim husband has complete legal obligations towards his second, third or fourth wife and their children.[37]

However, one important underlying fact in the whole debate concerning polygamy is that it is rarely practiced, and the majority of Muslim marriages remain monogamous institutions. Furthermore, polygamous marriages should be both accepted and sanctioned by the women involved.

The Hijab

Another aspect of controversy centers on the wearing of the **hijab** (here meaning veil) by Muslim women. Again, perspective is crucial here. Many western thinkers, particularly liberal feminists (Muslim and non-Muslim), may find the wearing of the veil almost demeaning to the Muslim woman. Controversy raged in the late eighties when a French school by the name of Lycée Collège Jean Moulin in Albertville refused to allow Muslim girls to attend the school wearing veils; the reasons revolving around the belief that as France is a secularist society, overt expressions of religiosity that degrade women have no place in the classroom. As a tragic consequence of this decision two Muslim girls were expelled for wanting to continue wearing the veil. Thus, it is important to remember that from the perspective of some Muslim women the wearing of a veil is far from degrading or oppressive but instead an expression of religious pride and identity, as well as an outward expression of modesty.

Among Muslim believers and thinkers we can find a wide spectrum of beliefs as regards the veiling of women. These range from those who believe that it is a religious obligation for all women (Ar. *wajib*) to cover their faces as well as their heads, to those who believe that the veiling of women is un-Islamic; and there is a position somewhere in-between which supports the view that while veiling of the head is required for all Muslim women, veiling of the face is not. The differences between these views depend largely on differing exegesis (interpretation) of the Islamic texts such as the Qur'an and *sunnah*. Zakaria Basher, in his Seminar Paper entitled *Muslim Women in the Midst of Change*,[38] helpfully categorizes these viewpoints into three main strands – (1) the traditionalist view, (2) the moderate view, and (3) the liberal view.

(1) In his discussion of the traditionalist view, Basher locates a number of reasons why traditionalists believe that the Muslim woman is required to cover her face as well as her head. These reasons are as follows:

(i) The interpretation of 33.59 suggests that a woman is required to cover all of her body including her face. Sura 33.59 reads:

> O prophet! Say to your wives and your daughters and the women of the believers to draw their cloaks close to themselves, so it is likelier they will be known, and not hurt. God is All-forgiving, All-compassionate.

(ii) The revelation of Sura 24.31, according to traditionalists, caused some women of Medina to cover their heads and faces. Sura 34: 31 reads:

> Say O Muhammad to the believers that thy cast down
> their eyes and guard their private parts;
> that is purer for them. God is aware of
> the things they work,
> And say to the believing women, that they
> Cast down their eyes and guard their private
> Parts, and reveal not their adornment
> Save as is outward; and let them cast
> Their veils over their bosoms, and not reveal
> Their adornment save to their husbands,
> or their fathers. . . .

(2) The moderates put forward a number of reasons why they believe that traditionalists are wrong in their interpretation of the Qur'anic texts. According to moderates, Sura 33.59 never explicitly prescribes that women should cover their faces and Sura 24.31 only refers to the covering of the bosoms, as in pre-Islamic times women used to leave their breast uncovered – and this Sura was revealed in correction of this. Two hadiths (which traditionalists believe are of dubious authority) are pointed out in favor of the moderate position; the first related by Abu Dawud and the second by al-Tabari. In both hadiths Muhammad is related as saying that when a woman reaches puberty she is required to cover up her entire body with exception of her face and hands.

(3) Liberals argue against the veiling of women. Fatima Mernissi approaches the hadith material from a feminist perspective and suggests that the original meaning of *hijab* was "curtain." According to Mernissi, the belief that a woman should be veiled goes back to a particular sura revealed during the fifth year of the *hijra* (AD 627) – Sura 33.53, which reads:

> O believers, enter not the houses of
> the Prophet, except leave is given you
> for a meal, without watching for its hair.
> But when you are invited, then enter; and
> When you have had the meal, disperse,
> Neither lingering for idle talk;
> that is harmful to the Prophet, and he
> Is ashamed before you; but God is not
> Ashamed before the truth. And when you
> Ask his wives for any object, ask them
> From behind a curtain; that is cleaner
> For your hearts and theirs.

Mernissi argues, using hadiths from al-Tabari, that the Prophet needed to protect the privacy of himself and his wives from various guests and therefore drew a
curtain between him and his guests. The verse was never meant to segregate women
from men or hide them under veils. Instead it was a response to social intrusions
from his companions, in this case Anas Ibn Malik.

So there is certainly no unified view when it comes to the issue of veiling. This
is because the sources are open to a multitude of different interpretations. Things
are more straightforward when we move on to a discussion of the third main area
of controversy – education.

Education

Islamic sources are fairly clear when it comes to the education of women.
Education is not a right denied to Muslim women, instead it is encouraged. In the
hadith material, the Prophet is reported as saying: "Seek knowledge even if it takes
you to China," and "Knowledge is incumbent on every male and every female."[39]
The Qur'an constantly encourages Muslims to seek knowledge. There have been
many Muslim female scholars throughout history, including the Prophet's own
wife Aisha.

Therefore, the situation in the **Taleban**-controlled Afghanistan, from where reports
speak of the dismal situation of women, denied rights to education and simple free-
doms, is un-Islamic (in other words the situation cannot be justified by either Qur'an
or hadith material). An article in *The Times Magazine* suggested that, in Taleban-
controlled Afghanistan, women could not get an education or show their faces, but
definitely *could* be isolated or starved.[40]

Divorce and inheritance laws

In the case of divorce and inheritance, Islamic law seems to lean more favorably
toward the male. For a man divorce is relatively easy (as compared with a woman).
In order to divorce his wife the husband has to tell his wife he divorces her three
times in front of a witness, though he must allow one month to pass by between
each pronouncement in order to ensure his wife is not pregnant. However,
twentieth-century reforms in family law in countries such as Egypt and India led
to the revoking of this practice (*talaq*) as detrimental to the rights of the woman
involved and also allowed greater rights to divorce for women.

A woman is entitled to half the inheritance of the man. However, it is important to remember the fact that this was an improvement to the existing rights of
women in pre-Islamic Arabia who were not entitled to any property. Furthermore, in a system where the husband is given the burden of responsibility when
it comes to maintaining his family financially and the woman's assets remain
entirely her own, the inheritance laws may not appear so discriminatory against
women.

Problematic passages in the Qur'an

A general belief of Muslims involves the idea that the Qur'an is the eternal word of God. Some passages in the Qur'an present a problem for modernist Muslims (in this sense meaning Muslims who seek to reconcile their Islamic faith with more modern elements), particularly those passages that seem to reduce the status of women in comparison with that of men. If the Qur'an is the word of God in the twentieth century then surely clear rulings such as Sura 4.34–8 present a problem:

> Men are the managers of the affairs of women
> for that God has preferred in bounty
> one of them over another, and for that
> they have expended of their property.
> Righteous women are therefore obedient,
> Guarding the secret for God's guarding.
> And those you fear may be rebellious
> Admonish; banish them to their couches,
> And beat them. If they then obey you,
> Look not for any way against them; God is
> All-high, All-great.

However, this is not to suggest that the passage itself is not subject to differing interpretation. John Bowker's *Voices of Islam* portrays a wide range of Muslim responses to this passage. One Muslim argues that the passage should be understood symbolically as Muhammad himself, in the hadith material, never literally beat his wives but instead tied two pieces of cloth together and symbolically beat them:

> In other words, beating her is symbolic. It does not mean that you hang her by her hair from the chandelier and beat her with a big cane or anything like that. You beat her, yes, but as a kind of physical pressure if psychological pressure does not work, to bring her to her senses. You do not abuse her with words, you do not say, "You are ugly, you are a cow" – this is forbidden. For God's sake, what is more harmful than to say she is a cow, that she is ugly, she is fat?[41]

Another problematic verse in the Qur'an occurs in Sura 2.228 where man is given rank over his wife:

> Women have rights over them of an honourable kind, but men have *darajab* over them.

Some Muslims have interpreted rank as chairmanship over the family.[42] If the husband and wife need to make a major decision and both agree, then no problem arises. However, a problem does arise if they disagree, and in order to prevent an ongoing battle, one of the partners must have the final decision. As the man has the financial responsibility over the family the decision concerning such matters as the house and finance should be his.

So although there are problematic passages in the Qur'an regarding women, these passages are subject to varying interpretations, many of which present the husband's role as one of care and responsibility over his wife rather than as a dictator or authority figure.

The importance of listening to the actual voices of Muslim women was emphasized at the beginning of this section. Again, there is no unified voice but those who affirm the positive status of women in Islam appeal both to the significant role women have played during the history of Islam and to the numerous rights and respect conferred on a woman in the family environment. There are of course other Muslim women who are much more critical of the treatment in Islamic countries (but it is important to remember that such treatment normally reflects social disharmony within the country itself rather than being a reflection of any Islamic precept derived from either the Qur'an or *sunna*). One fairly well-known Muslim female writer, who suffers at first-hand the mistreatment of women in Egyptian society, is Nawal El-Saadawi. In her book *The Hidden Face of Eve: Women in the Arab World* (1982) she writes that;

> As a girl I used to be scared of going out onto the streets in some of the districts of Cairo during my secondary school days (1943–8). I remember how boys sometimes threw stones at me, or shouted out crude insults as I passed by, such as "Accursed be the c_ _t of your mother" or "Daughter of the bitch f_ _ _ _d by men." In some Arab countries women have been exposed to physical or moral aggression in the streets simply because their fingers were seen protruding from the sleeves of their dress.[43]

However, as Akbar Ahmed is careful to point out in *Discovering Islam*, such degradation has no place whatsoever when it comes to the "ideal Muslim woman." According to Ahmed, "The ideal woman is in many important ways like her male counterpart – modest, pious, and caring for her family."[44] Ahmed also points out that women have many rights conferred upon them in Islam, such as the right to inheritance, divorce, and education. They have many role models to look up to, such as Khadija, Muhammad's first wife and the first person to believe his message; Aisha, another of the Prophet's wives, who fought at the Battle of the Camel in 656; and also Fatimah, Muhammad's daughter who played an active role in early Islam.

B. Aisha Lemu and Fatima Hareen, in their booklet *Women in Islam*, talk about the positive role of the woman as a mother and carer for her family:

> The Muslim woman's role in the home is a vitally important one to the happiness of the husband and the physical and spiritual development of their children. Her endeavour is to make her family's life sweet and joyful, and the home a place of security and peace. This and her early character training of the children have a lasting effect on the behaviour and attitudes of the next generation when they reach adolescence and adulthood. There is a well-known saying in Arabic – *al-umma madrasatun* meaning "the mother is a school," which conveys the importance of this role.[45]

The authors emphasize the fact that the Qur'an affirms the spiritual status of women, which is equal to that of the male. If both male and female live according to Islamic principles both will reap the rewards of salvation, for example Sura 33.35:

> Men and women who have surrendered,
> believing men and believing women,
> obedient men and obedient women,
> truthful men and truthful women,
> enduring men and enduring women,
> humble men and humble women,
> men and women who give in charity,
> men who fast and women who fast,
> men and women who guard their private parts,
> men and women who remember God oft-
> for them God has prepared forgiveness
> and a mighty wage.

They locate material from the hadith where the Prophet affirms the importance of the mother:

> Messenger of God, who is the most deserving of good care from me? The Prophet replied: "Your mother (which he repeated three times) then your father, then your nearest relatives in order."[46]

Also in the hadith material the Prophet stated that: "Paradise lies at the feet of mothers," which implies that salvation awaits those who treat their mothers with respect.

Modern Expressions

All religions have had to cope with the onslaught of modernity. Modernity is simply an ideology that gives prominence to scientific beliefs over and against religious beliefs. All religions have had to adapt to the effects of modernity, which tends to regard religion as an obstacle to the progression of society. Modernity has led the way for secularism in that religion is given a secondary role in society; it rarely has a decisive position in the running of the state. Its role in the public arena is limited. Islam and **secularism** seem to be mutually exclusive as Islam is not by its nature a private religion; it takes a very active part in the lives of its believers. Opinions vary as to how well Islam has coped in the modern world, and there are some very good texts that explore the issues surrounding Islam and modernity. Akbar Ahmed, *Postmodernism and Islam*,[47] F. Rahman, *Islam and Modernity*,[48] and Andrew Rippin offers a very good summary of the effects of modernity on Islam in his book *Islam: Belief and Practice (volume two)*.[49]

Whether or not Islam has been successful in coping with the effects of the modern world it is definitely on the increase in the West, attracting a large number of converts. A movement known as *The Nation of Islam* has, in the past decade, attracted a certain amount of media attention for recruiting a large number of converts among the black population in the United States. Reports suggest that it is also making an impact on the black community in Britain. This movement originates from the views of a man known as Elijah Muhammad (1898–1975) and his views are still being propagated today in the mouth of Louis Farrakhan. Although this movement has been praised for improving the social situation of blacks, particularly in the United States, it has been criticized for its racism toward whites. It has little in common with traditional Islam and is even blasphemous in suggesting that Elijah Muhammad was the final prophet (as in traditional Islam the prophethood ends with Muhammad).

Islam plays an important role in the lives of 17.7 percent of the world population. It is a flourishing religion, and this in itself suggests its ongoing contribution to the modern world. The religion is based on complete devotion to Allah as well as the principles of peace and justice and has much to offer in the realms of interfaith dialogue.

An important controversy that illustrates the clash between the Islamic community and the secular values in the West is *The Satanic Verses* controversy, and it is to the issues surrounding this particular altercation that we now turn.

The Satanic Verses *controversy*

The publication of the novel *The Satanic Verses*, written by author Salman Rushdie, in September 1988, caused immense controversy worldwide. In Britain, a vast number of the Muslim community demanded immediate censorship of the novel after certain passages were brought to the attention of Muslim organizations and ambassadors. The UK Action Committee on Islamic Affairs, formed after the publication of the novel, appealed to Penguin to carry out three demands. These were as follows:

1   To immediately withdraw and pulp all copies of the above mentioned title as well as to undertake not to allow to be published any future edition of this sacrilege.
2   To tender an unqualified public apology to the world Muslim community for the enormous injury to the feeling and sensibilities of the Muslim community.
3   To pay adequate damages to an agreed Islamic charity in Britain.[50]

No response was forthcoming from the publishers, so on January 14, 1989, Muslims aimed to draw media attention to their protest by burning a copy of *The Satanic Verses* on the streets of Bradford, Yorkshire. Media reactions were especially critical of both the subsequently named "Bradford Burning" and the demands for censorship by the Muslim community. Muslims were consequently labeled as "Nazis," "fundamentalists," "militants," and "extremists."

Events escalated when on February 14, 1989, the late Ayatollah Khomeini pronounced a death sentence against Salman Rushdie and his publishers. The declaration, which was broadcast over Tehran radio, read as follows:

> I inform the proud Muslims of the world that the author of *The Satanic Verses* book which is against Islam, the Prophet and the Koran, and all involved in its publication, are sentenced to death.

Tehran declared a state of mourning and Rushdie went into hiding. So why were some Muslims so opposed to the novel? The reasons are complex, but they can be summarized into two main points: first, Muslims object to the way in which they believe some people have distorted Islamic history, and secondly, they protest at Rushdie's characterization of the Prophet Muhammad (who they identify with the character Mahound in the novel).

Rushdie insists that his novel is not a deliberate attack against the Islamic religion and certainly not in any way an attack against the Muslim community, having been himself brought up amongst Muslims (Rushdie was born in India but moved with his family to Pakistan after the partition of India in 1947). He argues that his novel is rather a challenge to religious certainty, that is, religious affirmations that the world is a certain way and not another. It is a challenge to belief systems that seem to present the truth in a black and white manner. According to Rushdie all religions are guilty of this, but his novel focused on the Islamic religion as this is what he knows the most about. Rushdie argues that his book encompasses a wide variety of themes and is not really about Islam – rather it is a story about migration and loss and would appeal to the immigrant Muslim community in Britain if they could only appreciate its wider context.

In Britain (where the book was published), the arguments against the banning of the novel came mainly from the liberal intelligentsia and the media world (see, for example, Fay Weldon's *Sacred Cows*).[51] The most significant argument against censorship revolved around the issue of freedom of expression. In other words, in a democratic society an individual's freedom to express their views and ideas must be protected.

The fatwa[52]

Salman Rushdie was sentenced to death as an apostate by the Iranian cleric, the late Ayatollah Khomeini. An apostate, in Islam, is one who renounces his or her faith in Islam. Rushdie was born a Muslim but renounced his faith when he was still an adolescent. Thus Rushdie has been an apostate for a very long time. The concept of apostasy also includes those who have insulted the Prophet and it is likely that what was perceived as the insulting nature of the book, as regards the character of the Prophet, was the main motivation behind the *fatwa*.

Among Muslims, opinions vary greatly. In Britain, the majority of the Muslim community are Sunni and therefore did not recognize the authority of the late Ayatollah Khomeini, unlike the Shi'ite community of which the majority reside in Iran. A common reaction by Muslims in Britain was that the death edict was contrary to the law and spirit of Islam. Finally, the Qur'an is clear that those who renounce their faith, and those who insult the Prophet, will be punished but only in the next life by Allah:

The House of Imran (170)

Those who buy unbelief at the price of faith,
they will nothing hurt God; and there awaits them
a painful chastisement.

Women (135)

When you hear God's signs being disbelieved
and made mock of, do not sit with them
until they plunge into some other talk, or
else you will surely be like to them. God
will gather the hypocrites and the unbelievers
all in Gehenna.

Exercises

1. Examine the main theological themes within the Qur'an.
2. Critically evaluate the picture of Jesus in the Qur'an.
3. Discuss the significance of the Prophet Muhammad within the Islamic religion.
4. Discuss the significance of Shi'ite history during the Iranian revolution.
5. Do you believe that the French school was justified in forbidding Muslim girls to wear their headscarves to school?
6. Construct a debate between those who believe *The Satanic Verses* should be banned and those who are against censorship.

GLOSSARY

'Abbasids Arab dynasty which flourished between 750 and 1258 in Baghdad.

al-Buraq Winged horse that transported Muhammad on his night journey.

Badr Major battle between Muhammad and the Meccans in 624.

Fatwa A legal ruling in Islam.

Gehenna A term referring to hell.

Hadith A term referring to the tradition of the Prophet and his companions.

Hajj One of the Five Pillars of Faith. A term referring to pilgrimage.

Hijab Literally means "curtain." Commonly used in reference to a Muslim woman's veil.

Iblis Lucifer.

Ijma Consensus of the Muslim community. One of the four main sources of law.

Isnad Refers to the chain if authority, which must be secure for a tradition to be considered authentic.

Isra' Muhammad's night journey form Mecca to Jerusalem.

Ithna 'Ashari The majority Shia group who believe in the hidden Mahdi.

Itjihad A term which refers to independent legal judgment free of past precedents.

Jinn Mischievous beings in the Qur'an.

Mahdi A belief in Shia Islam where the hidden twelfth Caliph or Mahdi is expected to return and bring justice on earth. Literally means "the rightly guided one."

Monotheism The belief in the oneness of God.

Mujtahid One who has the authority to give independent judgments relating to law or theology.

Munkar One of the questioning angels in the tomb.

Nakur One of the questioning angels in the tomb.

Qur'an The holy book of Islam.

Qur'aysh The tribe that Muhammad belonged to in Mecca.

Salat One of the Five Pillars of Faith. A term referring to prayer.

Sawm One of the Five Pillars of Faith. A term referring to fasting.

Secularism A term that refers to our modern era where religion has been pushed out of the public sphere.

Shahada One of the Five Pillars of Islam. Refers to the confession of faith – a means of initiation into the Muslim community.

Shariah Islamic law.

Shias Minority of Muslims who accept 'Ali as the first Caliph.

Shirk Blasphemy in Islam such as the belief in more than one God.

Sufism The mystical strand within Islam.

Sunnah The example of the Prophet incumbent on every Muslim to emulate.

Sunnis Majority of Muslims who accept leadership of the first three Caliphs.

Taleban The Taleban are a Muslim army that successfully took over Kabul and subsequently implemented Shariah Law.

Tawhid Central Islamic belief in the oneness of God.

Ummayads Arab dynasty that flourished from 661 to 750. Established itself in Damascus.

Zakat One of the Five Pillars of Faith. A term which refers to almsgiving.

Notes and References

1 For a clear, succinct dictionary of Islamic terms see Ian Netton, *A Popular Dictionary of Islam* (London: Curzon Press Ltd, 1992).

2 Al-Tabari, *The History of al-Tabari: Muhammad at Mecca*, volume 5, trans. W. Mongomery Watt and M. V. McDonald (New York: State University of New York Press, 1988).

3 Essad Bey, *Mohammed* (London: Cobden-Sanderson, 1938), p. 65.

4 M. A. Pasha, *Sixth Century and Beyond: the Prophet and his Times* (London: Ta-Ha Publishers, 1993).

5 I have used a number of sources for this overview, but especially M. A. Pasha, *Sixth Century and Beyond*, and Michael Cook, *Muhammad* (Oxford: Oxford University Press, 1996), who bases his biography on Ibn Ishaq (one of the most notable collectors of material on the life of the Prophet – popular edited version by Ibn Hisham (d. circa 833).

6 Michael Cook, *Muhammad*, p. 17.

7 The actual religious movement appears to have emerged with Ja'far al Sadiq (ca. 700–765 – the seventh Imam) and we only know about detailed Shi'ite beliefs much later during the period of the twelfth Imam, where Shi'ite sources came into existence – see, A. Rippin, *Muslims: Their Religious Beliefs and Practices*, volume 1 (London: Routledge, 1995), p. 108.

8 Akbar Ahmed, *Living Islam* (London: BBC Books Ltd, 1990), p. 52.

9 From A. Rippin, *Muslims: Their Religious Beliefs and Practices*, volume 2 (London: Routledge, 1995), p. 107.

10 From Jean-Pierre Digard's article "Shi'ism in the State of Iran," in Olivier Carré (ed.), *Islam and the State in the World Today* (London: Sangam Books Ltd, 1988).

11 See also A. Ahmed, *Discovering Islam* (London: Routledge, 1980), p. 16, who makes this same point, though one must concede that many writings, such as novels for instance, are treated academically. It is also important here to note my approach to the Qur'an and its interpretation. In general my approach is fairly empathetic to mainstream Muslim interpretation.

12 See Ian Markham (ed.), *A World Religions Reader* (Oxford: Blackwell Publishers, 2000), pp. 303–6, for texts examining the characteristics of Allah.

13 This example is taken from Alfred Guillaume, *Islam* (London: Penguin Books, 1956), ch. 7, p. 128. This section is largely dependent on Guillaume's discussion of philosophy in the Islamic tradition, contained in chapter 7.

14 See William Montgomery Watt, *Islamic Surveys: Islamic Philosophy and Theology* (Edinburgh: Edinburgh University Press, 1962), p. 44.

15 Ibid., p. 118.

16 S. Thobani, "Indian Woman," in *Bulletin of Concerned Asian Scholars*, 21: 1 (1989), in Kim Knott, "Points of View," in H. Willmer (ed.), *20/20 Visions: The Futures of Christianity in Britain* (London: SPCK, 1992), p. 84.

17 For passages referring to Jews, see Sura 4.46f; 2.75; 5.15.

18 For specific Qur'anic texts relating to Jesus, see Ian Markham (ed.), *A World Religions Reader*, pp. 310–12.

19 See H. M. Baagil, *Christian Muslim Dialogue* (Birmingham: IPCI), p. 19ff.

20 Al-Ghazali, *Revival of the Religious Sciences*, in M. Ruthven, *A Satanic Affair* (London: Chatto and Windus, 1990), p. 131.

21 As discussed by D. Waines in *An Introduction to Islam* (Cambridge: Cambridge University Press, 1995), pp. 129ff.

22 Imam 'Abd ar-Rahim ibn Ahmad al-Qadi, *Islamic Book of the Dead* (Norwich: Diwan Press, 1977), p. 58.

23 See John Bowker, *The Meaning of Death* (Cambridge: Cambridge University Press, 1993, Canto edn.), p. 105.

24 Imam 'Abd ar-Rahim ibn Ahmad al-Qadi, *Islamic Book of the Dead*, p. 60.

25 Ibid.

26 Ibid., p. 69.

27 D. Waines, *An Introduction to Islam*, p. 130.

28 Imam 'Abd ar-Rahim Ahmad al-Qadr, *Islamic Book of the Dead*, p. 84.

29 See I. Markham, *A World Religions Reader*, pp. 314–19 for specific passages from the Qur'an and hadith.

30 Edward Said, *Orientalism* (London: Penguin, 1978).

31 B. Aisha Lemu, in B. Lemu and F. Heeren, *Women in Islam* (Leicester: The Islamic Foundation, 1978), p. 13.

32 Ibid., p. 14.

33 Rana Kabbani, *Europe's Myths of Orient* (London: Pandora, 1986).

34 Kim Knott, in *20/20 Visions*, p. 85.

35 A. Ahmed, *Living Islam* (London: BBC Books, 1993), pp. 27ff.

36 Annie Besant, *Islam* (London: The Theosophical Publishing House, 1992), p. 34.

37 B. Aisha Lemu and F. Heeren, *Woman in Islam*, p. 28.

38 Zakaria Basher, *Muslim Women in the Midst of Change*, Seminar Paper 5 (Leicester: The Islamic Foundation, 1981).

39 Sarah Sheriff, *Women's Rights in Islam* (London: Ta-Ha Publishers, 1989), p. 7.

40 *The Times Magazine*, October 12, 1996.

41 John Bowker, *Voices of Islam* (Oxford: Oneworld, 1995), p. 129.

42 See Bowker, *Voices of Islam*, pp. 125ff.

43 See Akbar Ahmed, *Discovering Islam* (London: Routledge, 1988), p. 187.

44 Ibid., p. 184.

45 B. Aisha Lemu and F. Heeren, *Woman in Islam*, p. 19.

46 Ibid., p. 23.

47 A. Ahmed, *Postmodernism and Islam: Predicament and Promise* (London: Routledge, 1992).

48 F. Rahman, *Islam and Modernity* (Chicago: The University of Chicago Press, 1982).

49 A. Rippin, *Islam: Belief and Practice*, volume 2 (London: Routledge, 1995).

50 From Appignanesi and Maitland, *The Rushdie File* (London: Fourth Estate, 1984), p. 59.

51 Fay Weldon, *Sacred Cows* (London: Chatto and Windus, 1989).

52 The term *fatwa* means any legal ruling in Islam but during *The Satanic Verses* controversy the term became equated with the death edict pronounced by the late Ayatollah Khomeini.

Bibliography

Studying Religion: Issues in Definition and Method

Bocock, Robert and Kenneth Thomson (eds.) (1985). *Religion and Ideology*, a Reader. Manchester University Press in association with the Open University.

Bowker, John (1999). *The Oxford Dictionary of World Religions*. Oxford: Oxford University Press.

Clark, Walter Houston (1958). *The Psychology of Religion*. New York: The Macmillan Co.

Freud, Sigmund; James Strachey (ed.) (reissued in 1989). *The Future of an Illusion*. New York: Norton & Co.

Gandhi, Mahatma (1995). *What is Hinduism?* New Delhi: National Book Trust, India.

Hinnells, John, Raymond Turvey, Reginald Piggott (1997). *Penguin Dictionary of Religions*. Harmondsworth Penguin Books.

Marx, Karl (1977). *Selected Writings*. Oxford: Oxford University Press.

Markham, Ian (2000). *A World Religions Reader*. Oxford: Blackwell Publishers.

Sharpe, Eric J. (1976). *Comparative Religion: A History*. London: Duckworth and Co. Ltd.

Sharpe, Eric J. (1992). *Understanding Religion*. London: Duckworth.

Smith, Huston (1999). *The World's Religions*. San Francisco: HarperSanFrancisco.

Otto, Rudolf (1969). *The Idea of the Holy*. Oxford: Oxford University Press.

Secular Humanism

Frederick Edwords, "What is Humanism?," http://www.infidels.org/library/modern/fred_edwords/humanism.html)

Matt Cherry and Molleen Matsumara, "10 Myths About Secular Humanism," *Free Inquiry Magazine*, vol. 18, no. 1, http://www.SecularHumanism.org/library/fi/cherry_18_1.01.html

Hampson, Daphne (1990). *Theology and Feminism*. Oxford: Blackwell.

de Lubac, Henri, trans. Edith M. Riley (1963). *The Drama of Atheist Humanism*. Cleveland and New York: Meridian Books, World Publishing Company.

Humanist Manifesto II can be found in Ian Markham (ed.), *A World Religions Reader*, second edition (Oxford: Blackwell Publishers, 2000).

Buddhism

Ajahn Chah (1982). *Bodhinyana. A Collection of Dhamma Talks*. Bangkok: Funny Press.

Bechert, H. and R. Gombrich (1995) (eds.). *The World of Buddhism*. London: Thames and Hudson.

Dharmachari Vessantara (1996). *The Friends of the Western Buddhist Order. An Introduction*. Birmingham: Windhorse Publications.

Gombrich, R. (1995). *Theravada Buddhism: A Social History from Ancient Benares to Modern Colombo*. London: Routledge.

Hamilton, S. (1995). "*Anatta*: a Different Approach," *The Middle Way* (May) 70, 1: 47–60.

Harvey, P. (1993). *An Introduction to Buddhism: Teachings, History, Practices.* Cambridge: Cambridge University Press.

Harvey, P. (1995). *The Selfless Mind: Personality, Consciousness and Nirvana in Early Buddhism.* Richmond: Curzon Press.

Keown, D. (1996) *Buddhism: A Very Short Introduction.* Oxford: Oxford University Press.

Kulananda (1996). *Thorsons Principles of Buddhism.* London: Thorsons.

Skilton, A. (1994). *A Concise History of Buddhism.* Birmingham: Windhorse Publications.

Young, S. (1993). *An Anthology of Sacred Texts By and About Women.* London: Pandora.

Illustrations from H. Bechert and R. Gombrich (1995) (eds.). *The World of Buddhism.* London: Thames and Hudson.

Buddhist Scriptures (1959). Selection and trans. E. Conze, Harmondsworth: Penguin.

The Dhammapada (1984). Trans. J. Mascaro. Harmondsworth: Penguin.

Vinaya Pitaka (1966). Trans. I. Horner. London: PTS.

Sikhism

Cole, W. Owen and Piara Singh Sambhi (1995). *The Sikhs.* Brighton: Sussex Academic Press.

Kohli, S. S. (1992). *A Conceptual Encyclopaedia of Guru Granth Sahib.* New Delhi: Manohar.

McLeod, W. H. (1978). *Guru Nanak and the Sikh Religion.* Delhi: Oxford University Press.

McLeod, Hew (1997). *Sikhism.* Harmondsworth: Penguin.

Massey, James (1991). *The Doctrine of Ultimate Reality in Sikh Religion.* New Delhi: Manohar.

Morgan, Peggy and Clive Lawton (eds.) (1996). *Ethical Issues in Six Religious Traditions.* Edinburgh: Edinburgh University Press.

Sambhi, Piara Singh (1989). *Sikhism.* Cheltenham: Stanley Thornes & Hulton.

Singh, Gopal (1987). *The Religion of the Sikhs.* New Delhi: Allied.

Chinese Religion

Cao Xueqin (1973–86). *The Story of the Stone (The Dream of the Red Chamber),* trans. David Hawkes and John Minford, 5 vols. Harmondsworth: Penguin.

Ch'en, Kenneth (1964). *Buddhism in China: a Historical Survey.* Princeton: Princeton University Press.

Falk, Nancy A. and Rita M. Gross (1980). *Unspoken Words: Women's Religious Lives in Non-Western Cultures.* San Francisco: Harper & Row.

Giles, Herbert A. (trans.) (1900). *San Tzu Ching (The Three Character Classic).* Shanghai: Kelly & Walsh.

Gregory, Peter N. (1991). *Tsung-Mi and the Sinification of Buddhism.* Princeton: Princeton University Press.

Hughes, E. R. (trans.) (1942). *The Great Learning & The Mean-in-Action.* London: J. M. Dent & Sons.

Lin, Yutang (1938). *The Importance of Living.* London: William Heinemann.

Lopez, Donald S. Jr. (ed.) (1996). *Religions of China in Practice.* Princeton: Princeton University Press.

Shahar, Meir and Robert P. Weller (1996). *Unruly Gods: Divinity and Society in China.* Honolulu: University of Hawaii Press.

Waley, Arthur (1938). *Three Ways of Thought in Ancient China.* London: Allen & Unwin.

Judaism

Books

Dosick, Wayne D. (1998). *Living Judaism: The Complete Guide to Jewish Belief, Tradition, and Practice*. HarperSanFrancisco, reprint edn.

Epstein, Rabbi Dr. I. (1992). *Judaism*. Viking Press, reprint edn.

Fackenheim, Emil L. (1994). *To Mend the World: Foundations of Post-Holocaust Jewish Thought*. Bloomington: Indiana University Press, reprint edn.

Forms of Prayer for Jewish Worship. *See* Reform Synagogues of Great Britain.

Fry, Helen P. (compiler and editor) (1996). *Christian–Jewish Dialogue*. Exeter: University of Exeter Press.

Gilbert, Martin (1993). *An Atlas of the Holocaust*. New York: William Morrow and Co., reprint edn.

Gilbert, Martin (1997). *Holocaust Journey*. New York: Columbia University Press.

Hertz, Joseph H. (ed.) (1997). *A Book of Jewish Thoughts*. Bloch Publishing Company.

Jacobs, Louis (1969). *Jewish Ethics, Philosophy and Mysticism*. Illustrated by Irwin Rosenhouse. New York: Behrman House, p. 151.

Jacobs, Louis (1995). *We Have Reason to Believe*. London: Vallentine Mitchell, fourth edn. With a New Preface.

Kung, Hans (1992). *Judaism*. London: SCM Press.

Kushner, Harold (1993). (Extract 15 in *A World Religions Reader*), *To Life: A Celebration of Jewish Being and Thinking*. London: Little, Brown and Co., pp. 54–60.

Lancaster, Brian (1993). *The Elements of Judaism*. Rockport, MA: Element Books Limited.

Levi, Primo (1987). *If this is a Man/ The Truce*. Abacus.

Moore, R. I. (May 1991). *The Formation of a Persecuting Society: Power and Deviance in Western Europe, 950–1250*. Oxford: Blackwell Publishers, reprint edn.

Neusner, Jacob (1990). *Torah through the Ages*. Philadelphia: Trinity Press.

Plaskow, Judith (1991). *Standing Again at Sinai: Judaism from a Feminist Perspective*. HarperSanFrancisco, reprint edn.

Reform Synagogues of Great Britain (1977). *Forms of Prayer for Jewish Worship*.

Scholem, Gershom (1996). *On the Kabbalah and its Symbolism*. New York: Schocken Books.

Wasserstein, Bernard (1997). *Vanishing Diaspora: The Jews in Europe Since 1945*. Harvard University Press, reprint edn.

Wiesel, Elie (1982). *Night* (a novel). Bantam Books, reissue edn.

Wiesel, Elie (1993). *Souls on Fire: Portraits and Legends of Hasidic Masters*. Simon and Schuster.

Wilkomirski, Binjamin (1996). *Fragments*. New York: Schocken Books.

Shintoism

Joseph Kitagawal, *On Understanding Japanese Religion* (Princeton: Princeton University Press, 1987).

Masaharu Anesaki, *History of Japanese Religion* (Rutland: Tuttle, 1963).

H. Byron Earhart, *Japanese Religion: Unity and Diversity* (Encino: Dickenson, 1974).

Ian Reader, *Religion in Contemporary Japan* (Basingstoke: Macmillian Press, 1991).

Helen Hardacre, *Shinto and the State 1868–1988* (Princeton: Princeton University Press, 1989).

Winston Davies, *Japanese Religion and Society: Paradigms of Structure and Change* (Albany, NY, State University of New York Press, 1992).

Index

Abd ar-Rahmin ibn Ahamad
  Qadr, 351, 352
Abraham, 7, 73, 102, 153,
  295, 348, 356
Abu Bakr (Caliph), 341
Abu Da'vd, 339
Abu Hanifa, 342
ad fontes, 333
Adam, 153, 154, 346, 348
Adhimutta, 204
Adi Granth, 218, 220
Ahamad ibn Hanbal, 342
Ahmad, Shah Abdali, 220
Ahmed, Akbar, 342, 364,
  365
Akal Purakh, 221–3
Akihito, Crown Prince, 302
al-Bukhan, 339
al-Ghazali, 347, 348, 351,
  353
al-Mahdi, Muhammad
  (Imam), 343
al-Musavi Khoeini, Ruhollah
  (Imam), 343
al-Nasa'i, 339
al-Tabari, 339
al-Taqi al-Jawad,
  Muhammad (Imam), 343
al-Tirmidhi, 339
'Ali (Caliph), 341
Ali (cousin and son-in-law of
  Muhammad), 80
'Ali abi Talib, 343
'Ali Shari'ati, 344
Allah, 78, 79, 80, 81, 110,
  112, 114, 115, 338–68,
  346
Allport, Gordon, 54, 56, 57
Amar Das, Guru, 217, 218
Amaterasu-o-mikami, 304,
  305

America, 104
Amitabha (Amida), 203
Ammerman, Nancy, 22
Amrit, 220
Amritsar, foundation of, 218
Anabaptists, 328
Analects, 246
Ananda (disciple of Buddha),
  206
Anatta, 197–8
Anchorites, 316
Angad, Guru, 217
Anicca, 197
Anselm, St., 13
anti-idolatry, Jewish, 280
Antony, The Great, Saint,
  316
Apocrypha, 75
Apologetics, 314, 332
approaches to the study of
  religion, 10–14
Aquinas, Thomas, 318
Arahat, 204, 207
archetypes, 52
Aristotle, 23, 318, 347
Arjan, Guru, 88, 218, 230
Arjuna, 83, 182
Arnold, Matthew, 139
Arnold, Sir Edward, 209
artha (success), 170, 177
arts, 117–38
Arya Samaj, 221
asceticism, 316
ashramas (Hindu stages of
  life), 177
Asian values, 268
Assagioli, Roberto, 49, 52
Atharva veda, 175
atheists, 26, 27
Atman, 170
Atonement, 8

attendant angels, 352
Augustine, St., 153
Avalokitesvara, 200, 203, 208,
  209
avatar, 179
Ayatollah Khomeini, 343,
  367, 368

Bahadur, Guru Tegh, 219,
  230
Bainbridge, William, 40
Baptism, 327–8
Barker, Eileen, 22
Barth, Karl, 127, 133
Basher, Zakaria, 360
Batson, C. D., 56, 57, 62
Baudelaire, Charles, 125
Becker, Ernest, 55
Beethoven, Ludwig van, 127
Bellah, Robert, 33, 39, 103,
  104
beloved five, 220
Bennett, Alan, 210
Berger, Peter, 34, 35
Bergman, S. H., 295
Bernard of Clairvaux, 318
Besant, Annie, 359
Bey, Essad, 339, 340
Bhagavad-Gita, 83
Bhago, Mai, 234
Bhajans, 84
Bhakti yoga, 181–2
Bhikkunis, 200–1, 207
Bhikkus, 200–1
Bhindranwale, Jarnail Singh,
  221
Bible, the, 74–8
Blavatsky, Madame, 209
Bocking, Brian, 300, 305
bodhisattva, 193, 203, 299
Bowker, John, 363

Brahma, 179, 184, 186
brahmacharya, 177
Brahman, 172
Brahmin, 191
Brahminical Hinduism, 179
Braud, William, 63
British Buddhism, 210–11
Bruce, Steve, 33
Brunce, William K., 302
Buddha, 3, 85, 87, 91,
　190–204, 300; four sights
　of, 195
Buddha nature, 194
Buddhas, plurality of, 194
Buddhism, 85–7, 98; contra
　caste, 205; doctrine of
　three bodies, 204; female
　deities, 208; humility,
　201; in/and the West,
　209–10; meditation, 202;
　non-ordination of nuns,
　208; pragmatism, 199;
　renunciation, 202;
　syncretic forms in the
　West, 212; view of
　normal existence in, 197
Buddhist realms of rebirth,
　200; ordination ceremony,
　204; precepts, 206
Burnouf, Eugène, 209

Calvin, Jean, 320
Calvinism, 320
Cao Xueqin, 261
capitalism, 22–4
Castaneda, Carlos, 61
Causton, Richard, 210
Chah, Ajahn, 201
Chalcedon, 324
Charlemagne (Charles the
　Great), 317
Cherry, Matthew, 149, 159
Chiang Kai-Shek, 267
China: chronology and
　calendars, 264; concept of
　reciprocity, 257; daily
　offerings, 263; egalitarian
　ethics, 258; ethical
　naturalism, 256; official
　atheism in, 265; pre-

modern "non-secularism",
　241; syncretism in Tang
　China, 249, 261; western
　views of, 266; women's
　societal roles, 260
Chinese religion: early
　characteristics of, 250;
　familial basis, 241;
　traditional house design,
　262; view of heaven, 251
Christendom, 8
Christian life, 325
Christian toleration, 321
Christian uniqueness, 335–6
Christianity, 74–8;
　colonialism, 322;
　distinctiveness from
　Judaism, 312; great schism,
　317; monastic growth,
　318; moral philosophy in,
　330; patriarchy in, 331–2;
　plurality in, 333; Roman
　Empire and, 313; view of
　other faiths, 335
Christians, persecutions of,
　313
Christology, 324
Church, 326
Cicero, 2, 9, 140
Citta, 197
civil religion, 33, 39, 103
Clarke, Walter Houston, 5
Classical Chinese (language),
　problematic nature of,
　242
Clement of Alexandria, 313
clerical celibacy, 319
Coenobites, 316
Cohen, Leonard, 86
Cole, Henry, 125, 126
communitas, 102
comparative religion, history
　of, 6–10, 100, 107
Compson, Jane, 212
Comte, Auguste, 29, 143,
　145, 146, 149, 157
confessional approach, 12–13
Confucianism, reinvigoration
　of, 267–8
Confucians, 98

Confucius, 3, 245, 246, 250,
　254, 257, 258, 267–8,
　270
Constantine (Emperor), 122,
　123, 314, 315, 316
conversion, Jewish view of,
　290
Conze, Edward, 198
Cook, Michael, 340, 341
Council of Trent, 321
Covenant, 281
Crusades, 317–18
Cubism, 133
Cultural Revolution, 261
culture, 106–12

Dalai Lama, 203, 211, 213
Dali, Salvador, 134, 135
Daly, Mary, 153
Dante, Alighieri, 127
Dao, 247, 254
Daoism (Taoism) ethics, 246,
　255–6; alchemy in, 248
Darwin, Charles, 9, 23, 26,
　100, 114, 141
David (King), 348, 349
Davie, Grace, 34
Davies, Winston, 297
Dawkins, Richard, 150
de, 251, 259
death, 55
definition of religion, 1, 30
Deists, 8
deities, Vedic, 178
Delaunay, Sonia, 130
Deng Xiaoping, 267
dependent co-arising, 199
Descartes, René, 55
Dhamma, 192, 195, 205
dharma, 2, 168, 170, 172,
　177
Diana, Princess of Wales, 34,
　104, 105
diaspora, 71
diaspora, Hindu, 183
diaspora, Jewish, 276–7
diffused religion, 243
dimensional approach, 3–5
Diocletian, 313, 314
Docetism, 350

doctrine, 4
Dominic (founder of the Dominicans), 318
Dong Zhongshu, 248
double fifth, 265
drugs, 60–1
dualism in Chinese religion, 250
Dubnow, S., 279
Duhkha, 171, 196, 197
Durkheim, Emile, 15, 17, 22, 24, 25, 26, 27, 28, 32, 35, 38, 100, 101, 103, 106, 107

ecclesiology, 327
Eckhart, Meister, 318
Ecumenism, 322, 334
Edward VIII (King), 236
Edwards, Frederick, 140
Einstein, Albert, 272
Eliade, Mircea, 15, 17, 18
Eliezer, Rabbi Israel, 276
Eliot, T. S., 330
Elizabeth II, Queen of England, 78, 104
empathetic approach, 13–14
Engels, Friedrich, 104
Enlightenment, 321
epics in Hinduism, 181
Erikson, Erik H., 49, 50, 51, 52, 56
Eucharist, 327–8
eurocentric, 100
evolution, 23, 100
Ezra, 275

Farrakham, Louis, 366
Fatwa, 367
feminists, 129
feudalism in China, 244
Feuerbach, Ludwig, 143, 144, 149
Fiqh, 342
Fischer, Roland, 60
five evil passions, 225
Five Pillars of Faith, 355
five relationships, 256
Four Noble Truths, 196
Frazer, Sir James, 100

Frederick the Great, 146
free-will, Karma and, 174
Freud, Lucian, 133
Freud, Sigmund, 5, 15, 48, 49, 51, 56, 66, 134, 144
functional approach, 5
functionalism, 106
fundamentalism, 22, 33, 34, 40
funerals, 122

Gabriel (Angel), 340
Galileo, 55, 141, 321
Gans, Herbert J., 108
Garhasthya, 177
Gautama, Siddhartha, 3, 190, 194, 195
Geertz, Clifford, 29, 30, 35, 97, 106, 108, 110
Gehenna, 354
Ghandi, Indira, 221
Ghandi, Mohandas K., 6
globalization, 108
Gonzáles de Mendoza, Juan, 242
Granth, Adi, 222
gratefulness, importance in Shinto, 297
Gregory IX (Pope), 318
Grunewald, Matthias, 133, 136
Guang Xu, 266
Gurdwara, 88, 231
Gurmukhi script, 217
guru (in Buddhism), 201
guru, 192
Guru Granth, 88, 218

hadith, 79, 81, 339
Hajj, 102–3, 356
Halakhah, 289
Hamilton, Susan, 198
Hampson, Daphne, 152
Han Confucianism, 248
Han Yu, 248, 258
Harappan civilization, 178
Harbhajan Singh Puri (Yogi Bhajan), 236
Hardacre, Helen, 300
Hardy, Alister, 59

Hareen, Fatima, 364
Hargobind, Guru, 218, 219
Harmandir, 218
Harvey, Peter, 196
Hasa al 'Askari, Imam (d. 873/874), 343
Hasan (Imam), 343
Hasidism, 276
Heaven, Chinese concept of, 251; Hindu notion of, 171
Hegel, Georg Friedrich, 8, 18
Heidegger, Martin, 11, 18
Herberg, Will, 39
heresy, 36, 323
Herod (King), 287
Herodotus, 6
Herzel, Theodore, 278
Hesse, Herman, 209
high culture, 117
Hijab, 360
Hillel, 275
Hillman, James, 52
Hindu "renaissance", 181
Hindu: philosophical schools, 179; 'trinity', 179; view of heaven, 171
Hinduism, 82–5, 98; Banyan tree model for, 163; diasporic, 183; goals of life in, 170; tensive equilibrium model of, 165
Hinnells, John, 2
Hirata Atsutane, 301
Hirohito, Emperor, 302
Hirst, Damien, 128
historical critical method, 73, 77
Hitler, Adolf, 274, 291
Holocaust, 277, 293
Holy Roman Empire, 315
Homer, 58, 121
homosexuality, 37
Hume, David, 142
humor, Jewish, 295
Husayn (son of 'Ali), 341
Husayn, Imam, 343
Husserl, Edmund, 11, 12, 18, 19

Huxley, Julian, 150
hymns, 89

Iblis, 346
Ibn Ishaq, 339
Ibn Maja, 339
icons, 99, 122
Ijma, 342
impermanence, Buddhist
  doctrine of, 197
indulgences, 320
Ingersoll, Robert G., 140
intentionality, 330
interfaith conversations,
  335
interpretative approach, 29
Isaac, 153
Ise pilgrimage, 301
Ise Shrine, 305
Islam, 78–81, 98, 123–4;
  divorce and inheritance,
  362–3; idealization of
  female, 364; judgment
  day, 352; monotheism,
  340; origins, 339;
  philosophical schools, 347;
  polygamy, 359; prophets,
  348; reverence of saints,
  341–2; secularism, 365;
  succession, 341–2; view of
  Bible, 348; view of Jesus,
  349; view of judgment,
  351; view of paradise, 354;
  view of post-mortem
  existence, 353; western
  perceptions, 338; women,
  357–65; women's
  education, 362; women's
  obedience, 363
Islam, Yusuf (Cat Stevens),
  79
Isnad, 339
Ithna 'Ashari, 343
Itjihad, 342
Izanami, 304

Ja'far al-Sadiq, Imam, 343
Jacob (patriarch), 153
Jacobs, Louis, 289
Jala ud-din Rumi, 344

James, William, 16, 45, 47,
  48, 56, 58, 59, 60, 62, 65
Japanese religion, "reality"
  of, 307
Jati (caste), 176
Jaynes, Julian, 58
Jesus Christ, 15, 17, 57, 77,
  79, 122, 133, 134, 137,
  153, 161, 275, 309; life of,
  309–11, 313, 316, 322–5,
  348–50
Jhana states, 202
jinn, 346
Jiva, 192
Jivan mukt, 226
Jnana yoga, 180
John of Damascus, 346
John the Baptist, 134
John the Evangelist, 331
jokes, 29
Judaism, 70–4;
  (Conservative), 291;
  diaspora, 276–7; ethical
  prescriptions, 288–9;
  festivals, 285–8;
  homeland, 283; identity,
  273–4; (Liberal), 73;
  memory, 274;
  monotheism, 280;
  (Orthodox), 287, 291;
  Praxis orientation of, 273;
  progressive (reformed)
  Judaism, 291; rites, 284–5,
  285–6; (Second Temple),
  287; self-definition, 290;
  "Theology", 279
Jung Chang, 260, 261
Jung, Carl, 15, 51, 52, 56,
  58
Junzi, 255

Kabbalah, 276
Kabbani, Rana, 357
Kada no Azumamaro, 301
kama, 170, 177
kami, 297, 304
Kang Youwei, 266
Kangxi Dictionary, 242
Kant, Immanuel, 11, 18
Kanwar, Roop, 185

karma (in Buddhism), 205
karma, 88, 169
karma yoga, 180
karuna, 203
kasina, 202
kaur, 220
Keown, Damien, 200
Kerouac, Jack, 210
Khadijja, 340
Khalistan, 221
khalsa, 220; authority in, 232
khandas, 197
King, Martin Luther, 37,
  329
kirtans, 89
Kobo, Daishi, 299
Kojiki, 304
kosher rule, 288
Krishan, Guru Har, 219
Krishna, 83, 182, 186
Kulananda, 196
Küng, Hans, 128
Kushner, Harold, 288

Lactantius, 2
laicization, 333
Laozi, 246, 247, 254
Lau, D. C., 255
lavan, 218
lectionary, 75
Lemu, B. Aisha, 357, 359,
  364
Lenin, V. I., 104
Leo III (Pope), 317
Leo the Great (Pope), 315
Leo X (Pope), 320
Levenson, Joseph, 267
li, 254
liberalism, Christian, 321
liminal, 102
Lipner, Julius, 166
Liu Shaoqi, President, 267
logical positivism, 26
Lotus Sutra, 208
lotus, as image of Buddhist
  teaching, 194–5
Lu Xun, 267
Luckmann, Thomas, 34
Luke, St., 331
Luther, Martin, 154, 320

Macartney, Lord, 266
MacIntyre, Alasdair, 27
Madhyamaka, 199
Magatsuhi-no-kami, 304
Magdalene, Mary, 134
magisterium, 320
Mahabharata, 181
Mahayana, 86, 193; view of women in, 209
Mahdi, 343
Maimon, Rabbi Moshe Ben, 279
Majushri, 203
Malcolm X (Malik al-shabazz), 102
Malik, 342
Malinowski, Bronislaw, 35
Mamun (Caliph), 347
Mandate of Heaven, 251
Mao Zedong, 267
Mara, 195; temptation of the Buddha by, 207
Marga, 180
marriage, 89
Martel, Charles, 317
Martinez, D. P., 306, 307
Marx, Karl, 5, 24, 25, 26, 27, 32, 36, 37, 104, 126, 131, 137, 143, 144, 145, 149, 161
Mary, mother of Jesus, 134, 316, 323
masands, 218
Maslow, Abraham, 58
Matsumara, Molleen, 150, 159
matsuri (Shinto festivals), 305
McLaren, Malcolm, 131
medieval use of art, 122–3
Meiji restoration, 301
Meir, Golda, 278
Mencius, 246, 250, 254, 255, 256, 257, 258, 270
mental illness, 56
Mernissi, Fatima, 361
Messiah, 77, 311
Methodism, 321
methodology, 29
Michelangelo, 133

Middle Way, 196
midrash, 74
mindfulness, 201
miri, 219
Mishnah, 71, 73, 275
moksha, 170–1, 177
monotheism, Islamic, 340
monotheism, Jewish, 272
Moore, R. I., 283
Moses (patriarch), 73, 272, 274, 278, 282, 286, 348
Mu'tazila, 347
Muhammad (prophet), 16, 78, 80, 81, 94, 102, 112, 337, 338, 339, 340; historicity of, 340, 350–1; life of, 340–1
Muhammad 'Abduh, 359
Muhammad, Elijah, 366
Mujtahids, 343
Müller, Friedrich Max, 9, 16, 18
multiculturalism, 108
Munch, Edvard, 131
Musa al-Kazim, Imam, 343
Muslim ibn al-Hajjaj, 339

Nagarjuna, 196
nam simran, 226
Nanak, Guru, 87, 215, 216, 217, 222, 225, 226, 228, 230, 231, 233, 234, 235
Narayana (Vishnu), 178, 179, 182, 184, 186, 189
Naths, 215
Nation of Islam, 366
natural religion, 7
Nawal El-Saadawi, 364
near death experiences, 56
Nebuchadnezzer, 274
Neo-Confucianism, 249
Nestorian divide, 323
Nestorius, 323, 324
New Age, 33–4
new religious movements, 28, 108
Newton, Isaac, 55
Nicea, 314
Nichiren, 210
nidanas, 199

Nietzsche, Friedrich, 143, 146–7, 148, 149
Nihongi, 304
nimitta, 202
Ninety-Five Theses, 320
Nirvana, 196
Noah, 348
Noble Eight-fold Path, 196–7
no-self, Buddhist doctrine of, 197
numinous, 12

Oedipus, 49
Olcott, Colonel Henry, 209
Old Testament, 70, 74–5
Oldenberg, Hermann, 209
Orientalism, 356–7
original sin, doctrine of, 326
Orpheus, 313
orthodox, 323
Orthodox Church, 315
Otto, Rudolf, 12, 18, 19

pabbajja, 204
Pachomius, 316
Paden, William, 97
Pahlavi, Shah Mohammed, 343
Pahnke, Walter, 61
panj kakke (five "K"s), 220, 227
panth, 220
paranormal, 62–3
Parousia, 311
Parvati, 178, 184, 187
Pasha, Abdula, 339, 340
paticcasamuppada, 199
Paul, St. (apostle), 77, 125, 312, 320, 326, 329, 330, 333
Pepin the Small, 317
period in the grave, 352
perspectivalism in Hinduism, 166
Peter, St., 313, 316
Pharisees, 275
phenomenological approach, 10–11

Phylacteries, 287
Picasso, Pablo, 129, 130, 131, 137
piri, 219
Plaskow, Judith, 280
Plato, 120, 121, 126, 131, 137, 347
plays, 121
Pontifex Maximus, 314
positivist approach, 29
post-Christian, 333
postmodernism, 46, 106–7
prajna, 196
prayer, Christian view of, 327
Presbyterianism, 320
profane, 101
Progressive Judaism, 287
Prometheus, 160
Providence, 8
psychokinesis, 62–3
psychology, 15, 44–67
psychomanteum, 63
Pure Land (Buddhist school), 203, 208, 300
Purusarthas, 170

Qi as foundational substance, 253
Qin Kui, 268
Qin Shi Huangdi, 248, 269
Qu Qiubai, 267
Qu Yuan, 265
Quant, Mary, 131
Qur'an, 16, 78–81, 112, 338, 344–5

Rahit Marayada, 228, 232
rahitnamas, 233
Rahman, F., 365
Rahner, Karl, 128
Rai, Guru Har, 219
Ram Das, Guru, 218, 229
Rama, 181, 186
Ramadan, 80
Ramakrishna, 183
Ramayana, 181
Raphael, 137
Rashi, 74, 281
Ravanna, 181, 187

Reader, Ian, 307
realism, 119
redemption, 325
reform movements in Hinduism, 183
Reformation, 99
Reischauer, Edwin O., 300
relativism, 27, 107
religious experience, 47, 58–9
religious traditions, family resemblance between, 168
ren, 256
Renaissance, 319
Rg Veda, 175
Rhine, Joseph, 63
Rhys Davids, T., 209
Ricci, Matteo, 8
Rippin, Andrew, 365
rishis, 168
ritual(s), 35, 38, 96–106
ritual offerings as guarantor for afterlife (Chinese), 251
Rossetti, Gabriel, 137
Roy, Ram Mohan, 183
Rushdie, Salman, 156, 366, 367
Ruskin, John, 118, 119, 124, 125, 126, 130, 138, 139
Russia, 104
Ruthuen, Malise, 351

Sabbath, 285
Saccidananda, Brahman as, 180
sacraments, 327
sacred, 101
Said, Edward, 356, 357
saints, 105
Salat, 355
Salvation, 330
Sama Veda, 175
Samadhi, 196
Samanas, 195
Samatha-yana, 202
samsara (in Buddhism), 170, 205
samsara, 215
sanatana dharma, 174
Sandys, Edwina, 136

sangats, 217
sangha, 200, 204
Sanskrit, 82
Sarasvati, Dayananda, 183
Sariputta, 204
The Satanic Verses (Rushdie), 366–8
sati, 185
Sawm, 355
Sayers, Dorothy, 130, 138
Scheler, Max, 12, 19
Schleiermacher, Friedrich, 8, 19
Schopenhauer and Buddhism, 209
science, 23
scripture, 68–95
Second Temple Judaism, 287
Secularism, Islamic responses, 365–6; Jewish attitudes to, 292–3
secularization, 32–4, 100
self, non-continuity of, 198
Sen, Keshab Chandra, 183
Septuagint, 71, 75, 282
seva, 217
sexism, Chinese, 260
Shaf'i, 342
Shahada, 355
Shahrastani, 7
Shaivite, 179
Shakespeare, William, 127
shakti, 184
shame, in Chinese religion, 258
Shari'ah, 79, 342
Sharpe, Eric, 109
Shema, 72
Shi'ites, 80
Shia, 341–4
Shingon, 299
Shinto: –Buddhist relationship, 299; creation myth, 304; "denationalization" of, 302–3; historical significance of, 298; national learning school, 301; origins, 299; reverence of nature, 299;

ritual purity, 299; Shrine Shinto, 305; syncretism, 300; view of suffering, 304; worship, 304
Shintoists, 98
Shirk, 344
Shiva, 178, 179, 184, 186, 188, 215
Shri (Lakshmi), 178, 184, 187
shruti, 82, 174
shu, 257
Shugendo, 300
Shumaker, Jack, 55
shun, 257
Sikhism, 5, 87–90, 98; contra sati, 218; early environment, 215–16; early martial history, 218–19; ethical prescriptions, 232–3; festivals, 230–1; grace, 226; as Hindu–Muslim conglomerate, 226; migration patterns, 236–8; modes of divine revelation, 225; rituals, 227–9; spiritual stages, 227; view of human nature, 224; view of karma, 235; view of women, 233–4; work ethic, 234; worship, 231
sila, 196, 204
Sima Dan, 244, 246, 247
Singh, 220
Singh, Guru Gobind, 219, 220, 222, 227, 230
Singh, Ranjit, 220
Sita, 181
six schools of Chinese philosophy, 244
"skillful means," 192, 205
Skilton, A., 192
Skinner, B. F., 53
Smart, Ninian, 2, 3
Smith, Adam, 146
Smith, Wilfred Cantwell, 31
smriti, 82, 175
sociology, 15, 21–43

Soka Gakai, 210
sola scriptura, 76, 99
Soteriology, 324
Spencer, Herbert, 23, 28
Spiro, Melford, 31
Spring Festival, 265
Starbuck, Edwin, 47
Stark, Rodney, 40
State of Israel, creation of, 294
State Shintoism, 301–2
Stein, Gertrude, 130
Stoics, 7
structuralism, 106
Sufism, 344
Sumedho, Ajhan, 211
Sunnah, 81, 338, 342, 350
Sunni, 80, 341–4
sunyata, 199
supernatural, 2
symbols, 112
synagogue, 275
syncretism, 110
syncretism, in Sikhism, 226; in Tang China, 249, 261; in western Buddhism, 212

taboo, 101
Talib, Abu, 340
Talmud, 72, 275–6
tanha, 196
Tao Yuanming, 254
tawhid, 348
Tefillin, 285, 287
telepathy, 62–3
Ten Gurus of Sikhism, 216–20
Tendai, 299
Tertullian, 153
theodicy, 35
Theodosius, 315
theotokos, 316, 323
Theravada Buddhism, 3, 85, 193
Theresa, St., 56
Tillich, Paul, 128
time, Buddhist conception of, 200
Tindal, Matthew, 142
tolerance in Shinto, 306

Tolstoy, Leo, 126, 127, 129, 138
Torah, 72–4; (oral), 274, 282
totem, 49, 101
totemism, 25
Tov, Rabbi Israel Baal Shem, 295
translation, 31
transubstantiation, 328
trikaya, 204
Trinity, doctrine of, 322–3
Tripitaka, 86
Turner, Victor, 102, 103
Twelve Links of Co-origination, 199

'Umar (Caliph), 341
'Uthman (Caliph), 341
upaya, 205–6
utilitarianism, 330

Vak Lao, 89, 90
Vaishnavite, 179
van Balthasar, Hans Urs, 128
van Eyck, Jan, 133
van Gennep, Arnold, 101, 102, 115
vanaprastha, 177
Varna, class structure of, 176
varnasramadharma, 176
Veda, 82, 174; elements of, 175; power of as scripture, 176
Ventis, W. L., 56, 57, 62
Victorian culture, 124–7
Vinaya, 192, 200; in Britain, 211
vipassana-yana, 202
Vischer, Friedrich Theodor, 125
Vishnu, 83, 215
Vivekanda, 183

Wailing Wall, 287
Warhol, Andy, 131
Watson, J. B., 53
Watt, William Montgomery, 347

Watts, Alan, 210
Weber, Max, 15, 19, 22, 24, 25–9, 32, 35–7, 42, 43, 99
Weldon, Fay, 367
Whirling Dervishes, 344
Whistler, James McNeill, 118, 119, 130, 138
White, Rhea, 59
Wiesel, Elie, 295, 296
Wilson, Bryan, 32
women and Islam, 357–71
women's roles in Shinto, 306
worldview, 35, 96–7

Wright, Frank Lloyd, 131
Wu Zetian, 248
Wulff, D., 65
wu-wei, 254
Wuzong, 248

xiao, 257
Xunzi, 246, 262

Yajur Veda, 175
Yang, C. K., 243
Yazid (Caliph), 341
Ye Dehui, 266
yi, 256
Yin and Yang, 252

Yuan Shikai, 267
Yue Fei, 268
yuga, 173
Yugoslavia, 38

Zakat, 56
Zayn al-'Abidin, Imam, 343
Zen Buddhism, 61, 87, 203; syncretism of, 193, 300
Zhang Yimou, 260
Zhou Dunyi, 253
Zhu Yixin, 266
Zionism, 278, 283–4
zongjiao, 243